THE STORY OF UNITY THEATRE

For Beth and Ben

The Story of Unity Theatre

Colin Chambers

St. Martin's Press
New York

First published in the United States of America 1989

Printed in Great Britain

ISBN 0-312-03580-2

Library of Congress Cataloging-in-Publication-Data

Chambers, Colin.
The story of Unity Theatre / Colin Chambers.
p. cm.
Bibliography: p.
Includes index.
ISBN 0-312-03580-2
1. Unity Theatre (Group)—History. 2. Amateur theater—England—London—History. I. Title.
PN3169.G82L84 1989
792'.0222'09421—dc20 89-33030
CIP

Alfie Bass

My pride was to be appearing for the cause. I can't imagine anything more inspiring than creating a play or revue with a real purpose ... It was special because it was collective.

Michael Gambon

As a six year old I used to play in the street outside Unity Theatre. In my late teens I played there again, but this time it was on the stage. It helped to give me a wonderful career and changed my life. Unity gave me and many others the chance to stand on its stage and act ...

Bill Owen

I learnt the basics of stagecraft at Unity ... It was my life.

Paul Robeson

Joining Unity Theatre ... means identifying myself with the working class. And it gives me the chance to act in plays that say something I want to say about the things that must be emphasised.

Contents

Illustrations 11
Foreword 13
Introduction 17

1 **Beginnings** 24
The Workers' Theatre Movement
Popular Front and Rebel Players
The Founding of Unity

2 **Britannia Street** 59
Waiting for Lefty
Taxi Driver Playwrights
Cannibal Carnival
The Fall of the House of Slusher
Mass Declamation
Spain

3 **Expansion** 91
Left Book Club Theatre Guild
Local Groups
Goldington Street
Building the New Theatre

4 **Golden Days** 124
The Communist Party
New Leadership Changes
Aristocrats
Living Newspaper: *Busmen*
Bury the Dead
Paul Robeson

5 **Political Pantomime** 162
Munich
Babes in the Wood
International Acclaim
Aiming for the West End

6 **They Never Closed** 188
Black-out Revues
Playing the Shelters
O'Casey's *The Star Turns Red*
The Match Girls
The Eastern Front

7 **People's War** 228
The Amazons
Ted Willis and *Buster*
New Talent
Winkles and Champagne
A National Society
1945

8 **A New Jerusalem** 263
Going Professional
Financial Problems
National Impact
Mobile Plays
What's Left?
The Ragged Trousered Philanthropists

9 **Out in the Cold** 314
UnAmerican Activities
The Cradle Will Rock
A Sartre Première
World on Edge

10 **The Final Years** 347
Changing Times
Brecht and Adamov
New Writing
Silver Jubilee Appeal
Counter-Culture
Fire

Unity Productions 1936–1983 403
Select Bibliography 419
Index 422

Illustrations

Between pages 128 and 129

Waiting for Lefty by Clifford Odets (John Vickers Theatre Collection)

Where's that Bomb? by two taxi drivers (photographer unknown)

Agitprop sketch 'Class against Class' performed on board ship bound for Leningrad (photograph provided by Maurice and Ray Braham)

Cannibal Carnival by Herbert Hodge (photograph provided by Maurice and Ray Braham)

Photomontage programme cover by John Vickers for *Bury the Dead*

Aristocrats by Nikolai Pogodin (photograph provided by Roy Battcock)

Plant in the Sun by Ben Bengal (John Vickers Theatre Collection)

Crisis programme cover by John Maltby and Gordon Hogg

Chamberlain caricatured as the Wicked Uncle in *Babes in the Wood* (John Vickers Theatre Collection)

Sean O'Casey's *The Star Turns Red* (Herbert Paul)

Señora Carrar's Rifles by Bertolt Brecht (John Vickers Theatre Collection)

Between pages 256 and 257

Bill Owen directs *The Match Girls* (Cyril Bernard, Unity Studios)

Merseyside Unity Theatre in *The Big Screen* (National Museums and Galleries on Merseyside – Museum of Labour History)

Glasgow Unity in *Men Should Weep* (Scottish Theatre Archive)

God Bless the Guv'nor by Ted Willis (Unity Studios)

The professional company in *Black Magic* (Unity Studios)
Performing *Winkles and Champagne* for the BBC at Alexandra Palace (Unity Studios)
Satirising Attlee's Labour government in *What's Left?* (Unity Studios)
A post-war adaptation of *The Ragged Trousered Philanthropists* (Unity Studios)
Fight aboard an American tanker in *Longitude 49* (Unity Studios)
Unity's Mobile coach (photograph provided by Eric Paice)
British première of Jean-Paul Sartre's *Nekrassov* (Henry Grant Collection: Museum of London)
World première of Arthur Adamov's *Spring '71* (photograph provided by Una Brandon-Jones)
Bloomsday, an adaptation from James Joyce's novel *Ulysses* (Kenneth Jepson)

Text Illustrations

	page
Programme design for first productions at Goldington Street	116
Programme cover for 1941 production of *Distant Point*	210
James Boswell illustration for *Jack the Giant Killer*	216
Publicity postcard for Leeds Unity's revue *It's Possible*	255
Programme for *The Enemies* by Maxim Gorky, a British première	296
Programme for *The Whole World Over* by Konstantin Simonov	298
Handbill for *World on Edge*	343
Programme for Arnold Wesker's *Chicken Soup with Barley*	379

Foreword

In choosing to write the story of London's Unity Theatre, I was deciding to fill an extraordinary gap in both theatrical as well as political history. It seemed odd that no one had done it before. I knew of references to Unity in various publications and found out later that the BBC had broadcast a radio programme on Unity's history; I had seen material on Unity theatres that functioned elsewhere in Britain and books covering the Workers' Theatre Movement, which preceded Unity, but no full-length study or record of London's unique left-wing theatre that had survived for 40 years and changed the face of British theatre.

After beginning my research I discovered that there had been a proposal in the 1950s for Lawrence and Wishart to publish just such a book; possible authors included Alexander Baron, Jack Lindsay, Leonard Peck, Montagu Slater and Ted Willis, all people who had been involved with Unity, but the idea had come to nothing. I also came across several Unitarians who had considered writing a history (and one had drafted a few chapters) but none was likely to see publication. Given the paucity of the existing coverage of Unity, I was determined to proceed but felt anxious at being an 'outsider' who had only seen one production there. Yet it was clear from interviewing more than 80 former Unity members and corresponding with another 50 that the disadvantages of the 'outsider' in trying to retell the story were heavily outweighed by the advantages. While lacking the authority of lived experience, an 'outsider' could bring other equally valuable and valid considerations to bear. Whoever had written the story would have had to carry out the immense research that was required to supplement and challenge individual recollection and bias. Although all accounts, including mine, are shot through with assumptions, the rigour of constructing the history from scratch has, I hope, given my version an adequate objectivity.

It is genuinely a people's history, not a literary one, and oral evidence was a major source of research, even though very little of what was said to me is reproduced directly. I matched the vivid but often self- and mutually contradictory accounts against whatever documents I could find, in scattered and incomplete archives, in personal collections and in libraries. The Unity Theatre Society files have suffered the depredations of time, the war and light-fingered members, and there are no Communist Party records that I could find relating to Unity. There are a few, brief, contemporary accounts of Unity's activities, some short references in later surveys and a handful of university theses concentrating on the early years, only one of which has been published and that was in German.

From these different sources, I managed to piece together most of the jigsaw, helped enormously by the great generosity of spirit that I met, from Unity veterans, from researchers working in related areas and from others whom I had to approach, such as librarians. It was not easy evaluating the source material – bulletins, programmes, leaflets, pamphlets, scripts, magazines, reports and minutes of meetings and conferences, reviews and photographs, plus the articles on Unity and the correspondence and interviews. All of it is coloured by the moment and conditions of its production, much of the printed matter is poorly dated or undated, and documents relating to the first half-dozen years bear the effects of Unity's collective anonymity. Also, memory is notoriously selective. Whether in talking to people or reading the documents, myths about people, about plays and about the theatre would figure frequently as gospel, with the authority that is conferred either by print or the seemingly irrefutable retort of 'I was there'.

As the outline and then the detail of the story emerged, I consolidated or revised my version in a process of comparing memory to document and document to memory until I reached a point at which the pattern and the substance were settled to my satisfaction or had to remain unclear through lack of further evidence. (I would welcome additional information that might correct any errors that have arisen.) All the conclusions, unless attributed, are necessarily my own.

In talking to former Unitarians, I was struck by the warmth of feeling still felt towards Unity, even by the few whose politics had changed radically since leaving the theatre. The enthusiasm of all the survivors sustained me throughout the writing of the book. Those with whom I spoke or corresponded, rather than being thanked here, are listed in the notes to the chapters for which their information was most relevant. Some are referred to in the text, and I was sorry not to be able to mention everyone, for this book is their story. My first thanks must go to them.

Secondly, I must thank those who were not involved with Unity but who have shared their research with me and made my task that much lighter: Jon Clark, Sue Crockford, Andy Croft, Robert Mackie, Malcolm Page, Steve Parsons, Mick Wallis, Don Watson and Betty Hunt, who did valuable work on the Sheffield Left Theatre before she died.

Thanks are also due to the following: Neal Ascherson, John Attfield, Anne Ball, Martin Banham, Bonnie Borin, Peter Borin, Hetty Bower, Noreen Branson, Chris Brunel, Janey Buchan, Norman Buchan, Alan Bush, George Byatt, Chris Chambers, Stuart Cosgrove, Helen Crome, Bea Cutler, Hymie Fagan, Stan Fitch, Joan Frood, Jim Fyrth, Clive Gehle, Florence Gersten, Alison Hindell, Bert Hogenkamp, Nick Jacobs, Ben Jancovich, Laura Jennings, Nesta Jones, Solly Kaye, Reiner Lehberger, Sid Lesser, Harry Lewis, David Margolies, John Mason, Jane Noble, Eileen O'Casey, Michael Orrom, Derek Paget, John Pitt, Denis Roberts, Ian Saville, Ken Sayer, Nicola Seyd, Ted Seyd, Simon Shepherd, Jo Spence, Jo Stanley, Barrie Stavis, Ian Steadman, Jack Sutherland, Sadie Thomas, Joanna van Gyseghem, Chris Whittaker, John Willett, Cecil Woolf.

Institutions that helped were: Actors' Equity, BBC Library, British Library, British Theatre Association (Enid Foster), Camden Libraries, Communist Party Library (George Matthews, Betty Reid, Francis Reid), Daniel Watney Douglas Young, ETV (Stanley Forman), *Fiction Magazine*, Gasters (Frank Loeffler), Imperial War Museum, International Brigade Archive (Tony Atienza), Institute of Laryncology and Otology (Robert Walker), *Listener*, Marx Memorial Library (Max Egelnick, Jane Rosen), *Morning Star*, Museum of the Jewish East End (David Mazower), National Film Archive (Elaine Burrows), Merseyside Museum of Labour History, National Museum of Labour History, National Sound Archive, *New Statesman*, Performing Rights Society,

Sheffield University (Philip Roberts), Southern Illinois University (Sheila Ryan), St Pancras Housing Association (Tom McCormack), Theatre Museum, *Tribune*, Unity Trust, Warwick University (Clive Barker), Working Class Movement Library (Edmund and Ruth Frow). Lastly, grateful thanks to the Eva Reckitt Trust for its grant and apologies to anyone whom I have omitted.

C.C.

Introduction

Tucked off the road behind King's Cross and St Pancras in North London, Unity, a tiny theatre of the left, rose, during its forty-year history, to national and international prominence. For a period it could justifiably claim to be the leading amateur theatre in Britain. Dedicated to making the world a better, fairer, more peaceful place, Unity Theatre relied for its remarkable survival on the enthusiasm and commitment of its practitioners and the goodwill and loyalty of its supporters.

The theatre began with irrepressible determination amid the political struggles of the early 1930s that were fought against the savage cuts in state benefit, the imposed means tests, the waste of widespread unemployment and poverty, and above all against the rise of fascism. Four decades later, when the theatre's auditorium was destroyed by fire, Unity had become a shadow of its former glories. Yet, despite its non-professional status and limited size, Unity made a major and lasting contribution to the British theatre through its own work and that of its members who became professionals. It pioneered direct political commentary on stage in its satires and documentary-based shows and developed a drama that represented working-class life and speech with insight and integrity.

As well as presenting countless mobile shows on tour, Unity mounted in its own theatre more than 250 productions, over half of which were new plays, many specially written for Unity, and a third of which contained original music – an astonishing productivity, especially for an amateur company. This encouragement of creativity produced some shows that, even if they did not endure beyond their moment, comprise an original and peculiarly English enrichment of indigenous drama, such as the comic *Where's That Bomb?* written by two taxi drivers, a Living

Newspaper called *Busmen* and a clutch of politically astringent pantomimes and revues. World premières of plays by Sean O'Casey and Arthur Adamov were staged, as well as British premières of some forty plays by foreign playwrights such as Jean-Paul Sartre, Maxim Gorky and Bertolt Brecht; the first Brecht play to be seen in Britain was a Unity production.

Unity was joined by many other groups that shared a common ideology and it led two national left-wing drama movements, first in the turbulence of the 1930s, when the left animated the cultural life of Britain, and then during the disruption of the Second World War which, in its own way, also released terrific cultural energy. The different groups were proudly independent and added their own batch of local plays to a repertoire stock that emanated from London Unity. These movements, which involved hundreds of people and at their height consisted of about 300 groups, contributed importantly to changes in British theatre after the war, such as the winning of public subsidy for drama, the resurgence of regional theatre, the widening of the content of plays, progress in drama training and advances towards a national theatre.

Unity's activities brought it into contact with the wider public beyond the confines of the left. The company's popular music hall show *Winkles and Champagne* appeared live on television and the theatre was featured in several radio programmes. National newspapers took an interest when voluntary labour built Unity's new theatre, with financial support from prominent theatrical and political figures. This interest was followed up a few months later when, at the height of his popularity, Paul Robeson turned down a starring West End role to appear at Unity in a strike play as just another member of the anonymous cast. The greatest press coverage came when Unity's record-breaking anti-appeasement pantomime *Babes in the Wood* outrageously lampooned the Prime Minister Neville Chamberlain. During the iciest moments of the Cold War, the news from Unity took a more sinister turn; a civil servant performing in a Unity revue lost her job because of Labour's anti-Communist legislation and there were attempts, linked by Unitarians to the US embassy and MI5, to put the theatre out of business while it was playing a satire directed against the American government.

Although Unity shared with other oppositional theatre groups the aim of challenging the kinds of plays theatres staged – and why they staged them, where, how and for whom – it was distinct in the ways in which it offered those challenges. Unity was a democratically run club with a committee for everything. Drawing on its communist and working-class roots, it attempted its theatrical revolution as part of a social and political one. Its ethos was rooted in a notion of collective, though hierarchically ordered, endeavour, the values of which were to be shared by performers and audience alike. With all its shortcomings, it was to be an example of a type of socialism in practice, anchored in working-class activity.

Although Unity was happy to receive middle-class support, it saw its main function as being an expression of the working class – a class that had been denied access not only to political power but to cultural production as well. Unity commanded tremendous support from individual trade union and Co-operative organisations, and earned itself an abiding place in the movement's history, yet it was clearly a theatre of the Communist left. It served the working class according to definitions shaped by the Marxism of the Communist Party and reflected the political movement of which it was an inseparable part.

Unity's aims were conditioned by changing historical circumstance but always included striving for socialism, even if the word itself was not used. The rule book, for example, that was born of Popular Front attempts to win the widest possible support, defines Unity's purpose as

> to foster and further the art of drama in accordance with the principle that true art, by effectively and truthfully interpreting life as experienced by the majority of the people, can move the people to work for the betterment of society.

The choice of name illustrates the theatre's awareness of political context and reflects its self-image. Unity did not describe itself as a Marxist or Communist theatre, because that would have been too restrictive. Whilst the term 'proletarian' belonged to the 'red' period preceding the foundation of Unity, from which Unity was trying to move away, the term 'workers' theatre' was acceptable and readily adopted. It soon gave ground, however, to the Popular Front description of a people's theatre which lasted throughout and after the war and which was given particular prominence following the Nazi invasion of the Soviet Union.

Whatever the description of Unity, there remained an aggressive pride in it being an amateur theatre. This was much more than a simple reaction to the fact that entry to the professional theatre, and the world it represented, reflected a narrow interest antagonistic to the working class. Unitarians believed that the purpose of Unity as a workers' theatre was different in kind from that of the professional theatre. Although they wished to attain technical excellence, they were not interested in reproducing copies of West End drama – the experience had to be different for those who were making the theatre and for those who were seeing it, both in the content of the plays performed and in the context of their performance. The experience offered both at the venues Unity visited on tour and at its own premises was to become more like an extension of a political meeting into the cultural field, with an assumed union of values between actor, audience and play.

Throughout Unity's existence, however, there arose the impulse to establish a professional Unity presence as a means of deepening and extending the theatre's influence, although the circumstances changed radically each time this occurred and there was always internal opposition. (When Unity was founded the state was not supporting drama of any kind, let alone that being offered by Unity, and later, when public subsidy was introduced for drama, it was not available for amateurs.) The successes of the early years led to the first possibility of creating, alongside the amateur theatre, a separate professional company, but this initial attempt was cut off by the outbreak of war. The next occasion came at the end of the war and a professional troupe was founded in 1946, only to collapse fourteen months later. The third and final attempt, in the 1960s, was rebuffed by a majority of members who equated professional expertise with commercialism and responded by electing a new leadership to run the theatre.

As a political theatre, Unity was subject to the ebbs and flows of the movement and to the pressures and conflicts within it, having constantly to negotiate the differing needs and functions of art and politics, the correlation of which was never as simple as it sometimes seemed. Unity had to give both performers and audience a sense of their place in history, as part of an onward march of progress whatever the temporary setbacks; its approach, therefore, was optimistic rather than self-critical. It presented many images of the working class that were emblematic of its traditional strengths. But, during the post-war fragmentation of the left, Unity found it difficult to understand the changes that were taking place in the composition and ideology of classes and how they were being reflected in the labour movement; consequently it failed to appeal to the emerging movements that were based in gender and race. Nevertheless, the theatre was not locked wholly into an uncritical 'workerism'; it tended to swing between adopting a vanguard role and embracing outright populism, but only once – in 1956 when it presented criticism of the Soviet Union's activities in Hungary – did it depart significantly from the positions of the Communist Party. This allegiance was the source of much external, and occasionally internal, rebuke. Yet, whatever the theatre's record, it is Communists who bear the burden both of its successes across nearly half the century and of its ultimate failure to renew itself.

Communist Party Marxism inspired its followers to believe that whatever they did was in accord with the truth because their materialist philosophy provided an analysis that was more 'real' than any other system of thought. Unity, therefore, pursued an artistic policy based on a realism that demanded that the plays it presented should explain the world better – ie, more truthfully – than traditional drama could. This approach, which was embraced by the leading British Communists active in cultural production, was antagonistic to 'art for art's sake' or modernism. It was rooted in a notion of conscious purpose, which, in Unity's case, meant stimulating people to take political action.

Whilst neither wanting to restrict Unity's role to that of an elite shock brigade nor wishing to expand its function to tackle mass forms of drama like the pageant, the theatre marshalled to its purpose an impressive range of forms. It drew on several different and contending theatrical cultures – from choral declamation, conventional naturalism and the critical reportage of Living Newspapers (using poetry, dance, film and drama), to pantomime, revue and socialist realism of the Soviet and Brechtian styles. Such diversity could embrace the interventionist side of agitprop – a Soviet-born contraction of 'agitational propaganda' – which says 'This is how the world really is; now that you can see it clearly for what it is, go out and change it'. And it could embrace the revelatory perceptions of naturalism, based either on working-class life and vernacular (the world the audience knows but which is excluded from traditional cultural representation) or on middle- or upper-class life as portrayed in the classics (the traditional world of the stage but seen from a progressive standpoint).

This variety led to a conflict that raged throughout Unity's existence on the suitability of certain aesthetic forms. It was a debate that frequently overlapped arguments on whether or not Unity was separating its art from its politics by reproducing either wholly or in part what were seen as bourgeois forms of play production and play going. These were the same basic differences that defined the internal struggles of Unity's predecessors in the Workers' Theatre Movement and that later surfaced again in the political theatre movement of the 1960s and 1970s.

Given the potent mix of intense political commitment and the passions roused by the drama, it is not surprising that Unity's history is fraught with such disagreements; for Unity was more than a theatre – it was a way of life, a means of politically conscious self-expression that was collective and provided a solution to individual alienation. Its activist approach, stemming from a Communist philosophy that gave due weight both to theory and practice, allowed anyone who shared Unity's aims to enter a complete world. Unity offered directly theatrical activities – a wide range of plays performed in different venues (and, for a while, children's and puppet theatre) – and a serious training through practice and study in all features of theatre, whether at Unity's drama school, in its classes or in the management of the many and various aspects of running a performing company with its own building. It also offered a hectic social and recreational life; at one time or another there were a choir, an orchestra, a film club, a camera club, a folk club, a poetry club, a soccer team, exhibitions in the foyer, a Unity magazine, members' bulletins, a bookshop, political meetings, raffles, bazaars, rambles, a camp, parties, dances, a bar and a Unitarians' network of pubs and cafés.

This world was a nursery for the nation's cultural talent. Many of Unity's members went on to work in theatre, film, television, radio, drama schools, journalism, publishing, the universities, as actors, playwrights, producers, casting directors, fight arrangers, technicians, stage staff, administrators, agents, critics, professors, teachers. Some of them became well known – like Lionel Bart, Alfie Bass, Michael Gambon, Bob Hoskins, David Kossoff,

Warren Mitchell, Bill Owen and Ted Willis. But, for most people, Unity was important as an 'open university' of drama, giving them self-respect and the chance to do something in the theatre for a cause in which they believed. The collective, prodigious and dedicated endeavour of the Unitarians – whether they were machine hands, engineers, dressmakers, bus drivers, labourers, furniture workers, turners, postal clerks, students, carpenters, architects, opticians, or even a landlord – has left a lasting legacy that not only affected deeply their own lives and the life of the left and the labour movement but also changed profoundly and uniquely the character and content of the British theatre in the twentieth century.

1

Beginnings

The founders of Unity saw themselves in a tradition of political theatre that reached back to the origins of European drama – Unity once likened its role to that of the ancient Greek playwright Euripides when he attacked the war policy of the government of his day. In publicity material they traced their roots to the medieval guild tradition, suppressed by the Reformation, of presenting Mystery Plays on carts. There were also historically closer, although unacknowledged, antecedents. These ranged from the Luddites and Chartists through cultural pioneers such as William Morris to the fighters for women's suffrage, who created dozens of propaganda plays and whose protests themselves often took on highly theatrical and dramatic forms.

The labour movement, by and large, was not particularly interested in theatre, but some of its organisations, such as the Clarion Clubs, did use drama to foster an alternative vision of life; as individuals, socialists had promoted Ibsen's New Drama, created a Fabian theatre of social concern and helped build the repertory movement.[1]

After the First World War commercial theatre atrophied as it became even less the province of theatre people and even more an attraction for making money. In the absence of the state support that had promoted innovative theatre in Europe, there was an expansion in the activities of private play-producing societies and in what became known as the 'little' theatres, like the Festival Theatre or the Gate, where audiences could see challenging new plays, often from abroad, and exciting experiments in staging and style, away from the restrictions of the Lord Chamberlain's censorship.

Within the labour movement, a broadly based repertoire was

being developed that embraced German expressionism as well as Shaw and Chekhov. Its thrust was primarily ethical and anti-militarist rather than directly political. Some on the left, however – mainly members of the newly formed Communist Party and the Independent Labour Party and people within Marxist educational institutions like the Plebs League and the National Council for Labour Colleges – proclaimed a more combative role for drama, based on class struggle.

The Workers' Theatre Movement

Inspired by the Russian Revolution and the cultural upsurge which followed in its wake, a Council for Proletarian Art was formed in Britain in 1924.

Two years later the name was changed to the Workers' Theatre Movement (WTM); this new name reflected the political aspirations of its founders rather than their class background.[2] Among the first WTM productions were two plays by the German playwright Ernst Toller, *Masses and Man* and *The Machine Wreckers*, and a Czech play, *RUR (Rossum's Universal Robots)*, by Karel Čapek, which satirises the machine age and helped introduce the word 'robot' – meaning 'unfree' labour – to Britain. In Scotland, miner Joe Corrie began writing plays for the WTM, including one of the strongest of the period, *In Time o' Strife*, which is set during the pits crisis of 1926. It was toured locally and performed in London and Germany, and in 1982 the socialist touring group 7:84 Scotland revived it.[3]

In its first stage, the WTM comprised a loose grouping of occasional activities around Britain, varying in scope, skill and choice of plays; some people were interested in the aesthetic value of drama and in its progressive heritage, others wanted to use drama for revolutionary propaganda purposes, and there were those who just wished to brighten up their political meetings. Differences of attitude hardened in the years following the General Strike and they reflected in many ways the growing divisions within the British and international working-class movements.

The Moscow-based Communist International (Comintern), which governed the general policy of all Communist Parties, adopted a sectarian 'class against class' approach that lasted officially from 1928 to 1935.[4] Everyone who was not within the revolutionary vanguard of the working class became an actual or potential enemy of that class, and therefore, objectively, an ally of the ruling class; on the political front, social democrats were denounced as social fascists, and on the cultural front, artists and intellectuals were abused as lackeys of the bourgeoisie. In the British context, such opinions were given credence by the betrayal of the General Strike by the leaderships of the TUC and Labour Party and by the record of Labour's two governments in the 1920s, which led to Labour being derided as the third capitalist party. The policies of the Labour Prime Minister Ramsay MacDonald, who split his own party and paved the way for the harsh rule of the National government in the 1930s, deepened such beliefs.[5]

As a loyal section of the world Bolshevik party, though not without internal divisions on the matter, the Communist Party of Great Britain followed the Comintern's lead and set up revolutionary organisations parallel to existing labour movement bodies. A self-supporting autonomous 'red' world was to be created, based on the then current premiss of scientific socialism that the death knell of capitalism had already been sounded (most notably by the Wall Street crash of 1929) and that proletarian revolution followed by the coming of a soviet state was inevitably the next item on history's agenda.

From the loftiest of ideals, and in the face of the relentless hardships of life, Communists kindled such a fighting spirit that they were able to found and sustain a daily newspaper and to launch a number of imaginative political-cultural initiatives, in education, recreation, sport, the book world and the cinema as well as in the theatre.

Within the WTM the catalyst for change was a London group led by a stockbroker's clerk H.B. (Tom) Thomas, who left the Labour Party to join the Communists after the defeat of the General Strike.[6] He had founded the Hackney Labour Dramatic Group which presented one-act plays that were, in his words, of 'social significance', like Susan Glaspell's *A Woman's Honour* or J.M. Barrie's *The Twelve Pound Look*. Later the group mounted full-length plays such as *In Time o' Strife, RUR* and Shaw's *Mrs Warren's Profession*. A major departure came in 1927 when the group staged Thomas's own adaptation of Robert Tressell's *The Ragged Trousered Philanthropists,* the forerunner of several notable later dramatisations, including a celebrated one by Unity Theatre. The group changed its name to the Hackney People's Players, and performed *The Ragged Trousered Philanthropists* some thirty times that winter to great acclaim. Success brought the group the means to expand: recognition, money and the stimulus to create its own material with direct appeal for the new audiences that it was seeking. Hackney People's Players decided to affiliate to the WTM, only to find that the WTM had collapsed. Charged with new-found confidence, the group became the core of the new WTM, with the energetic and dominating Tom Thomas as its chief ideologue and creator.

Thomas attempted to devise a popular political revue format, in such works as his pantomime skit *Malice in Plunderland* (1929), *Strike Up* (also 1929), which mixes dance, song and sketches, and *Their Theatre and Ours* (1933), which uses several techniques to comment on how culture affects people. This proved an inspiration to future work at Unity, although it was not consciously acknowledged by those who came later.

The new, mobile, flexible form of theatre that Thomas espoused was known as agitprop and had been developed by the international Communist movement. It began life in the Soviet Union where it permitted rapid and simple communication with a largely illiterate population. It had been taken up in Germany, and other European and Scandinavian countries, and in America too.

In Britain, Thomas led the WTM in supporting agitprop and rejecting the naturalistic tradition of theatre, which he believed merely reflected surface reality without being able to analyse deeper relationships or connections. Naturalism, therefore, could do no more than reproduce the status quo. Its static picture had no leverage on the future. Instead, Thomas embraced a materialist theory of drama and performance that was based on what he called the X-ray dialectical realism of montage. This was the basis of agitprop and it could intervene in the making of the future by offering just such a deeper analysis through a juxtaposition of slogans, chants, stereotypes, dialogue, mime, satire and songs. WTM groups developed their own style of mass speaking and expressive gesture, and shared their experiences in articles such as 'How is a WTM Sketch Written?' or 'How to Produce "Meerut" ' (a sketch about jailed trade unionists in India).[7]

It was after producing Upton Sinclair's *Singing Jailbirds* that

Thomas became convinced that a new dramatic form had to be found for the new workers' theatre. He thought that, like many other plays by left-wing writers, *Singing Jailbirds* this one was too pessimistic because the imprisoned sailors become martyrs instead of being freed. Thomas felt, too, that conditions were not right for presenting such work; the plays were full-length and that put them beyond the means of most non-professional left groups, especially if they were to attempt them on a regular basis; they needed to be played indoors, in halls or clubs with adequate facilities, which placed an undue burden on administration and economics; and they required audiences to come to the performance and not the other way round. This meant an unacceptable restriction on those whom the WTM could reach. Thomas came to believe that theatre groups should go out to their audiences and therefore not perform in theatres (or buildings resembling theatres) and that the performances should be free of charge.

The group, reflecting the 'class against class' politics of the period, changed its name in 1929 to Red Radio. Performances would begin with the chant:

We are Red Radio,
Workers' Red Radio,
We show you how you're robbed and bled.
The old world's crashing,
Let's help to smash it,
And build a workers' world instead.[8]

Red Radio dedicated itself to a set of theatrical ideas about the political use of drama that were soon to become guiding points of principle within the new WTM, although in practice these principles were often contradicted by those most vociferously promoting them. Thomas developed the ideological stance of the WTM and, as well as contributing regularly on theatre to the *Daily Worker*, wrote a great deal of material – plays, sketches, parodies, monologues – which was used by groups all over Britain and was designed for rapid performance on the street.

Although groups did perform indoors, the WTM saw itself as an outdoor movement, presenting its distinctive revolutionary messages on what it called 'open platform' stages – carts, lorries, steps, on street corners, in parks, at factory gates – often in a basic uniform of dungarees, sometimes bearing the hammer and sickle, and with no other costume or make-up. Megaphones might be used but props and scenery were frowned upon, and their use became the subject of stern debate and internal discipline. When they were required, they were portable and reduced to a minimum. The necessary aesthetic counterpart to an objective, scientific outlook seemed to require the utmost simplicity in all the elements of production to allow the sharpest focus on the purpose of the drama. Thomas dubbed the movement a 'propertyless theatre for the propertyless class', which became the slogan of the WTM – a workers' theatre of ideas instead of a bourgeois theatre of illusion.

Groups sprang up around Britain, mainly in big cities with high unemployment, and took names like Sunderland Red Magnets, Dundee Red Front Troupe, Southampton Red Dawn or Salford Red Megaphones. The greatest concentration was to be found in London, which at one time had some ten groups, including the Yiddish-speaking group Proltet, a four-woman group called Red Flag, and two groups whose members were later to form the core of Unity – Red Radio and Rebel Players – both based in Hackney. Some groups lasted a few years, others disappeared quite quickly.[9]

The WTM was never organisationally strong, but it made up in zeal and discipline what it lacked in numbers and administrative apparatus. It was a self-sufficient, non-professional, propagandist movement, openly hostile to all professional theatre workers and to other non-professionals who were not deemed to be revolutionary. It developed a strategy of frontal attack that assumed the world would change in its image and not the other way around. The overwhelming majority of its members were young, and while most were members of the Young Communist League, or the Communist Party, the troupes were not affiliated formally to any party. The party leaderships often looked upon them privately with condescension, indifference or even suspicion, seeing their work as at best marginal or at worst diversionary (and the weekly theatre column in the *Daily Worker* carried frequent criticisms of WTM groups). Political support tended to come at local level where group members lived, had good contacts and could respond swiftly to events of local importance.

Most impact seems to have been made when groups performed in connection with a political campaign, though little effort was made to get trade union bookings because the unions were considered to be part of the capitalist state machinery. WTM troupes played on Hunger Marches, at anti-war meetings and in the 1931 election campaign of the Communist candidate Willie Gallacher (himself a member of a Scottish WTM group). They also raised funds for the Lancashire cotton strikers in 1930. Their sketches dramatised many anti-capitalist and anti-imperialist themes, from factory speed-ups and evictions to problems of mining communities and the sailors' mutiny at Invergordon against the harsh cut in naval ratings' pay. Audiences were often difficult to attract at factory gates or on the street unless there was a high level of political activity around a local issue to which the WTM group was well connected. Those who did stay and watch, and especially those at political meetings, seemed to have been glad of the plays (although some party speakers at the same event as a WTM group feared the competition for the audience's interest). Frequent attenders were the police who would often harass or arrest the performers.

The WTM formed a national leadership which published a magazine in November 1931 called *Red Stage* (later *New Red Stage*). It lasted until December 1932 when it was superseded by a monthly bulletin that continued until the issue of April/May 1934. The WTM also had a reading committee, to tackle the habitual problem of creating suitable material, and members established related groups, such as a film section and a choir. The first national conference, held in London in June 1932, formalised the primacy of agitprop over naturalistic theatre, although the latter was not entirely ruled out and the wholesale rejection of the traditions of European drama was fiercely disputed. Nevertheless, the conference stridently attacked not only capitalist drama but also left-wing drama, Labour Party, ILP and Co-op drama, and sanctioned the WTM's isolation from the rest of the non-professional, as well as professional, theatre. The group that most openly challenged this line was the Rebel Players, which, at the All-London Show mounted on the Saturday evening of the conference, performed a realistic play.

Debates within the WTM continued, not just on the nature and importance of agitprop, but on a range of other, apparently settled, questions: the relative value of indoor and outdoor work, the role of the individual writer as opposed to that of collective creation, attitudes to other cultural forms like jazz, the involvement of professionals, who were generally castigated for being tainted by the bourgeois theatre for which they worked.

Agitprop's ascendancy was confirmed by visits to Britain of members of German left-wing theatre groups and by trips that WTM members made to Germany, where the influence of the 'workerist' Soviet theory of proletcult was still strong. Germany had mass working-class theatre organisations and the powerful Communist Party alone boasted 180 troupes.[10] Other international links, however, suggested different approaches to political theatre. The WTM was affiliated to the International Workers' Dramatic Union (IWDU), which, like similar Comintern organisations, was supposed to act as a central directing agency. Its first congress in 1930, attended by Tom Thomas, supported agitprop while warning against exclusive concentration on it. In 1932, at the second plenum of the IWDU's successor, the International Union of Revolutionary Theatres (IURT), German Communist Arthur Pieck attacked what he called the '*Hurrah-sozialismus*' of some groups and the schematism of much of their work, including the British.

The plenum expressed concern at the isolation of amateur workers' theatres from revolutionary elements in the professional theatre, at the under-estimation of bourgeois theatre, at the mistaken view of agitprop as the only form a revolutionary theatre could take, at the inability to create a united front of theatre workers, and at general artistic weakenesses, particularly the tendency to believe that revolutionary theatre could do without dramatists and replace them by collective writing. The IURT also criticised the editors of the WTM's *Red Stage* for not rebutting erroneous ideas.

Differences within the WTM came to a head in 1933 – the momentous, tragic year that Hitler became Chancellor and unleashed his terror on ever wider sections of the German population. An international Olympiad of workers' theatre groups was organised in May that year by the IURT, at a time when a new cultural orthodoxy was beginning to emerge in the Soviet Union with narrowing and prescriptive definitions of socialist realism.

The British WTM held a competition to choose its delegation for the Moscow event. Points were awarded for different aspects of work, with political activity scoring higher than artistic merit. Two groups were formed from those who were chosen and able to go, but it was impossible for them to present their work adequately because they did not have enough time to rehearse together as a team. The ad hoc groups performed four sketches – *Class against*

Class, Capitalist Rationalisation, Invergordon, and *Social Service* – which were praised by the Olympiad's international jury for subject matter but severely criticised for 'artistic-political' presentation. The jury's report on the work of the British delegation and its subsequent recommendations were a great blow to the esteem of the WTM and caused renewed debate on the return of the delegation, which, in any case, had found the whole experience quite confusing. (Their first taste of proletarian culture in the homeland of the revolution had been a visit to a classical ballet in Leningrad, which came as quite a shock because the WTM had been expelling members for such major transgressions of the revolutionary cultural code as using props. To have suggested producing anything as traditional as the equivalent of a classical ballet would have been heresy.)[11]

In the ensuing discussion, some argued the need to perfect the agitprop form rather than abandon it; others, while recognising its place in political theatre work, believed that different forms should be developed. The WTM resolution passed in Britain after the Olympiad reflects a compromise between the two camps. The primacy of agitprop was re-affirmed but other avenues were opened up, including the possibility of establishing a left-wing play-producing society and of working with professionals.

The first result of this debate was the reconstitution of the Rebel Players group. With the somewhat reluctant blessing of the WTM leadership, this group became a 'curtain stage' company presenting plays 'to win workers from other dramatic organisations' (in the words of the WTM resolution of July 1933 drafted by Rebel Players and carried by the WTM leadership). This move was designed also to help solve the WTM's financial problems and to aid 'the development of a repertoire to win other dramatic groups to the revolutionary line'.

Rebel Players had been formed in early 1932 (according to available information) but straightaway had suffered from personnel problems.[12] By November 1933, the reconstituted group announced that it was now on a sound footing and was happily working with professionals, most notably the actor-director André van Gyseghem, who, though often in the background, became a key figure in the development of British workers' theatre.[13]

Van Gyseghem had won a London County Council scholarship to attend the Royal Academy of Dramatic Art and worked with a

Co-operative drama group in South London. After three years' performing, he became in 1930 an actor at and artistic director of one of London's 'little' theatres – the Embassy at Swiss Cottage – and directed there, under Ronald Adam's management, several plays on important social issues. These included Hans Chlumberg's anti-war play *Miracle at Verdun*, Eugene O'Neill's *All God's Chillun Got Wings* and *Stevedore* by Paul Peters and George Sklar, the latter two with the outstanding black actor Paul Robeson in the cast. Van Gyseghem also established an experimental theatre, studied and worked in the Soviet Union with leading figures such as Meyerhold, Eisenstein and Oklopkhov, and visited left-wing theatre people in America.

He was a special visitor to the Moscow workers' theatre Olympiad and travelled on the same boat as the British WTM delegation, whom he saw rehearsing. It proved an exhilarating experience that changed the way he saw the function of drama. He later described his discovery of agitprop as 'an absolute eye-opener' and on his return to Britain he wrote to the WTM leadership, who were suspicious of him and decided to send him to the dissident Rebel Players. Van Gyseghem, who spoke at many meetings for the WTM about the Olympiad, worked with Red Radio and Proltet as well as Rebel Players, and helped bring other professionals into contact with the WTM. He directed three productions for Unity Theatre and became its first president. In the late 1930s he became a prominent director of mass pageants, both in South Africa (where he founded The Bantu People's Theatre and, it was said, signed up all its members as members of Unity[14]) and in Britain, including a 1939 May Day event that involved some 6,000 people in three South Wales mining valleys celebrating the centenary of Chartism. A Communist all his adult life, van Gyseghem had a distinguished professional career as an actor with major British companies and he was the first artistic director of the Nottingham Playhouse. In January 1934, along with Miles Malleson, Ina de la Haye, Lionel Britton and Barbara Nixon, he was a founder of the professional Left Theatre company, a private play-producing club like the Stage Society that invaded the heartland of the West End on Sunday evenings.[15]

Alongside the reconstitution of Rebel Players, the establishment of Left Theatre as the professional complement to the WTM was the other immediate effect of the 1933 post-Olympiad resolution. As a result, Left Theatre professionals worked with WTM groups while WTM members provided 'extras' in large-cast Left Theatre shows. Tom Thomas became the WTM representative on the Left Theatre committee.

Left Theatre wanted to stimulate the non-professional left wing groups to develop their own skills and choice of material by presenting at the highest possible technical level a repertoire of social concern but with wide appeal, and especially plays with positive images of the working class. Left Theatre's first production was of Friedrich Wolf's mutiny play *Sailors of Cattaro*, followed by John Wexley's *They Shall Not Die*, a protest at the racism of the American Deep South. The company performed Gorky's *Mother*, Montagu Slater's *Stay Down Miner*, with music by Benjamin Britten, and later a second version of this story (of a Welsh mining community trying to stop a train carrying strike-breakers) retitled *New Way Wins*. This amended version toured with another Slater play, *Easter 1916,* which had won a Left Theatre play competition held to overcome the lack of indigenous plays worth performing. The company also staged Ernst Toller's *Draw the Fires, Peace on Earth* by George Sklar and Albert Maltz, and left-wing revue, a link between the WTM tradition and the Unity repertoire to come.

Left Theatre sought labour movement backing and played in London County Council halls as well as in the West End, but it was not a permanent company and its members could only perform between their own professional engagements. More than 40 trade union bodies affiliated to it but the TUC refused to do so and a £2,500 appeal fell well short of the target. Financial problems, especially in meeting the wages bill, and organisational difficulties forced Left Theatre to fold in 1937.

Popular Front and Rebel Players

Despite the release of new energy following the post-Olympiad debate, the WTM itself began to drift apart under the pressures of the changing political situation. These had increased since the Nazis had seized power in the country which had once seemed destined to lead the Communist revolution in the west. The years 1933-35 were a period of transition inside the Communist movement and many of the 'class against class' policies had already been overturned in practice by the time of their official replacement in 1935 at the Comintern's seventh congress with an opposite approach based on alliances with other popular forces. The aim of this strategy was to build a united front on the left as the core of a People's or Popular Front against the main enemy, fascism.[16]

In Britain, membership of the Communist Party and the circulation of the *Daily Worker* were growing. The fight against unemployment and Mosley's fascists was strong. The Peace Ballot campaign (from the end of 1934 to mid-1935) involved more than 1,000 local committees with 500,000 volunteers and produced 11,500,000 votes in favour of the League of Nations and 10,500,000 votes for disarmament. The General Election of 1935 saw the first MP returned on a solely Communist ticket. While the Popular Front strategy produced fruitful results at local level and within newly created national bodies organised around particular campaigns, efforts to form an official pact at national party level failed (there were four main attempts between 1936 and 1939).

Leaders of the Labour Party and TUC had not forgotten the Communists calling them social fascists. They were suspicious of Popular Front organisations as vehicles for Stalinist domination, a view underlined by the experience of the Moscow trials and shared by supporters of Trotsky, who replaced the Labour leadership in the Communist lexicon as the latest 'objective fascists'. Nevertheless, the Popular Front strategy dominated anti-establishment politics of the latter half of the 1930s, particularly after the outbreak of the Spanish Civil War, and laid the basis for an extraordinary growth in political and cultural activity mobilised around the left, accompanied by unprecedented influence for the Communist Party.

After the workers' theatre Olympiad Popular Front ideas were actively discussed within the WTM; as early as 1934 there was a United Front Troupe in London's West Ham. During the 1935 General Election WTM groups supported United Front candidates. While some found the change of Communist line disconcerting and dropped out of activity, many adjusted with enthusiasm. However, they carried over ideas from the past which helped shape, and in their turn were re-shaped by, the new politics.

The WTM's isolation was breaking down. Rebel Players even

affiliated to Britain's main amateur theatre organisation, the British Drama League, which itself was enjoying the peak of activity since its founding in 1919, with an estimate of between 20,000 and 30,000 groups affiliated to it. In April 1935, the WTM responded directly to the changing situation by forming a broader umbrella body called the New Theatre League, with Tom Thomas as its secretary.[17] The name was borrowed from America, which had now become the pacemaker for left-wing theatre since the Nazis had taken over the German workers' theatre organisations and had banned all left-wing and liberal drama.[18] The New Theatre League was supposed to co-ordinate the work of all amateur theatre organisations concerned with plays of social significance, but it never amounted to much and faded away with the establishment of Unity Theatre as a Popular Front workers' theatre.

This transition from the WTM to Unity came mainly through the work of Rebel Players, which, as the WTM disintegrated, had begun to absorb members of other groups, notably from Proltet and Red Radio.[19] Attempts by the WTM leadership to discipline groups, which had always maintained a fair degree of independence, merely confirmed the break-up. Some WTM members pursued their special interests in new organisations; musicians and members of the WTM choir formed the Workers' Music League, which later became the Workers' Music Association. A dance/drama group was set up, and a group of people who had attended a film conference in Moscow during the theatre Olympiad, turned the film section of the WTM into a left-wing distribution company called Kino and were also involved in founding the Workers' Film and Photo League. Each kept contact with Unity, both as organisations and through the individuals concerned; the dance troupe performed at Unity, the Film and Photo League (having dropped 'Workers' ' from its name) distributed a record of a Unity play to accompany one of its films and Unity was present at the foundation of the Workers' Music Association just two months after Unity itself had been established.

Experiences varied in many places that were later to develop active left-wing theatres – Glasgow, Liverpool and Bristol, for example; the WTM either disappeared and had no connection with the subsequent group, as in Liverpool, or it survived in new companies with new forms of presentation. In Manchester, for instance, there was a direct link between the Salford Red Megaphones, through Theatre of Action, to Theatre Union (and after the war to Theatre Workshop).

Such changes were part of the wider creation by the left, through different organisations and magazines, of a cultural network of its own which attracted many people who did not come from traditional left-wing backgrounds.[20] The Popular Front strategy meant not only a new attitude to the trade unions and the Labour Party but also a new attitude to the middle class, especially the intellectuals who were no longer to be seen as the infected bearers of bourgeois poison. The 1929 slump had created thousands of unemployed among the middle class, many of whom would never again see their lives as stable and secure, nor the world as a safe place while capitalism was in crisis and peace was threatened by book-burning Nazis. There was also a new militancy among students, exemplified by the Oxford Union debate in 1933 at which the motion that 'This House refuses to fight for King and Country' was carried, much to the horror of the establishment. These wider sociological shifts were reflected even within the WTM, primarily in Rebel Players, which was bringing into its ranks people from a range of backgrounds.[21]

The core of Rebel Players consisted of young Jewish people, often the daughters and sons of families who had fled persecution and settled in London's East End.[22] They came from tightly knit communities which proved to be the seedbed of a distinctive revolutionary politics that was different from the predominantly Labourist political culture of the neighbouring, and mainly Catholic, docklands.

Many of the Jewish refugees had been involved in underground political activity in Tsarist Russia, Poland or elsewhere and in England they helped found a number of craft trade unions (some of the surviving banners of which are in Yiddish). With the overthrow of the Tsar, it was understandable that the young Soviet Union should become a symbol of hope for Jewish people, as well as for others suffering oppression; anti-semitism and racism were outlawed and the previously dispossessed were in control. The Communist Party, likewise, became attractive, offering the sense of belonging to an international family, with its own habits and way of life and complete conviction about victory in the future based on the rock-solid predictions of a scientific analysis. This struck deep chords for a community that traditionally felt it did not belong and that carried with it historically a correspondingly deep sense of loss. The Communist Party had a strong Jewish presence but the party's particular appeal lay precisely in its disregard for the barriers of religion or race – all workers were brothers and sisters under the skin, whether black or white, Catholic, Protestant or Jewish.

In Jewish communities, it was culture rather than country that provided identity; London's East End spawned an impressive network of classes, libraries and political meetings held in cafés, halls or on street corners, as well as a spread of cultural associations. It was not unusual for Communist Party branches to have cultural organisers and for comrades to listen to and discuss a symphony or opera played on a gramophone. There was also a tradition of Yiddish theatre, which had been established in the late nineteenth century and was opposed by the rabbis. The repertoire had been wide and had even included plays on political issues. It declined after the First World War and what remained, strong as it was, became associated with 'middle-aged' conservative – even Zionist – tendencies, keen on preserving the past and celebrating a culture under threat. Political theatre, on the other hand, was youthful and radical, educating its audiences in English – the language of the young Jews – to change the present and build a new future. (The Yiddish WTM group Proltet, however, was concerned with Jewish heritage, too.) It is not difficult to see the attraction of political theatre in such a milieu, shaped as it was by a religion whose rituals expressed the value of words and learning and the continuity of a shared experience. The religious ceremonies themselves are dramatised stories, presided over by highly theatrical figures – for example, the cantors, singing their solos as if in an opera (and the tunes were often very close, if not identical, to well known arias). This proclivity for performance could also be seen in the way speakers addressed open air meetings or street traders called to their customers and negotiated a deal. It was not surprising that it served Unity well, and that Unity became famous for its humour and its down-to-earth vigour, in striking contrast to the insipid West End.

Political theatre aimed at breaking down the barriers between people and there was nothing specifically Jewish in content in the repertoire of Rebel Players or Unity. The appeal was political. Rebel Players deliberately set out to attract people beyond the Jewish community of the East End, performing in areas 'up the social ladder' like Hackney or Stamford Hill and in central London.[23] Its members were tailors, furniture craft workers, labourers, the unemployed, clerks, civil servants, shop workers, hairdressers, skilled technicians. A few Oxford and Cambridge graduates joined the group, and for one woman the choice was to be presented at court or perform with Rebel Players – she chose the latter. Middle-class members were recruited, particularly during the Peace Ballot when Rebel Players performed Ernst Toller's *Requiem*, a mass declamation dedicated to the assassinated German revolutionaries Rosa Luxemburg and Karl Liebknecht, which was also known as *A Man and a Woman*. Toller saw one performance, in Holborn.[24]

Whatever the difference in social background or political experience, most members at this period joined the Communist Party if only because, in contrast to the Labour Party, it was actively fighting on the important national and international issues of the day. Communist discipline in Rebel Players was tight; members were penalised or expelled for misdemeanours, such as bad time-keeping or behaviour considered detrimental to the group. 'It was a commitment,' recalls Rebel Players' secretary Bram Bootman, himself a civil servant. 'As simple as that. If you were called out, you just went, wherever or whenever you were wanted.'

While everyone was united in a determination to raise artistic standards to better serve the labour and left-wing movements, Rebel Players lacked suitable material to perform and it decided to look back for ideas to the earlier period of the WTM before the concentration on agitprop. Despite having to abandon a planned production of *The Ragged Trousered Philanthropists*, which proved beyond the group's means, it was able to perform at the WTM conference in February 1934 another play from that earlier phase, a short anti-war play, *Gas*.[25]

This conference confirmed the different directions being taken within the WTM; Manchester's Theatre of Action, for instance, criticised Rebel Players for placing content above form and could only agree on the need to perform indoors and to have a proper base, then still a controversial point for a predominantly mobile movement with little finance.

Rebel Players included further material from the earlier WTM period in its repertoire, such as the sketch *RIP* (Rent, Interest, Profit) and two 1928 plays by Tom Thomas: *Women of Kirbinsk*, in which the women of a remote Russian village just after the 1917 Revolution take over the estate of a local landowner and subsequently find that their action has been legitimised by new land decrees of the Soviet government, and *The Fight Goes On*, set during the miners' lock-out that followed the General Strike.

The group had set up a repertoire commission to tackle the problem of new material, the political and artistic priority being to create new work about contemporary struggles in Britain. Out of the commission came *Fate or – !*, on the dangers of child labour, and *Slickers Ltd*, which shows workers challenging the intrigues of high financiers in profiting from war.[26] Attributed to John Hammer (most likely a pen name) and stylised in make-up and gesture, it looked forward to Unity material in its attempt to create a fast-moving, broad comedy on a serious issue drawing on an indigenous tradition. The commission also helped produce *Hunger Marchers* (by George Poles or Pole – probably another pen name), in which agricultural workers come to understand their own exploitation as they prepare to receive a hunger march in their village against the wishes of the local squire.

New productions also included two 'open platform' sketches: *It's a Free Country* by H. Baron, which represents an attempt to develop agitprop by taking character seriously in the story of a long-service worker who is dismissed and fined for assaulting a policeman on an unemployment demonstration; and a satire, *Dr Krupps*, contrasting wasteful capitalist agricultural methods to beneficial Soviet ones. There was a short comedy called *Twenty Minutes* by the Soviet writer Cheharkov on the speed of both marriage and divorce in the Soviet Union, and a campaigning play, *For Dmitrov* – in honour of the Bulgarian Communist who was tried for the Reichstag fire but who used the court proceedings to indict the Nazis instead. He was acquitted after intense international solidarity and became a renowned symbol of the anti-fascist fight.

Rebel Players performed six shows that were later to form part of Unity's early programme. Two were in the realistic style that set Rebel Players apart from the rest of the WTM. *The People's Court*, by critic and writer Hubert Griffith who was on the board of

Left Theatre, deals with the impartiality of Soviet justice. It was based on a visit to Moscow by the author who saw a woman judge try a paternity case brought against a member of the Young Communist League without letting his party membership sway her in his favour. Her judgement, combined with seeing the baby, make the father admit his responsibility. *The Secret*, written by the Spanish Republican novelist Ramón Sender, was based on an incident in Barcelona during the mass jailings of 1935 – a prisoner tricks his interrogator and chooses death rather than betray his comrades. Three of the plays were stylistically linked to the WTM: Toller's mass declamation *Requiem*; a collaboratively written skit *The Fall of the House of Slusher*, which was based on a WTM sketch, *Love in Industry*; and *Newsboy*, an extension of WTM sketches such as *Suppress, Oppress and Depress*, which were early attempts at drama documentary. *Newsboy* is an adaptation in Living Newspaper format of a poem by the American Communist V.J. Jerome. It displays the values of the Communist press in the face of the lies of the capitalist papers, as the 'truth' behind the headlines is acted out in brief, inter-cutting scenes. The text was changed constantly to keep up with events and the writer Simon Blumenfeld remembers scripting a completely new version at Unity.

The sixth play of this group turned out to be the most explosive newcomer of all, *Waiting for Lefty*, and was a mixture of both traditions. Inadvertently, the staging of *Waiting for Lefty*, and the controvery that it aroused within the dying WTM, hastened the founding of Unity Theatre and the beginning of a completely new phase in British political theatre.

Rebel Players had consolidated its organisation at its annual general meeting in March 1935. New members were joining but the group was finding it difficult to offer them challenging new work. It was decided to mount a special programme of shows to gain publicity and launch a campaign of expansion. There was even talk of looking for permanent premises, which, although felt to be desirable, was beyond the group's current means. The special evening was to be held in October and was to include *Waiting for Lefty*, a powerful short piece from America by Clifford Odets which had been published in *New Theatre*, the magazine of the American New Theater League. The play had already been performed in Britain by Manchester's Theatre of Action but without a licence. Rebel Players contacted both Odets and his agents for permission to stage the play, but this was not forthcoming, possibly because of Manchester's unlicensed performance. Nevertheless, Rebel Players went ahead with its plans to present the play during 'An Evening of Social Drama' at the Fred Tallant Hall in North London on Saturday 12 October 1935. Permission had still not arrived by 8 October and Tom Thomas, who had tried to help secure the necessary permission, wrote to the Rebel Players in his capacity as secretary of the New Theatre League. He said that to present *Waiting for Lefty* would be a 'violation of our principles', which would put off professionals and damage relations with American writers, 'to whom we look for the greater part of our repertoire'. He asked for the performance to be cancelled.

Rebel Players felt no moral obligation to comply because the group had done all in its power to obtain the licence. Counter arguments to Thomas's centred on the belief that *Waiting for Lefty* was essential to the group's survival. It was the only new piece of work to be included in the evening and without it the group could not sustain its growth in membership, its newly won contacts with the labour movement or its financial viability; in other words, to cancel meant the collapse of the group. Rebel Players went ahead with the evening under the banner of the Popular Front slogan, 'Art is a Weapon of the Masses'. The programme comprised *Twenty Minutes, Slickers Ltd, A Man and a Woman* and *Waiting for Lefty*, although, in deference to Thomas, the latter's title was not used. (A leaflet referred to a 'sensational play of a New York taxi strike by Clifford Odetts' – misspelt with two t's.) The evening was a success with *Waiting for Lefty* clearly the main attraction, and none of the problems arose that Thomas had predicted.[27]

At the next meeting of Rebel Players, Thomas was censured. A letter was sent to the IURT in Moscow explaining the argument and making a demand: unless Thomas resigned, the group would break with the WTM. The dispute had become highly personalised, as did most of Unity's later internal conflicts. Thomas supported some of the group's work but disliked a lot of it too. He came out in favour of using professionals, though not in leading positions, which is what he felt was happening with Rebel Players, and he believed that Rebel Players was trying to 'legitimise' the WTM and form a new power centre. Another meeting of the group later that October issued a call for a general meeting of the whole movement 'for an exposition of the New Theatre League' – a coded way of saying that Rebel Players had an alternative plan for the movement which it wanted debated and for which it would seek backing. The following day, 29 October, Rebel Players issued a formal notice saying that the 'WTM has ceased and officials retired and that individuals have constituted themselves as a provisional committee to formulate New TL.'

The New TL (Theatre League), though it did present some revues and shows and hold a few meetings and socials, rapidly became less important than the creation of a new theatre company with its own premises. It faded away at the end of 1936 when Unity had become established. While this signalled the final burial of the WTM, and the loss to the movement of several of its stalwarts like Tom Thomas, those who formed the nucleus of the new Unity did not abandon overnight all that the WTM stood for.[28] They never forgot their debt to the WTM, nor that Unity would never have existed without the WTM. It was always regarded a 'badge of honour' to have been one of those who had performed 'on the streets' and, as one of Unity's leading directors, John Allen, was to write a little later:

> It is important to know that those actors who are still the backbone of the club spent five years rehearsing in attics and cellars, and giving performances at street corners, from the back of lorries etc.; and it is my belief that the quite remarkable strength and vigour of these actors is due entirely to this training.[29]

Building on the experiences of the WTM, which had developed from a series of diverse and separate initiatives without any guiding model of revolutionary drama to follow, there was intense debate within old WTM groups, the New Theatre League, and sections of the Communist Party about the nature of the new theatre and of its organisation and ideology. The WTM, while aware of many of its problems, had stuck to its sectarian position and belief in mobile agitprop, convinced that if only the workers could be shown the truth then the socialist light would penetrate the capitalist fog of false consciousness.

The political basis of the WTM's position had been undermined by the rise of fascism and the Rebel Players' leaders were determined to break out of the isolation and narrowness of the approach that the movement found itself in. This required new forms of organisation and new repertoire choices. Rebel Players did not want to replace one dominant form – agitprop – with another but to embrace a variety of forms as long as they were appropriate to the pursuit of the Popular Front goals, which, in the context of the threat of fascism, were as revolutionary as those of the WTM. Rebel Players' members were fired with the same spirit of opposition, autonomy and intense dedication to a vital cause that distinguished the WTM. Certain beliefs were carried over into Unity, such as the overriding importance of non-professional status or the primary need to take plays out of theatre buildings to where an audience lived or worked, and these were to remain articles of faith for significant numbers of Unitarians throughout Unity's existence, even when they were not shared by the theatre's leadership.

But, by the end of 1935, the leadership of Rebel Players was openly committed to launching a permanent theatre. They knew that this was a big risk since the professional Left Theatre was having great trouble achieving the same aim, and subsequently failed. Also, other parts of the labour movement, in particular the Co-operative wing, which had the means to sustain such a venture, had resolutely rejected the idea. The answer was to lie in political commitment and the pursuit of a Popular Front strategy, an outward going policy led by Communist Party members aimed at involving increasing numbers of people in the political struggles of the day through their participation in a drama that was unashamedly propagandist.

A 1936 Communist Party pamphlet sums up the approach. Called *War and Culture: The Decline of Culture under Capitalism* it was written by poet and essayist Edgell Rickword. In a section called 'Peace and Culture are Indivisible', it reads

> The artistic creativeness of the workers grows up from, and is stimulated by, the political struggle. So let us make use ... not only of the organisational forms of struggle (which are of the first importance), but of the growing artistic forces of the movement. Let us use *our* theatre, *our* films, *our* poems and novels against the infectious influence of the war-makers, expressing confidence and hope against today's confusion and despair.[30]

Following the formal break with the WTM in October, Rebel Players concentrated attention on making the impossible happen –

finding a permanent base and setting up the necessary organisation to keep it alive. There was some respite from performing, as Odets still had not granted permission to play *Waiting for Lefty* and the group felt it could not present it on a regular basis without a licence. New members and more bookings, however, added to the frustration of not having a permanent theatre: Rebel Players had always been forced to use whatever places could be found for meetings and rehearsal – cafés, pubs, a baker's basement in Holborn, a room above a skin factory in Smithfield meat market, a bookshop in Whitechapel run by a former member of the Proltet group who had joined Rebel Players.

The lack of stability threatened the survival of the group, though the main drawback of acquiring a permanent theatre was also clear: it was felt with good reason that after an initial flush of enthusiasm the group would not have the artistic and organisational capacity to sustain both its own building and its mobile work, and that the ensuing effort to keep open the theatre would reduce or even destroy the politically vital touring activity. On the other hand, a permanent place could allow more continuity and could provide a focus for more efficient work and organisation, which would help improve standards and open up the possibility of gaining a regular audience. The group would then be in a stronger position to carry out its primary task of taking theatre to people who might not otherwise experience it – a priority that was to change in the years to come. A permanent base could also be a social place to meet and relax, discuss and argue, read and rehearse – a cultural centre for music, dance, cinema, poetry, and exhibitions, too, the success of which might lead to a renewal of the workers' theatre movement nationally.

The Founding of Unity

In December 1935 Jimmy Turner, a recent recruit to Rebel Players, telephoned Bram Bootman, the group's secretary, to say that he had found a possible site. It was near Kings Cross at the top of Grays Inn Road, opposite the new premises of the Co-operative Sunday newspaper *Reynolds News*. The area had a definite working-class identity, which largely derived from the transport industries, as well as Bohemian associations, mainly through the art world. It also lay outside the East End, which was important for Rebel Players in their attempt to broaden their appeal. Turner and Bootman went on Christmas Eve to see St Jude's Hall, Britannia Street. Built in 1842, it had been left derelict for nearly a year after the Methodist church next door, to which it had been attached, was demolished as a result of a parish amalgamation. The hall, situated on the second floor with an arched roof, had been used as a schoolroom, a mission and more recently for theatrical rehearsals; Bram Bootman remembers seeing piles of rubbish and the remnants of a dilapidated set for what he took to be something like *A Midsummer Night's Dream* when he and Turner were shown the hall by the vicar. Turner had found the vicar sympathetic – Bootman remembered him as a relative of the actor John Le Mesurier, and he became a great Unity supporter. They negotiated with him a long-term lease at £100 a year. The first three months were to be rent-free in exchange for the group renovating the hall.[31]

Rebel Players' committee met on New Year's Day 1936 and set up a working party to oversee the conversion of the hall into a theatre. The committee agreed the terms of the lease, which was signed by van Gyseghem and Bootman – both men being in work – but in the calculations the rates had been forgotten. It caused quite a shock when the demands came in and they had to be paid.

The committee also discussed the group's change of name and its constitution. Bootman recalls old WTM-type names being suggested, like Red Theatre or Theatre of the Revolution, and some that were too intellectual, like Alpha or Omega Theatre. They were rejected in favour of a name that summed up the prevailing political strategy of the moment, Unity, which, remembers Bootman, was proposed by Derek Blaikie. Blaikie worked for the *New Statesman* and was a friend from Oxford University days of the journalist and future Labour MP Tom Driberg who also became a Unity supporter.

A notice was issued to all Rebel Players' members the day after the committee meeting, using the Whitechapel bookshop address. It called a general meeting for that Sunday, 5 January, at 4 p.m. in Room No. 4 of the well known working-class meeting place Circle House, Great Alie Street, 'to establish the First Workers' Theatre in London!!' Letters were sent also to selected individuals, such as former WTM secretary Philip Poole, inviting them to the meeting in the hope of persuading them to join and donate money. Leading

WTM figures like Poole and Thomas did not become involved, however, believing that Rebel Players, always the odd group of the WTM, would establish a theatre so different from what they had been used to that they would not feel at home in it.

The Rebel Players' committee asked the general meeting to endorse proposals that were to be put to the inaugural AGM of Unity. The policy was to present Popular Front ideals and to combine touring with a repertoire presented at Britannia Street at a single, accessible ticket price. The theatre would be run as a club on the democratic centralist lines of the Communist Party and certain trade unions. A management committee, elected at the AGM by club members, would oversee a network of subordinate committees which would have responsibility for different aspects of the club's life, from stage management and repertoire to catering. Conduct of the club would be reviewed at quarterly general meetings. By becoming a club, the new theatre could avoid the censorship of the Lord Chamberlain's office as well as local authority restrictions and the ban on Sunday performing. (Forming a club was a well established practice in the theatre and had been used on the left in the late 1920s to show Soviet films that had not been granted a licence.)

This final meeting of Rebel Players' members endorsed the committee's suggestions and another letter was circulated, on notepaper headed Unity Theatre Club, Britannia Street, Kings Cross WCI, announcing 'The First General Meeting of UTC' to be held on Sunday 9 February, at 5 p.m. at the theatre itself. Invitations were sent to a range of individuals as well as to many organisations, such as trade unions, the Labour Party, the Communist Party, theatre guilds and amateur dramatic groups.

According to a Unity Theatre handbook, 360 people attended the inaugural AGM, of whom 60 became what were known as active members, who were eligible to vote and stand as officers, and 300 became associate members, who were entitled to buy tickets for club performances. This distinction between types of membership was carried over from the Rebel Players' constitution, which provided the basis for the initial Unity rule book. Membership cost 1 shilling, with an additional payment for the extra rights afforded active members and a reduced fee at the committee's discretion for the unemployed. The rules declared the club's business to be, quite simply, 'to produce, present, and exhibit to its members and their guests, stage plays and films of social significance and educational value, and to provide suitable premises and accessories for these purposes'. A six-person general management committee was elected to run the club's affairs comprising Derek Blaikie, Bram Bootman, Maurice Braham, Mark Chaney, Joe Stern and Jimmy Turner.[32] Leaders were elected for the various sub-committees which were to make monthly reports to the management committee. There was to be no artistic director and all important decisions were to be taken by vote. The meeting agreed to continue following the principle of collective creation by keeping the cast and production team anonymous in the programmes and also endorsed the decision to rent and renovate the old mission hall.[33]

Unity members and their friends, including skilled building trades workers, had been clearing the rubbish at Britannia Street and preparing the upstairs hall for use as a theatre. They climbed ladders to clean rafters, they scraped down and repaired walls, floor and ceiling, and they turned the pulpit into a stage that was built in sections to the specifications of designer Bagnall Harris who had worked at the Old Vic and with van Gyseghem at the Embassy. The height, shape and size of the stage could be altered at will. They wired up the long, thin hall (65 feet x 20 feet) for lighting and installed an inventive dimming system made of old stoneware drainpipes blocked off at one end and embedded with an electrode. These 'pots' were filled with sal-ammoniac acid and water into which was lowered another electrode on a cable, worked by a hand-wheel. Advancing the two electrodes together brought the lights up while separating the electrodes dimmed them. If left on full dim for too long noxious fumes wafted out of the pipes. One hundred or so repainted wooden seats from Collins Music Hall in nearby Islington were put in as well as, over the stage, a false proscenium arch made of canvas and painted black.

A sign over the street door read 'Unity Theatre Club'. Inside, a card table would be placed to serve as the box office while people queued on the pavement. The ground floor was available for hire and was used for rehearsals, committee meetings, cups of tea and the men's toilet. Up a spiral stone staircase, on the first floor was the theatre, the single dressing room used by all, and the women's lavatory. Bram Bootman, who became Unity's voluntary archivist and remained a Unitarian until his death, recalled that Jimmy

Turner became the club's first employee (as a 'clerk') and that Red Radio stalwart Joe Stern, who stayed with Unity until after the war, was employed as Britannia Street manager on £3 a week. His duties included taking bookings and general care of the building, which required him to sleep there from time to time.

Britannia Street – or 'Brit Street' as it was known – was officially opened on Sunday, 23 February 1936 by Dr Edith Summerskill, who had recently stood for Labour on a peace ticket in an important by-election. An enlightened manager, Anmer Hall from the Westminster Theatre, was on the platform too. The afternoon performance included Margaret Barr's Dance Drama Group, which was influenced by the German Mary Wigman and the American Martha Graham, and Unity's presentation of *Private Hicks*, by the American playwright Albert Maltz, which Unity had begun rehearsing in the continued absence of permission to stage *Waiting for Lefty*. Kino, the workers' film group, was to have shown a film but the projector broke down. Quickly, several Rebel Players veterans donned their blue jerseys, red kerchiefs and grey flannel skirts or trousers and presented Toller's *Requiem* instead.

This was not the only hiccup. With all the pressure of getting the hall ready for the opening, no one had remembered to print any programmes. Bootman and his assistant Celia Block (who had the job, she says, because she was the best, if not the only, typist in the group) rushed to the WTM/New Theatre League Headquarters in Great James Street and printed some programmes on the roneo machine just before the ceremony was due to begin. They returned with no time to spare, and Bootman, who had to introduce Dr Summerskill, could not shake her by the hand because she was wearing white gloves and his hands were still covered in ink. The official opening was followed by tea, coffee, cakes and sandwiches and then a dance. Although *Reynolds News* did carry a description of the conversion of the hall, Bootman recalls that no one had thought it important to invite the press to the launch and even the *Daily Worker*, which had run advertisements for the event, did not subsequently report it.

Unity's opening was low key. While Communists were in the forefront, as with the WTM, there was no direct involvement from the national leadership beyond internal discussion and agreement on the value of the project.[34] The Communist Party took culture seriously, and perhaps more so during the Popular Front years than at any other time, but its main thrust continued to be industrial. Its working-class leaders had not entirely shaken off a deep British scepticism of middle- or upper-class intellectuals. Unlike some other Communist Parties, intellectuals did not as a rule occupy positions of national importance in Britain.

As far as Unity was concerned, the Popular Front approach of the party and related publications, like the *Daily Worker* with its weekly theatre column or the magazine *Left Review*, was directed as much at winning the 'high' ground of art as at promoting workers' cultural self-activity. The two were not seen in contradiction but as twin partners in a common alliance of workers by hand and brain inhabiting separate though interconnected worlds. Professional Communist artists, who were active politically as well as culturally, and had their own meeting places and magazines, worked primarily in an hostile environment against the prevailing ideology and sought to be exemplary in their craft to demonstrate the superiority of their philosophy. They were keen and happy to support Unity while letting Unity organise and develop according to its own needs, aims and capacities. Unity welcomed and wanted their advice and help, but its world remained quite distinct from theirs. The youthful enthusiasm, ambition and self-confidence within that world of Unity's founders may have led to utopian self-assertion, yet it did not prevent them also from making realistic assessments of their place in the order of things.

Challenges to theatrical orthodoxy came from across the ideological and class board; there were signs within 'bourgeois' drama of liberating things to come – people's Shakespeare at the Old Vic, for instance, or the work of directors like Tyrone Guthrie, Barry Jackson and Michel Saint-Denis and productions at 'little' theatres such as the Festival Theatre, Cambridge. Amateur theatre had its pioneers too, most notably Nugent Monck at the Maddermarket Theatre in Norwich, and in both 'camps' ideals similar to those of Unity were being pursued – the London-based Group Theatre, for example, heavily influenced by the European avant-garde, set out to be a co-operative in which the performers were trained in common and which called for the theatre to be a social force breaking down the barrier between audience and actor. The difference for socialists and Communists was that the emergence of cultural and political movements allowed radical thought to become socially effective. Left-wing individuals and groups drew their strength from these movements in a constant process of defining and redefining themselves through political and cultural activity and in the process helped make those movements stronger. The few specifically socialist groups – like the Theatre of Action in Manchester, a shock troupe still concerned with developing its own aesthetic, Left Theatre, a bold but sporadic professional initiative, or Unity – were part of a political upsurge that addressed most aspects of culture.

Understandably there were ambiguities for Unity; the surviving simplistic impulses of WTM days did not always fuse easily with the more complex needs of the Popular Front, particularly in reaching out to new people. To take one case, Unity wanted to tour but less and less to appear randomly before its audience – at, for example, a factory gate – without the kind of adequate preparation that might begin with Unity being invited to the venue either by the workers concerned or following an approach from the theatre itself. Unity was convinced that for political theatre to progress from the often haphazard confrontation of the WTM period it must organise its audience and its context. This was the anchor of Unity's huge commitment to take on a permanent home along with and underpinning the touring activity, both as a symbol of the developing maturity and potential of the movement and as a practical basis for growth.

Unity wanted to overcome the working class's historical exclusion from the dominant culture by appropriating and transforming the 'best' that the bourgeoisie had developed whilst trying to create its own tradition too. Within this intention, partly in reaction to the extreme attitudes and isolation of the WTM and partly following the Popular Front approach, there was a strong current of thought that believed Unity should be taken seriously as a 'proper' theatre, a tendency that became more overt as Unity became more successful. This involved several paradoxes for the desired total theatrical revolution, aside from those thrown up by the unavoidable practical demands of keeping the premises open, which were always to be a drain on energy and resources. In terms of the auditorium, Unity's founders chose to build a conventional end-on proscenium stage rather than a more challenging configuration, for example, a theatre-in-the-round (which would have proved difficult though not impossible in the long, thin hall). The proscenium arch was the exemplar of bourgeois theatre, symbolising a stable picture frame world, the solidity of which was reflected in the apparent unchanging relationship between content and form and between the actor displaying illusion and the passive, voyeuristic audience.

A workers' theatre, drawing its audience from the left or into the left's orbit, could happily live with this actor-audience relationship because, it seemed to Unity, the values underlying it were different and opposed to those of the bourgeois theatre; whatever barrier might exist between stage and auditorium could be overcome by the content of the plays and by the ways in which the plays were presented. Not only would this mean using a range of styles, it could involve placing actors among the audience, or even decorating the theatre to change its appearance (for instance, one director of *Waiting for Lefty* made the auditorium look as if a trade union meeting were in progress). The auditorium did not boast traditional gilt-edged trappings and there were no footlights on stage. Not surprisingly, Unity also broke with the prevailing custom of playing the national anthem.

Unity avoided wholesale adoption of bourgeois theatre practices and conventional plays.[35] Minimalist standards of production reminiscent of the WTM were maintained at first, though these gave way quickly within the constraints of a restrictive budget to more visually exciting and imaginative effects. Nevertheless, respect for the skills of the bourgeois professional theatre, which for some became too reverential during the Popular Front period, did produce internal tensions that remained throughout Unity's existence.

Just one month before the meeting that set up Unity, an article in *Left Review* had called for the founding in Britain of a permanent theatre which would become 'an artistic centre for working-class and progressive audiences'. The professional theatre world could not provide this, public subsidy was not available, and only with the birth of Unity did this possibility become a reality. No one was sure if Unity would survive, let alone grow, and it took a hard year of struggling, fired by a rumbustious optimism and unceasing commitment, for Unity to become established within the left-wing movement.

Notes

Given the nature of the research for this book, which is described in the foreword, it would prove ludicrously unwieldy to cite every reference, especially from oral sources and newspapers. Notes are provided, therefore, to amplify points in the text or to guide the reader to the chief source or sources. Interviews and correspondence are cited for the main chapters to which they refer. Availability of plays can be found in the chronological list of Unity productions on pp. 403–418.

1. I do not know of any book that covers the history of rebel or alternative drama on a world scale. There are books and articles that deal with the nineteenth- and twentieth-century British traditions and specific movements, such as that of the repertory theatres or women's suffrage. An easy-to-read introduction with a manageable bibliography is Andrew Davies, *Other Theatres*, Macmillan 1987. Another introduction, bringing together experiments in Europe and America in the twentieth century, is David Bradby and John McCormick, *People's Theatre*, Croom Helm 1978. For the 25 years following the First World War in Britain, during which period Unity Theatre was founded, see Norman Marshall, *The Other Theatre*, John Lehmann 1947.
2. Chief sources for Workers' Theatre Movement: Howard Goorney, *The Theatre Workshop Story*, Eyre Methuen 1981; Howard Goorney and Ewan MacColl, *Agitprop to Theatre Workshop*, Manchester University Press 1986; Len Jones, *The British Workers' Theatre 1917-1935*, unpublished PhD thesis, Leipzig 1964; Reiner Lehberger, *Das sozialistische Theater in England 1934 bis zum Ausbruch des Zweiten Weltkriegs*, Peter Lang 1977; Raphael Samuel, Ewan MacColl and Stuart Cosgrove, *Theatres of the Left 1880-1935*, Routledge & Kegan Paul 1985; Richard Stourac and Kathleen McCreery, *Theatre as a Weapon*, Routledge & Kegan Paul 1986. *Red Stage, New Red Stage, Daily Worker*, WTM Bulletins.
3. Published in *Joe Corrie: Plays, Poems and Theatre Writings*, 7:84 Publications 1985.
4. Given the pyramid and international structure of the Comintern, policy changes took considerable time to be effected and were necessarily out of step with the thinking if not the practice of some of the constituent parties. After Lenin's death in 1924, there was also an increase in power of the central bureaucracy in Moscow as the annual congresses (from 1919-1922) became more infrequent. There were five plenums between

the 5th congress in 1924 and the 6th in 1928 and four plenums and three praesidiums between the 6th and the final congress in 1935. The change in line from 'class against class' to that of a united and popular front can be seen to have begun in 1933 by Dmitrov.

5. There are many histories of the period. A good introduction is Noreen Branson and Margot Heinemann, *Britain in the 1930s*, Weidenfeld and Nicolson 1971.

6. For Tom Thomas's work and thoughts, see *Theatres of the Left.* Interview with Jack Selford gave details of Hackney group.

7. See *Theatres of the Left.*

8. Recited to me by WTM veterans and quoted in *Theatres of the Left* and *Theatre as a Weapon*.

9. For references to individual groups, WTM activities, conferences, publications, see note 2. See also Philip Poole interviewed in *Red Letters*, No. 10, 1980; Jack Loveman, 'Workers' Theatre', *Red Letters*, No. 13, 1982; Kathleen McCreery, 'Proltet; Yiddish Theatre in the 1930s', *Race & Class*, Vol. 20 No. 3, Winter 1979. For the wider context, see also Alun Howkins, 'Class Against Class: The Culture of British Communism 1930-1935' in Frank Gloversmith (ed.), *Class Culture and Social Change: A New View of the 1930s*, Harvester Press 1980.

10. See *Theatre as a Weapon*; L. Hoffman and D. Hoffman-Ostwald, *Deutsches Arbeitertheater 1918-1933*, Henschelverlag 1972. For an account of Das Rote Sprachrohr, one of the German Communist Party's most popular troupes, see Len Crome, *Unbroken: Resistance and Survival in the Concentration Camps,* Lawrence and Wishart 1988.

11. See Jones, who quotes the report and recommendations, which were not printed in Britain until March 1934 although they were discussed and acted upon beforehand. Philip Poole gave details on André van Gyseghem and the Moscow trip.

12. *New Red Stage*, June-July 1932, mentions Rebel Players (and says the group wore uniform when performing outdoors but not inside). Rebel Players information from Bram Bootman and Philip Poole.

13. André van Gyseghem gives his own account of 'Theatre in the Thirties' in Jon Clark *et al.* (eds), *Culture and Crisis in Britain in the 30s*, Lawrence and Wishart 1979. Other professionals who worked with the WTM include Ina de la Haye, Joyce Bland and Shirley Wakefield.

14. André van Gyseghem wanted to visit Africa after working with Paul Robeson and he took with him records of Robeson singing. Van Gyseghem persuaded the government to let him use black Africans in the Empire Pageant instead of white people 'blacked' up. He founded the Bantu People's Theatre as a theatre run on socialist principles and directed O'Neill's *The Hairy Ape*, which was seen at the Bantu Men's Social Centre, an important centre for cultural activities among mainly middle-class black people. The Bantu People's Theatre did not survive the war. There is a reference to this in Robert Kavanagh, *Theatre and Cultural Struggle in Southern Africa*, Zed Press 1985.

15. Information on Left Theatre from interview with Mark Dignam; also see Davies, Lehberger, van Gysegham, *Daily Worker, Left Review*.

16. There are many books on the Popular Front. A useful introduction is Jim Fyrth (ed.), *Britain, Fascism and the Popular Front*, Lawrence and Wishart 1985, which contains references to Unity.
17. For New Theatre League, see *Daily Worker; Left Review; Theatres of the Left* and note 1. The provisional committee organised a conference on 30 January 1936 to put the League on an official footing. At this event there were performances by Margaret Barr's Dance Drama Group, the Labour Choral Union, Manchester Theatre of Action and the Battersea Players. Speakers included Gillian Scaife of the Group Theatre, William Armstrong of Actors' Equity and the Earl of Kinoull. The League held a few meetings and socials, such as the 1935 New Year's Eve Crazy Night Supper and dance. In the summer of 1936, the League moved into Great Newport Street with the Group Theatre but within months had ceased to function.
18. For American workers' and radical drama, see Malcolm Goldstein, *The Political Stage*, Oxford University Press 1974; *Drama was a Weapon*, Morgan Y. Himmelstein, Rutgers University Press 1963; Karen Malpede Taylor, *People's Theatre in Amerika,* Drama Book Specialists 1972; *Theatres of the Left.* Unity was affiliated to the American New Theatre League which folded in 1940.
19. Memories differ as to the timing and nature of these absorptions. *Daily Worker*, 20 February 1934, reports collaboration between Rebel Players and Red Radio. Maurice Braham says the two groups never formally united but the minutes of the Rebel Players's committee meetings of 1935 show members from both groups attending.
20. For background, see James Klugmann's introduction to *Culture and Crisis in Britain in the 30s*.
21. It is impossible to define accurately the class composition of Unity and I believe it is fruitless to attempt judgements on its value from that perspective, even though some commentators have tried to, using as their point of departure the assumption that Unity was less proletarian than its predecessor, the WTM. Leaving aside the absence of commonly agreed definitions, the ideological implications of the terminology and regional variations in make-up, there is insufficient evidence of the WTM's composition to define it sociologically as proletarian – and what evidence there is suggests a heavy leavening of non-manual workers, even if they would have placed themselves among the working-class vanguard. In any case, the core of Unity's early activists were ex-WTM members. Unity throughout its 40-year existence overwhelmingly comprised working people, often with differing ideological dispositions but who nevertheless combined behind a common aim.
22. The Jewish communities of London's East End in this period are best explored through the writings and other creative work of the people themselves, especially the novels. See, for example, Simon Blumenfeld's *Jew Boy* and *Phineas Kahn: Portrait of an Immigrant*, Lawrence and Wishart 1986 and 1988.
23. Main interviews/correspondence for Rebel Players and launching of Unity Theatre: Celia Baker (then Block), Bram Bootman, Maurice

Braham, Ray Braham, Kathleen Channing, Ted Channing, Edith Forsyth, Alice Holmes, Etta Stern, Joe Stern, Trudy Stern. See also Malcolm Page, 'The Early Years at Unity', *Theatre Quarterly*, Vol. 1 No. 4, October-December 1971; Ron Travis, *The Unity Theatre of Great Britain 1936-46*, unpublished MA thesis, Southern Illinois 1968.

24. Bram Bootman recalled that Toller was astonished and angry that his mass declamation was being presented as a peace play but Joe Stern remembered Toller saying that he had not realised what a moving play he had written until he had seen the Rebel Players' performance. Richard Dove, 'The Place of Ernst Toller in English Socialist Theatre 1924-1939', *German Life and Letters*, Vol. 38 No. 2, January 1985, says that Unity toured Toller's *Masses and Man* in 1937-8 in a production by André van Gyseghem but there is no record of this in Unity's papers and no one that I spoke to could remember it. Dove's source was a talk given by van Gyseghem.

25. Not to be confused with Georg Kaiser's *Gas 1* or *Gas 2*.

26. *Slickers Ltd*, became the basis of *John Bullion*, written by Ewan MacColl and Joan Littlewood for Manchester's Theatre of Action bcause they were dissatisfied with the original. In *Theatres of the Left* and *Agitprop to Theatre Workshop*, MacColl calls the original *Hammer* (as does Goorney in *The Theatre Workshop Story*), presumably after the author. There is also disagreement over the dates of the London performance. Merseyside Left/Unity Theatre Archive, Box 12.1, held in the Merseyside Museum of Labour History, has a copy of the play.

27. Contrary to some accounts, *Waiting for Lefty* was not first directed in Britain or in London by Herbert Marshall, who seems to be the source of the errors. Nor, as another account has it, was the play performed in London in March 1935 at the Longacre Theatre, which is in New York. *Waiting for Lefty* was published in the February 1935 issue of the American *New Theater* magazine. Theatre of Action seems to have been the first group to present it in Britain (though not, as Ewan MacColl implies in *Theatres of the Left*, in 1934 before it was written) and Shirley Wakefield appears to have been the first to direct the play in London, for Rebel Players in October 1935 and then at Unity.

28. According to Simon Blumenfeld, Tom Thomas stayed active for at least two more years in Unity's mobile work but others do not remember him being involved after the end of 1935. Jerry Dawson of Merseyside Unity Theatre says that Thomas eventually supported the move to a permanent theatre – and even called for a building fund for it – and that he recognised the Popular Front strategy as a wise and necessary one.

29. *Some Notes on the Formation of Left-Wing Amateur Theatre Groups*, the Left Book Club Theatre Guild 1937. Authorship was not credited but it was written by John Allen.

30. Reproduced in Edgell Rickword, *Literature in Society: Essays and Opinions (II) 1931-1978*, Carcanet 1978.

31. *Reynolds News*, 1 March 1936, reported that the rent was to be half rather than free for the first three months but Bootman insists that it was free.

32. Memories differ on the original six but having compared all the versions this seems the most likely group.
33. Anonymity was not the preserve of the left. It was a practice followed also at the Maddermarket Theatre, Norwich.
34. Some accounts have offered a more mechanical account of the involvement of the Communist Party in the establishment of Unity, presumably because that was its practice in other areas of work, but this is not borne out by those involved. Ron Travis in his thesis cites an undated letter, written around December 1935, from André van Gyseghem to Mark Chaney concerning a resolution submitted to Communist Party headquarters on the future of Rebel Players and the setting up of a new group. He takes this to mean that 'Unity Theatre was founded on an order from the Communist Party of Great Britain'. All it means in fact is that the Communists involved, and Rebel Players like Unity was run by Communists, understandably were keeping in touch with the party which supported them. Many Unitarians wished that the party had taken a closer interest in the theatre's activities while others were happy with what amounted to an 'arm's length' relationship. Travis wrote his thesis under the guidance of Herbert Marshall who, in the *Listener*, 22 March 1973, and in unpublished interviews, has given an incorrect account of the origins of Unity and of his role in the process. Bram Bootman in a letter to the *Listener*, 12 April 1973, set the record straight.
35. Later historians have tended to emphasis the break between Unity and the WTM, representing it as a dilution of proletarian and political purity. Unity is damned for abandoning the sharp revolutionary tool of agitprop in favour of the blunt reformist instrument of socialist realism associated with the proscenium stage of the Stalin era. Raphael Samuel in *Theatres of the Left* says that the founding of Unity marked 'a return to legitimate, conventional theatre' which 'for the most part was content with a fairly simple naturalism'. Politically, 'its aims were comparatively modest' (in contrast to the WTM) and 'the leadership of professional directors was accepted without question'. Samuel also believes that Unity's desire for 'finished staging and accomplished performances' was inherently at odds with any acceptable political intent. He is wrong on each count (as well as on the date of Unity's founding – January not March 1936, or April if one takes the first public performances – and on its location – Britannia Street not Goldington Square; it opened a theatre in Goldington Street in 1937). Samuel represents an influential voice in these matters and his version has been echoed by others (such as Valentine Cunningham in *British Writers of the Thirties*, Oxford University Press 1988) who likewise ignore: the diversity of forms used by Unity, including agitprop; its record of performing on tour, which continued with different degrees of intensity up until its demise; its artistic purpose, which did not involve a separation of technical achievement from its ideological aim but a fusion of the two with the former being better served the better the latter was realised – this was to be achieved with the help of professionals under Unity's elected leadership (ironically, Das Rote Sprachrohr, a model for the WTM troupes, was led by a professional actor); and its revolutionary

perspective – the defeat of fascism, and the replacement of the ills of capitalism, chiefly war, unemployment and poverty, by peace and socialism.

2

Britannia Street

After the opening of the Britannia Street theatre, permission to perform *Waiting for Lefty* finally arrived.[1] It was included in an American double bill with *Private Hicks* in Unity's first proper presentation, on 17 April 1936, following a few trial runs and outside shows. Both plays had appeared in the monthly American magazine *New Theater*, which some of the cast used as their script, and both were directed by Shirley Wakefield, who had worked at the Royal Academy of Dramatic Art and with André van Gyseghem at the Embassy Theatre.[2]

Albert Maltz had won a New Theatre League prize for *Private Hicks* in 1935. (He was later imprisoned as one of the 'Hollywood Ten', for contempt of Congress during the McCarthy anti-Communist witch-hunt and afterwards wrote to Unity asking for his royalty payments because he was hard up.) The play concerns a young man in the National Guard who chooses court martial rather than shoot strikers on a picket line, and is set in the store-room of a Midwest factory that is on strike. Off stage can be heard the noises of the pickets and the police: shouts, whistles, sirens, glass shattering, rifle shots. Hicks is brought in; he talks to one of the privates, seventeen-year-old James Lee, who is guarding him:

HICKS *(in a low voice)*: Aw ... I'm sick of the whole damn business. I ain't gonna be a strikebreaker.

LEE: For Godssakes –

HICKS *(jumping up)*: That ain't what I signed up for! I ain't a scab! *(He walks.)* My ol' man's been out on strike ... he had a damn good reason ... What the hell, if I get a job I'm liable t'go out on strike too, ain't I?

LEE: But Jesus, throwin' your gun down – that's a hell of a thing.

(There's a pause. Then Hicks sits.)

HICKS: Don't I know it? ... I musta been up in the air awright.

(A pause. Hicks jumps up again.)

HICKS: I'm tellin' yuh twenty or thirty got shot. *(He walks.)*
LEE: Yeah? My God! ... Yesterday there was a kid I saw –
HICKS *(interrupting)*: Yuh shoulda seen it, that's all – yuh shoulda seen it. I don't take that stuff. I just don't take it! *(A pause – his voice is low.)* An' since ten o'clock, that vomit gas ... right in the middle of 'em ... They ain't hogs! They ain't wild animals or somethin'!

The Major comes to question Hicks.

MAJOR: You're in the National Guard. You're not supposed to take sides.
HICKS *(with great excitement)*: Ain't we takin' sides? Ain't the National Guard in here on the side of the company?
MAJOR: [...] You don't know what you're talking about. You're being led by the nose. Those goddam agitators stirring everybody up. Jews most of them, foreigners ... Those men don't want to strike. They're being stirred up.
HICKS: [...] When my ol' man talked strike, there wasn't nothin' stirrin' him up but his pay check.

Hicks agrees to apologise for the sake of discipline but, when ordered to say that he would now be prepared to shoot, he refuses. His individual and isolated moral stand takes on a wider importance at the end of the play when Lee promises Hicks that he will pass the strikers' leaflets to the other National Guardsmen and tell the pickets of Hicks's bravery.

Maltz based the play on an incident in Ohio in 1934 when the National Guard used tear gas to break a strike. The brutality of American labour disputes gave the plays written about them an edge that was missing in their British counterparts. Maltz's play suited Unity because it was short, had a manageable cast size, was written colloquially in a realistic setting and had a moving, direct political appeal concerning a basic trade union issue. Joe Stern, who played a sergeant who kicks Hicks on the floor, remembers audiences being so caught up in the production that they booed him for maltreating the hero.

The play also addressed, albeit simply, the problem of moving from the antagonistic, aggressive theatre of the WTM to the more difficult arena of positive political choice, which, without being explicitly shown, was the seedbed of a militant Popular Front approach. Hicks makes such a choice, based on a residual labour movement consciousness that comes from his father, on a generalised humanist attitude toward the strikers as fellow citizens, and on a degree of personal courage. His refusal inspires others to change their ideas and become active on the side of the workers. Such plays provided an answer both to the irrelevance of the West End, with its 'anyone-for-tennis' entertainment, and to the limitations of agitprop.

'Waiting for Lefty'

The other half of the bill, *Waiting for Lefty*, had all the advantages of *Private Hicks* but a more daring structure and wider appeal. It excited even its political critics in both America and Britain, and from its first performance by the professional Group Theater in New York, which ended with the audience rushing the stage, the play became legend.

Waiting for Lefty is played on a bare stage with a committee of New York cabbies sitting in a semi-circle discussing strike action 'to get a living wage'. The members of the audience are cast as if they were also taxi drivers at the same meeting being asked to vote on the strike call. The strike is opposed by a tough, corrupt union boss Harry Fatt, who is accompanied by his gunman. The meeting is waiting for its leader, Lefty Costello. In the meantime, five of the committee step forward in turn, to tell through short, realistic scenes, a crucial personal story which explains why each of them is backing the strike. Odets described this moving back and forth, from and to the meeting in cinematic flashback, as being like a minstrel show in which performers present their own special acts one after the other. A chair is left empty for Costello while the other members of the committee, young and new to union affairs, act like a chorus commenting on the scenes.

The first 'story' is that of a driver, Joe, whose furniture has been reclaimed because the instalments have not be paid. Life is hard and he wants to work but Edna, his wife, threatens to leave him if he does not vote for the strike.

> EDNA: [...] when a man knocks you down you get up and kiss his fist! You gutless piece of baloney.
> JOE: One man can't –
> EDNA *(with great joy)*: I don't say one man! I say a hundred, a thousand, a whole million, I say. But start in your own union. Get those hack boys together! Sweep out those racketeers like a pile of dirt! Stand up like men and fight for the crying kids and wives. Goddammit! I'm tired of slavery and sleepless nights.
> JOE *(with her)*: Sure, sure! ...

EDNA: Yes. Get brass toes on your shoes and know where to kick!

In the next episode, 'The Young Hack and His Girl', a cab driver Sid is seen to be too poor to marry Flo and raise a family. Following a scene in which a company stooge opposing the strike is exposed by his own brother, there are episodes depicting people from other professions who have been forced into 'hacking': in the first, a scientist, Miller, is sacked for refusing to spy on his superior and make poison gas; next, a young actor gets turned down by a New York producer, but as he leaves, the stenographer offers him a dollar:

PHIL: It won't help much.
STEN: One dollar buys ten loaves of bread, Mister. Or one dollar buys nine loaves of bread and one copy of *The Communist Manifesto*. Learn while you eat. Read while you run ...

She tells him it is not the meek but the militant that shall inherit the earth: 'Come out in the light, Comrade.' (This scene was omitted in the 1939 collection of Odets's first six plays which was reprinted by Methuen in 1982.)

In the next scene, at a private hospital in financial trouble, a ward is being closed and a senior doctor loses his job, not because of economies, but because he is Jewish. He tells a colleague that he had thought of going to Russia.

BENJAMIN: The wonderful opportunity to do good work in their socialized medicine but [...] No! Our work's here – America! I'm scared ... What future's ahead I don't know. Get some job to keep alive – maybe drive a cab – and study and work and learn my place – [...] Fight! Maybe get killed, but goddam! We'll go ahead!

A militant driver called Agate stands and challenges Fatt. There is a tussle but he speaks on.

AGATE *(to audience)*: What's the answer, boys? The answer is, if we're Reds because we wanna strike, then we take over their salute too! An uppercut! The good old uppercut to the chin!

Agate comments on the stories that have been played out and asks: 'What are we waiting for? ... Don't wait for Lefty.' He is interrupted by a cabbie coming through the audience with news that Lefty is dead, a bullet in his head. Agate's response is a climactic call to fight:

> AGATE *(crying)*: Hear it, boys, hear it? Hell, listen to me! Coast to coast! HELLO AMERICA! HELLO. WE'RE STORMBIRDS OF THE WORKING CLASS. WORKERS OF THE WORLD ... OUR BONES AND BLOOD! And when we die they'll know what we did to make a new world! Christ, cut us up to little pieces. We'll die for what is right! put fruit trees where our ashes are! *(to audience)* Well, what's the answer?
> ALL: STRIKE!
> AGATE: LOUDER!
> ALL: STRIKE!
> AGATE *(and others on stage)*: AGAIN!
> ALL: STRIKE, STRIKE, STRIKE!!!

The ending invariably had the audience chanting 'Strike, strike, strike' in unison – a device that had been used before in workers' theatre but never with such success. Harold Clurman, director of the play's first production, aptly described its impact:

> When the audience ... responded to the militant question ... with a spontaneous roar of 'Strike! Strike!' it was something more than a tribute to the play's effectiveness, more even than a testimony of the audience's hunger for constructive social action. It was the birth cry of the thirties. Our youth had found its voice.[3]

Odets had hit the right note in his combination of realistic scenes and agitprop structure – a clear development of the Workers' Theatre Movement type of play; flexible, minimal in setting and costume, breaking down the barriers between audience and actor and focusing on a labour issue but using characters with whom the audience can readily identify. The play is simple, economical, detailed, direct and short. It is not analytical but, given the context in which it was produced, emotionally powerful, if sentimental. The characters are both real and symbolic, appearing strongly in cameo portraits that are often romanticised and do not allow for deep exploration. Fatt, for example, who wanders through the action puffing smoke menacingly, is clearly a representative of capital but also a convincing portrait of a ganster union boss; Joe, Edna, Florrie and Sid are the man and woman in the street but also individual characters experiencing familiar problems in their own particular, but recognisable, situations; Agate, with one glass-eye, is as the name suggests, crystal-clear in his analysis, unshakeable and the militant incarnate. However idealised, he is identifiable as the kind of rank-and-file leader who emerges time and again in working-class struggles.

The intercutting scenes, which were innovative then and showed the influence of the newly-emerging cinema, add up to a picture of a society in crisis in which everyone is affected and no one can be neutral – a common theme of plays in the 1930s. In a persuasive and primarily youthful statement of the Popular Front ideal (before it had become official international Communist policy), middle-class people are seen becoming politically active alongside working-class people, not for an abstract slogan like 'world revolution' but for an immediate and realisable aim, a strike. The strike, however, is still not the main point of the play, the burden of which is its emotional appeal conveyed with all the pent-up pressure of a fervent confession.

Odets was a member of the Communist Party of the USA and an unknown actor in the Group Theater when he wrote *Waiting for Lefty* at the end of 1934, reportedly in three nights, and won with it a New Theatre League competition for a short play on a labour subject. (Later, when giving evidence to the McCarthyite hearings in which he 'named names', Odets claimed that the competition had been fixed and that he had known nothing of the taxi drivers' strike of February 1934 that was said to have inspired the play.)

Waiting for Lefty marked the highpoint of the American workers' theatre, drawing as it did on native traditions and transforming them with a fresh openness that probably owed something to the absence of a censor.[4] According to Odets, in 1935 the play was being performed at the same time in 60 theatres across the United States. Numerous groups took it up in Britain where *Waiting for Lefty* became synonymous with left theatre.

Merseyside Left Theatre hit the headlines with one performance, at the Royalty Theatre, Chester, in a drama festival in 1938 when the theatre manager lowered the curtain while the play was still running and ordered the orchestra to play 'God Save the King'.[5] The reason he gave was an objection to 'extreme profanity' in the play, a reference to remarks by Fatt in warning the drivers to be wary of the strike committee: ... 'Give those birds a chance and they'll have your sisters and wives in the whore houses like they done in Russia. They'll tear Christ off his bleeding cross.' In court, ten members of the group were found guilty of presenting the play without proper permission from the Lord Chamberlain and BBC radio withdrew a planned broadcast.

London Unity made its reputation with *Lefty*, as the play was known, not because of extensive press coverage but by word of mouth and the hard work of Unity supporters in getting bookings for it. Unity was not yet open week in week out and only performed at Brit Street sporadically. The *Amateur Theatre and Playwrights' Journal* critic said, 'I have never seen an audience more profoundly moved,' but the tone of the few other reviews the play received, while welcoming, was more cautious. The *New Statesman*, the week following the opening performance wrote: 'Given by a highly trained company on an adequately equipped stage its effect would be shattering ... this performance is effective and the players ... command our respect for portraying characters with whom they are in sympathy.' Barbara Nixon in the May *Left Review* reported on the opening double bill of *Lefty* and *Private Hicks*:

> Both plays were well acted, and reached a standard I have not often seen in amateur productions. If the group can maintain this standard, it will play an important part in Socialist propaganda, and will be an encouragement to other groups.

And that is what happened. As Unity's new secretary, ex-seaman Tommy Foster, who had taken over from an exhausted Bram Bootman, wrote in the autumn of the following year:

> *Lefty* established us as it has established working-class theatre groups all over the world. And it was *Lefty* that enabled us to get through those difficult first summer months without losing ground.[6]

Unity staged *Waiting for Lefty* over 300 times before the war to more than 40,000 people, presenting it in many different types of venue around England, from the newly opened Players' Theatre at Charing Cross and West End theatres for Sunday fund-raising events to miners' hall and Co-operative clubs. There seems to be a consensus that it worked better in the latter than in the former – and, despite its mythological status, it should be noted that not all its performances were cheered to the echo by a full theatre. *Lefty* could play to a poor house too. Unity revived it in 1972 and 1980, as did some of the political theatre groups of this period such as CAST.

Lefty had several directors (or producers as they were known then) and many cast changes; for every performer who joined Unity in the early period, appearing in *Lefty* was the equivalent of doing national service. Not surprisingly, the piece figures in many anecdotes, from the mix-up with the music in the first performance, when a record of Shostakovich's second symphony that uses the factory hooter was left playing at the start of the intimate Sid and Flo scene instead of being replaced by the silky sound of Hoagy Carmichael, to the occasion when the innovation of an actor coming through the audience misled alert stewards in a strong Mosleyite area in West London to believe that they had a Blackshirt disruption on their hands.[7] At some performances the actors wore cab drivers' caps and sported trade union badges. They would hand out leaflets to the audience and ask the audience to produce their membership cards as if they were attending a proper union meeting. This idea was reinforced by keeping the 'house' lights in the auditorium full on for the opening scene of the play. During the Coronation bus strike of 1937, bus workers covered the theatre with posters and gave out information about their dispute. *Lefty* was played sixteen times at different garages during the month-long fight and helped win Unity considerable support among militant London trade unionists. In April 1938 Unity entered *Lefty* for the British Drama League's annual competition. The director, Herbert Marshall, had to reduce the playing time to fit the competition rules, which he did by rehearsing very quick scene changes with the actors carrying the props (not then the common sight it was later to become). He drilled the cast with military precision and when they had perfected the moves, they performed them with their eyes shut and then in blackout. It gave the production extra zip and Unity won its area round, which was held at the small Fortune Theatre. When it came to the national final at the huge Scala Theatre, the orchestra pit proved an insurmountable obstruction to the action which had to take place among the audience and the size of the auditorium dwarfed the production. Unity came second.

Lefty brought Unity more money than the activists of Rebel Players or Red Radio had ever dreamt of, although cash flow was always a problem: Unity's performing fee, due in advance, sometimes was not paid at all or was lowered to meet the pressing needs of a particular struggle. The 'movement' could not afford a lot at the best of times and any organisation booking Unity had to cover the fee, the hire of a hall and the cost of advertising before making any profit on what was bound to be a low ticket price. Much of the money raised by the theatre came during the collections that were held at the end of every show, and which were accompanied by appeals for new members. Unexpected rate demands, the general expenses of running Britannia Street and financing the unemployed members' fares all took their toll of *Lefty*'s income.

The play, however, attracted more than money. It won enthusiastic responses from audiences new to Unity who were excited by the challenge of its form and content. Using the auditorium as part of the action and breaking down the barrier between actor and audience was then quite startling, especially when allied to a militant call for political action across the classes. *Lefty* made Unity many new members and broadened the club's make-up well beyond the boundaries of the East End Jewish community. Everyone worked hard and turned their hand to any job that was asked of them. The well-provided transport system that served Kings Cross, including all-night trams, meant not only that audiences could return home after a show but that actors and stage crew could work through to early morning if necessary, which they frequently did.

Lefty also had enormous appeal for those in the professional theatre who were increasingly frustrated by both the narrowness of the commercial theatre and the collapse of other experimental outlets at a time when publicly subsidised theatre was still a decade away. The most important professional to join Unity through seeing *Lefty* was John Allen, who had come from Cambridge University to London to be an actor in 1931 and had become a founder member of the Group Theatre, later to present plays by Auden and Isherwood. He was to work with Michel Saint-Denis at the London Theatre Studio, one of the most advanced theatre schools of its day, and he turned out to be a very good teacher himself, which proved vital for Unity. Allen directed several important productions for Unity, including *Lefty*, helped establish the Left Book Club Theatre Guild and became its first secretary, as well as producing shows and pageants for the labour movement.

He became director of Glynebourne's Children's Theatre and after a short spell at the BBC was appointed HM Inspector of Drama and then Principal of the Central School of Speech and Drama.

Allen remembers feeling dissastisfied with the Group Theatre. He felt that it was politically dilettante but was not sure why. When he was taken to see Unity perform *Lefty* he found the answer: 'It was the most marvellous experience because this was the commitment that was missing from the Group Theatre. It knocked me upside down and sideways and it answered in me a personal worry.'[8] He responded to the obligatory end-of-performance appeal for more money and members and met two former Rebel Players veterans, Ben Glaser and Henry Burke. As Allen recalls:

> They invited me to join. They articulated quite clearly their attitude to me as a professional. If the bourgeois world had a technical ability that could help the working class then they would use it. A separate working-class culture was not mentioned as it might be in the 1980s. There was just a culture to be used to achieve power. The bourgeoisie had taken it over and they wanted it on their terms.

There was a strong sense of how the working class should use that culture, and, in so doing, that 'we' should have 'our' films, 'our' novels and 'our' theatre.

Following in the footsteps of André van Gyseghem and Shirley Wakefield, Allen brought in other professionals to 'our' theatre, like Margaret Leona, who taught voice work, particularly for the mass recitations. She and Allen found the Unity actors not only eager but passionate to learn from those who were in touch with latest theatrical ideas, just as they, in their turn, were keen to learn from their experiences at Unity.

Taxi Driver Playwrights

Waiting for Lefty also helped Unity tackle the ever-pressing problem of repertoire by stimulating the theatre's first home-grown playwrights. Unity knew that it had to stage plays by and about the British working class if it were to hold and build its own audience. Contacts made while performing *Lefty* had led to Unity renting out part of Britannia Street to the London section of the taxi drivers' union. A cabbie called Robert (Bob) Buckland had joined Unity after reviewing *Lefty* for the section's journal, and he had persuaded another cabbie, Herbert Hodge, to join too. They had written magazine stories together as well as on their own; Hodge's material, which earned him £2 a week, appeared mostly in women's magazines under various pen names.

Hodge was a colourful character and impulsive. He had left school at fourteen and had worked at sea, in a coalmine and as a harvester in the United States. He had stood in the 1931 election as a candidate for Mosley's New Party, attracted by its call for a classless society, but had left when its fascist character became clear to him. He had been active in the National Unemployed Workers' Movement yet had also organised cab drivers outside of the main union and run a newspaper for them. In his autobiography Hodge recounts his first meeting with the Unity repertory committee to which he had been invited by Tommy Foster.

> None of them looked more than twenty-five. I felt like Old Father William. They held manuscripts in their hands. It was obvious I'd interrupted a play-reading. I sat down. Someone gave me a manuscript and the reading went on. It sounded poor stuff to me. But they all looked as if they were enjoying themselves, so I tried to look interested.
>
> It was, I decided, just another of these amateur literary societies. Only instead of reading their stories and poems to each other, they read their attempts at plays. Just another of Bob's sudden enthusiasms. I'd stick it now, since I couldn't very well do otherwise, and get away if possible without committing myself to join.
>
> When they'd finished the reading, the chairman, a thin young man with a Birmingham accent, asked me what I thought of it. I thought it was rotten, but I didn't like to say so. I explained I didn't know anything about plays, and so hadn't been able to visualise it.
>
> The Chairman said it was difficult to know what to do about it. They couldn't make up their minds. No one thought much of it, but they couldn't go on playing *Lefty* for ever, and they hadn't yet been able to get anything to take its place. And on that note of indecision the meeting ended.
>
> Joe [Stern] persuaded me to pay sixpence and take out a membership card before I left, and I went off with the cab feeling annoyed at wasting an hour's working time.
>
> But Tommy Foster, the young man from Birmingham, had lent me a copy of an American magazine called *New Theater*, saying there was a one-act play in it they hoped to do shortly.[9]

The play was *Bury the Dead* by Irwin Shaw which so impressed

Hodge that he decided to go back to the next repertory meeting, only to discover that the agents were holding out for professional performance and would not let Unity present it. Hodge felt that he could do better than the script that had been read at the previous meeting, which, he presumed, was now next in line for production. An idea finally came to Hodge after a week of fruitless puzzling, when he was sitting on the toilet. This gave him the clue. He discussed it with Bob Buckland and they developed it into a political satire. Hodge talked to John Allen about the play in the local café, the Pioneer at the top of Grays Inn Road. One scene was ready the following evening, Hodge having missed a taxi shift to write it. Buckland and Hodge worked on the play for a week and had a script ready for the next repertory committee meeting at which they read it aloud.

An aero-engine fitter Joe Dexter has been sacked because his boss saw a poem of his printed in the *Weekly Worker*. Dexter owes rent to his landlady, Mrs Judd, and is harried by hire-purchase collectors for overdue instalments on furniture, clothes, books and his typewriter. A gentleman from the British Patriots' Propaganda Association visits and offers him payment for stories that would 'instil in the mind of the worker his duty to his employer, his duty to his country and above all, the dreadful danger of attempting to think for himself'.[10] He wants them written on toilet paper, which would be supplied free to all patriotic employers, because the association sees the water closet as the last bastion of a dangerous freedom where a worker can sit alone and think; the press, education, entertainment and the church take care of everywhere else. There is even a plan to have the National Anthem played every time a sheet of the toilet paper is pulled off. 'It'll be a bit awkward for patriots,' muses Joe, but he is re-assured by the gentleman: 'I'm sure all *true* patriots will rise to the occasion.'

Dexter agrees reluctantly and writes a Hollywood-style romance – 'Love Will Find a Way or the Strike That Failed' – but is visited in a nightmare by the stereotypes that he has created, who are brought up from hell by the Devil Money-Power dressed in top hat and frock coat with an enormous belly, hooves, a forked tail and horns. He introduces himself: 'I'm food – clothing – shelter. I'm comfort, I'm security. For me men cheat, rob, murder [...] I was a fool in the old days. I was for ever buying souls. But we've progressed since then, we're democratic. Hellions never shall be slaves! I only hire nowadays ...' He draws a redly-glowing telephone from his coat tails and summons from the literary department of Hell's Gates one Bolshy, complete with bomb, one hero, strong, silent, and simple, one boss's daughter, and one hero's mother, poor but patriotic. As the characters come alive and act out the story Joe realises what a mistake he has made and turns on Money-Power: 'There'll be no real cures,' he shouted, 'until you are smashed!' and his characters revolt.

Bolshy tears off his whiskers and choking with rage accuses Money-Power.

> BOLSHY: You know I wouldn't know how to *use* a bomb. You know I'm a respectable trade union member who wants another penny an hour. You know I've got a perfectly good case. You know everyone would support me if they knew the facts. So you dress me up in these ridiculous whiskers, and put a bomb in my hand, so that you can drown my arguments with cries of arson and rape ... I want a decent standard of life and I mean to get it. I don't want to be violent. I want to do things peaceably, reasonably ... but –
>
> MONEY-POWER: Peaceably! What do you take me for? A milksop? *(Laughs contemptuously.)* What I have I hold!
>
> BOLSHY: Well – if you want revolution, you can have that too.
>
> OTHER THREE CHARACTERS *(together – humanly)*: We want to live! We *will* live!

The characters drag Money-Power out. The boss's daughter dashes back in, asking 'Where's that bloody bomb?', seizes it and rushes out. There is an explosion and Joe wakes up to find four debt collectors demanding back the hired goods. Spurred on by the revolt of his characters whom he created to 'bolster up capitalism', Joe refuses to sell the story to the man from the Patriots' Propaganda Association and tears up the script. Accused of being foolish, Joe explodes:

> Why come to me for your toilet-paper propaganda – why come to me? Go to the Press Lords of Fleet Street. They've been printing the workers' toilet-paper for years.

A few days after the play was read to the repertory committee, and with another application for *Bury the Dead* refused, Allen led the committee in recommending production, but the play had no title. Eventually a line from the play provided the answer and *Where's that Bomb?* was ready to enter the repertoire under Allen's direction. Authorship also threw up problems and, after some debate, it was agreed to use two pen names, Roger Gullan (for Hodge) and Buckley Roberts.

Hodge takes up the story:

> Unity had sunk all it possessed in staging the *Bomb*. Everyone was lending a hand, building and painting the scenery, fixing up the lighting effects, making a trap, sewing costumes, and, of course, rehearsing the play itself. Every night for nearly a month I left the cab outside the door for two or three hours while I watched and interfered with rehearsals. I'd never have believed the tangles six actors could get into on a small stage if I hadn't seen it for myself. There were no moves marked on the script. We had to work them out as we went along. John Allen said he preferred it that way; it gave the producer a chance to produce. But I wouldn't have appreciated it in his place. I learned more about play-writing in those few weeks than I could have learned from instruction books in as many years.

The attic, with a steeply sloping ceiling (designed by Rivka Black) looked like a naturalistic setting (Joe's bed was used during the day by those who had nowhere to sleep at night) but John Allen gave the production a larger-than-life comic style that almost became burlesque while retaining the realism of Joe's situation. Under the able guidance of stage manager George Henshaw, the production used several bold effects; an ingenious trap built in the tiny stage and worked by two men brought on the fantasy characters who were lit appropriately – red for the Bolshy, green for the villain Money-Power – and there was a hidden maroon hung inside an inverted dustbin for the bomb explosion.

Ironically, the opening night was planned for Friday, 13 November. Hodge says:

> On Thursday, the twelfth, there were ten shillings in the bank, and two pounds rent due on the following Saturday. At the dress-rehearsal, everything that could go wrong went wrong, including the trap and the alarm clock. But everyone was quite cheerful about it except me. Nothing like a bad dress-rehearsal, they said, for a good first night. And, apparently they were right. The hall was full. The play went without a hitch. The audience laughed in all the funny places, were tense in all the tense places, and clapped enthusiastically whenever they got the chance. The alarm clock went off at the right time, and the trap shot up the toilet-paper characters from hell according to schedule, but I didn't feel safe until the bomb exploded. It was

something in a dustbin in the dressing-room, and blew the lid off and knocked a lump out of the ceiling. But no one minded that. All that mattered was the bang. The audience was delighted.

It was a great success, and all the more because it was Unity's very own and markedly 'proletarian'. It played to full houses for three weeks and collected encouraging press notices as well as praise from theatre luminaries like Tyrone Guthrie. The *Reynolds News* critic said the play struck 'an entirely new note in left-wing propaganda'. Its 'Falstaffian humour' was 'more effective than a million dreary speeches'. It 'would never be produced in a West End theatre, but it will be rapturously applauded wherever people are familiar with unemployment, poverty and the seamy side of the hire purchase system'. Even if a few members of the audience found the toilet references in bad taste, the cast was totally committed and *Where's that Bomb?* entered the repertoire to become a Unity favourite. The dedication and necessary improvisation required to keep a theatre like Unity functioning is typified by Hodge having to pick up Money-Power (Harry Ross, later to become a professional actor) each Saturday at 9 p.m. when he finished work as a barber in Ilford, and drive fast to the theatre where Allen would be waiting to make him up like a medieval devil in time for his second-act entrance.

Where's that Bomb? turned out to be just the boost that Unity needed, to prove that it could advance beyond *Lefty* and become a creative force in its own right. *Bomb* was revived a few weeks later, the comic foil to the heroic *Lefty*, and with the Odets play became one of the most popular of Unity's double bills, even playing the West End's Phoenix Theatre, under the sympathetic management of Sidney Bernstein, for a fund-raising event. A national tour and full West End production were stopped by the censor. Lawrence and Wishart published the script with 'Banned by the Lord Chamberlain' printed on the front cover. Hodge and Allen went to talk to the Lord Chamberlain's officer whom Allen remembers as an immaculately dressed major with the manners of a perfect gentleman. He had no objection to the politics only to the toilet references. With the scene moved to the bathroom and Dexter now writing on shaving paper, *Where's that Bomb?* was given a licence and was performed by other left theatres in Britain, which were thankful for some humour in their repertoire. By the time the play was revived by Unity in 1949, it had become dated, even though during the war the government had used toilet paper to print its propaganda on.

Buckland went on writing magazine stories while Hodge, who also continued writing, became better known for his radio talks, in which he decribed his own experiences and offered opinion on a range of topics as the 'man in the street'.[11] He became a 'personality', being invited to literary events, and, as cab driver 3306, featured in newspaper and magazine articles. He wrote a personal column in a socialist monthly, *Life and Letters Today*, but was asked to stop a year later because, he says, his unorthodox ideas, which he expressed in book reviews as well as in his column, brought him into conflict with the editor. Hodge is a good example of the autodidact and new breed of worker-writer, branching out from three autobiographical books into the novel as well as the drama. He sent Merseyside Left Theatre what he called a 'still-born satire on newspaper publishing', with permission to rework it for local conditions, which the group performed in May 1940, extensively rewritten, as *Strike Me Red*.

'Cannibal Carnival'

Hodge wrote a second play for Unity, which he began in February 1937, but this time on his own and using his own name. He composed much of the play by missing shifts or creating in his head while driving past his would-be fares. This time, he had hoped to avoid the censor, but he had no luck for *Cannibal Carnival*, a theatrical cartoon of a bishop, a financier and a policeman shipwrecked on a Pacific island, irresistibly became a satire on Britain, then in the grip of post-abdication fever.[12] Bishop Bartholomew Bumpus of Belgravia, wearing a clergyman's collar and gaiters and little else, Hungry Joe, with a walrus moustache, helmet, truncheon and boots, and Mr. Crabbe, in frock coat and carrying a leather satchel full of clinking money, decide that they must civilise the inhabitants of the island who appear to live happily in a state of primitive communism, eating loaves from a large breadfruit tree. The island's leader, Egbert, is the first to be 'civilised'. He holds a loaf from the tree!

CRABBE *(solemnly)*: Render unto Ceasar the things that are Ceasar's. *(He takes half the loaf.)*

EGBERT: What is that?

CRABBE *(taking a bite)*: Patriotism, my boy.

EGBERT: And then?

BISHOP: And then comes the most beautiful part of all.

CRABBE: Watch this, it's good.

BISHOP: And unto God the things that are God's. *(Takes the other half of the loaf.)* That's religion.

EGBERT: And what do you say then?

CRABBE, BISHOP and JOE *(in unison)*: God helps those who help themselves – hurrah for the British Empire!

(They all eat.)

EGBERT *(pondering)*: I see. God helps those who help themselves. Yes, I see. *(Running after them.)* And now will you please give me my loaf? I must take it home. I am already late.

BISHOP: Come, come, my son. You *have* no loaf. It's been transubstantiated.

CRABBE: That's the point. That's the beauty of it. Don't you see?

EGBERT: But I have nothing!

JOE *(seizing him)*: Then you're arrested for being without visible means of subsistence.

EGBERT: What is that?

JOE: Another white man's custom.

Egbert used this discovery to get a loaf from another islander, shouting: 'God-helps-those-who-help-themselves-hurrah-for-the British Empire!' The islander calls him 'thief', and he is re-arrested by Joe. Egbert explains that he was only behaving like the white man.

BISHOP *(to Crabbe)*: He means well, I think. But like all savages, he's simple and childlike. Utterly lacking in moral sense [...] He doesn't even know the difference between religion and robbery.

EGBERT: But I do, white man.

CRABBE: What is it, then?

EGBERT: When you take bread, it is patriotism and religion. When I take bread it is robbery and violence.

CRABBE *(clapping)*: Bravo! You couldn't have put it better if you'd been to Oxford.

Crabbe puts a fence around the tree and Joe nails up a notice 'Private Property – Trespassers will be Prosecuted'. A system of exploitation is imposed on the island, complete with prostitutes, pawnshops and most important, unemployment. As the bishop says: 'It's positively marvellous. Just like dear old England.' The system requires anti-communism, racial prejudice and a coronation to keep the islanders happy, though the royal procession gets mixed up with an unemployment demonstration and the monarch's jazz band has to play a little louder to cover the sound of Joe cracking skulls from his hobby horse.

Faced with the unrest that would follow another cut in wages to keep up profits, Bogus and Crabe get Joe to become Lord Chief Justice and declare an election with only two candidates: the Bishop as a Tory and Crabbe as a Liberal who agree to rule exactly the same way as each other. Democracy is seen as 'the right of every man to choose his own tyrant'. But Egbert wants to stand for the workers, and he wins. Martial law is proclaimed by Joe who arrests Egbert again while Crabbe and the Bishop divert the islanders with anti-semitic propaganda (despite the absence of Jews on the island). Egbert is found guilty of being a Marxist and a Jew and is sentenced to death. In a farcical ending, Joe cannot bring his axe down on Egbert's head because Egbert keeps on shouting 'Up the Workers'; Joe comes over 'all class-conscious', gives Egbert a cigarette and goes on strike. The islanders set fire to the courthouse and, after saying grace, put Crabbe and the Bishop in a cooking pot. Joe stirs the stew with his truncheon as the islanders sing and dance.

Cannibal Carnival, sub-titled 'A vulgar spectacle in seven scenes', had a difficult passage at Unity. It was planned to open at the same time as the Coronation but this also turned out to coincide with the London bus strike of May 1937. Hodge had written the play for specific actors, some of whom now were not available because they were playing *Lefty* at striking bus garages, and one of whom refused to play his role because he disagreed with the play. Parts were altered to fit a new cast, the director John Allen had to appear as well, and Hodge acted as prompter because the size of the cannibal chorus left no one else free to do so. Unity was in debt for the costumes and scenery, which included a tree that dominated the stage and took people off up into the flies to a precarious platform that was lodged immediately beneath the roof and from which there was no exit until the end of the show. The designer was Misha Black, a founder of the Artists' International Association, later knighted and a professor at the Royal College of Art, and brother of Rivka who was also active at Unity. The theatre had no option but to go on with the show to recoup some of its money. *Cannibal Carnival* was rushed on, before a proper second version could be completed, on a hot June evening. It was vigorous and colourful but not entirely successful, although it did arouse debate on the use of Utopia in literature and attempts to popularise Marxism in different forms. John Allen was aware of the problems: a lack of focus, the broad strokes of cartoon that make quick but not lasting points and cannot hold the stage for a full evening, the need for more preparation and technical skill to achieve the right balance between the formal patterns of the play and truthful, rather than empty, caricature.

Cannibal Carnival divided audiences, who either found it very funny or very crude. There were complaints about its attitude to the working class, its blasphemy and its attacks on the church when religious leaders were criticising government policy. An internal Unity meeting was held and the show came off after three reasonable weeks at the box office in which time a small profit was made. The play has been revived a few times and performed in America, including, according to Hodge, a production at Harvard.

Hodge only wrote once more for Unity, when participating in early 1938 with John Allen again and others in creating the Living Newspaper *Busmen*. Hodge's loss to Unity coincided with his greater involvement in radio broadcasting and a shift at Unity away from his kind of theatre. The ironic tone of *Cannibal Carnival*, mocking even the masses, was not liked by many at Unity and it only surfaced again, albeit in attenuated form, in some of Unity's later revues.[13]

'The Fall of the House of Slusher'

Times were hard at Unity; after six months there was 9s 8d in the bank, an £80 debt and still only twenty or so active members. Britannia Street was not playing all the time, although attempts were constantly being made to keep the theatre open and to fulfil its role as a cultural centre. Unity productions were interspersed with one-off presentations of plays – for example, Friedrich Wolf's anti-fascist *Professor Mamlock* – performances by the Dance Drama Group and Workers' Propaganda Dance Group, puppet shows and the screening of progressive films, such as *War is Hell* from Germany, *Dawn*, about the Irish war of independence, and the first real Soviet sound feature, *The Road to Life*.

Unity's repertory committee was having a desperate time

finding suitable new material – a task made harder by the political criteria invoked and the tendency to judge every play against the model of *Waiting for Lefty*. A cast, for instance, was already rehearsing Odets's *Till the Day I Die* when the committee decided that it was too inward-looking and cancelled the production. His *Awake and Sing* also fell foul of the committee, which found it too sentimental. (Both plays were staged later by Unity, in the 1940s.) Odets's monologue, *I Can't Sleep*, was accepted, however. [14] In the play, a New York Jewish businessman called Blitstein justifies to a beggar his own rise from poverty and persecution in Tsarist Russia through tailoring, reading Marx and Lenin, to his current prosperity. His own doubts are swelled by the accusing presence of the beggar. The justification turns into a confession and Blitstein discovers that he has become a moral beggar, pleading for forgiveness. As the silent pauper leaves, Blitstein cries out in vain: 'Look at me, comrade, just look at me.' In John Allen's production, the beggar was on stage with his back to the audience. At the end he turned and from his make-up (which Allen spent an hour doing) they could see that the beggar was Death. Joe Stern, who played the beggar, recalls: 'The shock was enough to draw gasps from the audience.'

The repertory committee did not want to rely on American plays and was most keen to present more British material. Hodge and Buckland were promising discoveries but were lost almost as soon as they were found. While ideas were plentiful, realising them on stage was a different matter. Many proposals fell by the wayside, such as John Allen's plan to adapt *The Peace* by Aristophanes. Others that did come to fruition sometimes proved less successful than expected, like *Home of the Brave*,[15] a satire on Nazism as descending from primitive tribalism, or *Not for Us*, a portrait of Britain under fascist rule, which was intended at first to be played to Hunger Marchers after they had arrived in London. Written by a research chemist Norman Lee (who used the pen name Levy) and directed by Ben Sharma of the Habimah Theatre, its original title was *Last Fight* but the repertory committee found that too pessimistic and had it changed. By all accounts, the play was cumbersome and over-ambitious. It was too bleak to be popular and soon came off.

Much of the repertoire for Unity's first eighteen months comprised double or triple bills; several productions were revivals of short Rebel Players' shows – *Requiem, Newsboy, The People's Court* and *Lefty* – which could be presented in different combinations and proved easier than mounting full-scale work, as the experience of *Cannibal Carnival* and *Not for Us* showed. (Some, such as *The People's Court* and *Requiem* were revived again in the 1940s.)

This practice of flexible programming encouraged Unity to develop the use of double casts wherever possible. In the non-professional theatre, a single cast with its own domestic and professional responsibilities outside the theatre, cannot perform regularly or in long runs whereas two casts playing the same production can.

A new 'homegrown' piece in the repertoire, *The Fall of the House of Slusher,* was an enlarged and rewritten treatment of a Rebel Players's skit, which itself was based on an older WTM sketch, *Love in Industry.*[16] Directed by Allen, this comic operetta was a development of the WTM's political 'song play', using and parodying popular tunes such as 'The British Grenadier' or 'After the Ball is Over'.

Slusher was written collectively and went through several versions, each centring on the need to lower wages in order to meet a difficult economic situation. Sir Sam B. Slusher appeals to his shop assistants, who agree to work a 24-hour day, singing:

> Boys and girls come out to work
> You know you'll love it and will not shirk.

But, of course, it turns out to be only a beautiful picture in a beautiful golden frame. In reality, the workers give notice of a strike – the breeding ground of Socialism, Communism and Bolshevism, according to Slusher and his friends, a general, a politician and a pressman, who try to help him find a solution. They suggest competitions in the papers, a coronation, elections, even wooing the workers with ditties like

> All things bright and saleable
> Machine guns great and small
> Bullets bombs and bayonets
> These things make work for all.

The workers refuse to be fooled or intimidated. They leap on Slusher and tear his clothes off, leaving him finally in nothing but his underpants. They sing the final chorus:

> We won't be beat and we won't retreat
> We'll win or else we'll know the reason why.

Like *Cannibal Carnival*, it was criticised for its political and artistic crudeness. Composer Alan Bush, for instance, offered comradely objections, as a member of the audience, to the use of the Hallelujah Chorus ('We mean to free the world/From ca-a-pitalism/Halleluhjah, Hallelujah') on the grounds that it was not the business of workers' theatre to debase classical masterpieces.

Mass Declamation

Another new piece was Jack Lindsay's mass declamation *Who are the English?* (seemingly then an acceptable term for British) which had been printed in *Left Review* as a May Day poem 'not English?' and issued as a pamphlet. Lindsay, born into one of Australia's most remarkable literary families, had settled in Britain in 1926 when in his mid-twenties, having made a name for himself in Bohemian Sydney as a critic and aesthete.[18] He became a distinguished classicist and prolific author of more than 150 books – poems, novels, biography, autobiography and translations as well as artistic, philosophical and political explorations. His interest in mass declamation, a form of choral speaking that owed much of its popularity to the German working-class agitprop groups, coincided with his discovery of Marxism and he remained a committed, if unorthodox, Communist thereafter.

Who are the English? arose from a concern on the left to be both experimental, as the most stimulating of European culture was then, and to reclaim a national popular heritage while answering the right-wing accusation that Communism was alien to Britain and its way of life. Written for a dozen or more voices, the poem offers an historical survey of native rebels who make up an alternative tradition to that presented by conventional historians. The men and women of the chorus are lying or sitting in different parts of the stage, dressed in overalls with red masks. The leader of the chorus stands higher, up stage.

CHORUS: Who, who, who are the English?
LEADER: Who are the English
according to the definition of the ruling-class?
All you that went forth, lured by great-sounding names
which glittered like bubbles of crystal in your eyes
till they burst and you burst with them.

Is it 'you, the ragged thief, fruit of the press-gang', the poet asks, or 'you toilers on whose cowed faces the heels of your betters have left bleeding badges as proof of your allegiance'? It is not the subservient and the pliant.

FIRST WOMAN: I call instead on those who are not English
according to the definition of the ruling class.
We'll step back first six hundred years or seven.

Lindsay goes from the Peasants' Revolt, to John Ball and Jack Cade, to the Lollards, to Cromwell's Ironsides and the Levellers, to the Luddites and the Chartists, up to the General Strike of 1926. He calls forth William Morris and Rhondda and Durham miners and, finally, with clenched fists raised:

FULL CHORUS: We who made it, we are making
another England, and the loyalty learned
in mine and factory begets our truth,
this compact linking us to past and future
[...] The disinherited are restored, our mother,
England, our England
England, our own.

Mass declamation or recitations used stylised movement, lighting and music. This word 'mass' referred to speaking in unison rather than the size of the audience and some Unitarians became specialists in this type of performance (such as Fernau Hall, later to be one of Britain's leading ballet critics). They were popular with workers' theatres because, in John Allen's words, a performer could feel 'the exalting sensation of addressing an audience with words in which he passionately believes, and that of communion with other people on the stage'.[19] They had the force of direct and collective appeal which assumed a common ground with its audience and invited them to share in the experience on the basis of class politics and shared interest rather than isolated, individual concern. Mass declamation also had the advantage of allowing the performer to participate at the level of her or his own capability; new members could learn a great deal in the chorus while older ones could play the single voices and refine their performances.

Lindsay saw mass declamations as a way of bridging the gap that had arisen under capitalism both between the spoken word and poetry and between art and the people.[20] He saw this form of verse as a springboard for a new poetry and, despite overstating his case as was common – and understandable – among the many intellectuals who discovered Marxism in the 1930s, he and many others working in the novel, poetry, music, the visual arts, pageants and drama did contribute to a radical culture that was both militant and popular. Among Lindsay's mass declamations performed by Unity and other left-wing theatre groups in Britain were *The Agony of China* (written after the Japanese invasion and known by some as 'The Agony of Unity'), *Salute the Soviet Union, We Need Russia* (written in late 1938 or early 1939 when collective security might still have saved humanity from a second world war), *Salute the Maquis* and, during the Greek civil war, *The Voice of Greece*. (The last two poems were also known as *Man of the Maquis* and *Cry of Greece*.) None of these mass declamations, however, was to achieve the appeal of Lindsay's *On Guard for Spain*, which was performed all over Britain as part of the solidarity movement with the Republic that was defending itself against Franco and his fascist supporters.

Spain

The election of the Popular Front government in Spain was itself an historic event which made the need to defeat Franco's rejection of democracy all the more urgent and important. Having of necessity broken with the prevailing pacifism of the left which followed the carnage of the First World War, the issue of Spain transformed the politics of the decade, giving a new coherence and scope to the left, and it defined the nature of the fight that was to erupt into world war. It had a lasting effect on those generations who were caught up in its struggle that helped shape both the victory over fascism in Europe and the political battles of many countries in the immediate post-war period. From the summer of 1936 to early 1939, solidarity with Spain – the sending of people, goods, equipment, money, and the fight against non-intervention –

became the rallying call for all those around the world who opposed what was wrong in the world. Solidarity was a focus for action which changed all those who took part.

It became the driving force of much that Unity did at this time, accelerating a process of growth that had been sparked off by the many performances of *Waiting for Lefty*. It brought into left theatre in general more people than ever before. Unity revived Ramón Sender's Spanish play, *The Secret*, to raise funds for Spain (and the performers often found themselves presenting this harrowing tale at the seemingly most inappropriate occasions – in the middle of a dinner and dance, for example – but it achieved its aim). Unity also performed *Spain*, a poem by the Communist writer Randall Swingler, as a mass declamation.

> People of England, while you ponder,
> The ring is closing, the iron ring that strangles us ...
> Hear it ... The voice of the people crying to the people:
> Today it is us: Tomorrow it will be you.
> People of England, what are you going to do?[21]

It lasted about ten minutes in performance and was not too successful, though it received a good notice in *Left Review*. Merseyside Left Theatre chose this poem for its first production and reworked it for performance. Unity, however, could not find the right style and presented *Spain* only a handful of times. The actors wore potato sacks as masks to represent abstract voices, proclaiming from a void.

When one of the cast, Fred Baker, read *On Guard for Spain* in *Left Review*, he felt that this might offer a better vehicle for Unity.[22] John Allen and Margaret Leona, who had worked on the Toller mass recitation *Requiem* and the Swingler poem, turned *On Guard for Spain* into a powerful mass declamation that came to symbolise Unity's stand against fascism. Lindsay wrote additional stanzas at Unity's request and different versions were produced; *On Guard* could last up to an hour, using one, two or three single voices set against a chorus. Leona's interest in Greek dance and Japanese Noh plays helped her shape the movement, small at first with the chronicler and then larger for the chorus.

> CHRONICLER: What you shall hear is the tale of the Spanish people.
> It is also your own life.
> On Guard, we cry.
> It is the pattern of the world today.

Lindsay tells of the changes that took place with the election of the Popular Front government in February 1936. Then comes the warning of the Franco rebellion followed by the fascist attack – 'the testing time of the people'. The war is underway, battles are listed and the author returns to the overriding importance of Spain to the world at large; the International Brigades who went to fight in Spain are fighting for democracy and progress everywhere:

WOMEN: Listen, comrades,
if you would know our pride,
CHRONICLER: Can you dare to know your deepest joy,
all that is possible in you?
Then what you see in Spain's heroic ardour
is your own noblest self come true.
CHOIR: On guard for the human future!
On guard for the people of Spain.

Performances would frequently end with audience and actors alike shouting 'No Pasarán' – 'They Shall Not Pass' – the cry of the Republican movement.

Unity first presented *On Guard for Spain* in April 1937, when the actors used pages torn from *Left Review* as their scripts.[23] In July, Unity performed it from the plinth at Trafalgar Square at a rally supporting the International Brigades, without microphones and wearing the red, yellow and mauve of the Republic. Sometimes uniforms typical of those the Brigaders might wear were used, and, when it was played indoors, special lighting created silhouettes of soldiers and peasants on a backcloth. On occasion, three groups of actors were used to present *On Guard* in the Mile End Road, East London, where Mosley's Blackshirts were active. The first group would begin at one street corner – and if the Blackshirts did not come the police would – then the second would take up the story, and, standing at yet another point, the third group would carry on. *On Guard* was reproduced as a penny pamphlet and a record of it was distributed by the Film and Photo League to accompany the film *The Spanish Dance* (also known as *Spanish Travail*) during its screening. *On Guard* was performed at many solidarity events, including a special presentation at the Phoenix Theatre with *Waiting for Lefty* and *Where's that Bomb?* at which the collection was taken by Isobel Brown, whose fund-raising activities and oratorical powers on behalf of the

Spanish Republic became famous on the left. Fifty years on, in 1986, there were a number of revivals of *On Guard for Spain* to commemorate the anniversary of the outbreak of the Spanish war.

Stephen Spender criticised *On Guard for Spain*, calling it 'effective recruiting propaganda' but 'supremely untruthful as poetry', a view shared by later literary commentators on the period.[24] Yet many in the labour movement, from Communist Party general secretary Harry Pollitt to Labour MP Ellen Wilkinson, paid tribute to its impact as a mass declamation, saying that they had rarely seen crowds so moved. R. Vernon Beste, later secretary of Unity, wrote of seeing *On Guard for Spain*: 'I not only knew *intellectually* that the Spanish people's fight was my fight, but for the first time *felt* that it was.'[25]

Unity had plans to stage other plays on Spain – for example, Manzani's *An Army is Born* and Ralph Meredith's *Spanish Aid* – but these came to nothing. When John Allen invited the recently formed Merseyside Left Theatre to visit Britannia Street in September 1937 the group presented two pieces on Spain, *Before Guernica* and *Insurgents' Aid Committee*. A year later Unity added to its repertoire Brecht's short play, *Señora Carrar's Rifles*, because of its Spanish theme. It is unusual for Brecht in that he abandoned temporarily his exploration of epic theatre and turned to a naturalistic style (or what he would consider a reactionary form) in order to intervene directly in a political struggle with a play that illustrated the desired political response.

Based on Synge's *Riders to the Sea*, the Brecht play tells the tale of Theresa Carrar, whose husband had been fatally wounded in the Asturian revolution of 1934 yet had made his way back to his Andalusian fishing village to die. She does not want the same fate to befall either of her sons and does not tell the elder one of a village meeting that has been called to organise support for the Republican government. Her brother calls and, while she is out, the younger son shows him where she has hidden her husband's rifles. On her return she refuses to give her brother the rifles which he wants for the Republic.

When her eldest is brought before her on a blood-stained sail, shot dead by a fascist patrol boat without a challenge or a warning, Carrar sends the mourners away, hands the guns to her brother and joins him and her youngest son to go off to fight.

Brecht's attack on adopting a neutral position toward the Spanish war appeared in a translation by Keene Wallis, which had been published in an American magazine *Theatre Workshop* (April-June 1938) and was directed by John Fernald, who later became director of Liverpool Playhouse and head of the Royal Academy of Dramatic Art. At the time of Unity's production, Brecht was little known in Britain; BBC radio had broadcast two didactic pieces and *The Threepenny Opera*, two films had been screened privately, and his only novel and two articles on theatre had been translated.[26] On stage, his ballet *Anna Anna* had been seen at the Savoy Theatre in 1933 and in 1936 the London Labour Choral Union (usually known as *The Measures Taken*) had performed his didactic oratorio *The Expedient*. Unity's was the first production in Britain of a Brecht play and later a second version, re-titled *Mrs Carrar's Rifles*, was staged using a new translation by the director Herbert Marshall and Fredda Brilliant, who had found the Wallis text linguistically and politically weak.

Señora Carrar's Rifles, like *The Secret* and *On Guard for Spain*, was taken on tour to raise consciousness, spirits and money for Spain. Unity gave special performances for Spain of other shows too, such as *Aristocrats* at the Phoenix Theatre in 1938. It was all part of the massive Aid Spain movement that swept through Britain in the late 1930s.[27] Despite the blocking activities of the TUC and Labour Party leaderships, hundreds of towns set up Spanish Aid Committees, drawing on a wide range of people well beyond the ranks of the labour movement and involving an extraordinary spread of cultural events, in which left-wing theatres and Unity played their full part. Individuals at Unity also made special contributions; a life-long Unity activist, Richard Polling, adopted two refugee Basque children and several people closely associated with Unity then and later fought in Spain. Among those who died there were Unity volunteers Edward (known at Unity as Henry) Burke, Ben Glaser and Bruce Boswell. Burke was one of the first British volunteers to go to Spain and fought in the early battle of Madrid University in 1936. A professional actor, he died at Córdoba in January 1937. A memorial was held for him later when Unity had opened its new theatre and a plaque was raised there to his memory. He had been a member of Left Theatre, had chaired Rebel Players meetings, including those which created Unity, and had been one of Unity's first directors as well as a founder member. Ben Glaser, a tailor and former member of Rebel Players, and Bruce Boswell, who had left Coventry to become a Unity actor, both wrote letters from Spain to Unity. In one, Boswell tells how he met up with Glaser and together they formed a Unity group in Spain called The People's Theatre. At a concert a few miles behind the front lines where they could hear the big guns pounding away, Ben performed Agate's fighting last speech from *Lefty* to great applause: 'And when we die they'll know what we did to make a new world! ... put fruit trees where our ashes are!' Both Boswell and Glaser died at the Ebro, in July and September 1938 respectively.

As well as encouraging individual members to join schemes such as the one run by the Dependents' Aid Committee to help families of returning International Brigaders, Unity played at an International Brigades reunion at St Pancras Town Hall in October 1938. After the defeat of the Republic Unity's links with Spain continued; Unity presented a reading of a play called *Give Me Liberty*, set in Spain before the fall of Madrid and written by E.P. Montgomery, Denis Weaver, a war correspondent in Spain, and a German émigré E. Klein. Unitarians helped stage manage a spectacle in January 1939 at the Empress Hall, Earl's Court, honouring the International Brigaders who had just returned to Britain.

In 1943, Unity's mobile group commemmorated the Battle of Jarama with a play, *We Fight On*, staged at the Scala Theatre under the auspices of the International Brigade Association.[28] Written and directed by J.S. Frieze, it tells in thirteen scenes the story of the International Brigades from 1936 to 1943 and required a cast and choir of 150 performers, including, alongside Unity members, people from the exile Free Austrian, Free German, Free Czechoslovak and Spanish Republican cultural groups. The event also called attention to the fact that three months previously the Allies had landed in North Africa but had not yet liberated the anti-fascist prisoners and International Brigaders who were still held there in concentration camps and labour gangs. In 1945, at the Coliseum, *All One Battle* by Unity president Ted Willis was performed for the International Brigades, showing how those who fought in Spain had continued the struggle, in Italy, Yugoslavia, the Soviet Union and Japan, as well as in Spain itself.[29] In the 1950s an International Brigader, George Leeson, became Unity's general manager. His play, *This Trampled Earth*, set in contemporary Spain and aimed at exposing the conditions of gaoled Republicans, was staged by Unity in 1946.[30]

Notes

1. Interviews/correspondence for this chapter: John Allen, Celia Baker, Alfie Bass, Roy Battcock, Bram Bootman, Maurice Braham, Ray Braham, Nat Brenner, Mark Clifford, James Gibb, Bobby Hilton, Kate Hilton, A.T. Jackson, Jack Lindsay, Margaret Leona, Joe Stern, Trudy Stern, Roger Woddis.
2. *Private Hicks, New Theatre*, November 1935, from which the later quotations are taken. *Waiting for Lefty* was published in *New Theatre*, February 1935 and also in America in Clifford Odets, *Three Plays*, Covici-Friede 1935, which was used by the cast too. Victor Gollancz published *Three Plays* in England in 1936 and quotations are taken from this edition. *Theatres of the Left* carries a Federal Theater Project version which omits the laboratory assistant episode, though this is not made clear in the book. The Federal Theater Project negotiated different versions of the play in different parts of the USA. Mostly the changes involved adding local references to make the play more relevant to a particular community but sometimes scenes were omitted.
3. Harold Clurman, *Those Fervent Years*, Denis Dobson 1946. For some of the many discussions on the play see Chapter 1, footnotes 1, 3 and 12. For a critical account of the play from the left, see Albert Hunt, 'Only Soft-Centred Left: Odets and Social Theatre', *Encore*, No. 31, May-June 1961.
4. The play contains American references that might have escaped a British audience, e.g. Agate's cry 'put fruit trees where our ashes are!' echoes the call of the American labour hero Joe Hill from his death cell. His ashes were placed in envelopes that were sent to supporters in every state except Utah, where he was executed, and to supporters around the world on the four continents who scattered the ashes on 1 May 1916.
5. See Jerry Dawson, *Left Theatre: Merseyside Unity Theatre*, Merseyside Writers 1985.
6. 'No Slump in this Theatre', *Daily Worker*, 28 August 1937.
7. Such is the nature of anecdotal evidence that while several people remember the wrong record being played there is a discrepancy as to which record it should have been. Some say Hoagy Carmichael's 'Stardust' while others believe that it was Duke Ellington's 'Solitude'.
8. Interview.
9. Herbert Hodge, *It's Draughty in Front*, Michael Joseph 1938.
10. Roger Gullan and Buckley Roberts, *Where's That Bomb?*, Lawrence and Wishart 1937.
11. As well as *It's Draughty in Front*, Hodge's autobiographies were

Cockney on Main Street and *Cab, Sir!*, all Michael Joseph. Hodge also wrote about himself in 'I am a Taxi Driver', *Fact*, 22 January 1939 and talked about his life in various radio broadcasts. Mick Wallis is researching his radio and brief television career and his unpublished thesis lists all the programmes that Hodge made.

12. Scene 5 from, and commentary by Herbert Hodge on, *Cannibal Carnival* can be found in E.A. Osborne (ed.), *In Letters of Red*, Michael Joseph 1938. Scenes 4 and 5 are available in the British Theatre Association. A further extract can be found in *New Masses*, 6 July 1937, in an article, 'The London Theater', by Eleanor Flexner. In the extract published in *In Letters of Red* the Bishop is called Bogus but in scene 4 he is called Bumpus, the name which Geoffrey McKeeman, who played the part, recalls as the one that was used.

13. For example, in a scene about *Waiting for Lefty* in a 1939 revue *Sandbag Follies*, the authors gently mock Unity's style of production, but the difference in tone to Hodge is striking.

14. Several sources (e.g. Unity's records, a 1957 Unity pamphlet *Here is Drama* listing all the productions, Travis) list *Awake and Sing* as having been performed but I could not find anyone who contradicted the account of its rejection. The quotes from *I Can't Sleep* come from a Unity acting text that I was given and which I have deposited in the British Theatre Association library.

15. Authorship unknown, although it is remembered as American. It has been mistakenly attributed to Arthur Laurents, who wrote a play of the same name years later, and in the Australian pamphlet, *New Theatre: 15 Years of Productions* (1948) to Albert Maltz and George Sklar (who might possibly have written it with another title). Nor is it the play of the same title written by Charles H Faber and performed in New York in 1939.

16. *Love in Industry, Red Stage*, No. 5, April-May 1932. I was given three versions of *The Fall of the House of Slusher*, all deposited in the British Theatre Association. Quotations used are the same in all three texts.

17. 'not English? A Reminder for May Day', *Left Review*, Vol. 2 No. 8, May 1936. Quotations are taken from a Unity acting script. A pageant called *We are the English*, which was commissioned by the London District of the Communist Party and filmed by Kino, was performed on 20 September 1936. It involved a march of some 4-5,000 people and a gathering in Hyde Park of some 15-20,000 people but any links with Unity remain unclear.

18. For Lindsay's life until the end of the Second World War, see Jack Lindsay, *Life Rarely Tells*, Penguin 1982. For an introduction to his early work, see Robert Mackie (ed.), *Jack Lindsay: The Thirties and Forties*, Institute of Commonwealth Studies 1984; and for general essays on him Bernard Smith (ed.), *History and Culture*, Hale and Iremonger 1984.

19. *Some Notes on the Formation of Left-Wing Amateur Theatre Groups*.

20. Jack Lindsay, 'A Plea for Mass Declamation', *Left Review*, Vol. 3 No. 9, October 1937. See also Jack Lindsay, *After the Thirties*, Lawrence and Wishart 1956, Don Watson *British Socialist Theatre 1930-1979*, unpublished PhD thesis, University of Hull 1985. (Watson has also written in *Artery*,

Vol. 5 No. 3, 1980 and the Bernard Smith and Robert Mackie collections of essays.)

21. Quotations from *Left Theatre: Merseyside Unity Theatre*. A slightly different but full version of *Spain* can be found in *The Spanish War Against Fascism 1936-1939*, the catalogue of the archive of the 1985 Merseyside Commemoration Tribute to the Merseyside volunteers in the International Brigade, Museum of Labour History 1987.

22. A first version was printed in *Left Review*, Vol. 3 No. 2, March 1937 and reprinted in Valentine Cunningham (ed.), *The Penguin Book of Spanish Civil War Verse*, 1980. I was given two acting versions which have been deposited in the British Theatre Association library. Quotations are taken from the longer of the two. Lindsay's *Collected Poems*, Chiron Press 1981, contains two versions of *On Guard for Spain* as well as versions of *Who are the English?, Man of the Maquis* and *Cry of Greece. Salute the Soviet Union* was published in *New Theatre*, No. 2, November 1937. Other mass declamations by Lindsay – *May the First, Summer Election* and *A Piece about Peace* (performed by London Unity) – are held in the Merseyside Left/Unity Theatre Archive.

23. The copy of *On Guard for Spain* held in the Lord Chamberlain's papers in the British Library was licensed for performance on 23 April 1937 at Shoreditch Town Hall, but there is no mention of this appearance either in a Unity report of activities for that April nor in the *Daily Worker*. The Unity report gives the first performance as being on 24 April at Granville Hall.

24. Spender quote in *After the Thirties*.

25. 'Mass Declamation', *Our Time*, Vol. 2 No. 11, May 1943.

26. The two articles were 'The German Drama; pre-Hitler', anonymously translated in *Left Review*, Vol. 2 No. 10, July 1936, and an essay on Chinese acting, 'The Fourth Wall of China', translated by Eric Walter White in *Life and Letters To-Day*, September 1936. Eric Walter White had also written, in *Life and Letters To-Day*, September 1935, an article on Brecht's writing.

27. See Jim Fyrth, *The Signal was Spain*, Lawrence and Wishart 1986.

28. Copy of *We Fight On* in International Brigade archive, Marx Memorial Library, Box 27B File C.

29. *All One Battle* (also in International Brigade archive Box 27B File C) was followed by the speech of farewell to the International Brigaders made by the Spanish Communist leader Pasionaria (Dolores Ibarurri). It was read by Megs Jenkins.

30. *This Trampled Earth* was based on a fact-finding trip to Spain by Leah Manning MP, Philip Noel-Baker and Monica Whatley who were investigating the numbers of political prisoners in Franco's gaols and their conditions. A copy of the play is in the British Theatre Association library. D. Corkill and S. Rawnsley (eds), *The Road to Spain*, Borderline 1981, contains a short biographical note on Leeson and an account of why he went to Spain.

3

Expansion

By its first anniversary, Unity had risen – in John Allen's words – 'from an organisation with no assets except a few actors with stout hearts and a vigorous but underdeveloped talent, to one that has its own theatre and equipment and two well-trained companies'.[1] The Unity Theatre Club claimed an active membership of 80 and an associate membership of 1,500. It was printing its own internal bulletins, programmes, tickets, leaflets and posters, and had mounted in September 1936 the first of three pre-war regional tours in a couple of old taxis that Jimmy Turner had bought for 50 shillings each. Unity played *Waiting for Lefty* and *Private Hicks* for a week in the North-East at a cost of £70. The tour was organised mainly through the local miners and included a visit to three miners' halls and to one of the leading amateur theatres of its day, the People's Theatre, Newcastle, which had been founded in 1911 as an offshoot of the Clarion movement. With each tour, Unity went up in the world; the second, in 1937, boasted a lorry and the third, in 1938, a coach. The tours were not easy to set up. Not only was there the cost and the organisation, Unity was an amateur company and the actors who had jobs had to arrange their holidays to coincide with the tours.[2]

Unity's appeal was evangelical, propagandistic and proudly partisan; its popularity sprung from an immediate political identification with its audiences, presenting plays about working-class issues in a direct, spontaneous way and in language that audiences could understand as being their own or belonging to their movement. In contrast to the bland and vacuous West End, there was even a certain advantage in being untrained; a rough, robust and vital quality was appropriate and telling. In this context, Unity would have amounted to little if it had not also challenged the theatre-producing and theatre-going habits and practices of the day. It swept away the paraphernalia of tradition – high prices, evening wear, the star system, footlights – that fenced off the theatre from its public, and forged social and political links with its audience.

Unity performers would meet and get to know people at their mobile shows, whether mounting *Waiting for Lefty* at a Tailor and Garment Workers' Union meeting, staging at the Peoples' Palace, Mile End Road, a benefit for old trade unionists in distress, or appearing at Abbey Wood on International Co-op Day. Unity members would carry the theatre's banner on marches, and on the evening of any major event, the Unity audience would most likely include people who earlier in the day had been on the same demonstration. Unity actors in costume were a familiar sight on such occasions – at a May Day event, for example, welcoming the Hunger Marchers to Hyde Park with 250,000 other people.[3] At one rally, a Unity actor wearing his military uniform from the show he was in was cheered by on-lookers who believed that at last the army had come over to the side of the people. Unity members could also be seen at political meetings – at Gardiner's Corner, Aldgate, at Cable Street stopping Mosley's Blackshirts or selling the *Daily Worker* at striking bus garages. Unity saw itself as inseparable from the movement in an honourable tradition that stretched back to the unions' predecessors, the guilds. At a time when there was no public subsidy for the theatre and a huge class divide across Britain's cultural life, with access to so-called 'high' art restricted to the few, Unity could offer a clear, caring message, and its commitment, sincerity and passion moved even those who might not agree with its politics.

Yet, beyond a solid, politically loyal, core organised mainly by the Communists, Unity's audiences had to be won time and again. There was no guarantee, for example, that Unity's popularity at a political gathering or trade union function would necessarily lead to increased bookings at Britannia Street, and the job of reaching beyond the Communist Party's ranks was made harder by the dislike of Unity expressed by the TUC and Labour Party leaderships. It was a tough struggle to survive, even in the 'red' decade, and there was a constant debate at Unity as to whether unalloyed politics or humour, or what mix of both, might be the key to gaining the new audiences. In trying to assess how broad the theatre's appeal should be, Unity found that working-class audiences could often find plays difficult to follow, not because of the content but through unfamiliarity with certain dramatic forms and conventions. They were also easily put off, either by their general lack of ease at theatre-going or by reviews that fell short of the fullest praise from what they regarded as an authoritative source, such as the *Reynolds News*, the *Daily Worker* or their trade union journal. On the other hand, middle-class people interested in culture could be drawn to Unity because it was daring or, on occasions, fashionable in some circles.

Left Book Club Theatre Guild

In February 1937, one year after the theatre's founding, the management committee decided to re-organise Unity in order to enlarge its operation. The cramped, inadequate conditions of Britannia Street were inhibiting any chance of development, without which the club could not survive. The nature of the expansion, however, turned out to be more ambitious than anyone at Unity had expected. It had two main facets. One was the opening and running of a new theatre, the other was to set up a national co-ordinating organisation that would take over the role of the Workers's Theatre Movement and New Theatre League.

Tommy Foster, Unity's administrator, had been receiving requests from all over Britain for scripts and advice on how to start left theatre groups. Many inquiries came from members of the Left Book Club (LBC), which had been founded in February 1936 by the publisher Victor Gollancz (after an earlier idea suggested by the Communist Workers' Book Shop had come to nothing).[4] The LBC became enormously important, not just because of its monthly book 'choices' with their distinctive orange covers, and its pamphlets and leaflets which were read by thousands, but also because, in the absence of party political agreement on a Popular Front, the club became the focus for much united left-wing activity. As such, it was spurned by the leaderships of the Labour Party and TUC as well as, more predictably, the Liberal Party. When the club's first book was issued in May that year, the LBC claimed 9,000 members and by March 1937 it had grown to a membership of over 40,000 with well over 200 discussion groups and a full-time organiser. These numbers were to rise up until the war, reaching 1,200 groups with around 50,000 members in 1939 when the Nazi-Soviet pact split the Club. The club was wound up in November 1948 when membership had dropped to 7,000.

On Foster's initiative, he and John Allen went to see Victor Gollancz to ask for help with the postage for Unity's replies to the various requests. 'VG' was sympathetic and offered more – £5 per week for Unity to run a drama organisation allied to the book club. The awkwardly titled Left Book Club Theatre Guild (LBCTG) was launched on 1 April 1937.[5] To some extent, it followed earlier models, such as the WTM or the Federation of Workers' Film Societies, but it outstripped them both, being more broadly-based than the former and more active than the latter. Allen became the LBCTG's first secretary or national organiser, and, with the help of other Unity members, sent out duplicated advice and scripts, and travelled the country addressing groups.

With a confidence then typical of the left, Allen believed that the socialist theatre movement would 'in a short time' surpass the bourgeois theatre in technical proficiency as it already had in the vitality of its content.[6] Its success in achieving this, he wrote, depended 'upon its ability to solve two straightforward, but immensely difficult problems – how to get plays and how to organise an audience'.[7] The LBCTG tried to do both. The main avenue for the advice that he was offering was a booklet called *Some Notes on the Formation of Left-Wing Amateur Theatre Groups* (also known more simply in different editions as *How to Form Left Theatre Groups*). In the booklet, Allen uses Unity's experiences to help others. He deals with practical guidance and information, and also examines popular theatre from an historical and contemporary viewpoint.

The guild explicitly embraced a Popular Front ideology, which Allen applies equally to actors and audience, citing Unity's *Waiting for Lefty*:

> The twenty or so actors who form the cast of this play number among them members of the Liberal, Labour, and Communist parties, members of Co-operative Societies, Trade Unionists, and so on. The audiences who come to the Unity Theatre Club are even more varied, for they are not solely confined to members of the working class. A theatre such as this is continually presenting left-wing opinions and problems to people who would never dream of attending a political meeting; and if those ideas are presented in a way that is theatrically

effective, they will have a considerable influence on those members of the audience.

Of crucial importance was the view that theatre 'is a practical means of furthering the cause; and the tremendous amount of co-operation that is needed among the different people concerned in putting on a play is in itself a splendid lesson in practical socialism'.

The guild differed in its assessment of agitprop from the WTM. Allen criticises 'the political pamphlet in dialogue form ... and plays in which earnest young things are obliged to choose between loyalty and the man, or woman, of their affection'. He knew that agitprop was attractive and good for recruitment but it did not allow the actor to develop, and many people joined left theatres to act. Agitprop was useful sometimes, if judiciously placed in a programme. He does not condemn propganda – 'where is the work of art of value that is not propaganda?' comments Allen – but, rather, affirms the fullest use of all the elements of theatre. 'If the propaganda is clumsily expressed it will probably be more painful to sit through than no propaganda at all,' adds Allen, who, quoting Gollancz, asserts that 'by far the most valuable possession a group can have is a reputation for putting on good shows.'

Starting in June 1937, Allen produced a monthly report of the LBCTG's growing activities for 'VG', which the publisher corrected punctiliously, and which appeared in the LBC's magazine *Left News*. (The February 1939 article is unsigned and from March 1939 to August 1939 the articles were written by Frank Jones.) Allen's first article reported a conference held at Britannia Street of London groups and cites Sheffield Left Theatre Club as an example to follow, with its 'double course' of 'productions of full-length plays with a broad liberal policy' and 'the establishing of a sort of "Flying Squad" of people who are willing to go out with one-act plays, short sketches, etc., to villages, rallies and political meetings, with the deliberate purpose of propaganda'.

In October 1937, Unity and the guild published their own joint bulletin which ran to ten foolscap roneoed pages. In November 1937, the bulletin became a penny monthly called *New Theatre*, which, it was hoped, would link up with the cinema and involve Kino and be known as *New Theatre and Film*, though this did not happen. The paper offered a means of communication for the groups whose activities it reported. *New Theatre* carried articles on different aspects of the theatre and its techniques, lists of books to read, editorials and interviews with leading theatre people like Sean O'Casey. He told the paper that until the trade unions had seen the need to build Unity Theatres in every town in England, Scotland and Wales 'our work is not half done'.[8] In March 1939, following some internal disagreements, the paper's name changed to *Theatre for the People*. Unity carried on with its own magazine using the old name *New Theatre* until the war closed down both.

Contact between groups was made through visiting performances as well as through the bulletins. In 1937, Unity and the LBCTG organised a tour to the Midlands and the North-East of *Waiting for Lefty, On Guard for Spain* and *The Fall of the House of Slusher*. The visitors were accommodated by local trade unionists, Co-operators and Left Book Club members. Such tours not only brought the work of Unity and the latest political news from the capital to those living outside London, they also encouraged the setting up of local drama groups – or the further development of existing ones. Those involved represented a broad range of political and theatrical experience, from former WTM members to people newly moved by the times they were living through who simply wanted 'to do something' on the side of progress and justice. It was a time of great hunger for knowledge and debate, as can be judged by, for example, the launch and spread of Penguin paperbacks or the increase in Workers Educational Association courses.

Estimates vary but the LBCTG claims to have comprised some 70 groups nationally in the summer of 1937 and 140 by that October. By the beginning of 1938, the guild claimed 208 groups, ranging alphabetically from Aberdeen to Woking and geographically from Dublin and Plymouth to Edinburgh and Brighton. London boasted some 20 groups and the East End eight alone, including one organised by the Tailor and Garment Workers' Union. By September 1938, the figures nationally had risen to 308.

Even if London Unity provided a stimulus and occasionally a target of excellence, the other groups, with their different cultural and political backgrounds, were independent in spirit and action, as had been the case in the WTM.[9] (Merseyside staged *The Dog Beneath the Skin* by Auden and Isherwood in 1940, for instance, a play that London Unity would never have performed.) There was resistance to centralised authority and to any imposed ideology beyond a broad agreement on the crisis of world capitalism and on the fight against fascism symbolised by the defence of the Spanish Republic.

Local Groups

Regional movements developed in South Wales, Yorkshire and Lancashire – based respectively, in Cardiff, Sheffield and Manchester – and regional area committees were set up which later sent representatives to a national committee that held its first meeting in Glasgow in October 1938. There was to have been an organiser for the North of England to complement the London-based staff but this appointment was shelved in favour of securing new offices.

In early 1938, John Allen had moved the guild offices out of Unity because of the inadequate conditions to what at first was even more constricting – a flat in central London belonging to a voice coach, Nelson Illingworth – and a few weeks later to Excel House in Whitcomb Street off Leicester Square. In late 1938, when Allen's work as secretary had been taken over by Paul Eisler, the guild offices were transferred to 14 Henrietta Street in Covent Garden, the home of Gollancz's publishing house and of the Left Book Club. Eisler was joined in running guild affairs from London by others, such as Jack Selford from Unity's Play Department, Meg Wintringham and Frank Jones. In early 1939, Jones took over from Eisler as secretary when the guild had become the responsibility of the book club's Groups Department which formed the organisational apparatus of the club's activities. The London-based team acted as agents and as co-ordinators both between theatre groups and between theatre, dance and music groups, and they helped make contacts with the left and labour movement to facilitate bookings.

London Unity successes were popular among guild groups. Along with *Waiting for Lefty*, there was *On Guard for Spain* (which the Glasgow group is reported to have staged in a more imaginative way than its London counterpart), *Bury the Dead, Where's that Bomb?, Private Hicks* and *The Rehearsal* as well as the Living Newspaper *ARP* (Air Raid Precautions) that took on different variations in the different localities. Other plays that were popular with guild groups were *Till the Day I Die*, Joe Corrie's *Hewer's of Coal*, Elmer Rice's *Judgement Day*, and *Six Men of Dorset* by H. Brooks and Miles Malleson. (This had been commissioned in 1934 by the TUC for the centenary of the Tolpuddle Martyrs and was toured under TUC auspices in 1937 by a professional company led by Sybil Thorndike and Lewis Casson.) The reliance on American material was clear, and, in the case of Bristol Unity, one member who lived in New York between 1937 and 1939 regularly sent back scripts and records to the group's leading figure, her sister Joan Tuckett.

Many groups staged their own plays, such as *The Bull Sees Red* in Bristol, *Clogs* in Sheffield, written by unemployed miner George Fullard, *Cold Coal* in South Wales by Caerphilly bus driver Eynon Evans, *UAB – Scotland* in Glasgow, or in Sunderland, the recasting in the local context of Simon Blumenfeld's *Enough of All This*, a Unity/LBCTG touring play about a rent strike. Such productions frequently showed the close relationship that the groups enjoyed with the local left and labour movements. Newcastle LBCTG, for instance, performed at the Durham Miners' Gala in 1939 – apparently the only time the occasion has been graced with a play.[10]

Groups were urged – particularly in the run-up to the proposed general election that, because of the war, never took place – to use a Left Book Club publication, *Tory MP*, as the basis for creating an agitprop play attacking their local Conservative MP, should they have one, and helpful notes on how to achieve this were printed in *Left News*. Some groups looked to the tradition that the WTM had briefly rejected, and performed plays by the likes of Shaw, Galsworthy and even – very boldly – Euripides's *The Trojan Women* (in Plymouth, using Gilbert Murray's translation). The LBCTG, which worked closely with Unity's Play Department in developing its repertoire, published a play list in 1939 that named more than 150 titles – evidence of fertile and diverse imaginations.[11]

The LBCTG placed a great emphasis on learning and organised talks, weekend schools and summer schools, which brought together people from different parts of the country. The summer school was a regular feature of many left-wing organisations, from the Fabians to the Independent Labour Party, and provided temporary escape from city life in a rural and communal setting. The first Unity-LBCTG summer school was held between 31 July and 14 August 1937 at A.S. Neill's progressive Summerhill School in Leiston, Suffolk. Author William Paul described the scene (in *Left News*) as a 'barbaric classless society in which nothing was run but a great many things happened' – his response to the democracy of the school, with its general meetings, twice-weekly wall newspaper (a regular feature at Unity before the Second World War) and searing self-criticism.[12] Each morning began with a set lecture on some aspect of culture. This was followed in the afternoon by workshops on music, dance and drama, involving acting exercises and the exploration of different techniques from *commedia dell'arte* to mass declamation. To supplement this, the school rehearsed three plays from different eras; *Noah's Deluge* (a medieval morality), a Molière play and *Private Hicks*. Those attending also performed *Waiting for Lefty* in the village to raise funds for Spain.

In 1938, the second summer school, also held at Leiston, had the Communist scientist J.B.S. Haldane lecturing on air raid precautions and helping prepare a Living Newspaper on the issue, a lecture by the film maker Paul Rotha, Will Lee of the New York Group Theater talking on Living Newspapers and discussions on two American shows, *The Cradle Will Rock* and *Pins and Needles*. There were also performances in Leiston for Spanish Medical Aid of Ben Bengal's *Plant in the Sun*, the air raid show and *The Fall of the House of Slusher*.[13] The school was typical of hundreds of gatherings up and down the country at which people developed their own skills and listened to the advice of prominent authorities. In London, leading Communist J.R. Campbell addressed the first meeting of the Unity Play Clinic and the Unity Left Book Club Theatre Guild Group, on the subject of 'The Political Crisis and *Bury the Dead*', Irwin Shaw's anti-war play which Unity was about to present.

There was always much heated discussion about theatre's heritage and the left's attitude to it. The *Daily Worker* printed a series called 'The Past is Ours', in which, while the Communist position was argued, it was admitted that the British party was still 'backward' on the subject, especially in relation to national characteristics. *Left News* carried an article on bourgeois society that summed up the party view, which was shared by the left in the Popular Front movement:

> There can ben no doubt about it that the plays of Shakespeare, the poetry of Milton and Shelley, the pictures of Hogarth and Turner, the writings of Dickens, Jane Austen, Galsworthy and Shaw are of permanent value to the British people. It is our responsibility to hand them down to the generations to come and to the new society which will follow the passing of the present order.[14]

This debate was central to the role that the LBCTG and its moving force, Unity, saw themselves playing. It was seen as politically necessary to show that theatre, like other art forms, had reached its peaks of achievement when it had expressed the finest spirit of its nation, whether in the work of Aeschylus, Molière or O'Casey. In this way, the past could validate the present (which meant, then, the Popular Front strategy) and, therefore, the efforts of the left to build the future as representatives of the whole nation and not just one class. The cultural component of a would-be national movement in opposition to a Tory-led National government that was testing air raid sirens and manufacturing gas masks while encouraging the fascists' appetite for war was seen as the basis for the renewal of a proper national culture. But how to balance the future vision with the immediate practicalities, the anti-fascist appeal with socialist ideals? Allen was clear on this. He wrote in *Left Review*:

> ... although it is not possible to draw many actors together on a pro-socialist basis, it is possible to get them on an anti-fascist one. Most of them have wits enough to realise from example that fascism is more an enemy than a friend of vital theatre, but they have not wits enough to perceive, nor intellectual courage enough to admit, that a socialist Britain would remove those conditions which make a career on the stage today absolutely untenable for anyone who really cares about the business.[15]

He related this issue to the question of using popular forms to represent socialist values, which frequently leads to an uncomfortable sacrifice of principle for the sake of winning an audience. This problem, exacerbated by the Popular Front approach, brought the guild up sharp against its relation to the middle classes and to the amateur theatre world which was drawn overwhelmingly from those classes.[16] Groups were often criticised for not making sufficient attempts to mount performances before large 'unconverted' audiences. For some, the problem was not knowing to whom, or how, they should address themselves. They found the political and cultural environment hostile, with a Conservative Party in dominance, the media stridently pro-establishment and the Labour Party, TUC and many union leaderships equally anti-Communist. A *New Theatre* editorial tried to encourage and persuade those who held to old ideas. While underlining the difficulties of increasing worker involvement, it identified a 'sort of snobbery' that found something was good simply because it was proletarian. What was needed was skill guided by political conviction:

> We do believe that it is the job of the theatre people to do theatrical work and not interfere with the politicians. We have stated with emphasis in almost every piece of propaganda that we have produced that the basis of our work is political. This does not mean subservience to a political party, but it does mean that our theatre is playing a large part in the struggle for the overthrow of capitalism.[17]

There was a contrary view that saw the LBCTG mechanically as a conveyor belt of ideas that came from Unity, which, in turn, was seen narrowly as a vehicle for the cultural policies of the Communist Party. In general this was not the case and it would be wrong to see too instrumental a relationship between the three bodies. Communists were in the majority at Unity and a few, apparently, did try to dominate the LBCTG but most guild and Unity activists shared a broad ideology with the Communist Party, whether as members or not, and were happy to be associated with its attempts to develop a national drama movement.[18] Interestingly, the non-political Crescent Theatre in Birmingham had tried to form an Association of Little Theatres and had failed, largely because of administrative troubles, whereas the explicitly politically motivated LBCTG had managed to succeed. It was not until 1938 that the British Drama League agreed, somewhat reluctantly, to establish a Little Theatre Committee, and it was only after internal dissent that the guild finally affiliated in early 1939 to the league, although the guild earlier had praised the league and urged members to take the initiative in getting all the theatre groups in their area to co-operate in staging peace plays. It was official guild policy to participate in amateur festivals and it was estimated (in *Tribune*) in 1939 that four-fifths of the 603 finalists in such events had mounted progressive plays.[19] Unity was successfully taking part in such festivals, winning the national

British Drama League cup in 1939, and it was represented on the Little Theatre Committee as well as on the league's Publicity Committee.

Despite the tensions caused by attempts to break loose from the security of the narrow, autonomous world of the left, the guild's willingness to tackle the problem underlines its wider contribution to drama. It formed an important network of creativity and became part of a formidable theatrical force, both in itself and through its links, for example, with Gollancz's play publishing – individual successes like *Waiting for Lefty* as well as the *Best Plays of the Year* volumes appeared under his imprint. The Left Book Club also had a professional actors' group; this numbered 300 members and sympathisers on its mailing list, including Lewis Casson, Michael Redgrave, Sybil Thorndike, and André van Gyseghem. It overlapped in membership and held meetings with the Communist Party actors' group, which comprised professionals and concerned itself primarily with the state and direction of the profession and with union matters.[20]

The ability of Unity and the LBCTG to stimulate such ferment depended on their own activities as part of the labour movement which were linked to an even wider range of cultural interests mobilised around the left at the time. This is best exemplified by the Unity-LBCTG Cultural Week held in May 1938. The most daring event of the week was a presentation of Handel's *Belshazaar* at the Scala Theatre; the brainchild of Alan Bush, the production was sponsored by the four London Co-operative Societies. It involved a chorus of 300 Co-operators and the Boyd Neel String Orchestra, one of the most distinguished of the day. The opera was conducted by Warwick Brathwaite and produced by John Allen under the stage management of Unity's Jimmy Turner with help from members of the Unity stage staff. At the Conway Hall, Holborn, a discussion was held on 'Literature and the People' while Unity played host to several other activities; an exhibition mounted by the Left Book Club Scientists' Group called 'The Frustration of Science'; '5,000 Years of Poetry', compiled by Jack Lindsay for the Left Book Club Poetry Group (and issued as a pamphlet); and 'Why I Paint', organised by the Artists' International Association, involving six artists – including Roland Penrose and the *Daily Worker* cartoonist Gabriel – talking about different styles and uses of art, from surrealism to industrial design.

At the heart of the week was a 'Theatre and Music Festival' which ended with a national drama conference that set up a provisional LBCTG national committee. The music events were held at the Fred Tallant Hall under the auspices of the Workers' Music Association, which had been founded just after Unity and with which Unity had – and continued to have – very close links.[21] The theatre events were held at Unity; there was a drama competition involving 22 groups in three sections – mass declamation, political sketches and one-act plays, which *Left News* had said should preferably be humorous. The winners of two sections were the London Workers' Circle group, with *Private Hicks* and the mass declamation *Stop Those War Drums*. (No details were published for the political sketch section and one veteran, who remembers delivering a monologue in this category, says there was no award made.) The Workers' Circle group went on to form Stepney Unity and showed again the strength of theatre activity among the Jewish community.

The political and artistic breadth represented by this week demonstrated the movement's strength. Different points of view were aired in a provocative though creative way. The tensions, however, were not always productive, particularly when the political situation changed sharply. Varying attitudes to the Soviet Union and the role of the Communist Party lay behind some of the internal conflicts; the Nazi-Soviet Non-Aggression Pact of 1939 brought the movement to breaking point and the war finally snapped it. Survivors continued in various ways to play an active part in theatre and politics, either through left-wing theatres like Unity, which at the end of the war set up another federation of groups, through other amateur or professional companies or through their own individual effort not related to any organised movement.

Even if many LBCTG groups existed only on paper or for very short periods, there is sufficient evidence to show that the work of the guild's members represents a tremendous achievement – one that is generally unrecognised because it failed to produce any world-class writers. That was never its intention; the Unity-LBCTG movement was not much more than a loose grouping and was frequently inefficient as an organisation, but it did give its participants the chance of self-expression, a sense of common identity and purpose and an inspiring feeling of belonging to a larger movement for the greater good. Although in the short-term this movement failed – to unite the left, win international collective security, stop the spread of fascism and world war – it did in the longer term influence the victory over fascism and help return the first Labour government with a clear working majority. In that important process, left-wing theatre played a considerable part.

Goldington Street

Unity's contribution can only be understood in relation to its own spectacular growth during this period. In 1937, at the launch of the LBCTG, this required the achievement of the other and complementary aim to that of forming a national movement – the securing of new premises, to be run on different economic lines to those operating at Britannia Street, using a block-booking system based on corporate affiliations. (This was an idea borrowed from the experiences of Germany and America.) The necessary reorganisation of Unity during 1937 coincided with the establishing of the LBCTG, and the two processes reinforced one another, each playing its part in the attempt to create an alternative drama that transformed what was being created as well as both the means of production and the conditions of production and 'consumption'.

The policy was to continue to combine productions at the new theatre with a full programme of touring, using Britannia Street for rehearsals, workshops, readings, extra-mural activities and meetings. However, the aim was now to tour all productions, of both long and short plays, and the financial underpinning of expansion had to assume such increased artistic capability. New premises would offer the chance of greater economic potential in accordance with an ability to extend the repertoire into more complex, full-length, productions than hitherto had been the case. The shows at Britannia Street raised most of Unity's income but they spent it, too. Seat prices were kept low, to attract the desired audience, but this meant a dangerously small profit margin, if any. One box office flop might need four or five hits to make up the losses incurred.

Outside performances – full evenings for some organisations and shorter shows for rallies or meetings – helped cover the club's expenses (sometimes!) but to extend their activities also required a sounder financial and organisational base. The economic problem threatened the artistic, and therefore the political, work of Unity, and this was compounded by the difficulty of finding good, suitable material to perform.

The proposed block-booking system entailed organisations – trade unions, trades councils, Co-ops, branches of political parties – affiliating to Unity and thereby becoming eligible to make a booking in advance for all or part of the theatre on any number of evenings at a reduced rate. The affiliates could then sell the tickets to their own members, either at the price they had paid Unity for them, which would be less than the box office price, or even cheaper still, should they wish to subsidise their membership. Unity, on the other hand, was assured a certain income before a production opened.

The system had political and artistic implications, as well as economic, and to make it work required considerable effort, both in the initial stages of persuading organisations to affiliate and then subsequently in keeping up their interest and showing that their affiliation had been worthwhile.[22] This groundwork was done by many on the left, although Communists were in the forefront, active in trade unions through party groups, in Co-operative societies and in their own party branches. But the system relied for its success on the shows themselves, which led to a consolidation of the relationship between the theatre and its audience, with the affiliates becoming an important factor in the calculations of the repertory committee. (This could be both positive and negative, and particularly after the war, when the political climate was less favourable to Unity, conservative tendencies within the audiences proved depressing and frustrating for those at the theatre who wanted to be more innovative.)

It was never envisaged that the block-booking system would provide the amount of money required for Unity to carry out fully all of its plans. In the absence of state support which, for example, the Federal Theater Project provided in America on a huge scale, such a level of finance could only come through massive subsidy from the labour movement, and this was not forthcoming either then or in the future. The block-booking system, however, did provide the basis for Unity's development in the late 1930s, which is remarkable as the theatre was often on the verge of bankruptcy, if not on occasion being technically insolvent. Despite the Popular Front strategy, little effort seems to have been made to win corporate affiliations outside the traditional labour movement – from the Methodists or Quakers, for instance – although there were new attempts to gain middle-class audiences on an individual basis. (One spur was the hope that they might contribute handsomely at the customary end-of-show appeals.) According to John Allen, the overwhelming working-class character of Unity's audiences up to this point changed as a result of this approach. It helped bring Unity new supporters and a wider fame but also led to internal tensions as there were always those who believed that the workers' theatre was compromising too far.

The reorganisation campaign was launched by a fund-raising show on 25 February 1937 for members of the theatre profession.[23] The evening comprised *Waiting for Lefty, Where's That Bomb?* and Herbert Marshall reading poems that included his own vigorous translations of Mayakovsky. It turned out to be a gala occasion, with Elmer Rice, Tyrone Guthrie, H.G. Wells, Beatrix Lehmann, Flora Robson, Michel Saint-Denis and Geoffrey Whitworth, founder of the British Drama League, in attendance. The event is remembered chiefly for Wells's high-pitched squeaky voice, rising above the rest as he shouted 'Strike, strike, strike' at the end of *Lefty*, and for the appearance in court that afternoon of Bram Bootman and Tommy Foster, who were fined for allowing tickets to be sold without the customs and excise stamp on the back that was required for entertainment tax. Wells also gave £25 in response to a challenge from Alan Bush who offered £25 if nine others did the same. Fund-raising continued during the year and included performances of *Lefty* and *Bomb* at the Phoenix Theatre.

While new premises were being sought, Unity had to change its rules to become a co-operative society with new powers of association and activity. Constitutionally, the distinction between active and associate membership was kept, along with the related rights, and two new categories were added of life and honourary associate membership. Members of the police and armed forces were excluded from the society, as were fascists (though this latter condition was not written into the rules). Each Unity member had to be over 16 and had to buy at least one share in the co-operative, which was still to be run as a club, and active members still paid an extra fee for their privileges. No one was allowed to hold more than £200 worth of shares and all surplus revenue went to the society.

The rules also were expanded. Alongside the club's desire 'to devise import and experiment with new forms of dramatic art' and 'to work for the regeneration of the commercial theatre' along the lines that Unity thought it should develop, the main business of the new society became:

> to produce and present amongst as wide an audience as possible stage plays, dealing with social problems and issues of interest to the working class, and acted by its own members and to attain such a standard of acting ability technical craftmanship and artistic production as to give shape and momentum to the liveliest movements and ideas for the progress and betterment of the world.

Special mention was made of 'the idiom of the workers as a vigorous literary form'. Among other things, the rules allowed for the purchase of new premises, the forming of a federation of theatre groups, the teaching of drama and affiliation to other bodies.

Unity saw itself as a focus for all the arts, and not just drama – a Popular Front cultural centre – which, it was hoped, would be open seven days a week. It continued its association with the dance drama groups, set up its own music group with an orchestra and a choir under John Goss, which became a popular feature of many left-wing rallies, and increased its social activities. It held more film seasons and launched its own theatre magazine, bookshop, and School of Dramatic Studies, which, according to a Unity handbook, was 'the only theatre school in Britain applying the methods of Stanislavsky'. André van Gyseghem remained president while the management committee was enlarged from six to eighteen, from amongst whom was elected a smaller executive committee that met weekly to run Unity's affairs with the help of new sub-committees. The first life member was H.G. Wells and fourteen distinguished individuals from the worlds of politics and culture – all men – were invited to join a new general council: Alan Bush, Maurice Browne, Lewis Casson, Sir Stafford Cripps MP, Victor Gollancz, Tyrone Guthrie, Professor Harold Laski, Miles Malleson, Sean O'Casey, D.N. Pritt MP, Alderman Joseph Reeves, Paul Robeson, Michel Saint-Denis and George Strauss MP.[24]

Unity's leadership had thought that the formation of the new Unity Theatre Club Limited, a process which had begun in February, would only take six weeks to complete, yet the club was not registered under the Industrial and Provident Societies Acts until 19 November 1937, just a week before Unity's new building was officially opened. The old Unity Theatre Club was dissolved on 6 December and transferred to the new body.

Tommy Foster was in charge of the search for the new premises, being spurred on, no doubt, by the frustrations of working at Britannia Street, which John Allen remembers him describing as a cross between a tube station and a waste-paper basket. He was looking in the Kings Cross area for sites as close as possible to Britannia Street, which Unity wanted to continue using. Not only was the transport excellent but the area had proud theatrical associations; it was long the home of George Bernard Shaw, who served on St Pancras's first local council, and it boasted several local theatres – the Camden Theatre (later the Hippodrome), the Euston Theatre of Varieties (later the Regent), the Scala, the Bedford and the Open Air Theatre in Regent's Park. There were notable amateur theatres linked to Edith Neville, a prominent local figure and social worker – the St Pancras People's Players and, more importantly for Unity, the Tavistock Players and strong youth club and Boys' Brigade drama; not far away could be found the headquarters of the British Drama League, the Royal Academy of Dramatic Art, Sadler's Wells, Collins Music Hall and the West End.

Foster found a former cinema and pipe factory, but the deal fell through, although an opening – with a new play by Herbert Hodge – had been announced. In August, Foster came across a larger site, less than a mile away from Brit Street in the densely populated but poor Somerstown locality (named after the family of Will Somers, jester to Henry VIII). The building lay behind St Pancras station beyond the railway arches at No. 1 Goldington Street and was a disused Methodist chapel hidden from the street between Victorian houses. It had its own asphalted alley lined by trees and a high wall as an entrance. A foundation stone by the main door bore the date 1850 (but did not tell the full story of how one James Nunn and friends had built a Zion Chapel beginning on 1 April that year to attract away from the gin palaces local rail workers and those living under the arches).

Unity faced competition for the premises, which were known as the Aldenham Institute. The local council had given conditional permission for the former warehouse to be used as a fascist meeting hall, but on 3 September this permission had switched to the Marconi Company, to run a technical training school for wireless operators. Others wanted the hall for a book-binding business. When Unity made its successful bid, the old Presbyterian chapel was being used as a mission for the unemployed and 'down-and-out' under the severe guidance of an ex-naval officer who offered his clients a strict routine of physical exercise on gym equipment rather than a diet of nourishing food.

Building the New Theatre

Despite an estimate for the conversion of the hall into a theatre of £3,000 to £4,000 taking six months, Unity members voted at a general meeting on 1 September 1937 to undertake the necessary work themselves as they had done at Britannia Street. The rules were changed to allow the management committee to take on a fourteen-year lease for £200, which was signed on 25 September just as the Unity tour to Lincolnshire and South Yorkshire was about to leave. During the conversion, Unity was unable to present shows at Brit Street but performed *Lefty* 23 times at various halls and a new mass declamation by Jack Lindsay, *Salute the Soviet Union*, in connection with meetings held by the Friends of the Soviet Union to celebrate the twentieth anniversary of the 1917 revolution.

The team in charge of the conversion was Tommy Foster, John Allen and Jimmy Turner; Foster had to find the money and raised £500 before the theatre was opened, Allen brought in the architect, Raglan Squire, and Turner, a do-it-yourself wizard who later ran a theatre lighting supply business, became the site manager. Oliver Dawson was the structural engineer, and often attended on site. The architect – the son of the writer J.C. Squire and a friend of Allen's from Cambridge University – was just beginning his professional career. It turned out to be his first and last theatre job, but one which he remembers with great fondness. It seemed an impossible job but he believed in the enthusiasm of those engaging him and in the cause itself. He drew up his detailed plans in the style that he had been taught, not realising that no one working on the site would have time to read them in that form. But, as he and Turner virtually lived at No. 1 Goldington Street from the beginning of work on 21 September to the opening of the theatre at the end of November, they forged a working relationship that overcame such minor problems.

When 'Rag' first showed the drawings to Turner, he replied, 'Thanks a lot, but I haven't time to look at them right now. Can you tell me how many screws we shall need?' 'What for?' asked 'Rag'. 'The whole job, of course,' answered Turner. 'I haven't the faintest notion,' came the bewildered response. 'Well,' said Turner, 'you ought to have; you are the architect. The point is that someone has offered to supply, free of charge, all the screws we need for the whole job. Can you work it out right away and let me know?'

Two hours later, with the help of two carpenters, 'Rag' gave his estimate, and next day the screws arrived in a lorry. No one took any notice of the original drawings after that; 'Rag' set out most of the work full size on a spare bit of wall or planking.[25]

All the material was begged by Turner in this way. Someone would be asked to pay for the timber, someone else for the lighting, someone else for the cement (Victor Gollancz, as it happened) and so on. Sometimes the material would come at trade price, sometimes free. Rich supporters were asked for donations and a few came to help as well, joining the small army of volunteer labour under Turner's careful eye who made their way over trenches and round concrete mixers through the wide front door with its original 'Welcome' sign still intact, sunk deep into the lintel.

Adverts were placed in left-wing and sympathetic newspapers asking for volunteers and appeals were made through contacts to the appropriate trade unions. (The *New Builders Leader* journal and the Building Workers' Sports Association were specially helpful and were thanked later when Paul Robeson sang at a special variety concert held by Unity to raise money for them.) Notices were put up in local labour exchanges which read:

> Anyone wishing to help build
> THE WORKERS' THEATRE
> please come to the Methodist Chapel
> Kings Cross at 9 o'clock
> FREE BEER AND SANDWICHES

According to the *Daily Worker*, some 400 people helped build the theatre at Goldington Street; the list included five architects, 34 artists and sign writers, seven dress designers, 115 carpenters, seventeen bricklayers, fifteen painters and plasterers, 41 electricians, thirteen engineers, eight metal workers, twenty upholsterers and nine plumbers. A barber came, whose contribution was to offer free haircuts to all, and there was another bevy of helpers (women) keeping the refreshments going under Ray Braham. They not only served the snacks but provided them as well. (It was taken for granted that this was a woman's job, remembers Ann Soutter, then a new recruit. 'We didn't think twice about the implications, only about being useful.')

Those in work came after work and stayed until midnight or took off time if they could; those out of work came all day. On Saturday nights, a new shift took over and worked until morning. George Lang, a sheet metal worker, was employed by a firm who had closed for a couple of days' stocktaking. He saw the advertisement in the *Daily Worker* and arrived to find the place knee-deep in plaster from the ceiling which had been stripped. His first job was to barrow the plaster out to a waiting lorry. The electrician Pete Bennett was about to lay the power cables and needed a metal trough to take them from the entrance to the stage area. He was going to approach a firm to have them made but Lang was able to oblige once the sheet metal had been cadged.

Another volunteer, R. Vernon Beste, remembers his first impression of naked working lights hanging from all manner of spurs that were jutting from the walls, with a round brazier in the centre of the site emitting a thin ruffle of white smoke. Wilfred White, who had come to London from Devonshire, took heed of a chalked notice to novices warning of the dangers of falling off the then only partly-built stage: ' "All the world's a stage," said Shakespeare, but he wasn't a builder.' White offered himself to Turner, who gave him a hammer and a cold chisel, pointed to a mark and told him to knock a hole in the 18-inch thick wall for the women's toilet water pipe, which came under the aegis of plumbers' union stalwart Tommy Sullivan. The entire workforce was kept sweet by the pure tenor of Harry Newton, the chief carpenter, whose rendering of 'Santa Lucia' was often the first sound to greet a newcomer to the site.

Complaints and encouragements were pinned up on a wall

newspaper which was changed weekly, though Sean O'Casey's message held firm until the opening night, when it was read out: 'I hope the Unity Theatre Club will smash the myth that culture and the enjoyment of art are confined to what is sometimes called the better classes.'[26] Advice and ideas mingled with strictures against bad language ('scaffold grammar') – a sensitivity that was due possibly to the increased interest shown in the venture by the press. Pictures and stories appeared, and not just in the left-wing papers; Jocelyn Herbert, later a prominent stage designer but then known as the daughter of the divorce reform MP A.P. Herbert, was photographed as a 'brickie' wielding a shovel and quoted as saying: 'It is to be a theatre for real, unvarnished plays of everyday life, you see, not the artificial, Hollywood conception of things.' Tom Driberg, the William Hickey columnist of the *Daily Express*, lent his support, and Eslanda and Paul Robeson visited the site to pledge their solidarity, which lasted throughout both their lifetimes.

When Unity took over the hall, it still retained many of the old chapel's features, such as the tall side windows and a small rear gallery.[27] It was wider and shallower than Brit Street, measuring 60 feet by 35 feet, and was immediately to be gutted. The old lath and plaster ceiling had to be removed to make way for a new sloping balcony. A new ceiling was installed, made in fully moulded light fibrous plaster, then the fashion in the super cinemas. The ceiling supported lighting, which flooded it to superb effect, and coved down to the front of the auditorium above the proscenium arch that frames the stage. This greatly improved the acoustics.

A major structural design problem of how to support the proscenium and the lighting with a bridge that could span the 35 foot width and provide access to the fly grid and galleries was solved by the construction of a wooden girder box, some 7 feet high and 4 feet deep, in which there was room to circulate and service the spots on what was known as the no. 1 batten slung beneath. The fly galleries, which spanned the depth of the stage, where situated either side and 10 feet below the fly grid, from whence backcloths and scenery could be flown (raised and lowered) on pulleys. The idea was abandoned of building a traditional fly tower, twice the height of the proscenium arch, and the original roof was left untouched though strengthened to carry the bridge, fly galleries and proscenium arch. The grid was positioned at the maximum height of 23 feet that was available and, for backcloths that were too tall to be flown flat, wooden cyclinders were provided around which they could be rolled.

Via a central walkway sloping up and back across the auditorium ceiling, the bridge also gave access to a remote lighting position at the back of the balcony that was rarely used and to the prompt (or left-hand) side gallery that was cantilevered out over the auditorium ceiling and housed the sound position. This was equipped with an amplifier and two turntables linked to the largest speakers then available set into the spandrels on each side of the proscenium arch – a lay-out that anticipated the earliest hi-fi systems. The isolated operator had to establish all sound levels during rehearsals and then adhere strictly to the sound plot under instruction from the stage manager 20 feet below through the only means of communication, the Standby and Go cue lights. The stage manager's prompt board used silent action stops modified from a Compton organ console, the manuals of which had been removed to leave just the semi-circle of white tabs (stops) below the cue lights. Amplifiers and speakers were connected in an intercom system to the lighting control 'spot box', the front-of-house staff and dressing rooms, making the traditional 'call boy' redundant.

The other major use of the bridge was to hold the no.1 spot batten. This afforded relatively sophisticated lighting possibilities, including sixteen circuits to light a collapsable canvas cyclorama which could be raised and lowered at the rear of the stage on scaffold poles by a system of weights and counterbalances. The spot focusing through the floor of the bridge was complemented by six lighting points in front of the balcony, four in the roof and two on either side of the auditorium for spot bars. The lighting was controlled from the 'spot box' at the back of the auditorium below the balcony which had a long, double-glazed window to afford an unrestricted view of the stage. This was then a rare feature in British theatres and had been copied from Michel Saint-Denis's London Theatre Studio in nearby Islington where John Allen worked. With help from Elstree film workers, Unity's chief electrician Pete Bennett installed a 48-way switchboard with up-to-date American controls, including twenty 1,000 watt dimmers, six 4,000 watt dimmers acting as group masters, six silent group blackout switches and two main silent blackout switches. The reconditioned resistance dimmers were a particular favourite of Turner's, recalls 'Rag', who says that George Bernard Shaw gave Turner the money for them, in contrast to his negative response when approached formally by Unity for a donation toward the cost of the new theatre. (This refusal had led to tart correspondence between Shaw and Unity's secretary that, unfortunately for Unity, was published in *Reynolds News*.[28]) A large trench sunk in the floor linked the board to the stage and a complete dual set of lighting allowed for pre-set cues and continuity throughout a performance. It is not surprising that Unity became well known for the quality of its lighting, much of the equipment for which had been bought from a sale of goods at a West End theatre, the Vaudeville. On the opening night, however, it was touch and go in the 'spot box' because no one had realised beforehand that the area was being switched from DC to AC on that very day.

The stage was built 3 feet off the original chapel floor and was raked (sloped) to improve the view from the stalls. It was extended at the back and faced with 'dance floor' parquet – a gift from a friendly supporter – and when a trapdoor with lift was installed to bring people or props on and off stage, the destruction of the polished oak brought tears to the carpenter's eyes. A hoped-for revolve did not materialise but the stage could be altered and extended by the addition of a moveable apron (or forestage) which was made up of a set of cubes for easy handling. The stage area of some 35 feet by 17 feet was huge in comparison to the stalls area of similar width but only 26 feet in depth. Wings 6 feet wide – known by John Allen as 'cod pieces' – projected out each side to mask the performers' entrances and exits.

Behind the stage, jutting out at right angles was a two-storey building measuring some 45 feet by 13 feet that had been a chapel. Throughout the building of the theatre, the lower floor had been a busy workshop and it continued in that function, housing a stage workshop and scene bay fitted with carpenters' and engineers' benches, a circular saw, power tools and a pillar drill. The scene bay could easily be found because of the smell of size, warming in a glue pot on a gas ring; it is used to seal and pull up the hessian covering of the flats (timber framed units of a set) prior to painting. Towards the OP (opposite prompt or right-hand side) and the stage door could be found the long props table set with whatever was needed for a particular show, from a dead comrade on a stretcher to the most everyday objects. Also on the ground floor was a bathroom and, running down the side of the theatre from the prompt side, the stage management, office space, a duplicating room, the LBCTG offices, the women's toilets and access to noisome cellars below. (The men's toilets were on the other side of the theatre, round the back, and they became notorious for their poor drainage.) On the upper storey, there was more office space, two dressing rooms – one for men and one for women, with hot and cold wash basins and side-lit mirrors – a rehearsal room, the wardrobe, the green (rest) room and space for a library of 2,000 books. The stage door could be found off a passage outside the theatre to its left that led down from the forecourt, in which a bookstall was set up whenever the theatre was open to the public.

Coming into the theatre from the forecourt, a wide central door opened onto a small foyer that housed the box office, which was on the left and under the balcony at the end of the 'spot box'. Beside and beyond it were doors to the stalls and to the right, a cloakroom and bar, which was not licensed until after the war, stairs leading up to the balcony and a side door to the offices. The auditorium seated some 180 in the stalls and 150 in the balcony (the capacity varied slightly from time to time). The tip-up seating was bought from the Vaudeville sale and upholsterers disembowelled it, 'beat up' the horse hair stuffing and recovered the seats as if new. The auditorium could also be used as a cinema, being equipped with a 16mm sound projector and loudspeakers with 18 watt output that were flown in from a grid behind a perforated screen with a black curtain surround.

The theatre was heated mainly by two coke-fired boilers that were adjacent to a convenient chimney in the workshop. One provided domestic hot water (for the dressing rooms, bath, basins and offices) and the other heated both the stage, by way of banks of panel radiators on either side, and the auditorium, through 4-inch diameter pipes running along alternate rows in the stalls. Elsewhere there were gas and coal fires. The system was designed, procured and part installed by A.T. Jackson, a twenty-year-old draughtsman working for a large heating firm, who obtained the materials and equipment at a large trade discount, which landed him in trouble with his boss. Sadly, owing to the flatness of the

Programme cover for the first productions at the new theatre in Goldington Street which opened in November 1937

system, the heating did not work properly on the November opening night (a fact remarked upon in the press) but this was soon put right.

Conversion took two months instead of six, thanks to the extraordinary efforts of the volunteer work force, and cost around £800 instead of the estimate of almost £4,000. It was a heroic and symbolic effort; workers 'by hand and brain' across the classes had joined together in useful, non-exploitative, non-alienating work to build their own theatre out of their own commitment and energies.[29] The very process of creative construction, the making of something of and for culture, carried its own cultural values and conferred upon the new theatre an almost religious significance.

No one left the building in the 48 hours before the opening, which found the foyer not quite finished, a few odd jobs still being completed and the smell of new paint not yet dry. Outside flood lighting and a sign in three-foot high letters made little impact through the smog on the evening of 25 November 1937. The souvenir programme showed on its cover two cloth-capped workers pulling open two huge red doors under the heading 'Opening a new Workers' Theatre'.[22] The real doors opened late on the foggy Thursday night but the proceedings began only fifteen minutes after schedule.

A packed and appreciative audience – invitation only – heard the London Labour Choral Union, conducted by Alan Bush, followed by the Workers' Propaganda Dance Group performing a piece on Spain called *A Comrade has Died*. Then everyone rose to their feet, clapped, stamped and shouted for five minutes as Paul Robeson appeared. 'I'm just as glad to be here,' he said, 'and you're gonna see a lot more of me from now on.' He sang half a dozen spirituals, explaining that Biblical references to Jericho or Jordan were symbolic of black struggle. In 'Ol' Man River', he changed the words 'tired o' livin' and scared o' dyin' ' to 'must keep strugglin' until Ah'm dyin' ' and finished with 'The Internationale'.

Bram Bootman, Victor Gollancz and Herbert Hodge appeared in front of the curtain. Speaking on behalf of the Unity leadership, Bootman recalled the theatre's origins in the Rebel Players and declared that 'our long cherished dream has become a reality. We are determined that nothing will stop our progress and that this theatre will remain open.' Hodge said that Unity now had a luxury theatre and warned against becoming respectable. Gollancz then officially opened the theatre. The aim of Unity, he said in reference to the LBCTG, was 'to build a chain of working-class theatres right across the country'. This would be possible because culture had become a working-class preserve; 'I can tell by all the cars outside,' he joked. Alan Bush, who with Robin Jardine had secured the lease of the building, made an appeal for money and raised £78 in ten minutes. By popular acclaim Jimmy Turner came on to the stage, wearing dungarees over his wedding suit – his bride was in the stalls. He thanked 'all the Bills, Berts, Paddys and Alfs who have helped to make the dream come true' – but whether or not he mentioned the Dorises remains unclear.

There was only one way to end the evening, with the play that had made it all possible, *Waiting for Lefty* (although there had been a plan to present instead *Salute the Soviet Union*). The performance by the original London cast was 'as vital as ever' said the report in *New Theatre*, describing the opening as a 'triumph'. In contrast to the quiet birth of Brit Street, No.1 Goldington Street received much press comment and many greetings messages – from embassies, journalists, cultural bodies and the world of theatre (Leslie Henson and Ronald Frankau, for example) as well as the world of politics (eight MPs and Communist leaders like Harry Pollitt and Rajani Palme Dutt). The *Daily Worker* heralded the launch of the new theatre as an 'historic moment in the development of the drama in Britain' and even *Harper's Bazaar* agreed. There was a good view everywhere, it said, and the new theatre was 'a model by any standards'. The article continued: 'The Movement of which Unity Theatre is the chief force represents the first genuine enthusiasm for the drama on any considerable scale that has occurred in England since the 1890s.' It is 'going to be the theatre of the future'. The *Amateur Theatre and Playwrights' Journal* believed that 'this amazing achievement' was important in the following ways:

> In the first place, the building of the new Unity Theatre adds one more to the growing number of permanent centres all over the country which have been created as the result of the activities of the non-professional theatre. In the second, this is, so far as we know, the first permanent theatre created by workers for the production of a workers' drama. In the third, it marks probably the most important forward step yet taken by the theatre of the left.

Night and Day reported on the 'excellent' results of the 'efforts of untiring people whose devotion was, happily, equalled by their competence'. The proportions and acoustics were good, and the lighting 'sensational'. For the correspondent of the *New Statesman*, the theatre was 'a very considerable achievement ... a good, modern, business-like looking piece of architecture, comfortable, efficient and thoroughly equipped'. The piece concluded:

> This new theatre is capable of playing a great part in theatrical history. Great subjects do not always make great plays, and thesis drama can be poorer theatre than musical comedy; but it is surely time that London audiences grew tired of their regular diet of marzipan. It is good to know that here is one theatre at least from which reality will not be excluded by the magic words 'No box-office appeal'.

Notes

1. *Fact*, No.4, July 1937.
2. Available accounts of the tours – by survivors and contemporary references in *Left News, New Theatre, Daily Worker* and *News Chronicle* – differ on details, e.g. dates, which plays were performed at which venues, the number of taxis used. The programme for the first tour gives its dates as 6-13 September 1936 and lists the venues as Stanley, Stockton (provisional), Victoria Hall (Sunderland), Murton (provisional), Jarrow Mechanics Hall, the People's Theatre and on the final Sunday Hawthorn Murton for a discussion; see Norman Veitch, *The People's*, Northumberland Press 1950. The second tour seems to have taken place in early October 1937 and to have been better organised, mainly through local Co-operative societies and Left Book Clubs, in Lincoln, Nottingham, Scunthorpe, Stainforth and Sheffield. *The Fall of the House of Slusher, On Guard for Spain* and *Waiting for Lefty* were performed. The third occurred in October 1938, taking *Plant in the Sun* and *Waiting for Lefty* to the Midlands, using Nottingham as its base, courtesy of the Co-op again.
3. In 1937, Unity joined the Left Book Club, the Film and Photo League, the Communist Party and some unions in a left May Day and in 1938, when there was a ban on processions in East London, Unity members 'walked' to the main demonstration in costume and with the theatre's banner.
4. John Lewis, *The Left Book Club*, Gollancz 1970, is a useful introduction to the club's history.
5. Information on, subsequent references to, and figures concerning the Left Book Club Theatre Guild come from: interviews with John Allen, Mark Clifford; *Left News; Theatre for the People; New Theatre; Daily*

Worker; Lehberger thesis (Lehberger also has contributed two essays that deal with the LBCTG, Unity and the 1930s to the German-English Yearbook *Gulliver*, No.4, 1978); Betty Hunt papers Sheffield University. See also note 9.

6. 'The Socialist Theatre', *Left Review*, Vol. 3 No. 7, August 1937.

7. *Fact*, No. 4, July 1937. Allen makes the same point in the *Left Review* article 'The Socialist Theatre' but less succinctly. The quotations from Allen are taken from these two articles, *Some Notes on the Formation of Left-Wing Amateur Theatre Groups* and interviews with him.

8. *New Theatre*, No. 4, February 1938.

9. For accounts of other groups; Douglas Allen, 'Glasgow Workers Theatre Group and the Methodology of Theatre Studies', *Theatre Quarterly*, Vol. 9 No. 36, Winter 1980; Dawson and *Jerry Dawson (1912-1988): A Celebration of His Life and Work*, a tribute published by friends; Betty Hunt papers (Sheffield); Angela Tuckett, *The People's Theatre in Bristol 1930-45*, Our History pamphlet No. 72, History Group of the Communist Party of Great Britain 1980; material relating to Bristol Unity Players from its director Joan Tuckett is held at the Modern Records Centre, University of Warwick; interviews/correspondence with Alec Baron (Leeds), Norman Draper (Cardiff), Anne Dyson, Eddie Frow, Ruth Frow (Manchester).

10. Footage of this event was shown in a 1978 BBC 2 television programme using home movies called *Caught in Time*. The amateur cameraman was seventeen-year-old Alfred Robson.

11. *List of Plays Recommended by Left Book Club Theatre Guild for Production by Left-Wing Amateur Groups*, LBCTG 1939. For a discussion of some of the plays listed see Watson.

12. *Left News*, No. 17, September 1937.

13. Jonathan Croall, in *Neill of Summerhill*, Ark Paperbacks 1984 writes: 'During one Unity Theatre Summer School an ambulance was paraded in the grounds. A converted Rolls-Royce, it was alleged to have come from the front in Spain, complete with the bullet holes in its sides made by the guns of Franco's army.'

14. *Left News*, No. 34, February 1939.

15. 'The Socialist Theatre', *Left Review*, Vol. 3 No. 7, August 1937.

16. This was much discussed – in *New Theatre*, the *Daily Worker* and other publications such as the Communist Party journal *Discussion*, e.g. 'A Real Workers' Theatre Movement' signed 'Actor', Vol. 3 No. 2, March 1938, in which the author says that the Workers' Theatre Movement died because of sectarianism.

17. *New Theatre*, No. 2, November 1937.

18. Tensions between the Communist and Labour parties and within the Left Book Club Theatre Guild and the book club itself have been written about in several books. Some have described the LBCTG and the LBC as Communist front organisations, though neither were. Communists were active and dominant in both and some did take an instrumental view of all organisations, seeing it as their duty as Communists to recruit wherever possible. However I have not been able to find 'the incontrovertible proof'

that the LBCTG was under threat of Communist takeover referred to in Ruth Dudley Edwards, *Victor Gollancz: A Biography*, Gollancz 1984, (and a letter to the author produced no reply) which takes up the theme from Hugh Thomas in *John Strachey*, Eyre Methuen 1973. The LBCTG arose from a Unity initiative and with its strong Communist leadership could hardly be in a position to be taken over by those who were already there and working locally and nationally alongside non-Communists. Communists were politically ambitious and attracted people because of their ideas, aims, organisation and discipline. It was natural for there to be tensions within any broad movement and for there to be differences of approach and strategy, yet, ironically, some of the most likely candidates at Unity for the role of villain saw the theatre's work within the LBCTG as a diversion from developing its own position in the wider movement and favoured more separation between the two not less. Sheila Hodges, in *Gollancz: The Story of a Publishing House 1928-78*, Gollancz 1978, charts from the 1930s through the 1940s (in *Betrayal of the Left* to which Victor Gollancz contributed and which he edited) to the 1950s (in his second autobiography *More for Timothy*) Victor Gollancz's attitude toward the role of the Communist Party in Left Book Club days until the Nazi-Soviet pact, and shows that he continued to support co-operation with the Communists. Gollancz himself, recalling the 1930s in his third autobiography, *Reminiscences of Affection*, says 'idealists ... are the salt of the earth'.

19. Sheffield Left Theatre won its area final once; London Unity won its regional finals twice and the second time added the national British Drama League cup too.

20. More research needs to be done on the groups in the Communist Party, although there are no party records in Britain that can throw any light on the subject for this period. The actors' group would have been the responsibility of the industrial department rather than the cultural committee and it had no relationship with Unity beyond offering individual support. Later, when Unitarians became professionals, they would attend Unity meetings when appropriate as well as the actors' group meetings but the two would still be quite separate. (John Slater, for example, was active in the leadership of the actors' group after turning professional in 1942 but not then at Unity.) Memories differ as to whether or not there was a party's writers' group as distinct from the Left Book Club groups or the Communist group organised around the magazine *Viewpoint* and its successor *Left Review*. This group was linked to the British section of the International Union of Revolutionary Writers, which folded in December 1935, and then the British section of the International Association for the Defence of Culture. However, Alick West in his autobiography *One Man in his Time*, George Allen and Unwin 1969, says that he belonged to a party writers group and in *This Narrow Place – Sylvia Townsend Warner and Valentine Ackland: Life, Letters and Politics 1930-1951*, Pandora 1988, Wendy Mulford says that Sylvia Townsend Warner was a member of a party literary group led by Edgell Rickword that once discussed what to do with Stephen Spender. Spender

himself in *The God that Failed*, Hamish Hamilton 1950, says he attended a small group of Communist writers. After the war, the groups took on a new lease of life. See note 10 to Chapter 8.

21. Workers' Music Association activities and left-wing musical events have been written about by John Miller (a wartime pianist with Unity) in WMA bulletin December 1975 and in an unpublished essay, and by Mick Wallis in *Left Pageants in Britain 1934-1944: Preliminaries to a Contextual Study*, unpublished dissertation, Manchester University 1985.

22. In July 1938 a bulletin gives the total number of affiliated organisations as 78, representing approximately 125,000 people, with 2,480 associate members. Figures given in an April 1939 bulletin show that in the first quarter of the year alone 91 corporate affiliates were obtained: 22 Labour Party organisations, 24 trade union bodies, 17 Co-ops, 5 Communist Party branches, 1 Young Communist League branch and 15 miscellaneous groups. Associate membership stood at 7,000 and the affiliated organisations represented 250,000 people.

23. Interviews/correspondence for the rest of this chapter: John Allen, Celia Baker, Alfie Bass, Roy Battcock, Bram Bootman, Maurice Braham, Ray Braham, Nat Brenner, Edith Forsyth, James Gibb, Bobby Hilton, Kate Hilton, A.T. Jackson, George Lang, Mary Peppin, Ann Soutter, Raglan Squire, Joe Stern, Trudy Stern, R. Vernon Beste, Wilfred White, Roger Woddis.

24. Bush, the only Communist Party member on the council, is a composer; Browne, a director, actor and playwright; Casson, an actor and director, married to Sybil Thorndike, knighted in 1945; Cripps, solicitor-general under MacDonald, a founder of *Tribune* with Laski and Strauss, expelled from the Labour Party in 1939 for advocating a Popular Front but later Leader of the House and Chancellor of the Exchequer; Gollancz, the publisher; Guthrie, innovative director, knighted 1961; Laski, leading left-wing intellectual; Malleson, actor and playwright, a great populariser; O'Casey, the playwright; Pritt, leading left-wing lawyer; Reeves, leading Co-operator; Robeson, the singer and actor; Saint-Denis, innovative director, influential teacher; Strauss, Labour left, later Minister of Supply, introduced Theatres Bill for the abolition of stage censorship, life peer 1979.

25. This anecdote is recorded in Raglan Squire, *Portrait of an Architect*, Colin Smythe 1984. A ground plan of Unity prepared by Squire was reproduced in *New Theatre*, No. 2, November 1937 and *Left News*, No. 21, January 1938.

26. Reproduced in *New Theatre*, No. 3, January 1938.

27. Technical details were carried in *New Theatre*, No. 2 November 1937 and in the programme for the opening ceremony. Additional information from interviews cited. Details and quotes from the first night come from the interviews and press reports. There are also several seconds of silent footage of the building of the theatre and its opening, showing people such as Robeson and Gollancz, which are held in the National Film Archive and logged as the Film and Photo League Fragments (FPL Mixed Neg Fragments Ref 603978A).

28. Correspondence reproduced in Travis.
29. For example, a bricklayer, Arthur Bernhard Beyers, is quoted in a Danish biography by Arvid Rundberg (*En Engelsk Arbejders Erindringer*, Tiden 1980) as saying that Unity was popular with London building workers and that he was one of a group of them who spent many hours voluntarily helping out alongside writers, students and actors. 'I would never have dreamed to carry around scenery ... together in fellowship with those type of people, yet they were just as enthusiastic for Unity as we were ourselves.'

4

Golden Days

Opening the new premises at No 1 Goldington Street marked the beginning of a period of expansion and success.[1] Unity moved from strength to strength, to a point at which further advance into a professional, as well as an amateur, company was only prevented by war.

Not long after the opening, Unity could boast a paid staff of six, whom the management committee (comprising a majority of Communists) deemed should earn the same rate as that of a full-time party worker, which was the wage of a skilled engineer. The new society was able to claim 300 active members and 2,000 individual subscribers. An enormous increase in activity led to the creation of four acting companies, which allowed duplicate casting for the production playing at Goldington Street, a new production to be in rehearsal, a group to tour, known as the Outside Show Group, and a group to rest, providing a pool of people who could be called upon at a moment's notice (not that life always worked out this neatly!).[2] There was a stream of publicity material, a wall newspaper called *Forum* produced by the Front-of-House staff, and regular internal bulletins, known for a time as The Weekly Epistle to the Unitarians.

Unity had made great strides quickly and its appeal was straightforward; as a leaflet, 'The Aim of Unity Theatre', put it:

> Unity is a workers' theatre, built by the workers, for the workers to serve as a means of dramatising their life and struggles, and as an aid in making them conscious of their strength and of the need for united action. The aim of Unity Theatre is a simple one. It is to help in the terribly urgent struggle for world peace and a better social and economic order and against fascism, by establishing a drama which deals with realities and reflects contemporary life, instead of plays which merely provide a dream world of escape and at best depict false ideas of life.

This approach was shaped by the politics of the Popular Front, which, in the British context, was anchored in the politics of the labour movement. Unity believed that progressive drama must have its roots firmly planted in that movement because the labour movement provided the impetus for social progress. Unity practised this belief in its repertoire choices rather than following an alternative policy of what an internal bulletin called presenting 'directionless productions in the mistaken hope of thus appealing to the middle classes'. Alongside repertoire choice, the other major plank of Unity's broad approach was its relationship to its audience. Unity saw itself as having an advantage here over the professional theatre and film world because its audience was its membership and its membership was more than just an audience. 'We help them to produce their own plays,' says the same bulletin, 'to become actors, producers, and playwrights. Our plays can be performed in every kind of hall, with little equipment and by ordinary people. This is the justification for our existence.'

Unity attracted in much greater numbers than Rebel Players people from differing social and political backgrounds, including theatre professionals disillusioned with the commercial set-up. This expansion was facilitated by the move to Goldington Street, which completed the break in identification with the East End that had begun when Rebel Players had become Unity and had taken premises in North London at Britannia Street. Most of the newcomers wanted to make their political contribution through drama and not through more traditional political methods, although some did both. Theatre offered a special kind of activity – social, immediate and personally satisfying.

Unity became a second – if not first – home, the place where people could come alive and feel useful after a deadening day either at work or on the dole. It could provide an escape – from lonely bed-sitter land, from oppressive conditions in the family, or from dull suburbia. People could act or use other skills – as carpenters, dress-makers, electricians, painters, accountants – with a freedom of imagination denied them elsewhere and for a cause in which they believed. Everyone would 'muck in', mending the toilets, sweeping the stage, sewing the costumes, painting the scenery – working together to get the show on in whatever capacity they could be of use (without, however, disturbing the sexual division of labour). Alfie Bass, to become nationally famous after the war as an actor, particularly in the television series *The Army Game*, used to bring up coal from the cellar when he first joined Unity, not quite sixteen years old. The youngest of ten children in the Bassonovitch family, he had acted in boys' club productions before joining Unity where he found a new way of life. 'Everyone was devoted, especially to keeping the theatre open,' he recalled. 'We saw it as the first workers' theatre and people had sacrificed so much to get it going that the philosophy of "the show must go on" was very strong. It was our duty to our audience,' he added. 'My pride was to be appearing for the cause. I'd do any part.' He left home in Bethnal Green to share a flat, live on the dole and put all his energies into Unity. 'I can't imagine anything more inspiring than creating a play or revue with a real purpose. Everyone participated, in the décor, the music, the acting. It was a rare thing. It was special because it was collective. No one dominated except the play and its purpose.'

That did not prevent continuous argument, often erupting into serious discord, nor, as Unity expanded, the development of a distinction between those who 'created' and those who 'administered', a greater distance between the leadership and the members, and a certain conservatism in the running of the theatre. Unity was prone to the personal rivalries and clashing egos common to most social activities and especially prevalent in both politics and drama. The mix was frequently explosive. Nevertheless, the feeling described by Alfie Bass was a common one and it inspired intense loyalty that on occasion was akin to religious fervour. R. Vernon Beste describes the unconscious attitude that pervaded Unity of not only telling the truth but of 'being' the truth. 'Ours was the earth,' he recalls. 'We not only had the message, we were the message.'

The spirit of commitment, however, was also a spirit of fun. Unity's social life was considerable. There were dances on Sundays, rambles, bazaars, weekend and summer schools and club trips to the theatre. There was a network of popular meeting places, from the (unlicensed) bar and the bookstall in the front yard to local cafés, such as the Pioneer, nearby pubs – the Pindar of Wakefield by Britannia Street or the College Arms and the Crown by the Goldington Street theatre – and the homes of members whose doors always seemed to be open for relaxation or revelry. While some members were morally severe, and rowdiness was rare on the premises, a fair amount of alcohol and mild drugs seemed to have been consumed by other Unitarians, no doubt to cope with the pace of life at Unity, which had a certain 'Bohemian' attraction for a few. Traditional social and sexual conventions could be flouted. Women easily outnumbered men and sexual partners were sought and changed frequently, usually on the men's terms. A favourite male ploy was to insist that not only was female promiscuity consistent with the values of Marxism-Leninism but that it was a positive revolutionary duty. Gay partnerships, both male and female, were accepted, though sexual politics were not discussed.[3] Many marriages were made at Unity, although a few that might have been were not and several more were broken. For the majority, traditional attitudes were the rule and the general position of women reflected their subordinate role in the rest of society. (The leader of Unity's second regional tour told one of the women in the company as they travelled north that she could not arrive wearing trousers and had to change into a skirt. Being a disciplined comrade, she did so, only to be greeted at the destination by her hostess sporting a pair of breeches.) The other side of this active social life inside and outside the theatre was the feeling of exclusion among those who were not party to it – a problem which grew as Unity's membership soared and the number of cliques increased correspondingly to the point where it was possible for two active Unitarians not to know of each other's existence.

The Communist Party

Communists played the dominant role at Unity and those who joined the theatre who were not party members were in the main happy for this to be the case. Many then became party members at Unity, however briefly. One of the theatre's pre-war highlights was the Unity Male Voice Choir under John Goss and Unity actors in *Plant in the Sun* performing before the delegates at the party's 1938 national congress in Birmingham.[4] In view of the pusillanimous leadership of the Labour Party, Communist activity on national and international issues was particularly appealing, and there was great rank-and-file solidarity across party lines on many key campaigns, despite objections from the labour movement establishment. The Communist Party, unlike the Labour Party, had a theory and a practice; it knew what it was doing and why it was doing it, whatever its blind spots. It seemed genuinely not only to represent the underdog but to have mobilised the underdog into action too – and, unlike the Labour Party, it was interested in culture. The effects of the Wall Street crash and the capitalist recession accompanied by the decadence of the rich also enhanced the status of the Communists and led to increased support for the Soviet Union as the first workers' state where society seemed to be planned for the benefit of the overwhelming majority. The Soviet Union was also aiding Republican Spain while the British government and others hid behind a bogus neutrality to watch fascism trample democracy.

The Soviet Union offered a psychological attraction; its very size seemed appealing. It was strong and decisive yet remote – and therefore not subject to the close scrutiny which might tarnish the image – and it was continually under threat, requiring constant and renewed solidarity, especially after the Nazi seizure of power in Germany; it was a socialist society triumphing over internal reaction and attempts by the strongest countries in the world to strangle it at birth. The terrifying price the Soviet peoples were paying was not fully known then and what information had emerged was swiftly accommodated in one way or another by Soviet supporters, whether Communists or not; some awful events were suppressed, some were dismissed as the fabrications of the enemies of socialism and some were even supported as necessary in the painful process of world emancipation. Those on the left who were sharply critical of the Soviet Union under Stalin did not as a rule come to or join Unity, which was known, and often attacked, as a Communist 'front' theatre, despite the efforts of the Communist-dominated leadership to dispel this notion.[5] The theatre's Popular Front character would be invoked and the broadly based general council cited as evidence. (The council was more symbolic than real, however, regardless of the genuine commitment to Unity of its individual members.)

The party was keen to bury its image as 'the red wreckers', which had been given credence in the early 1930s when it seemed to be *against* almost everything. It now placed the greatest priority on establishing new alliances but without abandoning the vanguard role of the party.[6] In this spirit, Unity was run as a democratic society governed by its rule book, which gave power in between annual and quarterly general meetings to the elected management

Waiting for Lefty by Clifford Odets, the play that made Unity's name and became the symbol of workers' theatre in the 1930s

Money-Power (*left*) raises from hell the stereotypes of ruling-class ideology, including a bomb-carrying Bolshy (*on the floor*), in *Where's that Bomb?*, a popular comedy by two London taxi drivers, Roger Gullan (Herbert Hodge) and Buckley Roberts (Robert Buckland)

Sailing to the Soviet Union for the 1933 Workers' Theatre Olympiad, the British delegation rehearses one of its agitprop sketches, 'Class against Class'

Herbert Hodge's 'vulgar spectacle' *Cannibal Carnival* mocks empire and the rituals of the British way of life

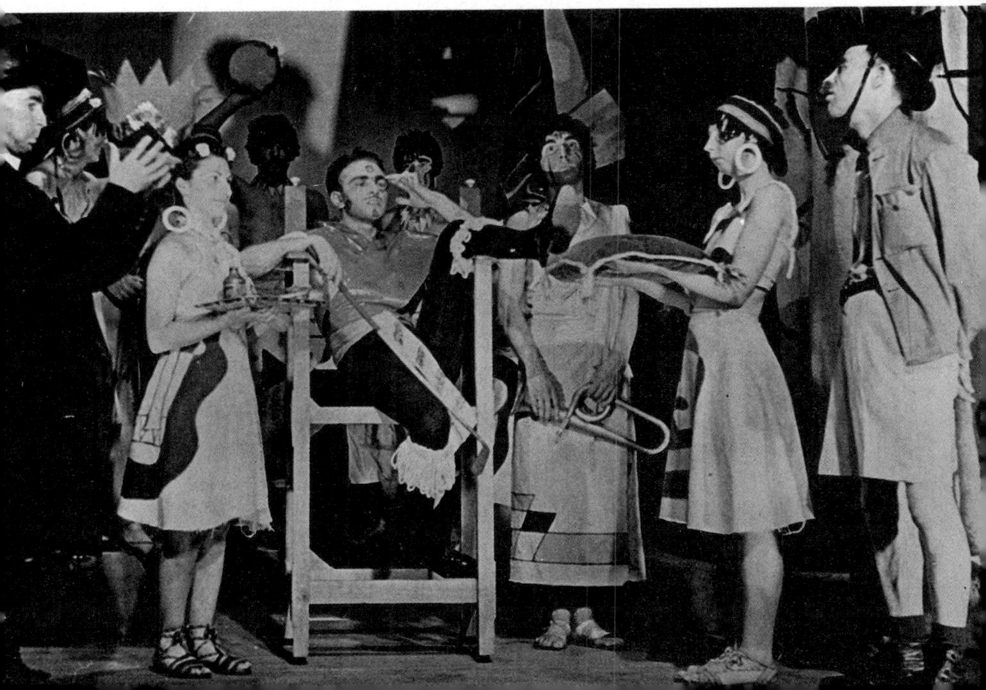

John Vickers' striking photomontage programme design for Irwin Shaw's *Bury the Dead* matches the play's chilling protest at the sacrifice of soldiers for causes which are not their own

Innovative use by director Herbert Marshall in *Aristocrats* of back projection, a technique not widespread in 1937

Shipping clerks prepare to do battle with thugs hired to break their sit-in strike in Ben Bengal's *Plant in the Sun*; even without Paul Robeson, the production won the British Drama League's annual cup

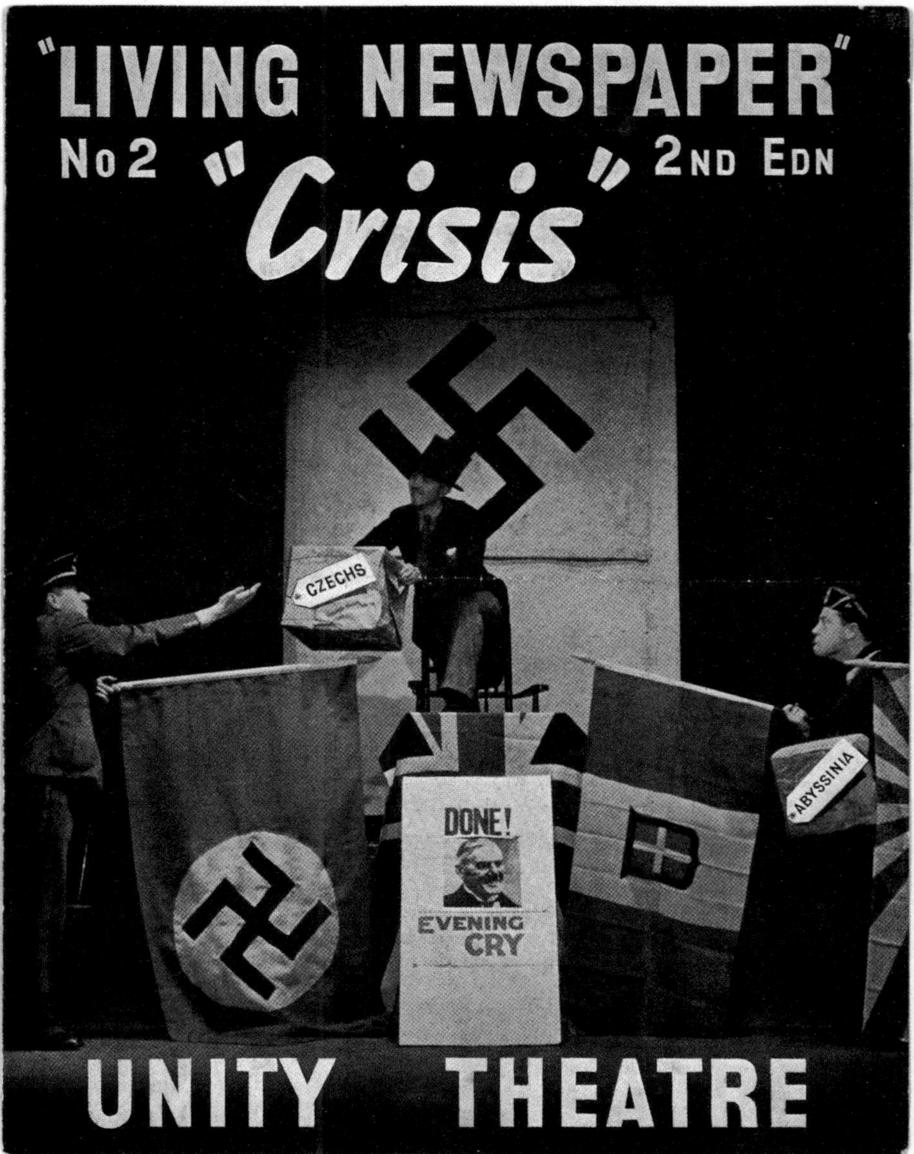

Britain hands the Czechs over to the Nazis – the programme cover sums up the terrible story of the Living Newspaper that opened the day Chamberlain flew to Munich

Unity became internationally famous for its first political pantomime, *Babes in the Wood*, which caricatured Chamberlain as the Wicked Uncle (here portrayed by Geoffrey McKeeman) and ran for six months

Two international landmarks: (*above*) priest confronts militant in the world première of Sean O'Casey's *The Star Turns Red* and (*below*) Unity presents the first play by Bertolt Brecht to be seen in Britain, *Señora Carrar's Rifles*, in solidarity with Republican Spain

committee serviced by advisory committees. The system was similar to the democratic centralist one of the Communist Party and there was an emphasis on the protocol of formal democracy with a distinct sense of the proper way of behaving within that democracy. Yet libertarian democracy of a kind co-existed with the centralised organisation; it seems as if every decision, from choice of director to the sweeping-up rota, was put to the vote in a multiplicity of little democracies that existed alongside the committee structure.

Party members in different departments – front-of-house, production, play clinic, for example – formed a party 'fraction' or group in their departments and met separately as Communists. All fractions held regular party meetings and education sessions, and the tutors would meet for their own training. Each department had a bulletin, but not a party one, and there was no general Unity party newsletter. All Unity party members were called to aggregate meetings, usually held at Britannia Street, to discuss important issues and to elect an overall Unity party leadership, which did not act as the management committee fraction but did have management committee items on its agendas. The power of the party groups inevitably led to friction and jealousy and there was resentment at the secrecy of the Communists, which seemed for some of them to be important as a means of conveying a sense of their special value. Most people, however, seemed content to avoid the burden of committee work and let those who enjoyed it get on with it. Party leaders would try and promote non-party people yet all too often they turned out to be party members or they would apply to join fairly quickly. There were outstanding Unity members who were not in the party, or who stayed in only for a short time, but it was the determination and organisation of the Communists that in the main kept Unity going and provided the bulwark of its audience too. Amid the proliferation of meetings and discussions and the personal competition common to all theatres, it was the discipline of the Communists – for good or ill – that, unlike the case in many another artistic venture, prevented Unity from being pulled apart by opposing camps or being run into the ground by the obsession of a single individual. The idea of Unity – or even the Communist Party – as a monolith conceals more than it reveals; what was extraordinary was the desire of so many high-spirited, tough-minded and often idiosyncratic people to sink their differences in a common aim. It did not suit everybody, and people were lost to

Unity because of Communist practice and policy. However, when internal conflicts did break out, they were as often as not related more to personality than to politics and were as likely to be among party members as between those who were inside and those who were outside the party.

Unity was the responsibility of the Communist Party's cultural committee, then chaired by the film-maker Ivor Montagu, and of the party's propaganda and education department run by Emile Burns. His assistant Dave Springhall was for a few years directly involved in Unity's affairs where he seems to have been a 'fixer' who also enjoyed the theatre's social life. Unity's relationship with the party centre at King Street and the London district of the party was often strained; Unity was unique – it was based in the capital yet clearly had national importance and its party members did not conform to the usual workplace or residential branch. Unity gained new members at an extraordinary rate but kept them away from the local branches that the party wanted them to work in. The party did not finance the theatre directly but many individual party members joined Unity as associates, if not activists, and many party branches became affiliates. Party members in and around London regarded support for Unity – and persuading organisations of which they were members, such as trade unions or Co-operative societies, to affiliate – as a duty as natural as the duty to sell the *Daily Worker* (which did not mean that everybody always did either).

Most Unity members, however, did not view the theatre as an adjunct of the party in any narrow or mechanical way and were angry when the party or the *Daily Worker* treated it as such. Nevertheless, they were also angry when the party or the paper criticised their work, which suggests that they saw themselves as partners within the same family who owed each other mutual concern and support. District and centre officials held regular individual discussions with the theatre's leaders, both party and non-party, many of whom they knew socially. Unity leaders in turn sought advice from the party on an informal basis, circulating scripts or raising serious problems that they felt required the party's authority or judgement to help settle. The most senior appointments would all be vetted by the party first. In the end, however, it was clear that the theatre's success depended on the quality of its productions and that depended on the people at Unity rather than on a committee or even a building.

New Leadership

After the move to Goldington Street, Unity's leadership seems to have worked more closely and more in line with the party headquarters at national and district level and this resulted in a dramatic change of personnel running the club following internal disagreements.

Broadly speaking the dispute resolved itself into two 'camps' – those responsible for overseeing the expansion of Unity (new premises and the LBCTG) and those who had been the core of Rebel Players, who had been joined by Play Department head Jack Selford and director Herbert Marshall, themselves never the best of friends. John Allen, in the former 'camp', was seen as theoretically wayward, too eclectic, and rather aloof, whereas Marshall, who had returned from studying in the Soviet Union and was keen to put his stamp on Unity with all the authority that coming from Moscow could then command, was believed to be advocating 'the correct line' on using drama in the service of the working class.

Disagreements had arisen over the viability of the new premises, which could be traced back to the highly acclaimed tour of September 1936. This had lost £80 and had forced Unity to undertake more activity than it was prepared for, which in turn had generated a rate of expansion that was too fast and too great for the club to cope with. The April 1937 balance sheet had shown a deficit of £60 and Foster had reported that only one third of the theatre's full members (who numbered approximately 150) were really active; by June, of 184 full members, approximately half were reported as active.

Those on the 1937 tour felt on their return to London that the future of Goldington Street had been taken firmly in hand by the Allen 'camp'. Exhaustion on all sides fuelled the differences, which sharpened after the opening of the new theatre. The overriding need to complete the construction work, which had united everyone, was replaced by jockeying for position. Early in February 1938, after a series of bitter meetings, Foster resigned as secretary and Turner was removed as production manager. Discussions were held with party headquarters and, despite misgivings at the proposed solution, Foster was replaced by Fred Roberts, remembered as a mild-mannered but anxious Midlander.

He was unknown to the Unity members, who were divided at the AGM on his appointment when he was produced at the meeting by Dave Springhall like a rabbit from a hat, as one veteran put it. (A Unity bulletin said that he was chosen from 100 applicants and it was good to have an outsider.) There was much protest and many of the 300 or so in attendance walked out, but to no avail. According to one who remained, Roberts said the first task was to sort out the Communist organisation at the theatre and the rest would follow. Discipline was tightened, and management committee minutes frequently refer to penalties or criticism incurred by members for breaches of proper behaviour, such as lateness. A new programme of classes was introduced to give theatrical talent its necessary political orientation and to control and direct the opportunism and individualism inherent in the theatrical activity. It was crucial that members knew what the theatre was for, who it was for and why they were involved in it.

The Unity leadership saw one of its main tasks as not only educating the new members politically as well as artistically but also welding the amorphous intake of individuals into a coherent whole; the Popular Front approach of alliances and broadening Unity's membership had nothing to do with encouraging the 'dilettante', as a *New Theatre* article in November 1937 makes clear. The education work was taken over by Jack Selford (then known as Solomons), who recalls that all sorts of people came to his sessions, from ushers to writers. The syllabuses were passed by the Communist Party centre and included some testing texts by Marx, Engels, Lenin, Stalin and Plekhanov, and by the British Marxists Ralph Fox, Alick West and Christopher Caudwell, each of whom had important books published in 1937. Notable intellectuals such as Francis Klingender, Rutland Boughton, Christina Walshe, Hymie Fagan and George Thomson would address weekend and summer schools and lecture on Marxism and its application to a range of topics, from Greek tragedy to the French revolution. Theatre specialists would deal with aspects of drama, especially the theories of Stanislavsky, which were studied alongside dialectics and the labour theory of value. Pamphlets and books could be purchased at the bookshop which had been set up in Britannia Street or at the bookstall in the forecourt of Goldington Street.

Debates at Unity on aesthetics were far from simplistic, even though they were conducted within a framework of basic certainties which marked the conventional Marxism of the day and which invited conclusions that, removed from the context of their arguments, were frequently simplistic. The traditional base/ superstructure model of the relation between economics and art was broadly accepted, with its attendant utilitarian notions of relations within the superstructure, such as a realist art serving a militant politics by exposing false consciousness, yet this by no means prevented original thought from thriving. The discovery of a materialist philosophy, even when structured mechanistically under the influence of dogmatic Soviet Marxism, produced a tremendous release of energy and provided a secure base from which more daring challenges to accepted values and ideas could be launched, especially when not related to issues that touched directly on the role of the Communist Party or Soviet Union. Maybe all the answers were not immediately evident, but Marxism gave the feeling that they were knowable and within the domain of human solution and control. With this courage, all the seeming confusions of the world could be put in their proper place.

All of Unity's activities, from choice of play to method of production, were to be analysed and assessed by what were considered to be immutable Marxist principles, but gaps remained between purpose and practice. The theatre's aims were presented in global and abstract terms – the struggle for world peace, social progress and freedom, through a drama dealing with reality rather than incorrect, bourgeois ideas – and when it came to finding and choosing plays, this idealist doctrine proved of less material use than it might otherwise have seemed. Still, it had meaning enough for those who embraced it, through learning, dispute and constant effort, and who were inspired with an exhilarating confidence that did not become apparent again in Britian with such intensity or scope until the late 1960s.

The novelist Elizabeth Bowen, as theatre critic of the magazine *Night and Day*, recorded her observations of the results: Unity was an 'important and vital' theatre which had a 'real purpose, so a real energy'.

'There still exists,' she said, 'a strong feeling, that few of us are quite clear of, against "propagandist art". Visit the Unity to see whether Art suffers.'

'Aristocrats'

Unity's first production at the new theatre was a clear challenge to any who felt anxiety about 'propagandist art' and an equally clear statement of the growing and often controversial role of Herbert Marshall.[7] Bert Marshall, as he was known, an ex-bricklayer and carpenter, was a large man in physique and temperament. He had won a five-year scholarship to study at the Higher Film Institute in Moscow at a time when Soviet art was in ferment before the repression of the Stalin years. He worked with leading Soviet artists such as Eisenstein, Meyerhold and Oklopkhov and met many prominent émigrés who passed through the Soviet capital, including Brecht. He directed for Soviet radio and the Foreign Workers' Theatre in Moscow and even took a production of *Waiting for Lefty* to the Finnish border where it played to English-speaking lumberjacks who had come to the Soviet Union from North America, many of Finnish origin. Marshall was put in charge of the Anglo-American section of the International Union of Revolutionary Theatres and helped organise the 1933 Olympiad, during which he was involved in tackling the artistic backwardness of the visiting British delegation.

Known at first as H.P.J. Marshall, to avoid confusion with the famous actor Herbert Marshall, he made a tremendous impact on Unity, directing there until the war, again in 1944 and 1950, and helping to design in the 1960s a proposed development of the Goldington Street theatre into a two-auditorium arts centre. He was a film-maker, noted translator of Russian poetry and in his later years a professor at an American university publishing an anti-Soviet digest. However eccentric and domineering, he brought to Unity a film director's eye and practical experience from some of the most advanced theatre people in the world. He provided a much-needed burst of energy for Unity when it could have gone stale through overwork and exhaustion. This was first apparent when he directed *Waiting for Lefty* for the British Drama League competition and improved the production through techniques that he had learnt in Moscow.

During this period, plans were being laid for him to direct at Unity a Soviet play, *Aristocrats* by Nikolai Pogodin. It was due to open in September 1937 but was delayed as Marshall had to return to Moscow to collect his belongings and wind up his affairs, which took longer than expected due to the climate of suspicion there attending foreigners and especially Communists. In his absence, Unity's internal disputes had sharpened. They concerned mainly the running and future direction of the new theatre, the opening of which at one point was to have consisted of *Waiting for Lefty*, *Where's That Bomb?* and *Cannibal Carnival*. This plan was dropped after the attacks on Hodge's satire forced it from the repertoire. *Aristocrats* became the opening production, on 10 December 1937. It not only celebrated the twentieth anniversary of the 1917 Revolution but also began the long association, involving seventeen productions, between Unity and Soviet theatre.

Marshall became embroiled in a bruising row in which the party centre tried to remove him from the production and have him replaced by the opera-trained Nelson Illingworth, who had taken a job as advertisements manager of the *Daily Worker*. Marshall had been in dispute with Emile Burns over his going to Spain and insists that Burns was behind the interference at Unity. Accounts vary as to how much of the production was directed by Marshall and how much by Illingworth, but it seems that in the end it was the cast who finally rejected Illingworth.

Aristocrats deals with the building by prisoners of the White Sea Canal, at the time the most lauded of Stalin's 'reform-through-labour' schemes; historians have since estimated that some 30,000 people died on the project. Pogodin, who waived his royalty fee for Unity, had been taken on an official visit to the canal and this gave rise to an account of the enterprise that was published under the name of Maxim Gorky and others. *Aristocrats* emerged from this book and Pogodin's own memories of the trip. According to the Unity programme, the play traces the remarkable effect of this experiment on the prisoners – 'notorious criminals and reactionaries' – and shows how by their treatment and contact with Soviet methods they are gradually transformed into loyal Soviet citizens. This 'construction of great works and the reconstruction of human beings ... stands in significant contrast to our own wretched prison systems'. The play on words in the title then becomes obvious: aristocrats are the enemies of the people, yet, in another sense, they are also the loyal Soviet citizens that the class enemies become as they work on the canal.

Aristocrats, which is described in the published version as a comedy, required three intervals and was much too ambitious for Unity, although Marshall had produced the play for Soviet radio, had worked as an assistant on the first stage production, knew the author and had visited the canal himself. He directed, designed and lit the production as well as creating the music score (and says he used his own translation. There is no translator credited in the programme.) He applied methods of rehearsal and interpretation that he had learnt in the Soviet Union, especially those associated with the actor-director Constantin Stanislavsky which reject external display in favour of finding through improvisation and study the inner truth of character and situation in its historical and social context. Marshall strove for cinematic fluidity in the action, most of which took place in small scenes that came to life out of black-outs in different parts of the stage and were played against a permanent set of scaffolding representing the canal lock gates. These were opened triumphantly in the finale, to let the water pour forth as if onto the audience, by means of clever projection. Billed as a Unity Theatre Collective Production, the *Daily Herald* said it was 'gripping from start to finish' and had 'humour, and vivid humanity, and an epic excitement'. A version was toured and a special performance given at the Phoenix Theatre for the Dependants' Aid Committee for relatives of International Brigaders. *Aristocrats* was performed five nights a week in December 1937 and two nights a week until the end of January. The other evenings were taken up by films, the London Labour Choral revue *Peace and Prosperity* and the dance/drama group, which had become a permanent part of Unity, although it was soon to move on. This opening up of Goldington Street was in line with the policy of making Unity a cultural centre for many art forms but it also met the difficulty of sustaining *Aristocrats* throughout the entire week.

The deposed director of *Aristocrats*, Nelson Illingworth, did not stay at Unity but instead proposed the establishment of an alternative theatre school to that run by Unity, which had as its chief lecturer the other protagonist of the production, Herbert Marshall. The new school was to be called Labour Stage, and Illingworth – an Australian who had taught voice at the New York Metropolitan Opera House and after the war helped train the newly-formed Theatre Workshop in voice technique – hoped, forlornly, that it would become the British counterpart to the

American Group Theater. The idea was to start an evening school near the site of the Globe Theatre on the south bank of the River Thames and to develop from that a professional repertory company. Other Unity members who were listed in the publicity material as being involved were John Allen (who cannot remember being a participant), Tommy Foster, Margaret Barr, Alan Bush, Randall Swingler, Jocelyn Herbert, Margaret Leona and Tess Gorringe, who publicly denied that Labour Stage was in competition with Unity.

Unity's own theatre school, the principal of which was Edwin C. White, an author on play production, was approved by the London County Council and supported by the joint education committee of the London Co-ops. It began as a series of night classes at Britannia Street and then expanded to premises in Netley Street, Hampstead. By Easter 1939 the school had trained over 250 people in acting, production, writing and stage management. The Chief Lecturer was Herbert Marshall and tutors included Alan Bush, Maurice Browne, Sybil Thorndike, André van Gyseghem, Hs'Ung, John Fernald, Lionel Britton, Flora Robson, Paul Robeson, Miles Malleson and Michel Saint-Denis. The school moved to Marylebone and continued for a while after the war making an important contribution to the training of theatre skills before drama schools became more accessible to the whole population.

Apart from the issue of the two drama schools, there were other ripples of mistrust or wariness at the time; for example, the LBCTG magazine changed its name from *New Theatre* to *Theatre for the People* while Unity launched its own *New Theatre* magazine; and a professional actress, Jean Shepherd, who had worked with Left Theatre and opposed Marshall, raised in the Communist Party professional actors' group the question of Unity using unpaid professionals. This reflected some old tensions between members of Left Theatre and Unity, but these were much less important than the areas of agreement and mutual support.

The end of the run of *Aristocrats* coincided with a Unity conference of Co-operative guilds, attended by 138 delegates representing 102 guilds, which recommended all guilds to affiliate to Unity. This was symbolic of their close links, which could be seen in the make-up of Unity audiences and in the work of individuals associated with Unity, such as André van Gyseghem or

John Allen, in the cultural life of the Co-ops – for example, in events like the 1938 Wembley pageant *Towards Tomorrow*, commemorating the Sixteenth International Co-operative Day, which was directed by van Gyseghem, written by Montagu Slater and used music composed and conducted by Alan Bush.

Aristocrats was replaced by a revival of *Where's That Bomb?* and a dance/drama performance – a programme chosen to celebrate Unity's second anniversary.

It was also a programme associated with those who had just lost the leadership of the theatre and who had criticised the choice of *Aristocrats* as having too little relevance to the British working class. They had proposed instead of the Soviet piece a new play by Hodge that never materialised, just as several other plans had fallen through, for example a production of *Clogs* by the Sheffield miner George Fullard, Brecht's *Roundheads and Peakheads, The Mouse Trap* by Gustav von Wangenheim and Lionel Britton's *Animal Ideas*. Again, the problem of repertoire had re-asserted itself and the theatre's Play Clinic – an echo of the Rebel Players repertory committee set up to stimulate the writing of British plays on Britain – had yet to provide Unity with any productions, although it had received many scripts and was holding regular workshops.[8]

The clinic, which was a section of the Play Department along with the Playwrights Group, the Revue Committee and the Living Newspaper Group, received mountains of scripts, many of them handwritten. One, remembers Jack Selford, came inscribed on wallpaper. The system for dealing with the scripts changed from time to time but the basic idea was to have them read and reported on by more than one person, followed by a letter of reply to the author from Selford. In one six-week period in 1938, 47 people read 102 scripts.

Scripts were read for political attitude as well as artistic merit, and changes were suggested on both counts. Even Sean O'Casey was offered the benefit of the clinic's advice, as were other writers like Geoffrey Trease and James Hodson whose plays were performed at Unity. Selford's own preferences played their part; he disliked verse drama – and turned down a play by Ronald Duncan on a stay-down strike in Derbyshire pits despite a favourable report from a reader, while on the other hand he recommended *Charley's Aunt* as a revolutionary comedy attacking pomposity but was overruled by the management committee. Plays could be rejected for not conforming to previous Unity success, like *Waiting for Lefty*, or because their message was wrong – too pessimistic, too great a divergence from the Communist position, too vague, or dealing with a subject that the Communists did not have any position on at all. On one occasion, a virtual certainty was disqualified after the author refused to make changes that had been requested by the Play Department. A former miner, Jack Jones, who had left the Communist Party, surrendered after much soul-searching, it seems, to the persuasive tongue of Herbert Marshall and agreed to let Unity stage his play *Rhondda Roundabout*, which was based on a novel of his about the Welsh mining valleys. A Unity bulletin reports that permission had been given for the Play Department to amend the script 'as we think fit' – and this involved seeking the advice of the Communist Party in South Wales, the leadership of which suggested some changes. Marshall says this happened without his or Jones's knowledge and was seen by Jones as a betrayal. The play had been given several readings and had been cast but was dropped when the changes were not made. It appeared in the West End instead.

Selford organised workshops for writers every weekend, which could involve at this time up to 100 people; Saturday was devoted to debate and watching rehearsals, Sunday to specialist classes. (Lecturers included Stephen Spender, Randall Swingler, André van Gyseghem and Hubert Griffith.) Plays would also be given readings. Selford says that the main problem for the clinic in both reading scripts and encouraging writers was fighting sectarianism and

> stopping plays ending with the Red Front salute. We had to go beyond agitprop but there was still a tendency not just to be against West End commercial theatre but against all 'bourgeois' theatre. We were for a working-class drama which did not then exist. Unity wanted plays that portrayed working-class life but they still had to have the right 'message'.[9]

It was an attitude that for some left-wing writers simply replaced one form of sectarianism with another and which, together with the paraphernalia of party control, put them off playing a more active part in Unity than they otherwise would have.

After the revival of *Where's That Bomb?* came the clinic's first production at the end of February 1938. Called *The Case of the Baffled Boss*, it was a modest piece of irreverence directed by Jean Shepherd and written collectively under the guidance of Jack Selford (who had appeared in Tom Thomas's production of *The Ragged Trousered Philanthropists*) as a sequel to *The Fall of the House of Slusher*. The great detective Sheerluck Bones is hired by the dreadful boss Sir Samuel Slusher to spy on the workers and expose 'red' plots. Described by *New Theatre* as a 'politcomedy' in five scenes, it traces back a line to the WTM and attempts to mix agitprop and parody in a cabaret-cum-operetta style. It was light-hearted, short and designed to be toured. Its format allowed daily comment to be improvised by the actors in between the parodies and original songs, such as 'Let's Mingle with the Masses', which satirises the fashion for Mass Observation, a new form of social investigation which relied on first-hand reports from observers who recorded people's daily lives.

BONES: Let us mingle with the masses,
With the lousy lower classes,
Let us live their mingy, mangy, mouldy life,

Watch 'em eat their bread and cheeses,
See 'em catch their hoppy fleas..es.
Let us mingle with the worker and his wife.

CHORUS: Oh, ming-le
With the mass-es.
With their rotten-cotton, ill-begotten chassis.
We will spy them out and track 'em,
Then Sir Samuel can sack 'em.
Let us mingle with the masses in the morn.[10]

Living Newspaper: 'Busmen'

The Case of the Baffled Boss shared the bill with a production that had been planned since the previous summer, but had been delayed by the work of the LBCTG and opening Goldington Street because of John Allen's involvement as its director. Originally called *Bus Strike* and now re-titled *Busmen*, the show was a Living Newspaper based on the Coronation bus strike of 1937, and in its techniques it showed the more serious side of Mass Observation. *Busmen* turned out to be a unique contribution to

British drama – an original Living Newspaper on an indigenous dispute written collectively with the help of those who had led the fight and presented in the most challenging theatrical styles of the day.

The idea of the Living Newspaper – a live representation, drawing on documentary sources, of an important, contemporary issue – had come from the Russian revolution via America, though distant antecedents can be traced in popular nineteenth-century British theatre. People at Unity had read the American Living Newspapers, and had corresponded with their creators. A few Unity members, such as André van Gyseghem, had been able to visit America and see for themselves, and one of the form's chief proponents, Arthur Arent, author of the influential American Living Newspaper *Triple A Plowed Under*, came to Unity to share his experiences. He pointed out that Living Newspapers should not be a substitute for a pamphlet and could not be dashed off in 24 hours or even 24 days.

John Allen, who had directed *Newsboy* for Unity, was keen to attempt a wholly British Living Newspaper in which 'we would be more adventurous than the Americans in the use of music and verse and dance'.[11] He was determined not to patronise his audience. The starting point was the Coronation bus dispute, which had become the largest industrial action in the country since 1932 and signalled a new stage in the internal battles of the trade union movement.[12] The union's general secretary Ernest Bevin was obsessively anti-Communist, while the party's greatest success in initiating a strong rank-and file movement was among London bus workers.

The bus workers, totalling 25,000, had a rank-and-file monthly paper (edited by Emile Burns) with a circulation of about 10,000. They enjoyed some autonomy within the union because they had formed their own branch under the umbrella of the Central Bus Committee. The problem for Bevin was that the rank-and-file movement had become the majority on this committee and had members on the union's executive, thereby being able to challenge the union machine on its own terms. The bus workers were in no mood to accept the increased stress caused by bigger buses, higher volume of traffic, tighter schedules and irregular meal breaks. A claim for a seven-and-a-half hour day was rejected by the London Passenger Transport Board and the committee wanted to strike.

Bevin was against but the union executive was for. The bus workers came out on official strike on 1 May 1937, just as London prepared for the Coronation. One of their slogans was 'the right to live a little longer'.

A court of inquiry found a case for investigation, which led the union executive to call for a return to work, but this was rejected by the rank-and-file movement, the Central Bus Committee and the garages. The executive reluctantly accepted this but ordered the tram and trolley bus workers to stay at work. This undercut the solidarity of the strike and it collapsed four weeks later when the executive revoked the powers of the Central Bus Committee to run the strike, suspended the machinery of the bus section and ordered the garages back to work. A union inquiry led by another anti-Communist Arthur Deakin, later general secretary, declared the rank-and-file movement to be a subversive, Communist-dominated body, and expelled three leaders from the union and debarred four others from office. One of those expelled led a breakaway union which lasted nearly a decade but was opposed by the Communist Party. The dispute ended in bitterness and a setback for the whole movement; the bus workers returned on terms that they had rejected already and failed to win a shorter working week. *Busmen* was written as a living report of the dispute but also to counter the breakaway and was performed at meetings that were organised to campaign for unity in the union.

Unity had made close contact with the strikers when playing *Lefty* at the garages and had made plans to work on a Living Newspaper on the strike as soon as it had finished. Allen was aiming now for a first anniversary production. He chaired a group of some ten people, including two of the expelled bus leaders, Bert Papworth and Bill Jones, the Communist writer Montagu Slater and Herbert Hodge. The group engaged in a process of 'total' theatre in which form and content were shaping each other under the impact of diverse influences. They wanted to emulate on stage the effect of *The March of Time* newsreel documentary from America which, despite censorship, was making a big impact in the cinemas. The bus workers provided information, checking on the naturalness of dialogue and the authenticity of the costumes, Slater wrote the verse and Hodge dictated to Allen scenes between a bus driver and his wife reminiscent of Odets. The minutes and transcripts of the various hearings were consulted. Following the trend set by Mass Observation, anecdotes overhead in bus queues and on buses were inserted. 'We stuck all sorts of bits in with scissors and paste,' says Allen, 'and I went home and edited it.' Alan Bush composed a score and Louise Soelberg, a dancer with the experimental American Kurt Jooss ballet, was the choreographer.

The style of production owed much to the work of German theatre – Piscator, Kaiser, Toller – and was explicitly non-naturalistic.[13] The back of the stage was painted with a honeycomb of eight foot squares which corresponded to different levels of a three-dimensional constructional set and formed separate acting areas, including rare use of the projecting cubes at the sides of the stage to bring actors out into the audience. These different areas would be lit in turn, alternating with action forestage, to give a cinematic quality to the juxtaposition of scenes. Details of the dispute were projected in graph form and the Voice of the Living Newspaper, offstage in the flies above, would comment and link the action like a chorus.

'Living Newspaper No. 1', as it was known, begins with a steel foundry overture fading to voices shouting 'Busmen! Busmen! Bus strike latest' and a ballet depicting industrial speed-up, accompanied by relevant figures and the names of some of the giant firms responsible, like Rolls Royce, de Haviland and Handley Page. There are 24 sequences set in different locations, covering the whole dispute. They move from the House of Commons, a hospital ward and a conductor's home to an Aldgate bus queue, a union meeting and the Coronation. In one scene (by Montagu Slater) a driver is discovered alone in a pool of light, under pressure and with only two minutes' 'stand time' at the end of his journey.

> It isn't as though there was anything wrong with a chap's nerves, it's the ... Red, amber, green. Stop. Take on. Start in. Stop again. If we weren't so late I'd get a cup of tea at the turn-round ... and if I'd hit that trike there'd ha' been jam for tea. If somebody'd give us fifty yards we'd sprint. Bell again. The deceased, who took his bus over the water-jump, said he'd a tip for the National and was five minutes late.
>
> *(The chorus stands all round the stage in the shadows and speaks the refrain.)*

What is my trouble and strife?
That blasted bell.
What regulates my life?
That blasted bell.
What is the word between
Stop, Go, the Red, the Green –
What runs the whole machine?
That blasted bell.

At the end of *Busmen*, after the union's finance and general purposes committee has recommended the expulsions and disciplinary action which the executive council accepted, the busmen discuss their fate. The Living Newspaper closes with an appeal to stay in the union, secure the re-instatement of the expelled and suspended workers and defeat the Transport Board. The final call is 'end reaction in the Transport and General Workers' Union. Is it a go, boys?' to which everyone shouts 'YES!' Reviewers in the *Daily Worker, Reynolds News, Tribune* and *Left Review* praised the production but the *Times* found it 'inexcusably dull' and documentary film-maker Paul Rotha, writing in *World Film News*, while being encouraging, criticised the continuity of action, the length of the script and the relation between the Voice of the Living Newspaper and the events on stage.

Busmen was not safe or romantic but it was clearly partisan. It overlooked the division of opinion that existed on the role of the party and the nature of the defeat yet it put the dispute into its social context and argued a position of unity, even though the main story concerned events a year old and therefore, strictly speaking, was not appropriate for a Living Newspaper. Allen recalls the show's political naivety stemming from the direct link that it had with those engaged in the struggle, while acknowledging that this involvement contributed immensely to the Living Newspaper's verve and edge. The build-up of sequences, some entirely visual, was exciting and the interplay of fact and fiction and of the personal and the public was powerful if lacking in self-criticism. The influence of the cinema was clear both in terms of montage and editing and in the search for realism and accuracy. The result was technically innovative but with broad appeal, a vindication of the Popular Front strategy of alliance between the forces of culture and labour. It was based on a coincidence of interest between performers and audience – many of whom had been involved in the strike. This was Unity's hallmark and produced a quality not to be found anywhere else at the time.

Busmen played six nights a week from the end of February until the next show in March and after that four nights a week to the beginning of May. Allen's wish for an anniversary show came true and the Phoenix Theatre was filled on 30 April 1938 for a celebratory performance of *Busmen*, the proceeds of which were given to an important campaign of the time, China Relief. At the same event, according to Herbert Marshall, the first documentary film was screened of Japanese atrocities in China, called *Nanking Captured,* which had been smuggled out after the fall of the city. The script of *Busmen* was published in the American *One Act Play Magazine*, thus at last beginning the export of plays from Britain to the US instead of the other way around and, in the words of a Unity bulletin, restoring the balance of trade.

The success of *Busmen* led to a debate in the *New Theatre* magazine on the potential of the Living Newspaper form and to the idea of creating a group of actors who would use rapid reporting and improvisatory techniques in regular, instant dramatisations of contemporary events – a development of the WTM's agitprop form. There was a plan to combine films and drama documentary, and discussions were held with Communist film-maker Ralph Bond of the GPO Film Unit, but came to nothing. Another avenue to explore was to work with Mass Observation. Allen had collaborated with Tom Harrison, a founder of Mass Observation, on a short play about an important by-election, but it was 'terrible', according to Allen. 'We hoped to learn from that and mix inventive dramatisation and close analysis of social behaviour to achieve in theatre what *Picture Post* did in journalism,' he says, yet his own distance from Unity at this time prevented any proper development from *Busmen* along these lines. Apart from a piece on air raid precautions and Living Newspaper No. 2 on the Czechoslovak crisis, none of the plans came to anything. A research department was set up under Sam E. White, which was linked to the Left Book Club Theatre Guild, but to little effect. Appeals for researchers (or 'legmen' as the Federal Theater in America termed them) went unheeded. Living Newspapers on Spain, crime and housing were abandoned, one on unemployment never took off at all, and then the war came.

Documentary-based drama continued at Unity both through the

war, with such productions as *India Speaks*, and afterwards, with *Black Magic* in 1947 and *World on Edge* in 1956. The form became more widespread during the war through groups such as the Army Bureau of Current Affairs Play Unit, often with the help of Unity personnel, and later was acceptable in the West End and the nationally subsidised companies as well as being developed on television in the technologically sophisticated 'factions'. It was also developed in a different direction by the pioneers of oral or verbatim theatre, from Ewan MacColl's Radio Ballads with Charles Parker to Peter Cheeseman's work at Stoke-on-Trent.

Despite the achievement of *Busmen*, the differences of opinion within Unity and the related repertoire problems made running the theatre difficult. Its next two productions were due to come from outside, the first from the English Group Theatre, with Stephen Spender's poetic drama *Trial of a Judge*, and the second from the French company Théâtre du Peuple, bringing Rolland's *Les Loups* and Gorky's *Mother* (which London audiences might have known from the film of Gorky's novel). The French visit had to be cancelled through lack of money but the Group Theatre production went ahead, largely because its preferred theatre, the Westminster, was not available.[14]

Founded in 1932, the innovative Group Theatre had won a reputation as a radical company and stood for many of the same ideals as did Unity.[15] The guiding light was the dancer Rupert Doone, who pioneered in Britain the application of the principles of classical ballet to the training of actors. His vision was to create a permanent ensemble performing a new drama of poetry, music and movement, but this was not to be. Nevertheless, several of the group's members were to become highly influential writers, directors, musicians and painters, and its work, particularly at the Westminster Theatre under Anmer Hall's management, helped lay the basis for modern British poetic drama through the plays of T.S. Elliot, Louis MacNeice, Stephen Spender and the notable team of W.H. Auden and Christopher Isherwood.

Trial of a Judge, like the Auden-Isherwood plays, embraces an explicit if unconventional Marxism. Spender had begun the play in 1933 but had changed it since going to Spain and joining the Communist Party.[16] The play is based on the murder of a Polish Jew by the Nazis and their subsequent interference with the court process. The judge has convicted the Blackshirts but also passes the death sentence on three Communists for carrying guns. His wife and a government minister urge him to reprieve the Blackshirts, which he does, but later changes his mind and is tried and shot along with the Communists. Spender wanted to move away from propaganda drama to explore the dilemma of justice – the crisis of liberalism in the face of the fascist threat. Like other writers on the left, he chose to idealise the action, abstracting time, place and characters, who are given names like The Judge, The Wife, The Red Leader, and who sit in one of the two opposing camps that the world has been divided into. Directed by Doone and designed by John Piper, who was making his debut in stage work, *Trial of a Judge* ran for nine days; the prices had been raised and the audiences stayed away, according to one report.[17] The play had been staged with Unity's co-operation in true Popular Front spirit – the character parts were played by professionals and some chorus parts were taken by Unity actors – yet there was friction between Unity and Group Theatre people. It seems to have been a clash of temperament and style of work as well as a clash of politics. Unity staff felt that the Group Theatre lacked discipline and seriousness (although the play was deeply serious) and in debate after the show, Unity members heckled Spender for what they considered to be his liberal retreat into symbolism and mysticism.[18] The show, it should be noted, opened just five days after the Anschluss, the forcible union of Nazi Germany and Austria. The *Daily Worker* echoed those who objected to Spender's poetic drama. Spender 'seems to have lifted himself to Olympian heights above our problems, and his writing has the wildness of clouds and rarefied air', it said. Given the welcome accorded to Spender by the Communist Party general secretary Harry Pollitt on joining the party and the Popular Front attitude to working with intellectuals, it is instructive to see on what terms and with what limits this was applied at Unity. It was not a rejection of complex language, as the success of *On Guard for Spain* showed, nor was it an undiscriminating acceptance of anything that was offered by the intelligenstia, as John Allen can testify on Unity's attitude to another Group Theatre writer, W.H. Auden:

> They do not attack Auden's exclusiveness, his eternal adolescence, his boy-scout-motherlove complexes, his irritating neuroses, his lack of

> anything positive or forthright, judging that if that's the way he feels about things, that's the way he should write. The feeling is simply that he is speaking another language, writing for another class. He is the author of the dissatisfied bourgeoisie. His perceptive pen clarifies their bewilderment and prejudices; and these sentiments have little interest for the positive spirit of the militant working classes.[19]

'Bury the Dead'

It was the dramatic failure of *Trial of a Judge* as much as the personal clashes that left Unity members feeling low and despondent. They did not object to symbolism as such but to what was being symbolised, as the next production proved with such power when Unity at last was able to stage Irwin Shaw's *Bury the Dead* after two years of waiting. The theatre called on its president André van Gyseghem to direct this first play by Irwin Shaw, a former American 'pro' footballer who had turned to writing children's serials on radio and then plays, which were later to include the Pulitzer Prize-winning *The Gentle People. Bury the Dead* had been presented first by an amateur cast that had transferred to Broadway where it became an overnight success, much like *Waiting for Lefty*, and Odets shared a similar New York Jewish background to Shaw's. (During the Korean War, however, Shaw forbad performance of the play because he felt it was being used in an anti-American way.)

Unity billed *Bury the Dead* as 'the greatest peace play yet written'; rhetoric aside, and despite its strong pacifist style, its target is not war as such but those who wage wars against the interests of the people who have to fight and die in them. Inspired by Hans Chlumberg's *Miracle at Verdun*, which van Gyseghem had directed at the Embassy Theatre, *Bury the Dead* likewise shows soldiers who rise from their graves and question the morality of the warmongering that has cost them their lives. It is set in 'the second year of the war that is to begin tomorrow night'. Behind a pile of sandbags and a platform that runs the width of the stage, a burial detail is digging a common grave, shovelling out the rats, borrowing cigarettes, moaning about army life. They hear a groan and six corpses stand up, a cross-section of soldiers, all privates but from different social and religious backgrounds. The captain reports the incident to the generals who want it suppressed as the news would be bad for morale. The captain tries to reason with the corpses but to no avail.

CAPTAIN: Men must die for their country's sake – if not you, then others. This has always been. Men died for Pharaoh and Caesar and Rome two thousand years ago and more, and went into the earth with their wounds. Why not you … ?

FIRST CORPSE: Men, even the men who die for Pharaoh and Caesar and Rome, must, in the end, before all hope is gone, discover that a man can die happy and be contentedly buried only when he dies for himself or for a cause that is his own and not Pharaoh's or Caesar's or Rome's …

CAPTAIN: Still – what is this world, that you cling to it? A speck of dust, a flaw in the skies, a thumb-print on the margin of a page printed in an incomprehensible language …

SECOND CORPSE: It is our home.

THIRD CORPSE: We have been dispossessed by force, but we are reclaiming our home. It is time that mankind claimed its home – this earth – its home.[20]

The war department censors the press, businessmen demand action but the generals and churchmen cannot get the soldiers to lie down. Finally, the woman closest to each of the men is brought to the grave to try and persuade them. They tell their stories in turn: no one wanted to cause trouble but the act of dying has taught them that they died unjustly – they want to go on living. When the often harrowing entreaties of the women have failed, a general orders the burial detail to take up position with a machine gun. They refuse and he fires it himself, but the corpses just walk past him into the auditorium to tell their message to the living.

Unity preceded *Bury the Dead* with either a revival of *Who are the English?* or a sketch by Vance Marshall on air raid precautions called simply *ARP*.[21] Marshall was an official air warden in Soho, where he lived, and he wrote the sketch as a confrontation in a working-class living room between the family and a warden who has come to carry out a census. It attacks militarism, poor social conditions, and the futility of the government's defence preparations. Under the guidance of the scientist J.B.S. Haldane, who had seen the effects on civilians of bombing in Spain, the piece was re-written as a Living Newspaper at that year's summer school to cover the First World War, disarmament, the arms race and local council compromise on ARP; it was performed and modified by Left Book Club Theatre Guild groups around Britain, especially at left Labour events. Haldane, it appears, was the world's worst actor but a superb propagandist. He was leading the Communist Party's campaign on ARP and his efforts led to the formation of a broad-based committee (banned by the Labour Party executive as subversive) that put pressure on government and local authorities. It was only after the blitz had begun that they responded properly.

The programme for the *Bury the Dead* evening broke tradition by using for its front cover a montage of photographs of the play instead of the usual workers opening the theatre's massive doors to let in a new audience. It was felt that by this time the new audience had arrived. The programme also named for the first time the director and his assistant, though the actors and production team remained anonymous. The photographs that were used were taken by John Vickers, an assistant to the renowned photographer Angus MacBean who lent Vickers the equipment. Vickers took outstanding theatre pictures and helped change the way drama was recorded visually. He used to watch a rehearsal all the way through and then take his pictures on a second run, knowing exactly the moment he wished to capture.

Bury the Dead touched a raw nerve in the left-wing movement. It had been profoundly shocked by the horrors of the First World War but had been forced to confront its anti-war sentiments in the need to fight fascism in Spain.

Van Gyseghem's production, with Rollo Gamble as assistant, is remembered as one of Unity's most striking. *Bury the Dead* from its first night, which was booked by the London district of the Communist Party, revived Unity's spirit and gathered up the momentum that had been generated by *Busmen*. It ran for six nights a week throughout its run. As with the montage effect of *Busmen*, its expressionistic style contrasted sharply with Herbert Marshall's muscular socialist realism, yet in each case the colloquial dialogue of the shows delivered by Unity's actors made the pieces powerfully convincing and 'real', showing once again what Unity could achieve that was beyond the means of the flaccid West End. The *News Chronicle* review of *Bury the Dead* commented: 'The passionate sincerity which the unpaid workers who compose the casts of Unity Theatre productions throw into their acting makes it not acting but living reality.' *Reynolds News* said the production 'attains the degree of perfection we are becoming accustomed to at Unity – striking settings, adroit lighting, perfect grouping and disciplined acting'.[22] The play's life elsewhere was hampered, though not killed, by the censor's objections to 'bad' language and the appearance of a prostitute. The Lord Chamberlain also cut all but the last lines of the scene between a disfigured private and his mother. When she sees his shattered face, she breaks the silence with a low moan that rises to a wail, then a scream that persists in the black-out. At Unity this moment frequently produced loud gasps from the audience.

Unity chose *Bury the Dead* to launch a special event held at the Cambridge Theatre to raise money for capital expenditure. The event marked a highpoint for Unity, demonstrating that the years of training and apprenticeship both inside and outside the Club's own theatre truly had paid off. The other play on the bill was an even more famous Unity production, *Plant in the Sun*. It had brought the theatre greater publicity than ever before because of the presence in the cast of Paul Robeson.

Paul Robeson

Before turning to the performing arts Paul Robeson had enjoyed outstanding academic and athletic success at Rutgers and had studied law at Columbia.[23] He appeared in several plays in Britain in the 1920s and 1930s, two of which had been directed by André van Gyseghem. In 1928, he played Joe in *Show Boat* at Drury Lane singing 'Ol' Man River', which became his signature tune, and after the production had ended its run he toured Britain with his song recitals. He played an historic Othello at the Savoy Theatre in 1930, the first black actor to perform the part since Ira Aldridge in the 1860s (who, according to the records, was the first black actor ever to play it). Robeson's film career began in 1930 and was soon troubled by racial stereotypes. Yet he made some memorable appearances, including the unemployed stoker in the British film *The Proud Valley*, written by Herbert Marshall and Fredda Brilliant, in which he is taken in by a mining community in South Wales, just as Robeson himself had been during the making of the film in the Rhondda. He was above all one of the world's leading concert singers from the 1930s onwards, despite the damaging withdrawal of his passport by the US authorities during the Cold War which led to a successful international campaign to win its restoration.

It was in Britain particularly that Robeson developed a Marxist view of history and politics, putting his own stand for black rights and his deep interest in black and African culture into a global and class context. In Britain, he became the friend of many Communists, left-wingers and leaders of the anti-colonial struggle such as Jomo Kenyatta, Kwame Nkrumah and Pandit Nehru. Robeson dedicated his life and art to the fight for socialism. His epitaph reads: 'The artist must take sides. He must elect to fight for freedom or slavery. I have made my choice. I had no alternative.'

Robeson made the promise to appear at Unity in Moscow in 1934 when he was discussing with Eisenstein the possibility of making a film and he met Herbert Marshall who was acting as interpreter. Three years later, at the height of his fame – he was voted Britain's most popular radio singer in October 1937 – he was able to deliver his promise by joining Unity's general council and agreeing to act as soon as possible in a play at Goldington Street, which he would do, like everyone else, for nothing. To appear at Unity he had to turn down the star role in Basil Dean's production at Drury Lane of *The Sun Never Sets* and other West End roles. Naturally this prompted many press inquiries as to why? He would reply: 'My father was a slave. Can I forget that?' To *Reynolds News* he said:

> The plays I shall do will deal with Negro and working class life. As an artist ... I must have a working-class audience ... The Negro is never cast as an equal ... Most scripts which are sent to me to read go into the wastepaper basket because they do not deal with ideas of social progress.

He developed this line in an interview in the *Daily Worker*:

> This isn't a bolt out of the blue. Not a case of a guy suddenly sitting down and deciding that he wants to join a workers' theatre. It began when I was a kid – a working-class kid living in that shack. It went on from that beginning.

His troubles in films made him realise that he could not overcome the prejudices of the system from within; the industry was too powerful for one man and he knew that he had to find other ways of expressing himself:

> Joining Unity Theatre ... means identifying myself with the working class. And it gives me the chance to act in plays that say something I want to say about things that must be emphasised.

Robeson's decision to appear at Unity was both an inspiration to the hard-working Unity activists and a validation of all for which they had been struggling. Those who acted with him or met him at Unity remember him as a giant of a man, literally and metaphorically, and describe him as gentle and great, larger than life. Everyone seems to have a Robeson anecdote and feels that at one time or another he sang just for them. Trudy Stern, who was in the cast of *Plant in the Sun*, remembers the management committee debating whether to build a special dressing room for him, but he declined the offer and insisted on being included on the rota for sweeping the theatre. While being much appreciated, this request was turned down after a vote, as the dust would have seriously affected his superlative voice. His great support was Eslanda Robeson, who also had to be his watchdog. Ann Soutter, the administrator's secretary, remembers that she often had to answer a telephone call from Eslanda if Paul had not arrived home in the taxi that she had sent to pick him up after the performance. He would frequently stay after the show, talking in the dressing room or entertaining those who remained in the theatre. Bram Bootman's vivid memory is of Robeson standing still, towering above everyone else, slowly tapping his foot to get the rhythm, putting his hand to his ear and singing 'Water Boy'. Dressed in a heavy overcoat thrown over his shoulders, despite it being the height of summer, he would also chat to the local children who waited for him every night at the theatre's gates. He visited Unity members in their homes, even after he had left *Plant in the Sun*, and came back to the theatre in the years to come, most notably after winning his passport back. The campaign for the return of Robeson's passport was particularly strong in Britain, and Unity figured prominently in the protests. Robeson, who had sung at the opening of the theatre, became a symbol of Unity, standing alongside *Waiting for Lefty* as synonymous with the best that the theatre had achieved.

Preparations had already begun at Unity for the play in which he was to appear by the time that he returned to London after a visit to Spain to sing for the International Brigades. Herbert Marshall had spent weeks looking for the play and, as with *Lefty, Private*

Hicks and *Bury the Dead*, the solution was found in the American *New Theater* magazine. On the face of it, Ben Bengal's *Plant in the Sun* did not look ideal for the 40-year old Robeson. It had won a New Theater League competition for plays about youth and told the story of a group of teenagers in the shipping department of a New York sweet factory who hold a sit-down strike when one of them is fired for 'talking union'. Robeson was to play the central figure of the man who is sacked, a nineteen-year old of Irish descent called Pewee, a role usually played by a white actor. Robeson, as it happened, had once worked in such a factory and true to the spirit of the enterprise and to the Stanislavskian approach of the director, the important factor was not whether he looked right but how he acted.

Drama, the British Drama League's magazine, reported:

> There is not a star part in the play. Robeson is simply one of the cast – no more and no less. And he is very happy about it. In spite of several difficulties, such for example as the fact that rehearsals can take place only in the evenings and on weekends since the members of the cast are at other times occupied in their several workaday tasks – carpentry, book-keeping, stenography, and so on – Robeson has thrown himself heart and soul into rehearsal, and it is certain that a salary of £1,000 a week could not have drawn from him greater effort or deeper conscientiousness.

To Unity, the naturalistic aspects of the Stanislavsky method had nothing to do with the West End's decadent naturalism of adultery or suburbia. *Plant in the Sun* was a play of social realism and, like *Lefty* and *Private Hicks*, turned on a strike, making a similar Popular Front appeal for unity across the everyday divisions of class, ethnic background, gender and sectional interest. The actors broke the play down into its thematic episodes and analysed the characters in terms of aims and actions. Marshall arranged lectures on the nature of spontaneous working-class struggle and on the social conditions of those portrayed in the play. He showed documentary film on stay-down strikes and took the cast to two sweet factories, one old, one new. The actors looked at American magazines for pictures of strikes and workers, and they practised the New York East Side dialect, which they modified while trying to retain its main features. This process of all-round examination continued after the show had opened by holding discussions with the audience at the end of the performance, a practice common at Unity, particularly with Herbert Marshall's shows.

Plant in the Sun opens with five shipping clerks arguing furiously over whether or not they should hold a strike in support of Pewee.[24] Only the week before, another clerk, Danny, had been dismissed for 'talking union'. The clerks believe that there must be a sneak in the factory, who turns out to be Henry, a filing clerk from another department who is nicknamed 'Susie' because he is seen as 'effeminate' and rather proper. He confesses and says he was driven to it by being excluded and treated as a baby by the other clerks. Pewee turns this revelation against those who were responsible, showing how the personal parallels the political. Henry agrees to spy for Pewee instead of the foreman who sacked him – an example of building workers' solidarity, which is shown to be more important than petty differences. Pewee applies this lesson to overcome the antagonisms felt by the shipping clerks against other departments, such as the packers, and to combat the sexist attitudes they have to the 'dipping girls'; both sections come with money collected by them and the filing clerks to help the strike – unity has brought strength. 'It's growin' fellas,' says Pewee to his mates, 'like a plant in the sun.' Roberts, the managing director, brings in a cop who cannot handle the situation alone, and the foreman threatens the workforce. The clerks telephone the union and Danny answers, telling them that only united action by the whole factory will work. He advises asking for more pay and shorter hours, to which Izzie, a clerk who is usually whining, responds with one of the play's best known lines 'That's a perfect combination.' What finally wins over the whole factory is the arrival of hired thugs. They turn out the light because the door to the other departments has been chained open by the shipping clerks to let everyone see what happens to them. The room is emptied after a terrific fight but the plan has misfired. Roberts ends the play: 'My God, they're *all* sitting. The whole damn factory.'

Marshall's spirited production began sharply with a flashing neon sign saying 'Candy Factory' projected onto New York skyscrapers. Full lights came on to reveal the row in full flow and that set the pace and tone of the evening. There was considerable scope for improvsed humour, at which Unity actors excelled and which gave edge to its gradual transformation into the steadfast courage required to resist the violence of the foreman. At the climax of the play, when the thugs clear the room, Marshall used a black-out followed by a single illuminated bulb swinging from side to side – a cliché in years to come but then a simple, powerful effect. This moment also needed a nightly recruitment of available men to make up the gang of thugs, dressed in old mackintoshes and battered trilby hats.

It became clear early on in rehearsal that *Plant in the Sun* would not fill an entire evening as the repertory committee had at first believed. One of the actors, Nat Bliss (who, as Nat Brenner, was to become principal of Bristol Old Vic Drama School) went back to old copies of *New Theater* and discovered *Rehearsal*, another play by Albert Maltz, author of *Private Hicks*. It was highly appropriate. A workers' theatre group is rehearsing a mass chant about a demonstration in 1932 in Detroit at which four men were shot dead. One of the women cannot get her part right and life is complicated by her personal relationship to the director. Suddenly she snaps and tells of her brother who had his back broken by the Coal and Iron Police during a strike and was dumped by them in nearby woods. She had not talked about the incident for twelve years, but now that the 'stone' in her breast was out, she could finish the rehearsal and make her role in the chant work. 'BROTHERS, SISTERS, HEAR ME! Remember the dead by organising the living.'[25] Directed by Barbara Nixon of Left Theatre, it made a formidable double bill with *Plant in the Sun*.

The programme for the evening continued the practice of using a photograph on the front cover, by John Vickers again, and named the directors but this time also credited the designer of *Plant in the Sun* (Herbert Marshall, executed by Elizabeth Watson). A note said that the actors remained anonymous and any part could be played by different actors without notice. 'This is due to the fact that the actors are workers whose hours of work vary and we therefore always have a double cast.' There was a plea for money to complete the new premises and help fund a building for the training school.

There was considerable nervousness at Unity on the opening night because preparations for the production had not been as smooth as expected. It had been difficult to gauge the humour of *Plant in the Sun* during rehearsal without the presence of an audience and the anticipation generated in the press by Robeson's involvement could easily have lead to an anti-climax. The critics came (from more than twenty publications) and praise flowed forth. The *Times* review said that it was 'refreshingly human', the *Daily Herald* that it was 'one of the most exciting plays to be seen in London' and from *Reynolds News*, 'I shall see this play three times.' The *News Chronicle* found that it 'has a vitality and tenseness that makes it tremendously exciting', and *Era* that it was a 'gripping piece of work in which the propaganda is skilfully interwoven with a good story and in which the characters are particularly well developed'. A significant change was noted by *Everybody's Magazine*: 'Although solid working-class folk form the bulk of the audience, the West Enders are almost falling over themselves to get inside.' Harold Nicolson made a broadcast about Unity, a group of MPs, as well as other important political figures, including Nehru, visited the show and in the two weeks following its opening 400 new members joined Unity Theatre.

The production went on a successful regional tour to the Midlands and the North, and on one occasion the cast had to perform without scenery or props after the police tried to stop the show from proceeding. (On another occasion, the venue had no entrance backstage. The only way to reach the stage, which was upstairs, was through the auditorium. Trudy Stern remembers planks being fixed from a window in the building opposite to a window in the hall and 'we had to clamber across, one at a time'.) Even without Robeson, who only played in London, the production retained its vigour – a tribute both to Robeson's ability to become part of a team and to the others in the cast whose work together could withstand his departure.

Plant in the Sun won the Welwyn Garden Festival competition and, along with nearly 600 other productions, was entered in 1939 for the fourteenth British Drama League Community Theatre Festival competition, in which the year before Unity had come second nationally after winning the regional round. This time Unity won both – the Cecil Hardwicke Trophy for its area contest and, at the Stoll Theatre, the Howard de Walden Shield in the national final. It was a tremendous achievement for the three-year old theatre and a moment of special pride when the victory was announced by the judge Tyrone Guthrie. Alfie Bass as Izzie and Joe Stern as Pewee were singled out for mention (actors' names were printed in the League's Festival programmes). To Unity this triumph was the culmination and vindication of its Popular Front approach – to be deemed the best amateur theatre company in the country, presenting a strong political play about the need for a union and the value of a strike.

An equally proud moment came when members of the internationally famous American Group Theater – the main inspiration for many in the British left-wing theatre movement – congratulated Unity on its production of *Plant in the Sun* and returned to see it twice. The Group Theater represented the best of American drama, and with writers such as Clifford Odets, Irwin Shaw, Albert Maltz and Ben Bengal, had been the main source of Unity's repertoire. The Group Theater was in London for a West End run of Odets's *Golden Boy* and came straight from docking in Southampton to join a distinguished first-night audience that included Esmé Percy, Robert Morley and Ellen Wilkinson. Odets, who gave Unity the book rights of *Golden Boy*, spoke from the stage.

Morris Carnovsky demonstrated acting techniques and many discussions on the role of theatre and its relationship to political struggle were had with Elia Kazan, Harold Clurman, Will Lee, Luther and Stella Adler and Lee J. Cobb.[26] There were fierce arguments with Unity members about the self-imposed anonymity of the cast. Alfie Bass remembers clearly:

> They thought that this was doing the ruling class's job for them. They said that if we were as good as we thought we were then we had a duty not only to become known, but to become even better known by as many people as possible.

In line with this, the Group Theater actors, whose company had more business than trade union contacts and no theatre of its own, believed that Unity should establish a professional wing – an idea that two years earlier would have seemed heretical, if not mad, but which, within six months, was being put into practice. Plans were made to take *Plant in the Sun* to New York, but, although accommodation had been arranged, the money could not be found to finance the visit.

Nevertheless, the meeting with the Group Theater came at a time when anything and everything seemed possible for Unity. It had gained a new and commanding confidence based on the collective hard work of a core of people who had been with Unity from its earliest days. The new theatre had been opened successfully and despite the many difficulties and various tensions, Unity had engendered a fast-growing nationwide left theatre movement and had presented a remarkable run of shows, each one of which was different in form and tone to the other.

In the summer of 1938, a meeting was held at the House of Commons, chaired by John Jagger MP, to ask for new support. Members of the Group Theater attended with Unity general council members, including Paul Robeson, MPs such as Ellen Wilkinson and A.P. Herbert, and other supporters like Kingsley Martin, editor of the *New Statesman*. An appeal on behalf of Unity, signed by MPs, confirmed what Martin had written in the *New Statesman* of *Plant in the Sun*: 'The Unity Theatre has found its feet; we may have here the germ of something as important in our national life as the Old Vic.' This declaration was underlined by the great Old Vic performer, Sybil Thorndike, who, on seeing the production with *Bury the Dead* at the special Cambridge Theatre performance, said that she saw 'as the greatest hope for the stage in this country the rise of Unity Theatre, realising that the real art of the theatre always was, and always must be, bound up with the life of the people'.[27]

Notes

1. Details for this chapter from Unity bulletins, publicity material, *New Theatre* and interviews are substantially the same as those listed in Chapter 3 note 23, plus Alison Macleod and Jack Selford.
2. One of the four companies was a troupe of more experienced members and was called the Shock Brigade. It was supposed to act as a catalyst and vanguard but was disbanded in October 1938 because this concentration of seasoned performers led to problems in and a weakening of the other companies. The experienced members were then distributed between all the companies.
3. Zelda Curtis, in '"Private" Lives and Communism' in Eileen Phillips (ed.), *The Left and the Erotic*, Lawrence and Wishart 1983, confirms the lack of discussion about sexuality while recalling the sexual boasting. I was told many anecdotes relating to sexual activity and what they said about Unity can be summed up by one which tells of a woman who was notorious for wearing knickers embroidered with hammers and sickles.
4. Silent footage of Unity and the choir at the congress, shot by Ivor Montagu, is held by Stanley Forman at Educational and Television Films Ltd, London.

5. A right-wing digest, *The Red Network: The Communist International at Work,* Duckworth 1938, in Appendix 1 lists Unity under 'Organisations Affiliated or Working in Close Association with the Communist Party'.
6. For an introduction to Communist activity and thinking in this period, see Noreen Branson, *History of the Communist Party of Great Britain 1927-1941*, Lawrence and Wishart 1985.
7. Marshall corresponded with me until he stipulated in a letter that further co-operation would be impossible if my book were 'in any way connected with the Communist Party, or if you are in any way linked up with that organisation.' I did not reply. His own and frequently incorrect account of Unity and his time there is contained in: unpublished interviews conducted by Betty Hunt, Jon Clark and Stuart Cosgrove; Ron Travis's thesis; articles in the *Listener* (to which Bram Bootman wrote a correcting reply) and correspondence with Unitarians and researchers to which I have had access.
8. The search for indigenous plays was constant and frequently emphasised in bulletins or elsewhere, e.g. John Allen 'Where Are Those New Dramatists?', *Daily Worker*, 21 June 1937.
9. Lionel Hale, for example, reported in the *News Chronicle*, 13 September 1937: 'There are satirical cartoons on the walls, bare boards on the floor ... Actors take curtain calls with right fist clenched in salute.'
10. I was given a script which I deposited in the British Theatre Association library.
11. Interview.
12. For an account of the dispute, see Ken Fuller, *Radical Aristocrats: London Busworkers from the 1880s to the 1980s*, Lawrence and Wishart 1986.
13. See John Allen's introduction to *Busmen* in the Nottingham Drama Text version (1984), from which the subsequent quotations from the play are taken. *Busmen* was published in the American *One-Act Play Magazine* in 1938. See also Watson and his '*Busmen*: Documentary and British political theatre in the 1930s', *Media, Culture and Society*, No. 4, 1981.
14. Bradby and McCormack have a paragraph in *People's Theatre* on the Théâtre du Peuple.
15. See Robert Medley, *Drawn from the Life*, Faber and Faber 1983, and Michael Sidnell, *Dances of Death*, Faber and Faber 1984.
16. Spender's brief membership of the Communist Party has been much written about to no great purpose by, among others, Spender himself (in *The God That Failed*, Hamish Hamilton 1950 and in his autobiography *World Within World*, Hamish Hamilton 1951), Valentine Cunningham (in *The Penguin Book of Spanish Civil War Verse*) and David Caute (in *Fellow Travellers*, Weidenfeld and Nicolson 1973. Caute gets Unity wrong – the audience was reared on Soviet 'girl-meets-tractor' stuff, he says, presumably without bothering to research his assertion). *Trial of a Judge* tends to feature in such accounts, as it does in John Lehmann, *New Writing in Europe*, Penguin 1940, which carried photographs of the production and of other shows at Unity, and in Julian Symons, *The*

Thirties – A Dream Revolved, Faber and Faber 1975, which also is illustrated.

17. Julian Symons in *The Thirties – A Dream Revolved*, who says sympathetically but incorrectly that Unity and the Group Theatre 'embodied the only new ideas of dramatic production in Britain'. Richard Findlater, in *The Unholy Trade*, Gollancz 1952, calls Unity the successor of the Group Theatre and traces a development from the latter's poetic revue to Unity's satirical pantomime, living newspaper and documentaries.

18. A view from the right by Harry Kemp, in Harry Kemp and others, *The Left Heresy in Literature and Life*, Methuen 1939, said that Unity had to turn to liberal plays because left-wingers were no good at writing. Kemp fought for the fascist side in Spain.

19. John Allen, 'Writing in Revolt', *Fact*, No. 4, July 1937.

20. *Bury the Dead*, Random House 1936.

21. One script of Marshall's *ARP* which I was given (now in the British Theatre Association library) includes the Air Warden referring to political suspects in Russia being sealed up in rooms ... 'It's little wonder we get all these fantastic confessions,' he adds. Sonny, a class-conscious youth, retorts: 'That's a lie. That's Tory propaganda.'

22. Van Gyseghem's prompt copy, which is held by his daughter, bears out the *Reynolds News* assessment of the care and detail that went into the production.

23. For introductions to Robeson, see Philip S. Foner (ed.), *Paul Robeson Speaks: Writings, Speeches, Interviews 1918-1974*, Quartet 1978; Marie Seton, *Paul Robeson*, Dennis Dobson 1958; Ron Ramdin, *Paul Robeson: The Man and his Mission*, Peter Owen 1987, all of which deal with Unity. On the question of Robeson's 'anonymity', Unity did advertise his name at the front entrance; see Martin Bauml Duberman, *Paul Robeson*, Bodley Head 1989.

24. *Plant in the Sun* quotes from *Three American Plays*, New Theatre Play Service 1946.

25. *Rehearsal* quotes from *Three American Plays*.

26. In the 1950s, Unity general manager Heinz Bernard contacted Odets's agent to inquire about the rights but was rebuffed curtly (apparently Odets had not committed his pledge to paper). Also, permission was refused for Unity to perform *Awake and Sing*. I wrote to the agent to confirm the details of these two incidents and did not receive a reply.

27. Quoted in *Unity Theatre Handbook* 1939.

5

Political Pantomime

As ever, Unity's repertoire and fortunes followed the turn of political events. In the latter months of 1938 the left was mobilising to counter the dangerous international situation. Britain and other democracies had already allowed the Japanese to invade China, the Italians to conquer Abyssinia, the Germans to annexe Austria and the Franco forces to gain the upper hand over Republican Spain, thus bringing Europe to the brink of war. Prime Minister Neville Chamberlain and his National government, which had shown little interest in the Soviet Union's proposals for joint talks on collective security, now faced new demands from Hitler for the largely German-speaking area of Czechoslovakia, the Sudetenland. On 15 September, Chamberlain flew to Berchtesgarden to negotiate with Hitler and a week later, saw Hitler again, only to find that the terms had been altered, much to Hitler's advantage. When Chamberlain announced a third trip, to Munich, Communist MP Willie Gallacher was alone in the Commons in his opposition.

Chamberlain's first visit had coincided with the fifteenth congress of the Communist Party, which was dominated by Czechoslovakia and the threat of war, and at which Unity appeared. The party view was that, while war was becoming ever more likely, Chamberlain's preparations – issuing gas masks, testing air raid sirens, digging trenches in parks, preparing ration cards, making evacuation plans – were all a bluff to scare people into accepting his appeasement of the fascists, the motor of which was anti-Communism.

Munich

Unity's management committee, chaired by bus conductor Charles Donnelly, met a week after the congress on Monday 26 September, three days before the premier's proposed third and final visit, and decided to mount a Living Newspaper on the worsening situation. The management committee issued a statement, explaining how the theatre could make a 'powerful contribution to peace' and appealing to professionals to co-operate with Unity to produce the play. The next day, a European war seemed imminent; the Czechoslovak government rejected the terms that had been agreed by Britain and France and the British Fleet was put on alert. By Wednesday morning, a Living Newspaper team had been assembled under Herbert Marshall, which included the writers Montagu Slater and Randall Swingler and Unity actor-turned-scribe Roger Woddis who was to bcome a noted writer and poet. They were joined in the next 48 hours by other authors and journalists, including a Czech who wrote a scene set in the Sudetenland. A first rough draft was completed in one 24-hour session. Actors who had to go to work the following day stayed all night and tried to put a shape to the script that was still being written and rewritten upstairs. Nearly all the moves and cues had to be improvised, with scripts in hand, yet Unity managed to open Living Newspaper No. 2, *Crisis*, on Thursday 29 September, the day Chamberlain flew to Munich.

Crisis opens with an explosion and red fire light. Men's voices chant 'War!' and are answered by the shout of 'Peace!' from women's voices.[2] The vocal tussle is broken by a fanfare of trumpets and the figure of Hitler, arm raised, delivering a speech on Nazi ambitions (taken from an actual diatribe). The focus switches from the public to the private, a family being visited by an ARP warden who shows them how to use their gas masks. The Voice of the Living Newspaper interrupts editorially: 'War can be stopped. Not by spreading panic and dread of war but by truth. Democracy is strong! Together, the peoples of democratic countries are a force no bullying dictator can dare attack.'

Britain is depicted centre stage in between the democracies to the left, including Czechoslovakia, the Soviet Union and Republican Spain, and the fascist governments to the right, Germany, Italy and Japan. Each bears a placard displaying its military details with its size in proportion to its armed strength. Cliveden, home of the Astor family, is identified as the British seat of fascism's invisible friends, whom Germany has invoked in response to Czchoslovakia's claim that democratic unity can win the day. Outside No. 10 Downing Street shadowy figures scuttle in and out and a crescendo of voices reveals the Anglo-French plan which the Czechs roundly reject. A cartoon sequence follows sketching out the chronology of recent events, with fascist states planting flags on their conquests and marching off behind a Non-Intervention screen helpfully provided by Britain. *Crisis* ends with a call for peace, which can only be ensured 'when the people of the world act in unity for freedom and democracy', and the cast asks the audience, 'Where do you stand?'[3]

The Living Newspaper included a poem by Bertolt Brecht (translated by Herbert Marshall), which Unity had already used as an introduction to his *Señora Carrar's Rifles*. The poem comes from a series called the *German War Primer* and begins:

> General, your tank is a strong chariot.
> It breaks down a forest and crushes a hundred men.
> But it has one failing; it needs a driver.[4]

Crisis used the techniques and performance style of agitprop (simple and symbolic costumes such as top hat and tails, for instance) alongside cameos of individual responses to the situation. It drew on documentary material – BBC broadcasts, politicians' speeches, military statistics – to explain the difference between democracy and fascism and British responsibility for the spread of fascism. At the same time, it fictionalised people's reactions, both as individuals, in the home, preparing for air raids, reading the papers, and in groups, demonstrating and demanding action.

Unity played *Crisis* (also known as *Czechoslovakia*) through October and early November, as Hitler occupied the Sudetenland, alongside revivals of *Señora Carrar's Rifles, Waiting for Lefty, Where's that Bomb?* and *The Fall of the House of Slusher*. Credited to the Unity Theatre Play Department, *Crisis* had a rough and urgent energy as well as moments of humour, though it needed cutting and firmer shaping. The *Daily Worker* review said 'obviously one is not going to go into detailed criticisms of such a miracle of production. The important point is that Unity did such a thing at this time.' *Cavalcade* noted that it was a 'dramatic presentation of tremendous force and sincerity'.

The Living Newspaper coincided with many meetings organised by the Communist Party on Czechoslovakia and it was constantly updated to include new events; when, for example, Duff Cooper, First Lord of the Admiralty, resigned over Chamberlain's actions, it was reported that evening in the Living Newspaper before many in the audience had heard the news. Unity was only able to make such revisions because of its club status, and, although the Living Newspaper was performed elsewhere, its intended 'public' life was curtailed by the censor who was becoming increasingly sensitive to political issues.

Crisis, however, was not able to lessen the theatre's debt, which had grown in the autumn to £1,200 after *Señora Carrar's Rifles, I Can't Sleep* and a revised production of *Waiting for Lefty* had played to almost empty houses at the start of the new season following the summer break. (*Lefty* had been revived to mark the West End run of Odets's *Golden Boy*, his popular play about a young man who has to choose between the boxing ring and the violin. During this revival, Unity celebrated its 300th performance of *Lefty* and invited the Leyton group from East London, identified by *New Theatre* as one of the best of the Left Book Club Theatre Guild companies, to perform the play at Goldington Street.) An appeal fund was established, which, in the belief that Unity was contributing to the development of drama generally, was aimed directly at the theatre profession as well as at Unity's usual supporters.

'Babes in the Wood'

Unity's next show after the Living Newspaper *Crisis* did more than lighten the theatre's debt. It wiped it out and brought Unity international fame as well. To the unsuspecting, the show might have seemed harmless, a Christmas pantomime called *Babes in the Wood*; but, as audiences were to discover to their huge enjoyment, this was no ordinary nursery tale.

Plans for the pantomime had been made earlier that summer when meetings were being called to discuss the repertoire problem. Geoffrey Parsons, lyricist of *Babes in the Wood*, remembers the debates:

> Some of us were wondering whether we could find a way of using Unity's considerable acting talent in a more light-hearted manner, feeling that it might be possible to induce even our political opponents to come and be subjected to the rapier of wit, whereas they would not venture within reach of the battle-axe of realistic drama.[5]

At one of the meetings, a post office civil servant called Robert Mitchell cut across the theorising with a practical suggestion. Instead of talking about new theatrical forms, why did not Unity adapt a traditional form to its own purposes? There were worried looks as he mentioned the word pantomime – he had studied nineteenth-century pantomimes and had directed successful versions of this supposedly decadent form for the much respected and neighbouring amateur group, the Tavistock Players. Anxiety deepened as he proceeded to read from the first draft of a piece he had written, but in the end there was no argument. 'Robert's script,' says Parsons, 'which he had produced so modestly, was a brilliant rendering into pantomime terms of the progress of appeasement.' The Babes stood for Austria and Czechoslovakia; the wicked uncle was Chamberlain; his two robber accomplices were Hitler and Mussolini; Robin Hood, the rescuer, was the Popular Front against fascism, uniting with Marion as the people. As Parson says:

> There, ready-made was a perfect vehicle for satirising Munich and the post-Munich situation. Add for full measure the Cliveden Set, a rumbustious Dame, a chorus of Stormtroopers, and finally Robert's own brilliant invention of the Fairy Wishfulfilment, and what *Vogue* subsequently described as Unity's 'political, scurrilous boiling-hot fun' was ready 'to lead the field'.

An advertisement was placed in the *Daily Worker* of 5 October 1938:

> Unity Theatre preparing its first pantomime will hold a Talent Finding Night Monday 10 October at 8.15. Dancers, singers, jugglers, instrumentalists, entertainers of all kinds invited to appear. Send your name to Variety Department ...

It was to be Unity's biggest and most ambitious show, involving a minimum of 72 people to provide a double cast – companies A and B – and a chorus. *Babes in the Wood* was announced to the press on 29 October and opened early for a panto on 15 November.

It ran for a record number of 160 performances until 22 May 1939, playing six nights a week to just under 48,000 people.[6] It was sold out to the end and only came off because of the strain on the actors, most of whom had full-time day jobs, and because the next production had missed several opening dates already and could not wait any longer. The show played outside London, though a planned Chicago production did not happen. Four songs from the pantomime were published and two were recorded by Decca. In addition to a mass of comment in the national press, Unity listed 73 foreign publications that ran pieces on this 'pantomime with a political point', as it was sub-titled, and boasted proudly that on 35 occasions the entire house was booked by an affiliated body. The engineering union took the house for six successive nights and there were more than 350 large block bookings. It was a unique achievement for a non-professional company, and only one year after the new theatre had been opened.

Such an ambitious project required a remarkable degree of discipline and co-operation under the guidance of a determined production team. Mitchell, an adjudicator at British Drama League festivals, became the director as well as being the author. Geoffrey Parsons and Berkeley Fase were deputed to write the lyrics and score respectively. They were all new to Unity and were neither weighed down by the internal wrangles nor tired from previous productions.

The production committee issued a ten-point notice on how to behave at rehearsals; with the size of company, many of whom were newcomers, an agreed code of conduct was essential.[7] The notice stressed punctuality, the importance of chorus work (which was not to be seen as secondary to that of individual, named, parts), the need for distinct speech, and the finality of the director's word. It was suggested that ideas should be written down and not used to interrupt rehearsal. Rehearsals, however, were known to stop in order to allow necessary visits to the local (Camden Town) labour exchange. Rules for behaviour on and off stage had to be learnt, too, and there was a new insistence on the showing of passes at the stage door.

The company had to be drilled in techniques that were quite different to those of the Stanislavsky method. Few had any experience of chorus work or of singing to anyone other than themselves in the bath. Peggy McLean as dance mistress and

Mervyn Vicars as chorus master tackled these two problems with help from Fase at the piano. There were running skirmishes between Fase and some senior Unity figures, like house manager Janet Harvey, which ended with her keeping him out of meetings and him trying to keep his singers out too, so that they could practice.

Fase was also responsible for obtaining two baby grand pianos for the show. He and Geraldine Peppin (who with her sister Mary was musical stalwart of Unity) went to Harrods to choose the two pianos which were delivered without prior payment. He remembers the theatre receiving bills for them seven or eight years later, by which time they had been so bashed in that they were of no use, except to Unity. Pianoforte arrangements for the show were by band leader van Phillips, Mervyn Vicars and James Gibb (who, to relieve the routine of the long run, used to weave pieces from other scores into his accompaniment).

Babes in the Wood was the outcome of a huge collective effort. It is credited in the programme as being written by the Unity Theatre Play Department, which at least meant that no royalties were incurred, unlike, for example, the cost of *Plant in the Sun* at £2 per performance or *Bury the Dead* at £3. The Play Department both helped and hindered the script, which went through many changes before and after the opening night and was taken to Communist Party headquarters for consultation. Parsons and Fase remember receiving good advice from Ivor Montagu, chair of the cultural committee, and from a perhaps surprising quarter, R. Palme Dutt, the leading theoretician, whom they recall as having a quick sense of humour. On the other hand, they remember Emile Burns, whose department was nominally in charge of Unity, as having no sense of humour and simply applying the criterion of 'would it offend the bus conductor's wife?' Mitchell, Parsons and Fase were the chief creators; one song that was used, 'We're Members of the Aristocracy', was sent in by Clarence Thorne and Lance Sterling and the words to another, 'Strike While the Iron is Hot', were written by veteran pantomime artist George Browne.[8] A request for designs brought in some 30 offerings; *Daily Worker* cartoonist Gabriel designed and painted one setting, George Haslam another and Lawrence Gowing, later knighted as an eminent painter and teacher, the rest. Stage management came under T.B. (Tris) Stack, lighting Pete Bennett, sound Joseph

Lines, and costumes Jo Hall, Joy Davidson and the wardrobe department under Pauline Elliott. Unity's advertising, under Arthur Soutter, became much more professional for this show, and the programme, designed by S. John Woods and the publicity department, broke new ground with its pictorial representation of 'Innocence Outraged'. Also, it was the first show for which stage management received programme credits.

While much of the show was rough – including the chorus and ballet work – its great strength lay as ever in the actors' energy and commitment, and in the wit and topicality of the whole piece, which was constantly up-dated. Like most pantomimes, the script does not read very well; the plot is thin, and the jokes are broad, obvious and dated. 'The whole point,' says Parsons, 'was to use the pantomime absurdities for our own purpose.' Clearly it worked at the time, offering a political satire that could not be found anywhere else and a theatrical vindication of the Popular Front approach at a time when politically it was in deep trouble.

Babes in the Wood opens in the land of Wonderwhy outside Tumbledown Towers which the Babes have inherited.[9] 'Glad to see you before us,' sings the chorus to the audience:

While you're seated at leisure
We perform for your pleasure
We shall give you a full measure and we hope a good time
We've taken an old-fashioned theme
And brought it up to date
That Unity's our watchword
We shall demonstrate.

The chorus lives on the estate; it acts as narrator and commentator, directs events and interviews characters, like Maid Marion, who appears first. The chorus wants to stop the Babe's wicked uncle from turning them off the land. Robin enters to learn that the wicked uncle (known at one point in rehearsal as Chamberstrain and also Chambermusic) wants to hand Tumbledown Towers over to the two robbers (known in rehearsal scripts as Hit and Muss) but has to win over the Babes to the idea. On comes Dame Nanny Nicknack, a figure of basic, rough-cast humanity, who has been thrown out of the Towers by the uncle because she did not like his friends, the robbers.

MARION: I hope they haven't molested you.
DAME: I'm not that sort of a girl – asking me if I'm a 'airy 'un, indeed.

Enter the wicked uncle to the tune of a yodel as the chorus rushes off. He calls for silence and introduces King Eustace the Useless and Queen Quarantine and the two robbers. 'Silence,' says the wicked uncle, 'I like German sausage and hate Russian tea, and my sister-in-law runs errands for me.' She is the Fairy Wishfulfilment, the embodiment of the Fleet Street columnist, spreading illusions and 'disinformation'.

Along with the monarchy, the aristocracy and the Prime Minister-uncle, she plays her part in bamboozling the Babes. (The Church is notably absent from the list of villains.)

Robin, the Dame and Marion decide to fight back, and sing one of the show's most popular numbers 'Strike While the Iron is Hot':

Times are bad, days are sad, we may wonder why
What's the use of wondering, to change 'em we must try.

The first half closes with a traditional 'grand transformation' scene as the two robbers chase the Babes into a wood where they fall asleep. Fairy Wishfulfilment appears and, instead of leaves, a shower of leaflets falls from the trees as she finishes her song. The Babes awake to read the message: 'Join Robin Hood – Make the rich pay – The Wicked Uncle Must Go.' The fairy tries to stop them: ' … Nice children believe in fairies – do you believe in fairies?' 'No,' reply the Babes and the fairy vanishes in a puff of smoke. Robin appears with his merry men and they sing 'The Unity March':

Come comrades sing with us
Join in the people's chorus
Come comrades march with us
Victory lies before us.

The second act begins in the palace backyard which has a dustbin, a clothes line and a toilet with No. 10 on the door. While the soloists read capitalist newspapers, the chorus sings a parody of 'Oh, dear what can the matter be?' with the catch refrain 'Nobody happens to care.'

Robin and Marion come on and hand out the *Daily Worker*, and the song changes from 'nobody' to 'Somebody happens to care.' The Dame, won over for unity, puts out the washing, which includes a pair of gents' large trousers or a pair of ladies' drawers bearing swastikas and takes a gas mask from No. 10 to sing the affirmative, superstition-defying 'Let's all Linger under Ladders'.

After the Cliveden set has shown its support for Hitler in a four-part harmony to the tune of 'We Plough the Fields and Scatter', stormtroopers are found in another part of the wood:

We're following our leader and we don't know where
We don't know who we're shooting and we don't much care
We know we've got to kill you though we don't know why
But blood must flow and heads must roll and you must die.

The wicked uncle enters to the sound of an aeroplane in a comic descent: 'After this I go back to my tricycle' (a reference to the British media's obsession with the fact that when Chamberlain first flew to meet Hitler he had never been airborne before). The problem for him is how the robbers are to grab the estate. He and Fairy Wishfulfilment favour persuasion; the robbers prefer outright violence, but for this to work the Babes have to be kept away from Robin. The wicked uncle suggests that the robbers threaten the Babes so that he can present himself as the kind uncle and advise them to surrender in order to save their lives. 'Peace at any price,' sings the Fairy.

In front of the curtain, revue-style, two young lovers complain to each other; all that life offers is 'Love on the Dole' – a foxtrot that took its cue from Walter Greenwood's novel of the same name in a situation that echoed a scene in *Waiting for Lefty*. It became the hit of the show and a popular song in its own right.

Love on the Dole,
That's a luxury we can't afford,
For they don't approve of love on the dole
On the Unemployment Assistance Board.
We've no room of our own,
There's nothing but the benches in the park
Where we can sit alone and hold our hands
And whisper in the dark.
We can't do the things
That other lovers do.
And it's hard to live on nothing but dreams

When the things you dream can never come true.
There's not much sense in life for us it seems:
Funny romance, though we love each other body and soul,
In our hearts we know we haven't a chance,
For there's no such thing as love on the dole.

Finally, the two opposing camps are drawn up against each other. The Dame and Robin argue for unity and the chorus responds with another foxtrot hit, 'Affiliate With Me' – a clever play on the traditional pantomime resolution of marriage for the two young dejected lovers who join in the song.

Our sentiment is sympathetic
To your society
We need your aid
In our crusade
To work for Unity [...]
Without doubt the motion's carried
We're no longer two
'Cos I agree
That you make me
Affiliate with you.

The finale includes a tap routine and a ballet number, the reprise of previous songs and a pay-off for each character. The robber and the wicked uncle are driven off stage to a reprise of 'The Unity March' and the closing chorus:

We must bid you goodnight now
Since they've learnt to unite now
Both the babes are alright now
Unity has won.

Robin, dressed in Soviet costume, makes a final appeal:

When strife disturbs and wars corrupt our age
Keen satire is the business of the stage.
When the curtain falls upon our pantomime tonight
Join with the workers in the social fight.

International Acclaim

When the first night came, the show began quietly. The curtain went up on the opening chorus and the exchange between Robin,

Marion and the Dame (played in company A by an Australian Harry Haddy who was unemployed and always walked to the theatre across London from his home south of the river). Then on came the wicked uncle, backwards. He turned to the audience with his toothy grin and the theatre exploded in delight. It seemed as if Chamberlain himself had come on stage, although this was not what Robert Mitchell had intended. During rehearsals, Mitchell had insisted that all references to real people should be implicit rather than explicit. This was intended to cover both visual and verbal allusions; direct imitation was ruled out, and the actors playing the robbers did not make up to look like Hitler or Mussolini.

This, however, had puzzled Geoff McKeeman, the actor playing the wicked uncle in company A, and he decided to apply to his part in the panto what he had learnt at Unity of Stanislavsky's approach. He investigated his character and then developed the appropriate physical elements. He read all that he could find on Chamberlain and watched him in the House of Commons. He noticed his peculiar voice, which seemed to come from high in the throat, and his remarkable moustache and eyebrows. McKeeman practised at home in front of the mirror until he achieved the right effects and gestures. He was a good mimic and, after much experimenting, hit upon the solution to the eyebrows and moustache by cutting a few stiff bristles from a kitchen broom. Other attempts had made him look too much like Chaplin but now, with his facial features accentuated by greasepaint, he looked suitably sinister. To gain height, he wore wellington boots stuffed with newspapers and this gave him a funny walk that helped too. He wore a top hat, although Chamberlain did not do so as a rule, and carried a rolled umbrella. For variety during the run, he also wore a fishing cap and carried a fishing rod, which he lent to Dave Bliss who was playing the same part in company B. (Angling was one of Chamberlain's favourite pastimes.) What McKeeman achieved was not a naturalistic likeness – the bland bank-manager look of the newsreel Chamberlain – but the bedraggled yet evil figure reminiscent of the Low cartoons in the *Evening Standard*.

Two nights before the opening at a dress rehearsal, Mitchell was not happy when he first saw McKeeman's creation, which, he thought was too exaggerated and would overshadow the larger roles of the two robbers. According to McKeeman, Mitchell believed that the effects would be toned down for the first night but 'I disobeyed and it was terrific.' The audience took several minutes to settle down before the show could continue but its success was assured. As Geoffrey Parsons says: 'Chamberlain was a catastrophe for the country but a gift from the gods to Unity' and he updated the script every time the Prime Minister issued another fatuous statement. McKeeman also took this liberty upon himself, without telling anyone else beforehand, and earned himself the distinction of appearing as picture of the week in *Life* magazine as the character that made *Babes in the Wood* internationally famous.

It is difficult to imagine the situation then, before the development of political satire on television and the ending of the censor's powers in 1968; it was one thing to lampoon foreign dictators like Hitler and Mussolini, which had already been done by Shaw in his play *Geneva* and in the America garment workers' revue *Pins and Needles*, an important source of inspiration for *Babes in the Wood*, but it was quite another to impersonate prominent living British figures, especially the Prime Minister.[11]

Political hindsight also makes it harder to realise that attacking Chamberlain at that time was not universally popular. Most of the press supported the 69-year old Premier and treated him as a hero. Unity had private information that a Tory MP wanted to take parliamentary action against the theatre and a question was asked in the House of Commons, clearly aimed at Unity though without naming it, concerning the status of club theatres. Legislation was threatened restricting their rights but nothing came of it. Berkeley Fase recalls that later he was told by Sir John Vansittart, a playwright and politician (who had resigned from the government after quarelling with Chamberlain) how furiously angry Chamberlain had been, not only about the production but particularly at his caricature picture being reprinted around the world. He and his friends believed that Unity had to be stopped – either fined or closed down – but had to back off when they were advised that the theatre was acting within the law.

Unity also ran into trouble over the depiction of the monarchy. Alfie Bass as King Eustace the Useless wanted to sport a beard resembling that of George V, but this was blocked as going too far; yet, in the *Daily Mirror, Babes in the Wood* was still attacked for guying the the crown.

The pantomime kept its freshness by being changed with events and responding to the audience. In true pantomime style, opportunity was taken for audience participation and singing, which paralleled the references from the stage to translating the message of the show into political action outside the theatre. The key figure in the updating process was Fairy Wishfulfilment, the wicked uncle's sister-in-law, who was created in company A by Vida Hope, a copywriter for a mail order firm. Parsons used to telephone the theatre from his work to add to or change her couplets; it might be a political reference or a mention of a person or group in the audience that evening – a particular union, a Left Book Club party or an MP. Vida Hope was taken into the West End from *Babes in the Wood* by the revue producer Herbert Farjeon. She was nicknamed 'Unity Annie' in the profession and later sang two Unity songs at the Duke of York's in a Binnie Hales revue. She directed the first production of Sandy Wilson's *The Boyfriend* and is said by Andrew Lloyd Webber to have taught him how to stage musicals.[12]

Critics were mixed in their responses. The *Times* found the show 'irresistibly funny' but the singing and dancing 'quite unambitious'. The *Observer* reviewer was 'disappointed' and thought the sentiment was 'doctrinaire', while the *Cork Examiner* railed that it was a 'bitter travesty of the jolly spirit of pantomime'. The *Daily Mirror* critic was 'exceedingly shocked' and found the show in 'bad taste', urging 'any decent man or woman' to 'boycott the theatre'. They all agreed with the *Manchester Guardian's* comment that it was 'not like other pantomimes' and though the *Spectator* found the 'politics better than the pantomime' even the *Daily Telegraph* admitted 'the show had ingenuity'. Goronwy Rees, in *New Writing*, reported that whenever the Wicked Uncle appeared 'the audience is transfixed by a horrible fascination'. He called the Fairy Wishfulfilment 'a genuine creation of popular art' and felt that in these two characters Unity 'has succeeded completely'. *Picture Post* ran a special feature while Lord Beaverbrook (target of the Fairy Wishfulfilment invention) was rumoured to have banned any mention of the show. Bookings were poor for the first few nights. It took the reviews to change that and then the popularity of *Babes in the Wood* owed as much to word-of-mouth as to the press. Unity could brandish the *News Chronicle* – 'point, pith and pungency. Wickedly witty songs and brilliantly satirical dialogue', yet it was clear from the membership applications that Unity had become a talking point across the political spectrum.

New affiliations more than doubled from 130 organisations and

3,500 individual members to 289 organisations and nearly 8,000 members. Coaches from the co-op guilds would jostle for parking space next to Daimlers and Rolls Royces. The box office could not cope as the queues stretched out of the foyer, down the entrance drive, and onto the road. Many personalities came and the most unlikely people to find at Unity could be seen laughing heartily at Chamberlain's antics, from Foreign Office civil servants to Churchill's son-in-law, Duncan Sandys, who was proposed for the theatre's membership by two Unity general council members and Labour MPs, Sir Stafford Cripps and D.N. Pritt. Sandys told Parsons that McKeeman had captured the Prime Minister perfectly, 'the way he licks his lips, like a snake'.

Babes in the Wood changed Unity and became a reference point for success and failure ever after. It was the culmination of many years hard work and experimentation, going back by way of slight pieces such as *The Case of the Baffled Boss* and *The Fall of the House of Slusher* on the comic musical side, and direct political productions like *Crisis* and *Busmen* on the other, to the days of the Workers' Theatre Movement with its cabaret agitprop. *Babes in the Wood* was a unique creation, entirely of its day and for its day, combining contemporary political comment and calls for action with fun, wit and entertainment on a much broader basis than Unity or the WTM had hitherto achieved, thanks to its Popular Front ideology and its successful exploitation of the traditional pantomime form. The show was a welcome revelation to those outside the left that socialists could have a sense of humour and a salutory reminder to the left itself that politics and pleasure were not mutually exclusive. It also marked a new stage in the 'professionalisation' of Unity, in the attitudes towards the work of all departments, and it attracted many new people to the theatre, for whom the show was a turning point in their lives – like Bill Owen, known then as Bill Rowbotham, who came with Vida Hope from Tavistock Players and was playing one of the robbers. He was to remain associated with Unity for the rest of its days, as actor, writer, director and chair of the Unity Trust, while he also became a well known stage, television and film actor.

The Parsons and Fase team continued to contribute in stunning form to Unity's work during the next decade as the Gilbert and Sullivan of the left, creating the nearest that the English – and it was very English – came to the political cabaret of continental

Europe. Parsons was general manager of EMG Handmade Gramophones when he wrote the pantomime libretto; his poems appeared in several magazines, he had a novel published and a short play performed by Unity during the war. With Fase, he wrote the revue *Sauce Tartare*, which played in the West End in 1949 and was televised, and subsequently he was the writer, co-writer or translater of some 200 popular song lyrics, several of which became chart-toppers and 'standards' including 'Auf Wiedersehn' sung by Vera Lynn, which won the first golden disc by a British singer, 'Smile', 'If You Go', 'Autumn Leaves' and 'If You Love Me'. Fase at the time of *Babes in the Wood* was a freelance musician, playing piano mainly and writing songs.

They teamed up together in 1934 and were taken to see *Bury the Dead* by one of the cast, Denis Waldock, who later wrote successful revue material for Hermoine Gingold. He introduced them to André van Gyseghem who brought them into Unity. They taught themselves the craft of revue songwriting, moving back and forth from skilful parody to clever originals. The art, they discovered, was to know how to produce songs with lyrics that were politically apt but could also be sung easily. Audiences would be hearing a song for the first time and would have to understand it immediately, which is especially hard if the song is trying to carry a political message. Their music was smooth but pointed and when they worked in the West End they found that both content and style were affected adversely; many professionals did not like or understand the content, and the way they performed the songs – including ones that had been presented at Unity – altered or neutralised the meaning. They retired from the revue scene gracefully when television and a shift in musical taste changed its ground rules.

Aiming for the West End

It was an unsual situation for Unity to be presenting only one show for six months and the actors who were preparing the next productions became increasingly frustrated. Unity's mobile work continued during the run of *Babes in the Wood* and a group appeared in a film made by Ivor Montagu called *Peace and Plenty* (from the slogan of the Communist Party's fifteenth congress in September 1938), which the Communist Party had commissioned as part of its campaign for the General Election due in 1940. The film was released in March 1939. The next show after *Babes in the Wood* had an impossible task. There was no way of following the panto. James Lansdale Hodson's *Harvest in the North* took Unity back to solid social realism and the Stanislavsky approach, this time under the direction of André van Gyseghem, assisted by R. Vernon Beste. Hodson was a journalist and novelist – a feature writer for the *Manchester Evening Chronicle* – who had been born in a small village six miles from Manchester. He was the only one of his family not to have worked in the cotton mills.

Harvest in the North, which had been performed first in Manchester in 1935, is set in a Lancashire mill town called Chesterford, part of a 'depressed area' suffering rationalisation and the dole. Apart from a prologue that gives a national context to the decline through the voices of a Scot, a Welshman and a Lancastrian, and the epilogue at the local war memorial, the action of the play takes place in the living room-cum-kitchen of one family, the Renshaws. The play shows the effects of recession through the changing lives of this family, the catalyst for which is the sacking of Peter, a mill engineer.

The strongest character is Harriet, Peter's daughter-in-law, who says that 'It's like t' war o'er agen.'[13] When asked by a friend 'What can *tha* do?' she replies 'I can win a bit o' peace for mysel'. When I've tried myself out rantin' or goin' collectin' or sewin' for them as can't sew – I feel quiet inside then.' She ends the play at the war memorial with a stirring speech:

> Our machinery they've smashed up with sledge-hammers. They conna smash us up – but they're waitin' on us rustin' away [...] There's a war on [...] a war against starvation and misery and degradation, and we are part o' the army feightin' it [...] We want 'em to know we're Englishmen and women, same as anybody else, entitled to a livelihood in the country we belong to and which belongs to us, the country some of our men died for [...] We're not givin' in – not ever.

Van Gyseghem said:

> I made the actors think more deeply about the characters as individuals by writing their biographies as they saw and felt them. I took the cast up to a Lancashire mill town to get the 'feel' of living in this environment – cobbled streets – clogs – shawls – the 'hooters' for work starting – this constant fall of smoke from the mills.

The set, which became drabber as the times became harsher, was the first of Unity's attempts at a thorough-going reproduction of real life. Designed by George Haslam, it was a genuine forerunner of post war 'kitchen sink drama' with a glowing fire, a plumbed-in sink with working waste pipe, and a tap from which the kettle was filled before being boiled on a real gas ring. Hodson was present for many of the rehearsals which spread over three months, during which time probably too much attention was paid to detail and not enough to the overall dynamic of the piece. The general verdict on the show seems to be that it was honest and worthy but not fresh. Nevertheless, the critic Harold Hobson noticed that, 'To an outsider, the evening's most striking feature was the audience, infallibly attentive, quick in response, warm in appreciation, and enthusiastically uncritical.' Unity also received a publicity boost during the run of the play when Herbert Hodge broadcast a radio programme on the theatre.[14]

In July came *After the Tempest* and *Colony*, which had been scheduled for Easter but had been shunted down the calendar to accommodate the success of *Babes in the Wood*. The two plays were written by Geoffrey Trease, social worker, journalist, teacher and novelist, best known for his children's books.[15] He was then in the limelight because of the recent publication of a satirical novel, *Such Divinity*.

The short play, *After the Tempest*, set twenty years in the future, had been written for a local Oxford drama group and it had proved a prize-winner at the Welwyn Garden Festival. Four English castaways are seen on a Pacific island two decades after an apocalyptic war which they survived and were shipwrecked. Three of them represent Britain's old ruling class and cannot adjust to their new situation; they sustain the ideology and symbols of empire. The fourth, who grew up on the island with its inhabitants, does not carry this imperialist baggage of class and racial prejudice. An Englishwoman lands in her aeroplane and tells them of the new society that has arisen since their shipwreck, which was caused not only by the war but – somewhat mystically – by a tempest of 'barbarism, famine, plague'.[16] Only the castaway who grew up on the island is seen to be fit to return to the new Jerusalem. Fredda Brilliant, a fine sculptress to whom Herbert Marshall was married, directed with assistance from Elizabeth McCormack.[17]

Unity decided to run *After the Tempest* with *Colony* as an evening about imperialism. *Colony* is also set on a fictitious island, this time in the contemporary West Indies, but is recognisable as a Caribbean country such as Jamaica. The action takes place on the seaward terrace of Government House and the play tells the story of the island's sugar workers who are striking for a fair wage, better conditions and the right to organise in a trade union. Their leader, O'Riley, is reminiscent of Alexander Bustamante, who founded the Jamaican Labour Party in 1943. The strike coincides with the visit of a British fact-finding delegation comprising scientist Professor Hamilton, a right-wing National Labour MP Sir Albert Upward, knighted for his trade union work, and a 'firebrand' Labour MP Jane Stevenson (based loosely on Ellen Wilkinson MP and played in one cast by Anna Zolk who became a film actress).

Miss Davis, an idealist missionary trying to raise funds to clothe the black children at her school, tells the scientist Hamilton about the island's diseases – typhoid, malaria, leprosy, hookworm – revealing a picture in stark contrast to that of the 'Paradise Island' notion held in Britain. The Governer, a well-meaning civil servant, meets the leaders of the sugar workers, who are angry at not being able to negotiate directly with the sugar bosses.

The workers, led by O'Riley, refuse the governor's offer of land settlements instead of a living wage. Solidarity spreads to a general strike, martial law is introduced and a warship is called to the island. The cruiser fires warning shots that spell disaster as one shell hits the sea wall and causes a flood, killing 36 people. O'Riley, who has been arrested despite trying to stop bloodshed, runs to the waterfront to organise the rescue and calls off the general strike to save lives.

MISS DAVIS: After all the hard words and hatred ... to see the Governor and O'Riley working side by side to rescue a child. They weren't enemies any longer, they weren't black and white, they were just two men. If we can only keep the spirit there's been tonight, I think the colony can solve all its differences.

JANE: But we can't keep it

MISS DAVIS: Why not? If anyone had told me yesterday that I should see ...

JANE (*rousing herself*): It's no good deluding ourselves. The class differences lie too deep. Times like these do touch the hearts ... even of the capitalists ... and they're stirred suddenly into being

> human. But the impulse fades again, and by the time the bodies are buried, it's all forgotten.[18]

Jane Stevenson is proved right. O'Riley returns voluntarily to the Governor's house but is given no concessions. The Labour MP promises to stir public opinion on her return to Britain, Miss Davis says that she will denounce the bombardment as un-Christian and the Governor is persuaded to consider new legislation to improve the welfare of the colony. O'Riley, whose initial rejection of all white people has now taken on a class perspective, turns to Jane:

> O'RILEY: We shan't forget this missie. It'll be mighty useful, coming at this time. It'll help us to build up our organisation stronger than ever, ready for the next round. Thanks for giving us a hand – we shan't forget.
>
> JANE: I'm beginning to think you can help us, too. When you break your chains, ours are that much weaker ... I was reading something the other day ... How did it go? 'A people that enslaves others cannot itself be free.'
>
> O'RILEY: We gotta learn to fight together, you in England and we here. Come on, the dawn's breaking. Let's get back to the job.

The production was topical because a report had just been published that outlined the poor health, property-owning pattern and violence meted out to strikers in Jamaica. The programme carried a note on the situation in the West Indies that was culled from this report and added a plea for literature on trade unionism, and on economic, social and political subjects to be sent to the islands. 'If tonight's play has inspired you to do this', it read, 'or to help them in any other way, then we, who have performed tonight, will not have acted in vain.'

There was considerable interest in the production which was well and widely reviewed as 'powerful' (*Cavalcade*), 'effective' (*Era*), an 'indictment of racism and class prejudice' (*Daily Worker*) and praised for its 'strongly-drawn characters' (*News Chronicle*). Director Herbert Marshall, who also designed an impressive colonial set, and his assistant Eric Capon, applied the Stanislavsky techniques in rehearsal and even issued the cast with a questionnaire after the first read-through.

While *Colony* was another Unity play that affirmed the need for collective action, its handling of racism was still something of a rarity, as was the presence of several black actors. The part of

O'Riley had been written for Paul Robeson who had said that he would be interested in returning to Unity if a suitable part could be found, but he had gone back to the USA to appear in *The Emperor Jones*. His part was taken by the Caribbean actor Robert Adams, who had played leading roles in *Song of Freedom, King Solomon's Mines* and *The Emperor Jones* and during the war founded the short-lived London Negro Repertory Theatre, which, according to another Unity activist Peter Noble who was involved, was probably the first black theatre company in Britain.[19] Adams, who once earned his living as a wrestler while studying for the bar, had appeared with Robeson in van Gyseghem's production of *Stevedore* in 1935 and was to double for, as well as understudy, Robeson in the film *Proud Valley*; he joined Unity's professional company in its opening production in 1946 and soon after returned to Guyana as a headteacher. There were difficulties in finding black actors for *Colony* and, with the delays in opening of the play due to the extended run of the pantomime, even more difficulties in retaining them. Peter, then known as George, Noble, who became a well known journalist and editor of the influential magazine *Screen International*, recalls the difficulties of finding suitable candidates and the personal rivalries that ensued. Such tensions were not confined to *Colony*, however, as individual competition was common; in Noble's case, for example, he says his main battle was with Ken Hughes, who went on to become a successful film director.

It was during the run of *Colony* that Unity's publicity department launched its glossy *New Theatre* magazine 'devoted to the interests of the modern theatre and associated arts'. The first issue, dated August 1939, was edited by John E. Cross, cost 6d., ran to 32 pages and carried advertisements from the theatre profession as well as from Schweppes. It was funded by the income from the pantomime. The editorial opposite a striking picture of Paul Robeson in *Plant in the Sun* (taken by John Vickers) said: '*New Theatre* is outspoken and independent, it strives for the complete emancipation of the stage and its workers.' There was news – the Parsons-Fase-Mitchell team was writing a new show – reviews, a play-writing competition, a picture spread of *Babes in the Wood* with a page of press comments, and articles on censorship of newsreels, on three Soviet films, on ballet, pageants, and television (a recent development, which showed Unity was alive to new influences in culture). Sybil Thorndike and Walter Hudd offered new perspectives on the theatre, Roger Woddis wrote on Michel Saint-Denis, film star Louise Rainer was interviewed on commitment, and Maurice Browne and James Hodson contributed on the question 'Is the theatre dead?' The second issue, in September, continued the broad coverage – music, records, books, films, amateur theatre, and reviews. There were articles on Welsh drama, German drama, the Old Vic, theatre as propaganda, Indian dance, the Players Theatre, an interview with Soviet director Oklopkhov, a look at stage censorship, and a letters page. *Calvalcade* estimated *New Theatre*'s circulation to be 4,000, but any chance to develop from this encouraging start was cut short by the war.

The success of *Babes in the Wood* had led to another proposed expansion – the establishment of a professional company to work separately but alongside the amateur company at Goldington Street. This idea represented a complete break with the past when Unity's exclusively amateur status was a source of pride and accepted as axiomatic. Only months before, Unitarians had been arguing fiercely with members of the American Group Theater against the idea of a professional company. The pantomime had transformed the situation and now Unity's leadership argued that the move represented a consolidation of the advances that the theatre had already achieved. Unity had brought drama back to the people by spearheading the rising amateur movement and had influenced the professional theatre to include in its repertoire an increasing number of social plays. There were detractors, however, among whom political and practical objections overlapped; the expansion would accentuate the effects that acquiring a permanent base had already had in making touring more difficult and in absorbing a great deal of time, energy and money simply to keep the building open, which had led to a proliferation of committees. Opposition was also expressed to the notion of the professional company being run by one individual (who probably would have been Herbert Marshall), which would have challenged the collective nature of Unity's activities, although the plan was to make the venture co-operative. Nevertheless, confidence was in the air and it was infectious. Unity's progress seemed as unstoppable as it was remarkable. Analogies were drawn with Soviet practice in combining amateur and professional work and the plan won the support, with whatever degree of reluctance, of even those who had been members of the Workers' Theatre Movement before Unity. A prospectus was issued in May 1939, outlining the decline of the commercial theatre and Unity's belief in its ability to revitalise it. A launch date of 1 September was announced.

Goldington Street was not big enough to accommodate what Unity described as the largest organised audience of any theatre in Britain, although the amateur theatre was to remain there was a private club and as the mainspring of all Unity's activities. The new company was to be the British equivalent of New York's Group Theatre, with a theory of production and standard of excellence in keeping with a policy of staging new plays not seen before in Britain. There were plans to co-operate with leading figures in other performing arts such as Anthony Tudor and Benjamin Britten to mount ballet and opera. Unity believed that a mix of revue, ballet, opera and pantomimes as the musical compliment to the plays would provide the necessary basis for acquiring a permanent theatre. The Lyric, Hammersmith, was mooted as a venue but in the end Unity West End Ltd, a limited liability company set up to protect Unity if things went wrong (with Fred Roberts and Jack Selford as directors), took a lease on the Kingsway Theatre (later to be the choice of the English Stage Company before settling on the Royal Court). Unity wanted a medium-price policy for its medium-size theatre (it seated 600) and revived the idea of turning the theatre into a social and arts centre, showing films and holding exhibitions. Discussions were also held on opening a suburban theatre to house musicals as a complement to the Kingsway and to launch suburban Unity groups focused on a particular locality in contrast to the national aspiration of Goldington Street.

The rules of the society had to be altered to allow for the changes and on 31 July 1939 Unity Theatre Society Ltd was established with a new wording for its main purpose that was to remain as its credo for the duration of the theatre's existence:

> to foster and further the art of the drama in accordance with the principle that true art, by effectively presenting and truthfully interpreting life as experienced by the majority of the people, can move the people to work for the betterment of society.

At the same time, Unity issued an illustrated handbook, giving a history of the theatre and an explanation of its intentions. The foreword, by Sybil Thorndike, said that theatre in its infancy in England had expressed a faith but that it had then slid away from its proper function. 'I think that Unity Theatre is proving itself the real heir of this old living theatre,' she wrote.

> Maybe the technical equipment of its actors is not up to the highest professional standard, but it has the more important quality – something to say – without which technique is just dead and boring. Unity Players are building their own technique because amongst them are capable and humble artists. It is the most exciting movement in the theatre of our day.

Unity's confidence was shaken when the first play to be presented at the Kingsway, Ernst Toller's *Pastor Niemoller* in a production by Lewis Casson, was considered too anti-Nazi by the Lord Chamberlain's office to be granted a licence. Deliberately, it had been Toller's agent and not Unity who had sought the licence but nevertheless it was refused. (Virtually penniless, Toller was to commit suicide in New York when he heard of the outbreak of the Second World War.) The new revue from Parsons, Fase and Mitchell was not ready, and, in any case, this too ran into trouble with the censor, who objected to the appearance of Queen Victoria in a sketch, implicit references to Lord Beaverbrook and Chamberlain, and to a song 'Every Father his own Führer'. 'Führer' had to be changed to 'dictator', 'Heil' to 'hail', actual words spoken by Hitler altered and Father 'must not be made up to resemble Hitler'. A further reference to 'German housepainter' had to go also.[20]

Unity turned to *Colony*, hoping to attract Paul Robeson as O'Riley and Beatrix Lehmann to play Stevenson, with Unity players Alfie Bass, Bill Owen, Vida Hope and John Slater in the cast too. The play was rewritten for the West End and posters were pasted up in tube stations asking 'Have You Heard About The Kingsway?' but all plans and Unity's further growth and wider acceptance were interrupted by the declaration of war.

Notes

1. New interviews/correspondence for this chapter: Una Brandon-Jones, Berkeley Fase, James Friell (Gabriel), Geoffrey McKeeman, Peter (George) Noble, Bill Owen (Rowbotham), Geoffrey Parsons, Geoffrey Trease.
2. Quotations from script that I was given which has been deposited in the British Theatre Association library. Script also held in Lord Chamberlain's Plays (Stage Plays Submitted But Not In Accordance With The Theatres Act 1843, And For Which A Licence Was Not Therefore Issued) 1938 Vol. 8, wrongly titled *Living Newspaper No. 2 ARP*.
3. Instructive anecdote from Una Brandon-Jones who, while not supporting Chamberlain generally, did believe then in his efforts to negotiate a peace. Her position did not produce outrage, she recalls; she was simply released from the show at her own request.
4. Marshall's translation of *The German War Primer* also appeared in *Our Time*, Vol. 1 No. 11, February 1942.
5. Quoted from Geoffrey Parsons, 'Robin in *Babes in the Wood*', *Nothing is Lost*, a tribute to Ann Lindsay by the Communist Party Writers' Group 1954.
6. There are different accounts of how many performances *Babes in the Wood* had. Geoffrey Parsons says 159, a Unity bulletin (June 1939) says 160 but Bram Bootman and a Unity Handbook published later in 1939 say 162. The bulletin also gives the number of people who saw the show as 47,647 and the number of block bookings as 374. All the figures need to be raised when the touring productions are included but I have found no records from which to make a final tally for *Babes in the Wood*.
7. The notice accompanied the script and is lodged in the British Theatre Association library.
8. Browne is credited in the programme but in the published sheet music it says on the cover that Parsons wrote the song while inside Mitchell is given as the author. Parsons says that he did not write the song and thought that Browne was a pen-name of Mitchell's. However, Jack Selford remembers Browne as a professional actor and pantomime specialist.
9. Quotations are taken from a script that I was given and have deposited in the British Theatre Association library, which consists of fragments and occasionally alternative versions of the same section. The order and the words of the script were frequently changed and what appears here is only, therefore, an approximation. Script also held in Lord Chamberlain's Plays (Stage Plays For Which A Licence Was Not Granted) 1939 Vol. 25 (stamped 24 May 1939 but entered in catalogue 30 May).
10. Branson and Heinemann in *Britain in the Nineteen Thirties* remember the tune as 'Land of Hope and Glory' but the words do not match, e.g. 'We own the press and scatter/Confusion in the land/Reaction's fed and watered/By our exclusive band.'
11. *Pins and Needles* was first performed in 1937 in New York by the Labour Stage Inc. which had been set up by the International Ladies'

Garment Workers' Union. It transferred to Broadway and enjoyed a record-breaking run at the time of 1,108 performances. There were three versions and two tours, including an appearance at the White House when the black members of the cast were removed. Parsons and Fase remember hearing and reading about it before *Babes in the Wood* and are able to recall one 78 rpm recording from the show being available in Britain. At least one Unity favourite came from the show, 'Sing me a Song of Social Significance' (originally 'Why Sing of Skies Above'), and in 1972 Unity staged a rewritten version of the show itself. It was revised for its 25th anniversary in America, with Shelley Winters in the cast and Barbara Streisand recording from it. See Harry Goldman 'When Social Significance Came to Broadway', *Theatre Quarterly*, Vol. VII No. 28, 1977.

12. Interview in the *Guardian*, 12 May 1986. Vida Hope also devised and directed *The Punch Revue*, produced by Unity member Oscar Lewenstein and Wolf Mankowitz with some material by Parsons and Fase and with Alfie Bass in the cast.

13. *Harvest in the North*, Gollancz 1935.

14. Herbert Hodge rewrote Unity's history for the occasion and even departs from the account that he gives in his autobiography.

15. See Trease's two autobiographies, *A Whiff of Burnt Boats*, Macmillan 1971, and *Laughter at the Door*, Macmillan 1974, both of which contain references to Unity.

16. It is available in the British Theatre Association library in J.W. Marriot (ed.), *Best One-Act Plays of 1938*, Harrap 1939.

17. An example of Brilliant's work is her sculpture of Gandhi in Tavistock Square, London.

18. There are two versions, one in Carbondale, from which the quotations are taken, the other, rewritten for the West End, in the British Theatre Association Library.

19. *Our Time*, Vol. 3 No. 3, 1943 says that the company was to perform next month at the Arts Theatre but Peter Noble recalls that it only played at Colchester Rep where it presented O'Neill's *All God's Chillun Got Wings*.

20. Script given to me and with Lord Chamberlain's comments is in the British Theatre Association library.

6

They Never Closed

Unity's leadership had discussed what action it should take in the event of war, yet when Chamberlain finally made the announcement, different assessments of the war and its likely outcome, on top of the daily pressures of running Goldington Street while planning to open at the Kingsway Theatre, meant that little of practical use had been achieved.[1]

Many Unity activists heard the news during the third summer school, which was being held later than usual because of the knock-on effect of the success of *Babes in the Wood*. The school, held at Clayesmore School, Dorset, was organised by Wilfred White, who recalls:

> For less than £70 per week we had the use of a 60-acre park, tennis courts, cricket field, boating lake, swimming pool, a theatre with cinema projector, a gymnasium, squash courts, music rooms, lecture rooms, dining hall, plus a large library whose excellent floor was used mainly for dancing. There was a domestic staff of 15 which we took on and I took with me from London an administrative staff of five: a catering manager, an entertainments manager, a tuckshop salesman, a chauffeur to drive the hired car and my personal secretary.

In the midst of this relative calm came the first explosion. On 23 August, Germany and the Soviet Union signed a non-aggression pact. White remembers: 'We sprawled on the sun-baked grass puzzling over the implications of this shattering event, which upset the habits of thought of years past.' It had come as a sharp surprise not just to the world in general but in particular to the Communist Parties, which, despite loyalty to the Comintern, had been told nothing in advance. Plain-clothes detectives called and took away an experimental radio transmitter (which had nothing to do with Unity but belonged to one of Clayesmore's pupils).

On Friday 1 September, the day before the Unity school was due to end, Hitler invaded Poland. Over the radio came the government's instructions: teachers to return to schools, windows to be blacked out, theatres to close. Two days later war was declared.

Back in Goldington Street, equipment and files were moved out to members' homes. Papers were fed into the boiler amid talk of going underground in case Unity activists were rounded up and the theatre closed down, either by Chamberlain or by Hitler, should he invade. A secret bank account was opened to finance future illegal guerrilla theatre, though this fact was known to only three people, and one group in the leadership argued that extra funds for such activity could be raised by not paying Unity's creditors. Suspicion was rife in this atmosphere and the society's secretary disappeared. Plain-clothes policemen had from time to time visited Unity (usually to try to break the club's rules by buying tickets for the same evening instead of waiting the statutory week after joining) and it was generally believed, it seems, that surveillance was stepped up after 3 September. People took it for granted that Unity's telephone was tapped and its mail likely to be interfered with. It was also commonly assumed that Unity, like the Communist Party, had been infiltrated by the 'intelligence' services, and one joke ran that no one minded as long as the secret agents could sing and dance as well.

War changed Unity, as it did everything else. The majority of those who had built and sustained Unity were called up at one point or another; for some, war became a convenient point of departure from Unity and others drifted away. Whatever the heartache and suffering, war also provided unforeseen opportunities for a fortunate few. A number who turned professional – Harry Ross, Alfie Bass, Bill Owen, Vida Hope, John Slater – returned from time to time to help out in different capacities, with other professional colleagues, such as Beatrix Lehmann, Walter Hudd, Patrick Hamilton, Rodney Ackland, Patricia Burke, Michael Redgrave and Freda Jackson. Turnover in people was high and new blood had to be found quickly and continuously, yet what was lacking in continuity and experience was more than compensated for in commitment. Remarkably, while many other initiatives collapsed, Unity kept going throughout the war, closing only for the first two weeks of September 1939 as required by law. Its achievements stand in remarkable contrast to the atrophy of the West End, which, with few exceptions, was inimical to new ideas. Unity provided a repertoire as continuous as, and a more varied and interesting one than, that of the Windmill Theatre, whose 'we never closed' boast became a famous slogan. Many London theatres left for the regions after a period of playing matinées only and, while some club theatres survived the immediate onset of war, only a handful lasted longer, mostly sporadically and none on the same scale as Unity.

After initial difficulties and readjustments, the theatre regained its influence as one of the leading amateur companies in Britain (if not the leading one) and even attracted many people who saw it as providing a sound training ground for a professional career. Despite unprecedented problems, particularly in the middle years of the war, Unity remained a beacon for the alternative theatrical values and managed to relaunch a national movement of left-wing theatres. Most of these groups had been forced to disband or to function fitfully and in isolation, although in several places, Glasgow and Leeds, for example, new Unity theatres emerged to lead vigorous, independent lives.

Tensions within the left, mainly concerning the Soviet Union, had sharpened with the defeat of the Spanish Republic and came to a head with the Nazi-Soviet pact and the Soviet invasion of Poland just over two weeks after the Nazis. Two members of Unity's general council, the pro-Soviet Sean O'Casey and Labour MP George Strauss, argued their contrary positions in the left-wing press. Meetings were held at the theatre addressed by Communists from the party headquarters to try to explain the shifts in policy. At first the party declared the war to be a war 'on two fronts', against fascism and imperialism. General secretary Harry Pollitt wrote a pamphlet published on 12 Septmber supporting this view and emphasising that it was a 'just' war. But on 3 October, after learning of the Comintern's views, the party executive did an about-turn and declared that it was a war between imperialists. On 11 October Pollitt stood down.[2]

Division of opinion was evident at Unity as elsewhere on the left. There were those who had felt misgivings at what they saw as the unnecessary compromises of the Popular Front strategy and thought that the pact had at last clarified matters and restored a proper sense of revolutionary realism. Chamberlain's 'phoney war' was taken as confirmation of this position. Others took an opposite view, arguing that there was now even greater need for popular and international unity against fascism. Some left the theatre while others stayed if only because keeping Unity alive was more important to them than party political disagreements. Unity's supporters were also affected, though given all the other pressures on surviving in wartime it is hard to say exactly how the change in Communist policy influenced audience figures. The theatre lost the support of some on the left and in particular those associated with the *Tribune*, from the columns of which the Communist Party was accused of aiming for civil war and the military defeat of Britain.

Although the Communist Party was the political organisation principally associated with anti-war sentiments, such views were not confined to party members, either at Unity or in other left-wing theatres. In Manchester, for example, the police stopped a tour of Theatre of Action's Living Newspaper *Last Edition* because its final scene depicted the war as a class war and said the workers' real enemy was at home; this was the current Communist line, although the leaders of the group had left the party five years earlier and were often at odds with the local party committees.

The pact radically changed the political climate so that it was never the same again, yet, despite the ideological differences that beset Unity thereafter, it managed to hold on to much of its support while the Soviet Union stayed out of the war.

Black-out Revues

For most Unity activists, the overriding aim was to get the theatre open as soon as possible and to mount new shows. Nothing was possible until the ban on theatres had been lifted, which for those outside the central London radius happened nearly two weeks into the war when they were allowed to open until 10 p.m. under certain conditions. Unity lay just clear of this radius and, in the middle of the row over the Nazi-Soviet pact, immediately began assembling a revue which was to be called *Sandbag Follies*.

There were many practical difficulties to overcome. The Kingsway Theatre's rent had to be paid and Unity's finances were in complete chaos, which angered Emile Burns at the Communist Party centre who had to help sort out the mess and tackle an argument about what had happened to money made by *Babes in the Wood*. Personnel had dispersed, including the missing secretary who was not to be seen again, and members could not be contacted, both because address lists had been destroyed or removed and because there was no money to issue circulars to those whose whereabouts were known. Instead, a press conference was held at which Unity announced that it would be the first theatre nearest to central London to reopen since the declaration of war and that it would present a new show in three days' time.

An advertisement in the *Daily Worker* asked active members to contact the theatre, and as many Unity people as possible were visited or telephoned. Anyone who could be reached came and helped, old and newcomers alike – Alfie Bass, Una Brandon-Jones, Mary Carr, Jimmy Gibb, Doris Levenson, Bill Owen, Randall Swingler, Roger Woddis and Barnet 'Doggie' Woolf, a scientist who came to specialise in animal genetics and who was responsible for much of the material that went into the show, a lot of which was taken from pieces that had been written already at the summer school. Well known band leader van Phillips auditioned people and wrote much of the music for the production. Songs from *Babes in the Wood*, like 'Love on the Dole', were added, with two sketches from the proposed Parsons-Fase-Mitchell Kingsway revue and some variety turns.

The show was rehearsed as it was being typed up; often the first that a performer knew of a sketch was a sheet of paper thrust into his or her hand just as he or she was about to go on stage. Bill Owen, who knocked it all into some sort of shape as writer, producer and compère, remembers falling back on his skills as a holiday camp entertainer. At one point he told the audience 'You know as much about this as I do,' and assured them jokingly that actors 'carrying bits of paper' were not holding scripts but trying to put out incendiaries. He recalls the show costing 6s 9d, which was the price of a tin of black-out paint.

The revue opened on 19 September 1939. It was an 'anti-jitter' show, debunking the rhetoric of a compromised government which was exhorting the population to fill sandbags and put them over lower windows as protection against bombs. The opening number arrived not long before curtain up. It was written by Woolf and van Phillips using the pseudonyms Arthur Pooley and John Berry:

Bread and cheese are going up in price,
We can't live on turnips and rice;
Everyone is saying in the country and the town
'Make them put the wages up
And bring the prices down.'
Fags are up, glad rags are up and ARP sand bags are up;
Neville said no profiteering,
But Neville sold us all a pup, pup, pup, pup.[3]

The show challenged official secrecy and bureaucracy, and satirised life in the blackout, at work and in the army. One sketch, attacking the drive for increased production through time and motion studies, had the tag line of the harassed worker (Alfie Bass): 'Yes, and if you give me a broom to put up my arse, I'll sweep the bloody floor for you!' Another, 'Pay Parade', was played throughout the war:

OFFICER: Private Jones, according to your pay account the position is as follows: barrack damages 3 shillings, voluntary attachments 4 shillings, company distress fund 6 pence, by Royal Warrant one day's pay 3 shillings, regimental fund …
JONES (*interrupting*): Here you are sir, take this tanner and call it quits.

The attitude to war was clear:

There'll be tin hats and brass hats and uniforms galore
But the brass hats sit where the bombs can't hit
While the tin hats win the war.

Yet the war was worth fighting;

We are the men of Britain; we toil and sweat and fight.
In our life's blood is written the tale of Britain's might.
This time we won't be bitten; we know for what we fight.

Nevertheless, there was a pub scene in which two workers argue the Soviet viewpoint. Attitudes to the war remained a source of friction, especially as Britain was standing alone against Hitler, however ineffectually, without the backing of any major power. It was difficult to attack Chamberlain's 'phoney war' against fascism while at the same time supporting the anti-imperialist war position. After the *Royal Oak* was sunk in October, Unity agreed at Harry Pollitt's suggestion to alter a line in *Sandbag Follies* that referred to Chamberlain hitting Hitler 'with a feather'.

Most of the show was on surer ground: a Noel Coward parody (two aristocrats determined to help win the war, but 'it is such a frightful bore'), for example, or a skit on Odets called 'Waiting for Lucy', which was played in three different ways, showing that Unity could laugh at itself; the first style mimicked a West End presentation, the second a modern, constructivist staging and the third Unity's own production values, with no money to spend on the show and no props. Characters such as Wally the Warden from Wandsworth or the man from the Ministry of Malformation, who always interrupts the compère, were introduced in between sketches. Songs like van Phillips's 'When Peace will come to Primrose Hill' were popular or 'Hungry Blues' sung by Doris Levenson with her distinctive deep strong voice that was to become synonymous with Unity's wartime entertainment. Some songs were witty – 'The Old School Tie's Gone Red', for instance – and some were sentimental – 'An Air Raid Shelter for Two'.

Sandbag Follies was raw but full of energy, and, like *Babes in the Wood*, it was Unity's own. It ran for a month to practically full houses despite the black-out. *The March of Time* newsreel reviewer even preferred it to *Babes in the Wood* while *Drama* found that it had 'neither point, wit, nor subtlety'.

Tiredness and continuing confusions caused by the change in the Communist Party attitude to the war brought the show to a close,[4] but the management committee, with its new secretary R. Vernon Beste, was determined to keep the theatre going, although he had to sack the paid staff because Unity could not afford the wages bill. Vernon Beste, who had worked at Goldington Street since helping to build the new theatre, was the only senior Unity member left from a group that had been set up to run the theatre in time of war. He was agreed as secretary by the Communist Party without opposition.

It was decided to stage another revue which would be better prepared than *Sandbag Follies* and more skilfully produced. The revue format was preferred because it allowed for swift changes in personnel and material whereas the 'straight' plays that Unity might perform needed a stable cast to rehearse for a fairly long period of time. It was also felt that for the moment entertainment with a point was more likely to win audiences and new recruits to Unity than the social realism of plays like *Colony* or *Harvest in the North*. There is no evidence to suggest that this approach was determined by the Nazi-Soviet pact, though the prevailing political climate, in which the pact played a major part, was obviously crucial. (The theatre was not affected by the pact in the same way as the cinema. According to one veteran, the anti-fascist film *Professor Mamlock* was withdrawn from distribution by Kino on Soviet orders.[5])

The new revue, *Turn Up the Lights*, opened in November, two weeks before the Soviet Union invaded Finland. It took its title from George Bernard Shaw, then aged 83, who had said that the black-out was unnecessary because Nazi bombers could find their targets by radar. The first number in the show was sung in the dark with the cast waving torches:

> We can make a start
> Tear the veil apart
> Turn up the lights.[6]

The main themes were continued from *Sandbag Follies* and some songs, like 'Fags are Up', were included again; the 'phoney war' was exposed and in the show's twenty scenes the political manoeuvring behind the smokescreen of a war effort was attacked. Unity boasted that it was the first theatre since the time of Euripides to challenge government war policy during a war. Characters from *Babes in the Wood* were revived to satirise censorship; the Babes were now the people, being kept in the dark deliberately by the government. Through glancing reference, this sketch also makes fun of the TUC owned newspaper the *Daily Herald* and of Leon Trotsky (who was living in exile in Mexico with less than a year to live). Both were linked to the Fairy Wishfulfilment's propaganda campaign that was designed to hide the 'real' situation. Another sketch, 'Nothing but the Truth', amplifies this theme, revealing the distortions of the media, while another shows that war means 'Business as Usual' for a scrap merchant. The most successful aspect of *Turn up the Lights* however, was its songs, many of which became favourites in the movement. The main thrust of the revue was typified in 'The

Profiteer's Song' by Woolf and van Phillips, which was sung by the concert bass Martin Lawrence.

> I'm a simple sort of fellow, with nothing to conceal –
> I dabble a little in sandbags, in butter or in steel;
> And as I wend my wealthy way, one thing I learn is true
> There's one eternal Golden Rule, the profits come from *you*!

Another Woolf-van Phillips hit, 'Ladies in Uniform', lampooned upper-class women slumming it in the forces and a third, 'Old Age Pensioners', which was sung many times in the war, was particularly apt as the government had just announced cuts in home spending to help finance the 'phoney war' effort. 'A Lullaby' contrasted the way in which the war affected a working woman with a baby, a rich woman with a Pekinese dog, a banker nursing his money bags and Chamberlain nursing to sleep the Labour politician Arthur Greenwood (who was to join the war Cabinet) as a friend 'paid to appear to oppose'. A song by Parsons and Fase from the Kingsway revue, 'Brother, Brother,' also became well-known, and like 'The Profiteer's Song', 'The Old Age Pensioners' and 'Ladies in Uniform' was published by the Workers' Music Association. 'Brother, Brother', sung by Martin Lawrence, was recorded by Topic Records and the words were printed as 'Prelude and Song' in the magazine *Poetry and the People*. The show's finale was appropriately rousing with echoes of Shelley:

> Here we come!
> We've left our woes behind us
> The Chains that bind us
> Are breaking.
> Here we come!
> We want to build a new world
> This old and blue world forsaking.

Bill Owen directed again, with many of the *Sandbags Follies* team in the cast as well as some newcomers. The programme told patrons that 'Air-raid shelters are situated in the cemetery and the trenches opposite the theatre, and in Bass's warehouse, St Pancras Way.'

A second edition of *Turn Up the Lights* was produced in February 1940 to give the show new life and keep it in shape. The order was changed, with 'Brother, Brother' becoming the finale, some items were dropped, like the *Babes* sketch, and new material was added; in homage to the Bard, 'The Witches' War Aims' joined 'Sir Hamlet Anderson' (a reference to the man officially responsible for ARP) and 'The Pressmen of England' (by Parsons and Fase) was taken from the Kingsway revue to join 'Nothing but the Truth' in exposing the media. Four journalists are reduced to drinking, smoking and playing cards because:

> We try to do our duty, but we find it very hard,
> Of Empire, home and beauty, almost every subject's barred.

Two other pieces came from the Kingsway revue: 'I Pin My Faith on the Pools' (Mitchell and Fase), and 'Anything Goes in a Song' (Parsons and Fase):

> Why must we sing about love all the time?
> Love's had the music too long!
> You don't have to drag in the moon for a rhyme!
> Anything goes in a song.

Playing the Shelters

The programme advertised Unity's services for touring local shows, offering established successes like *Plant in the Sun* or *Waiting for Lefty*, or entertainments comprising excerpts from such productions with songs and sketches from others, like *Babes in the Wood*. This marked the beginning of what was to be one of Unity's main wartime contributions – the extraordinary work of the Outside Show Group which had links with Unity's 'extra-mural' activities that lay outside of play-producing at Goldington Street, such as the symphony and string orchestra, Unity Singers and Male Voice Choir, play competitions and the social events, such as the weekly dances.

Unity's energy had flowed from *Babes in the Wood* into *Sandbag Follies* and *Turn Up the Lights*, creating a new band of stalwarts with an expertise in revue. They set up their headquarters in Britannia Street, which reopened on 21 January 1940 for rehearsals, weekend try-outs, visiting shows and bazaars – a standard feature of any self-supporting organisation. (The fourth anniversary bazaar in 1941 received a good deal of publicity, for no apparent reason: there was a fair that included a Bearded Lady, the Fattest Woman in the World and the Original Aryan, old time music hall, a puppet show and three variety shows.)

Later, the Outside Show Group, renamed the Mobile Group, moved to 9 Newport Street. Towards the end of 1943 there were moves to wind up the group, as it was thought by Unity's leadership to be too independent of Goldington Street, and soon it became the Variety Group. The outside work became intermittent but continued and throughout the war Unity presented more than 1,000 such performances, providing a bridge from pre-war Unity, as well as continuity through the 1940s, and playing a crucial role in helping Unity to survive.

Unity had written to local councils and the government urging them to provide evacuation and shelter entertainment, and offering Unity as a centre for such activities. The only reply came from the local borough council which thought that its citizens would prefer to sleep in the shelters rather than be entertained there. Unity disagreed and had to proceed on its own, which was nothing new, but nobody was very sure how to.[7] There were personal contacts with shelter committees that were being formed but nothing like the formal relationships that had applied when Unity had been booked to take out shows in the past. Unity activists were having to learn how to make contact with a new audience all over again, just as when the theatre had started.

Ann Davies, who had played an outstanding Robin in *Babies in the Wood*, wrote in a Unity Bulletin in August 1940, under the suitable title of 'London After Dark', about the breakthrough of the Outside Show Group, then run by Dave Abrahams.

> The first effort was at Tilbury ... an enormous goods yard on the edge of the East End where up to 15,000 people bed down every night. We had contacted a few friends there, and they promised to prepare things for us. We threaded our way in, stepped over legs, bundles, prams, past stacks of margarine boxes, round trucks and carts and initially settled on some bales of paper. There wasn't much light and nobody knew how to start. Then the guitar began to strum and community singing was started. It went over quite well, but there was something wrong. When we went over it afterwards we decided that we couldn't tackle the job merely as 'Unity Theatre doing shows'; we must become a part of the organisation of the shelter committees, and our work must harmonise with theirs, and help with their activities. So when a call came for a show over the weekend, I got down to the job of contacting

> the committee to find out what was wanted, and under what conditions we should be expected to work …
>
> Sunday came and six of us set off again to Belsize Park [underground station]. We arrived too early. We went out for a cup of coffee, so that we wouldn't be cluttering up the place before they were ready for us. We had a very narrow shave when the back of the café was blasted when several bombs fell just behind it. But we finished the coffee and hurried back to the Tube … They were anxious to forget the horrors outside and were ready for anything … We had to ask people to squash even closer together and allow us to pile up on their rugs and coats. They very readily did this and off we went. 'Swanee River', 'John Brown's Body', 'Roll out the Barrel', etc., got them interested … prepared the way for a couple of sketches, solos, songs and jokes. Ten minutes at one end of the platform, and finally a show at each end of the liftshafts. Even when these items had to be done sideways on, with occasional trains roaring through, they went over big, and the crowd was almost as pleased as we were.

The use of tube stations as shelters had been forbidden – from the outset of war, the tube trains had been kept running. After the first air raid on London in mid-august 1940, people ignored this ruling and, as in the First World War, they bought the lowest price ticket and stayed on the platforms until the 'all clear'. The London district of the Communist Party agitated for the tubes to be opened up as shelters, which led to police raids on the party offices and bookshops. Following the nightly bombing of the capital from early September, a mass civil disobedience campaign grew in defiance of the police who guarded the gates of tube stations. As the sirens sounded, thousands of people forced their way in and down to the platforms; by the end of the month 79 tube stations were being used as shelters; by October, the government had accepted the situation and began to organise sleeping, sanitary and refreshment facilities; in November, the government acceded to another Communist demand and announced that tunnelling would begin to extend the deep shelters. The tubes continued to be used for shelter after the Blitz had finished.

At one of the first tube shows, in October 1940, a casualty was brought in while the station was being shaken by explosions. Unity members helped distribute cocoa and performed six shows. Unity had to entertain against the noise of both trains and audience, who were usually stretched out in a long thin line on the narrow platforms. Mostly all that Unity managed to achieve was something akin to mobile busking, although on one occasion the

Outside Show Group performed a full-length show of revues and sketches on an improvised stage to an audience seated on chairs in an unfinished tunnel extension.

Results were also mixed at other venues. One trip to the enormous railway arches at Stepney, East London, which provided refuge for hundreds, ended abysmally as Unity players could not complete with the murmur of conversation, the smell, the snoring, coughing and wailing of children. Unity could, however, fill the Grand Palais, a centre of Yiddish theatre on the Commercial Road in East London, but at the cavernous town hall in Staines only six people turned up to watch. There could also be unwelcome attention; one night a Unity actor was stopped for questioning on his way home after a performance. In his bag he had a German uniform that he wore in a sketch, but his explanation was not believed and he was taken in by the policemen who thought him to be one of the much-feared Nazi parachutists who were supposed to be dropping on Britain at any moment.

Shows for labour movement or left-wing organisations had to offer entertainment with political bite whereas in shelters the performers had to rely on creating an immediate rapport with an audience who had not chosen to be entertained. Unity had to become popular in the simplest meaning of the word and songs were usually the key, like, for example, 'The Landlord's Song' by Woolf and van Phillips which was recorded by Topic Records with Alfie Bass singing.

> So pity the downtrodden landlord,
> And his back that is burdened and bent,
> Respect his grey hairs, don't ask for repairs
> And don't be behind with the rent.[8]

Also popular was Randall Swingler's poem '60 Cubic Feet', which comments on the restrictions of body and soul throughout life and in death by examining the minute area allowed a miner from birth to the grave. A sketch that had general appeal (and could be endlessly updated) showed a radio listener trying to tune the set and receiving three different stations cutting into each other; the BBC, the American NBC, and the fascist propagandist Lord Haw-Haw, all giving differing accounts of the same events or producing unintentionally amusing effects through the dovetailed dialogue.

A favourite joke with the shelter audiences told of an old man who was rescued from his council flat after it had been bombed. He is found smiling. 'What's the joke, grandad?' asks one of the rescue team. 'These blasted jerry-built places,' he replies. 'You goes into the little room, pulls the chain and the whole bloomin' lot collapses over yer 'ead.'

Unity became very skilful at pitching its shows to an audience's requirements and giving them a comforting sense of having had their own feelings expressed. People would join in songs, laugh at political jokes and often organise their own entertainment after a Unity visit.

Unity was in even greater demand after the Nazis attacked the Soviet Union in 1942 and the Communist Party backed the war effort. Shows would then either begin or end with a Soviet song or an item related to the Soviet Union – for example the mass declamation *Homage to Vatutin* (a Soviet general), a Living Newspaper, *Russia's Glory: The Red Army*, or a 'dramatic presentation' showing how Russian women aided their men. National songs and dances from occupied Europe were also performed. Factory bookings came pouring in and the range of venues at which Unity performed expanded rapidly, from the St Pancras Hospital near Goldington Street and the Royal Mint, where the actors had to sleep overnight among shining new coins, to the High Wycombe camps for the homeless and the luxury Duchess of Bedford flats that were being squatted in after the war. Unity played at rest centres in civil defence depots, in parks, barracks and canteens, at Second Front rallies, Aid for Russia meetings, Royal Ordnance hostels for munitions workers, and at National Fire-fighting Service stations, often performing three shows a day in quick succession. Sometimes, Unity played through the night – war had ended unemployment and large factories worked round the clock. Bill Owen remembers one visit in Greenford where they stayed for 24 hours to give performances to every shift. At one aircraft factory, a Unity visit organised by the women's shop stewards committee resulted in a rise in production of 10 per cent on the second half of the shift. It was the time of 'Music While You Work' and Unity's contribution was to sing songs with lines like 'We're turning out tanks for Russia'. The repertoire was huge: excerpts from *The Taming of the Shrew*, O'Casey's *A Pound on Demand*, old time music hall numbers such as 'The Houses in Between', political sketches, mass declamations – like Jack Lindsay's *Salute the Maquis* or Ted Willis's *Gabriel Peri* (foreign editor of the French Communist newspaper *L'Humanité* who was shot in 1941 but had smuggled out of a prison a letter reaffirming his beliefs that was used by anti-facists around the world) – spirituals learned from Paul Robeson records, or compilation shows such as *A Stitch in Time*, which comprised Randall Swingler's play *The Sword of the Spirit* and a revue *A Trip to the Big Store*.

In February 1943, Unity presented at the Scala Theatre in commemoration of the Battle of Jarama an ambitious show called *We Fight On*, the story of the International Brigades. Two scenes – one in a concentration camp in North Africa and one in a Madrid square where people were demonstrating against Franco – were banned by the censor. The slogan for Unity's 'Grand Revue' (a compilation show of highlights) that year was 'Let the people laugh and sing! While fascism feels death's last sting' and during 1943 Unity presented 50 two-hour shows around London, stretching from the industrial wilds of Willesden, Acton and the docks (where credentials had to be checked rigorously at the gates), to local events in different boroughs sponsored by the government's Holidays at Home programme. The Mobile Group played the Scala Theatre again in March 1944, with a compendium show called *Shop Window*.

Bookings were received also from the forces, sometimes when they were fed up with what ENSA – Entertainments National Service Association – was offering. In one huge hall on a thick foggy night, the Army Pay Corps greeted Unity with loud cheers because most of the professional entertainers on the bill had failed to turn up. At a Canadian camp, it took the Unity performers a little while to overcome the shock of discovering some way into the show that the audience was entirely French-speaking, while at US bases, where the attraction was eating food that was unobtainable elsewhere, Unity had to play to segregated audiences. One way of making a political point in these circumstances was to sing songs like 'Strange Fruit' about lynching in the South, or a song like 'It Ain't Necessarily So' from *Porgy and Bess* and to tell the white audience that it came from a black opera (or 'all-negro' as it was called then).

Throughout the war, Goldington Street acted as a social centre for those on leave or for visiting foreign servicemen and women who were looking for a place to discuss politics, see a politically orientated show or relax. Unity members who were in the armed forces were sent the Unity newsletter the *Call* and they carried on their peacetime activities, staging shows, holding and attending classes in Marxism and participating in political debate such as in the forces' parliaments which prefigured the result of the 1945 General Election. Unity bulletins carried letters from around the world where British forces were fighting, detailing such events and bringing news back home to complement the popular forces page in the *Daily Worker*. Theatrical activity in the armed forces was widespread; army groups even affiliated to the British Drama League and the army education syllabus recommended *Waiting for Lefty*.

The Army Bureau of Current Affairs, founded in 1941 to provide the military with an educational service, set up a Play Unit in 1943 which presented several notable productions and included on its small staff of writers Jack Lindsay, Ted Willis and André van Gyseghem, all of whom were closely associated with Unity.[9] The unit's leader, Major Michael Macowan, later drama director of the Arts Council, approached the Unity people because of the theatre's experience in propaganda and Living Newspapers. Along with Miles Tomalin, who had worked with Unity and the Left Book Club Theatre Guild, Bridget Boland, Stephen Murray and Macowan – all of whom had been involved with anti-establishment theatrical ventures before the war – they formed the core of a team that perhaps not surprisingly Churchill had investigated for political bias. ABCA's Play Unit also drew on the services of the Indian Communist writer Mulk Raj Anand, another Unity associate, and J.B. Priestley, who joined Unity's general council, as well as building on Unity's years of playing in 'non-theatre' venues. In its first six months, the unit had performed 58 shows to 20,000 troops in a variety of locations, from nissen huts and NAAFI canteens to gun sites. (Unity's influence on this type of work can be seen in a compilation show *Drama Documentary*, devised by Andrew Campbell after the war, in which extracts from such plays, including, for example, *Busmen*, are presented together.[10])

O'Casey's 'The Star Turns Red'

Problems at Goldington Street were dire but the repertoire, however, curtailed, included bold ventures – none more so than the show to follow *Turn Up the Lights*, the world première of Sean O'Casey's *The Star Turns Red*, a play that would have made most theatres, professional or non-professional, run for cover. O'Casey, a member of Unity's general council, had been working on the play for some time when he finished it in the summer of 1939. He revised it again after war was declared and later after it had been performed.[11] He offered the play to Unity free of royalty.

Like a medieval morality play, *The Star Turns Red* is an allegory of the fight between two opposing forces, Fascism and Communism, in which O'Casey not only traces the dialectic of the struggle but presents the victory of the workers' revolution. It is a fantasia, set on 'Christmas Eve, tomorrow or the next day', moving stylistically from realism to expressionism, from colloquial dialogue to rhetorical free verse. Throughout the play a silver star is seen in the background by a church spire; on the other side of the stage can be seen foundry chimneys.

The play opens in the home of an old man and woman – the working people whose support is vital for whichever side is to succeed. Their two sons ('always at each other's throats for the sake of a slogan') can only agree on the need to kill each other. Kian, the younger, has joined the fascist Saffron Shirts while the elder Jack is a supporter of the Communists who are led by the workers' leader Red Jim. The fascists and the Communists are preparing for final battle. The Lord Mayor, the Purple Priest and the Saffrons' leader visit the home to pronounce an end to Communist heresy. In the process they have Julia, who is to marry Jack, whipped because she slapped the fascist leader after he had called her a 'painted pansy' for wearing a bright pierrette dress which she had put on for a fancy dress dance. Her father, Michael, one of Red Jim's activists, rushes at the fascist and is shot dead by Kian.

As the Lord Mayor is trying to finish preparations for a victory ball to celebrate the complete seizure of power by the fascists, a bugle call signals a general strike. Factory hooters sound and the silver star turns red. Armed workers arrive to make the Mansion House their headquarters and the final battle takes place to the ballet music of the Russian composer Glazounov; Jack is killed and Kian, with a white flag, comes to the body, stunned by his brother's death.

RED JIM: We fight on; we suffer; we die; but we fight on.
Till brave-breasted women and men, terrac'd with strength,
Shall live and die together, co-equal in all things;
And romping, living children, anointed with joy,
Shall be banners and banneroles of this moving world!
In all that great minds give, we share;
And unto man be all might, majesty, dominion, and power!

The priest of the poor, the Brown Priest, who up until now had been used by the Purple Priest to help subjugate the people, changes sides and stands with Red Jim. News comes that the soldiers are joining the workers; Julia, in her green and black pierrete dress, raises a clenched fist and everyone sings the 'Internationale' except Kian who is gazing into his dead brother's face.

The play, dedicated to the 'men and women who fought through the Great Dublin Lock-out in 1913' sweeps and swirls in a curious blend of allusions and heightened moments. O'Casey draws on the streets of Dublin and the fight against the blueshirt fascists in Ireland but there is also an abstract evocation of Germany in 1933 when Hitler took power and a hint of Mosley with the flash on his insignia. Lain over this frame is reference to the backing of fascism by the Catholic hierarchies of Ireland, Spain and Italy, which is thrown into relief by suggestions of the Spanish Civil War and more prominently the battles of the Soviet Union; the storming of the Winter Palace, Lenin in the Smolny Institute, and the civil war with the White Guards. While trying to appropriate the New Testament for the proletarian cause, O'Casey's language also reverberates with Shelley and workers' songs as if in conscious tribute to an agitational tradition of left-wing art. *The Star Turns Red* is an extraordinary conceit, essentially a personal poetic statement of belief rather than reasoned argument or an intellectual analysis.

These are not real Communists, trade unionists, priests or fascists, and they are not meant to be. In Red Jim can be found elements of the younger Larkin, the great Irish trade union leader of the lock-out and of O'Casey's acquaintance, but – the name aside – such references would be meaningless to any but an Irish audience of a particular generation. In the play he stands, somewhat awkwardly, as a symbol: in contradiction to the play's basic premiss, he becomes an indispensable and idolised hero, a Communist Christ figure, rather than a leader of and with the people. Similarly, O'Casey wills the workers' revolution to be a carnival but he knows that the price in human terms is the highest that anyone can ever pay. Jim's final words to Julia, referring to the dead Jack, close the play: 'He fought for life, for life is all; and death is nothing!'

A Unity member, writing in the *Daily Worker*, described the play as 'the greatest thing we ever attempted' and it is O'Casey's most extreme, ambitious work, written in the heat of his own conversion to Communism. But there were many discussions at Unity before it was agreed to stage the play. Frank Lesser, who had been a political commissar in Spain and who was put into Unity by the Communist Party to oversee its internal disputes, remembers a meeting with several other leading members of the theatre that lasted for 36 hours during which time the play was dissected and its merits argued against those of other plays on offer. From O'Casey's correspondence, it can be seen that it took him even longer (from August to December 1939) to allow Unity the right to present his play. He was visited by Unity members, like Jack Selford, who put the theatre's reservations to him.[12]

There was concern over its general line; the Popular Front approach had called for alliances with all democrats in the fight against fascism and not an insistence on workers' revolution. Failure to make such a distinction had contributed to the disaster of Hitler's coming to power in the first place. There was worry at the play's attitude to trade unions, to the church – the left had being trying to combat anti-clericalism in order to win this broad unity – and at the role of Julia, the play's heroine, who is seen at first as being rather 'free' in her attitude to sex. (She mocks a Catholic flag-wagger Joybell, a member of a confraternity, who can't stop looking at her when she is dressed only in a petticoat, bodice, stockings and shoes, finally kissing him 'madly till she is breathless and frightened'.)

Nevertheless, *The Star Turns Red* went ahead, a decision that was not only daring artistically but politically too, because in March 1940 when the play opened, the Nazi-Soviet pact and the

Soviet war with Finland had changed many people's attitudes to Communists quite sharply.

Unity debts had to be settled first, which was achieved by prominent supporters, such as Sidney Bernstein, the solicitor W.H. Thompson, and Stafford Cripps donating £100 each. An appeal was issued to fund the O'Casey play, which received generous backing (though not from Bernard Shaw). Directors were interviewed and John Allen was welcomed back to Unity to work with Alan Bush as composer, Louise Soelberg as choreographer (the *Busmen* team) and Lawrence Gowing as designer. In one letter, O'Casey pays tribute to Gowing's impressive constructivist set, which was built from timber that was brought over from the Kingsway Theatre. The design apparently opened the author's eyes to the influence in the play of the spire, the chimney and the star.

Allen remembers the production as a triumph for British amateur theatre and not just for Unity, which had approached the British Drama League and other amateur groups in order to cope with the huge numbers required – double casts were still being used. (The programme thanks the British Drama League, Toynbee Hall, the Midland Bank Dramatic Society and the Company of Ten.) Sadly, O'Casey was too ill in Devon to attend rehearsals (which began with a half-hour warm-up and particular attention paid to voice work). He appointed an artistic 'minder', Peter Newmark, a student at Trinity College, Cambridge, where O'Casey had lectured, who had helped persuade O'Casey to let Unity stage the play. He had to watch over the production and to report back to O'Casey on the proceedings.

Just as commentators on O'Casey's work have rarely liked the play, the newspaper critics attacked it too. Ashley Dukes paid the theatre a back-handed compliment by blaming Marxism for making 'failure after failure in putting individual plays' on Unity's stage yet, 'success upon success in presenting its view of the world in topical revues and pantomimes'. Stephen Spender, who had rapidly become politically disillusioned after leaving the Communist Party, found *The Star Turns Red* negative, 'a play with characters who exist only as symbols to expound on morality'. Shaw, however, compensated for his financial abstinence by writing to O'Casey that the play 'shewed up the illiteracy of the critics, who didn't know that like a good Protestant you had brought the language of the Authorised version back to life. Splendid!' The play received a rave review from an unexpected quarter – O'Casey's previous adversary, James Agate, whom John Allen remembers in the Unity foyer at the interval arguing furiously against Communism. He was moved to write in the *Sunday Times*:

> Mr O'Casey's play is a masterpiece ... a magnum of compassion *and* a revolutionary work ... No Shavian nonsense here, whereby the protagonists, in this case meaning antagonists, put their knees under the mahogany and obligingly put each other's cases ... The most vital theatre in London is to be experienced in a back-street theatre in Kings Cross.

John Lehmann, in *New Writing for Europe*, describes *The Star Turns Red* as 'the most impressive of all Unity's productions'.

Unity wanted to enter the third act of *The Star Turns Red* in the Welwyn Garden City Festival but discovered that the Lord Chamberlain had banned the play from public performance because he did not like its theme – a view shared by the New York office of O'Casey's publishers, Macmillan, which refused to have it printed. (Unity entered for the festival instead a poor rendering of Toller's *A Man and a Woman*.)

The Star Turns Red brought Unity up against another kind of authority. One of the volunteer cast from another amateur group was a policeman who brought with him to rehearsal a rifle which he had purchased from a sale at the old Stoll studios. It was needed for the production to complement rifles that had been used in *Bury the Dead* and other shows and which had been carried over to Goldington Street from Britannia Street. A local superintendent heard about this stockpiling of arms by the Communists and interviewed Unity's secretary Vernon Beste, who readily confessed to the existence of the policeman's rifle, which, he assumed, was the reason for the visit, but it turned out to be a useless German relic from the First World War. He did not think to tell the superintendent about the rack of other rifles, wrongly believing them to be harmless guns used as props. The superintendent reported their discovery to Scotland Yard's firearms branch and told Vernon Beste that possession of each rifle was worth two years in gaol. A compromise was reached and the rifles were taken to a gunsmith after the production.

When *The Star Turns Red* came off, the Nazis had occupied France, Hitler had put an end to the 'phoney war' and Churchill had replaced Chamberlain as Prime Minister. The two casts of the production wrote to O'Casey.

> In these very difficult times it will have been running continuously for over 85 performances. That Unity has been able to do this is due to the greatness of your play, and the two casts wish to tell you how much they have enjoyed performing it.
>
> It has given them a great opportunity to take part in the production of a poetic masterpiece which represents a new step forward in the development of our drama, and which has widened our understanding and quickened our enthusiasm at a time when so many other means of expression are closed to us. We are under no illusions that we amateurs can do full justice to the quality of this magnificent play, but we have done everything that hard work, enthusiasm and sincerity can do.[13]

Despite the problems of the war, Unity remained determined, although it could not mount again a production as ambitious as the O'Casey. Hit hard by the call-up, the management placed an advertisement on the front page of the *Daily Worker* for sixteen men before it could proceed with its next production, which was of a finely detailed play called *Distant Point* by the Soviet writer Alexander Afinogenov who died only a year later in an air raid. The play was originally turned down by Unity, because of the poor translation of it which appeared in an American magazine, but Unity found acceptable a version by Hubert Griffith, author of the Unity show *The People's Court*, that had been performed in 1937 at the Gate Theatre. *Distant Point* is a well constructed piece of socialist realism using a naturalistic technique that shows considerable maturity. A Red Army general, whom it is revealed is dying of cancer, is held up by accident at a railway station in a remote Siberian village. His temporary presence there becomes the catalyst for a debate about human values, life and death, comradeship and dedication to the revolutionary cause. The general is asked a haunting question by a renegade priest, 'why do people fear death?'[14] The answer comes later in the play with the general's inscription in a book: 'We have only one Distant Point, a world in which all men shall live their lives in freedom and happiness. We all think of that, live for that – to the very last second of our last hour. And when death comes – why we'll all die alive.' Afinogenov shows ordinary Soviety people in a way that was then rarely seen in Britain (a situation that changed little in the subsequent four decades). He caught their ability to laugh at

The Soviet Union was not yet in the war when Unity staged this naturalistic Russian play by Alexander Afinogenov

themselves, to be prey to foibles as well as great passions, to be loyal and also selfish, and this undercut both the heroic image of perfect Bolsheviks that was frequently found on the left and the negative view of enslaved automatons promoted by the right. Afinogenov reveals a more complex picture. The play was performed during the Battle of Britain at a time when the government had forbidden strikes and was moving against the Communist Party because of its anti-war line. *Distant Point* was not very well reviewed, with some notable exceptions such as James Agate again, who by this time had joined Unity's general council, and Nancy Cunard in *Our Time*, who called it 'a page of reality out of Russia'.

Distant Point was designed by Rivka Black and directed by Eric Capon who had taught at a German refugee school in South-East England in the 1930s where he and the students had built their own theatre and played an avant-garde continental repertoire. He had attended Herbert Marshall's classes and assisted him on *Colony* before directing *Distant Point*, a play that he was to choose for his first production at the Citizens Theatre, Glasgow, when he became a joint resident producer just after it had been re-opened in 1943. That year, he published a four-part series on 'A Marxist Approach to the Theatre' in *Our Time*, a cultural magazine founded in 1941 with a similar editorial policy (and many of the same contributors) as the now defunct *Left Review* and likewise associated with the Communist Party. He was also briefly the artistic director of Unity. He directed *Buster* and *Spanish Village* at Unity and the première of Sean O'Casey's *Purple Dust* while at the Liverpool Playhouse, he ran the pre-RADA school and became the first full-time director of drama at the Guildhall School of Music and Drama as well as its deputy principal.

Capon's Unity production of *Distant Point* was reworked by Herbert Marshall a year later at Goldington Street after Hitler had invaded the Soviet Union and the Russians had become a mighty ally. The run of the revival was cut short to allow a professional production by André van Gyseghem to proceed.

'The Match Girls'

As the Battle of Britain raged, the Blitz began, which made it hard for people to get to Goldington Street and for the theatre to function properly. Some were killed making the journey and it was never certain that there would be a cast until the actors turned up – which, on occasion, they did not and replacements had to be found on the spot. Unity, only a quarter of a mile from two main rail termini, was hit four times during the war but it was never closed for long. There was one fatality (at least) when a workman who was undertaking repairs fell off the roof and was killed. Communist Party discipline came to the fore during the bombings and helped Unity survive and adjust to very difficult and changing situations. New routines had to be introduced, like playing only on Fridays, Saturdays and Sundays, or performing in the afternoons to finish early and beat the sirens. A fire-watching rota was started, which meant sleeping in the upstairs office under old blankets with Unity's highly active fleas. Those on official air raid duty could often be seen leaving the theatre in a hurry dressed in their uniforms. Vernon Beste remembers the starlings gathering for migration against the sound of bombing while *The Match Girls* by Robert Mitchell, the next production after *Distant Point*, was being prepared to open. Backstage volunteers were ignoring air-raid warnings and, sustained by sandwiches, were working through the night on the production when the roof was hit. Those who were working in the theatre managed to put out the fires and began emergency repairs. The opening of *The Match Girls* was only delayed by a day and the roof did spring leaks, which, at one afternoon performance, led to the audience watching the show holding umbrellas.

The 'match girls' of the title were unskilled workers in the late nineteenth century at the Bryant and May match factory in London's East End whose dangerous and exhausting work included dipping sticks into crude phosphorous. The 'girls' had to eat at their benches, which were contaminated with phosphorous, and many died of related diseases such as 'phossy jaw' poisoning, and were sacked the moment its symptoms became apparent. One fifteen-year-old girl became bald because she carried trays of matches on her head. They worked a twelve-hour day for an average wage of 5s 6d a week and were subject to fines for unspecified misdemeanours. A weekly socialist paper, the *Link*, attacked the owners, who included Liberal MPs, and three women were sacked for allegedly having talked to the journal. Others were ordered to sign 'contentment' statements and refused. With the help of Annie Besant and Bernard Shaw, the 1,400 who had gone on strike in 1888, demanding union rights and better conditions, won their dispute and founded the Matchmakers' Union. Their victory influenced trade union struggle, particularly among the unskilled and unorganised, through the degree of public support that they won and paved the way for later historic battles such as the dockers' strike of 1911.

Mitchell had roughed out a version of the story in 1938 for the Tavistock Players but had put it aside to produce *Babes in the Wood*. He rewrote it for Unity after many discussions. Much of the research was carried out by Helen Dibley, who visited the factory, libraries, museums and those few survivors she could find. Advertisements were placed in the *Daily Worker* for period costumes and a dress worn by Nellie Farren, a burlesque star of the time, was among those forthcoming for the show, which had in its cast a former suffragette and noted poet Caron Rock, who became something of a Unity institution remembered for her kindness, advice and unerring ability to spot a fake.[15] Mitchell wrote a line for her – 'The rich think the poor *likes* soup' – which became the play's signature.

Mitchell discussed the play with everyone he could find – the repertory committee, the play clinic, the technical staff, the performers – and even sent a script to Shaw. The show's composer, Berkeley Fase, recalls that Shaw did not comment on the play when he returned it but added a scene showing 'a funny bloke in ginger whiskers' arriving in a hansom cab for a strike meeting with Annie Besant (whom Shaw was to use as his model for Raina in *Arms and the Man*; according to some accounts, Shaw paid another tribute to the strikers by drawing on one of their leaders, Kate Slater, for Eliza Doolittle in *Pygmalion*).[16]

The Match Girls, directed by Mitchell and Dave Dawson (who was to turn professional) was a brave attempt to dramatise an important episode of working-class struggle that was said at the time to be the first women's strike and which Engels described as 'the light jostle needed for the entire avalanche to move'. The play was politically appropriate for Unity – working-class self-activity in alliance with members of other classes throwing up working-class leaders who were politically in advance of their middle-class supporters (Annie Besant rejected the idea of the strike at first). Despite its interest as an example of documentary drama history,

The Match Girls lacks form as a play. Mitchell's belief in collective creation meant that he needed more time than he had available for a strong enough play to be devised from the process. The changes in the text came too slowly and too late and the whole enterprise was severely hampered by the Blitz. Sadly, Mitchell was to die in 1942, aged 42, when he went for a swim in the West Country and did not return. *The Match Girls* was revived by Unity in altered versions in 1947 and in 1957, and in 1966 Bill Owen's musical version, with music by Tony Russell, played in the West End.

Mitchell was to contribute to one more Unity show, which opened on the first Sunday afternoon after Christmas in 1940, following a stop-gap run of Old Time Music Hall by the Outside Show Group when *The Match Girls* had finished. Rehearsals for the show, *Jack the Giant Killer*, were interrupted by bombing raids, which robbed the theatre of electricity and for one week forced the company to move to other premises. The new show was a sequel to *Babes in the Wood*, written by the same team of Parsons, Fase and Mitchell, who was using a pseudonym, Peter Quince. The 'second pantomime with a political point', originally planned for Christmas 1939 but now rewritten to support the Communist campaign for a People's Convention, openly attacked capitalism, imperialism and the government's promotion of a false and oppressive freedom.

The People's Convention was a national movement that called for a People's Government to ensure a People's Peace (in place of the current unrepresentative power bloc that included 'Men of Munich', whose appeasement of fascism, it was feared, would lead Britain to suffer the same fate as France and fall to the Nazis).

Jack was the united front against capitalism and fascism. The giant did not really exist but was a convenient bogey that was used to frighten the people into continued subservience. A beanstalk rose at the back of the stage in the form of letters that spelled the words S-O-C-I-A-L S-Y-S-T-E-M which Jack chopped down. The show was an uncompromising celebration of a political position that, through its association with the Communist Party, was then widely unpopular but which still commanded substantial backing.

Act One opens on the village green with the familiar chorus, introductions and jokes:

> DAME: Here we are – pushed here, plagued there, evacuated, drilled, ticketed, docketed, chivvied, worried, frightened, attacked …

BARON MOUTHPIECE: Excuse me –
DAME: Granted!
BARON: Madam, I must remind you that such remarks are calculated to spread alarm and despondence. I shall report *you* ...
DAME: Who the Hammersmith are you anyway? ...
BARON: I'm money power, monopoly. I work everywhere. You can't do anything without me, from fixing the bank rate to appointing a bishop. I'm the man behind the scenes, so –
DAME: Are you a member of this perishing government?
BARON: I'm not in the government – I'm *behind* it![17]

The Dame encourages everyone to 'go to it' and to complain about the state of affairs through union meetings. Two Bad Boys enter, representatives of the TUC and the Labour Party, who are proud to be serving in the wartime Cabinet and aim to do well out of it and to be treated like the Golden Boys of the ruling class which they are bent on helping. The Dame, Jack and Jill attack the Bad Boys in a song (to the tune of 'The Minstrel Song'). After Jack and Jill's duet 'Me Without You' (taken from the unperformed Kingsway revue and used by the Outside Show Group), there comes an attack on the Men of Munich still holding power, which was written as a parody of Tennyson's 'May Queen' (and was printed in *Our Time*):

You must wake and call me early, call me early,
Mother dear,
For the Führer's landing tomorrow and he may
even land right here;
He's sent me a special message, dropped from a
Messerschmidt fighter –
And tomorrow I'll be Gauleiter, Mother, tomorrow
I'll be Gauleiter.

When the Dame decides to sell Daisy (the traditional pantomime cow), she suffers various deductions (accompanied by references to bureaucracy, the Milk Marketing Board and class collaboration) and is left with nothing but beans. Enter Fairy Wishfulfilment's sister, the Home Front Fairy, with verses added or changed as events warranted. She tells Jack that the beans he was given for his mother's cow are fairy beans, but he does not believe her. She waves her wand and the beanstalk grows forming the words 'social system', but he is not going to climb it. 'I don't want to get to the top of the social system – I want to get to the bottom of this giant

Before Communists supported the war effort *Jack the Giant Killer* attacked Churchill's coalition government; programme design by James Boswell

business!' Jack and the chorus sing 'A New World Will Be Born'.

The second act opens at the Baron's Castle, with a chorus and the Dame getting the audience settled, for example with half-time scores in the European finals – The Germans have occupied the pitch and the English have scored one de Gaulle. The Fairy tries to stop Jack slashing at the stalk by threatening him with the giant but all they hear are noises made by Baron Mouthpiece and the two Bad Boys.

JACK: So you *were* the giant all the time!
BARON: Yes, but only the British branch.
JACK: And you two, you are the junior partners, I suppose?
BAD BOY 1: Yes, but the Fairy said we could work our way up.
BAD BOY 2: So we practised our own climbing –
JACK: On the backs of your own workmates? ...
DAME: Strikes me we're the real giant – us and our sort on the other side ...
JACK: We'll form a collective ourselves ... we shall start by setting our own house in order –
DAME: You mean India?
JACK: And the colonies – everywhere ... once the workers decide to shake off their chains, no matter how hard the struggle, nothing can stop the new world being born.

The show ends with refrains of the 'New World' song and others, and the cast and the audience sing the Unity march from *Babes in the Wood* with new verses added.

Jack the Giant Killer, produced (according to the programme) by the Unity Theatre Collective, opened the day of a terrible fire raid on the City and played during the Blitz; it was the first show to be restricted to Saturday and Sunday matinées, although it later played early evenings as well. The programme, designed by the *Left Review* cartoonist James Boswell, said that in the event of an air-raid warning those who wished to could proceed to the local trenches but the show would go on, and it did, to good reviews and full houses for four months – a remarkable achievement in wartime, especially when the prevailing political climate was hostile.

Unity's 'second pantomime with a political point' was a further extension of the Workers' Theatre Movement 'cabaret' tradition and was closely linked to *Babes in the Wood*, both in overt reference and in stylistic development (Baron Mouthpiece, brushing aside demands to open the tube shelters, is carrying on where the Wicked Uncle left off). It was more strident and didactic than *Babes*, explicitly following the line of the Communist Party and *Daily Worker* in openly attacking the Labour Party and TUC for their part in the wartime coalition government. Yet, beyond providing an enjoyable, sustaining and self-fulfilling entertainment for a beleagured political position, its cutting edge clearly left its mark.

Graham Greene, writing in the *Spectator*, preferred it to *Babes in the Wood* and praised in particular the Tennyson parody: 'The strength to non-Communists lies in its humour more than in its idealism; but the idealism, even if we disagree with its details and distrust the blind belief in modern Russia, is young and fresh.' He compared the show favourably to the current Farjeon revue in the West End (which, as it happened, included the original Fairy Wishfulfilment, Vida Hope) and said: 'Unity Theatre is the nearest thing we have to the experimental theatre of New York.'

T.C. Worsley, in the *New Statesman*, found the show 'thoroughly subversive' although he warned that the reader might 'find its political morals pretty murky'. He recognised that the achievement would not have been possible without a permanent theatre and a constant audience and said:

> As so often, the Labour Movement being what it is, the Communists and their fellow travellers are given a clear field when anything enterprising and politically educative needs to be done. So it has been left to them to re-establish, after about a century and a half's neglect, the tradition of political satire on the English stage.

Jack the Giant Killer, which also toured, remained topical, with constantly updated allusions to the issues of the day – the People's Convention, air-raid precautions, the campaign to open the tubes for shelter, the struggle for colonial freedom and the arrival of Hitler's Number Two, Rudolf Hess, who parachuted into Scotland during the play's run. One of the most important events that had to be included was the banning of the *Daily Worker* by the Labour Home Secretary Herbert Morrison. In spite of Communist support for the Nazi-Soviet pact, the party's influence was still strong and throughout 1940 it had caused the government much embarrassment. It had campaigned against Keynes's 'deferred pay' scheme, which was withdrawn; it had campaigned on the seven-day week and the Factory Acts, arguing that munitions output would drop, which was later admitted and the Acts amended; and it had continued its campaign for proper protection, including the successful actions to force the use of tube stations as shelters. The Cabinet threatened to suppress the *Daily Worker* when the paper called for a People's Government in support of the People's Convention. As the movement for a new government took hold nationally, the TUC general council refused the *Daily Worker* admission to the 1940 annual congress, and the Labour Party outlawed the convention as a Communist organisation. A Scottish edition of the paper was launched in November that year and in December there were calls in the Commons for the *Worker* to be banned. The People's Convention met in London in January 1941 and was attended by 2,234 delegates representing 1,304 organisations. The next day, there were twelve regional conferences. One week later, the paper was banned. Unity issued a press statement attacking the ban and Parsons added a couplet to *Jack the Giant Killer*:

> Our press they have banned for the truth in its pages,
> They want to conscript us to force down our wages.

Herbert Morrison (played by Johnny Hewer who was to become well known in television commercials as Captain Birdseye) was lampooned as one of the Bad Boys, the other being the notorious anti-Communist Ernest Bevin (played by Ron Bevan). Parsons recalls that Unity had no actor suitable to play Churchill so Baron Mouthpiece was invented instead (and played by Maurice Sweden who turned professional). As the programme said, 'All the characters are factitious.'

Rehearsals for some of the rewrites were attended by Michael Redgrave, whose contact with the left had been given new impetus by his strong support for the People's Convention and who lent strong backing to Unity. (On one occasion, according to Bram Bootman, the show was helped out by the actress Rachel Kempson, who was married to Redgrave.) The *News Chronicle* plastered Redgrave's name on its front page, attacking him for his beliefs. He was subjected to much abuse in the media and, like other performers who backed the Convention, he was banned by the BBC. (This was lifted after a campaign was mounted in his support and Churchill intervened on his side. Others were less fortunate.[18]) Just after the Convention, Redgrave recorded the pantomime's theme song, 'A New World Will Be Born', which, as with other songs from the show, was also published and sold widely. Another Unity recording was made at this time, of the Fairy Wishfulfilment song, sung by Vida Hope at the Adelphi Theatre for a People's Convention matinée.

Damage to the theatre in the spring of 1941 towards the end of the pantomime's run, when a landmine exploded nearby destroying many neighbouring houses, led to a £500 appeal for a new roof. The money was also to be used to rehouse and re-equip the Mobile Group, and for publicity material to regain access to the labour movement. The roof was re-slated by those involved in the pantomime in order to keep the show going and more substantial repairs were carried out in time for the opening in June of the first English production of Maxim Gorky's *Dostigaeff and the Others* (also known as *And the Others*), the second in a series of three plays on the October Revolution which had begun with *Yegor Bulichev*. (He was never to complete the third play because of his death in mysterious circumstances.) Unity was to perform five Gorky plays, including *Yegor Bulichev* in 1965, before his place in British theatre became associated with the Aldwych productions of the Royal Shakespeare Company. Two of the Unity productions were British premières.

The Eastern Front

Two weeks after the Gorky play opened, Hitler turned his troops on the Soviet Union and changed the course of the war. A trial of strength between the fascists and the Soviet Union was exactly what Chamberlain and the 'Men of Munich' had hoped for, and yet now that it had happened Churchill was attacking it instead of welcoming it. His immediate backing for Stalin brought Unity and the Communist Party into line with the government on the war effort.

This transformed the political situation for the Communist Party and Unity, neither of which had ever found themselves in tune with the government of the day, and it threw up a curious parallel; because the Cabinet's longer-term aim was a return to the pre-war status quo it had to support the Soviet Union and the resistance movements without being seen to support Communism, whereas the Communist Party had to back the war effort run by the government without seeming to back the system. Tensions arose over British-Soviet campaigning, with the government keen to keep the Communist Party on the sidelines in order to minimise its political exploitation of the situation and the Communist Party wishing to maximise its capital in this unusually fertile situation. The problem for the government was that much of the cultural material relating to the Soviet Union that could be used in the nationwide events that were held to celebrate the new alliance were in the hands of the Communist Party or bodies sympathetic to or run by Communists, which took the lead in organising many such activities, often under the umbrella of local government support.

On the industrial front, Communist policy on the need to reorganise and become more efficient coincided with the government's war requirements. This policy now found wide favour, in the absence of initiatives from the quiescent Labour Party and because the reversal of the Communist war position brought its industrial thinking within politically 'acceptable' bounds for many. Communists remained active in industry, especially in engineering, fighting for greater productivity and better conditions, though often in conflict with others on the left who posed workers' control as the prime concern.

Unity's next productions, a revival of *Distant Point* and *This Our World*, seemed to have been presented in a spirit of vindication, implicitly saying that Stalin had been right all along to sign the Hitler pact. The inference was that he had protected the Soviet way of life and had gained a breathing space for the Red Army to prepare for combat (presumably ignoring the decimation in the late 1930s of the Soviet military leadership which left the armed forces seriously ill prepared, accepting the division of Poland in 1939 as necessary to protect the minorities on the Soviet western border, and underestimating the role of nationalism as opposed to political conviction in the defence of the Soviet Union). *This Our World* comprised four short plays: *Hop Pickers* by Norman Bailey (a young man who seems to have passed through Unity quickly) set among town workers harvesting hops for a mean farmer who stand up for their rights; a revival of *The People's Court* (showing the superiority of the Soviet judicial system without any complementary commentary on the gross violations and contempt for legality under Stalin); *According to Plan* by Geoffrey Parsons, which deals with the frustrations and rebellion within the Nazi army on the eastern front as the Red Army approaches; and *Erma Kremer of Ebenstadt* by John Bishop, in which a German woman learns from the Soviet radio that her husband has been killed. A local Nazi threatens her because it is illegal to listen to enemy broadcasts but the family drives him out. As *Frau Kremer of Ebenstadt* (one of several titles), it was performed by the Outside Show Group and F.J. Brown writing in *Our Time* paid tribute to the 'tense hush' and 'electric silence' of a shelter audience engrossed in the play. Also in *Our Time*, Nancy Cunard reviewed *According to Plan* with the same observations on the audience's involvement and identification – its impact was 'little short of devastating emotionally'. *According to Plan* and *Erma Kremer of Ebdenstadt* were published together under the title *The Theatre is Our Weapon* in the Russia Today Society series as part of a drive to persuade labour, and especially Co-operative, movement organisations to stage their own productions. A German version of *Erma Kremer* was performed at Unity as part of a larger revue by the Free German League of Culture (based in Hampstead, North London), an organisation run by German exiles with whom Unity maintained links and at whose own theatre the Mobile Group performed.[19] This was an important act of solidarity in a country where refugees had been interned.

John Bishop was a pen-name for former vehicle builder Ted Willis, who chose it, he says, because it was the name of his closest friend in the army and he wanted to keep his political self separate from his artistic self. His 'political self' was considerable, including being the former leader of the Labour League of Youth who had taken the League out of the Labour Party to join the Young Communists after wrangles with the Labour leadership over Popular Front activities. He had spoken at the People's Convention in battledress and had been thrown out of the army not long after, to become chair of the Young Communist League, editor of its magazine *Challenge* and something of a 'personality' in left-wing circles.[20]

Erma Kremer was his first contact with Unity as a writer. His second was almost his last. He had met Vernon Beste, Unity's secretary, who had complained that no one in Britain was writing about the war. Willis, again using the name Bishop, wrote a play in three days called *Sabotage!* which deals with a British commando raid on an occupied French coastal village to save members of the Resistance who have blown up a bridge that is vital to Nazi transport needs. The Play Department turned it down – poor construction, too simplistic, halting dialogue – but Vernon Beste persuaded the management committee to support it on the grounds that Unity needed plays that were topical and should encourage its own writers. He did not know how topical it was going to be. *Sabotage!* opened the day after a British commando raid on a German radar station at Bruneval, on the French coast just north of Le Havre, and during the play's run there was a raid on St Nazaire when the destroyer *Campbeltown* was exploded in the French port's dock to hamper the movement of the Nazi's huge battleship *Turpitz*.

Sabotage! followed the December 1941 production of Odets's anti-Nazi resistance play *Till the Day I Die* (with John Slater in the lead and an upbeat epilogue by Randall Swingler), which coincided with the German's failure to capture Moscow. A fifth anniversary show had just been mounted at the Scala Theatre and although it was not always certain that there would be a sixth, energy was galvanized by the Soviet rebuff to Hitler and the campaign to launch the second front in Europe to relieve the pressure on the Red Army. This was reflected in the two remaining shows of 1942, *Get Cracking* and *Let's Be Offensive*, and in *Lift the Ban*, a dramatised history of the *Daily Worker*, written by Miles Tomalin and presented at the Scala Theatre just before the paper was allowed to reappear.

Get Cracking opened in June 1942, the same month that the Soviet Union and Britain signed a treaty of friendship, and it focused on war production and backing the Soviet Union. It was a revue comprising nineteen items compiled by Geoffrey Parsons, who was called up five days after the show's opening. Music was by Berkeley Fase (corresponding with Parsons from his RAF camp and rehearsing on leave), Michael Percival and Arnold Clayton, additional lyrics by 'Doggie' Woolf, Michael Percival and Una Brandon-Jones, with closing scenes by Randall Swingler. The show also included Hanns Eisler's 'Solidarity Song' (with the words by Brecht unacknowledged).[12] The programme said that in the revue:

> you'll find all the 'uncareless talk' which may be heard at any factory bench, in any canteen, in any barracks. Unity believes in the theatre as a social force. That is why our revue is entitled 'Get Cracking' – we feel it is the phrase on the lips of the people; we have turned it into a gay revue – with a serious message.

The opening chorus set the tone:

> Oh for that day,
> What a day that will be,
> When the church bells start to ring.
> Hi there neighbour
> Don't stop your labour
> Oh no.
> Oh for that day
> It's Unity on the job.[22]

There were sketches and songs that poked fun at bureaucracy, 'blimps' abroad, the rich, the way the war was being fought (in a football match between Commando Raiders and Brasshat Brigadiers), and at unquestioning obedience ('King Alfred invented blanco to counteract the dangerous habit of thought which had made him burn the cakes'). There was the new theme – all pulling together with the Soviet Union to win the war, as in 'Women in Industry' which the Mobile Group performed a great deal:

> Oh we're turning out tanks for Russia
> At the fastest rate we can;
> We're making frames of aeroplanes
> For the RAF to man.

This new enthusiasm for the war was summed up in the finale, which spanned resistance to fascism around the world.

The politics of *Get Cracking* were much broader than those of *Jack the Giant Killer*. *Daily Herald* journalist Hannan Swaffer and J.B. Priestley, established writer and popular wartime broadcaster who was to join Unity's general council, came on stage on the first night. The show had gone down well, but, as the run went on, it could not keep abreast of events. With the *Daily Worker* back in circulation and Communist Party membership up to 55,000 – almost treble the figure of a year before – a new confidence affected Unity, even in the most testing of situations. Its next show, *Let's Be Offensive*, which was aimed at support for the second front campaign, roared its message loud and clear:

Let's go – get on the attack
Let's go – we're turning them back
Get off the defensive and let's be offensive
And smash our way to victory this year.

Playing during the North Africa drive, the show took its title from a revue presented by Leeds Unity earlier in July, and was directed by Peter Wesley. There were many collaborators behind the twenty sketches and songs, including Honor Arundel, Miles Tomalin, David Martin (later to write a full-length play for Unity), Rogger Woddis, 'Doggie' Woolf and, unattributed, pieces from Parsons and Fase who had both been called up to different RAF camps. One of their sketches, 'Trouble at Tussauds', has the inhabitants of the Chamber of Horrors objecting to the presence of Hitler. Another unattributed item called 'The Nazi's Wife' was a poem by Brecht, written in America at the end of the previous year, which became one of his best known songs under its full title of 'The Song of the Nazi Soldier's Wife'.[21] The programme also included a favourite Outside Show Group sketch, 'Pay Parade', and a song written by Roger Woddis for Bill Owen, 'You Too Can Have a Body Like Mine', which became one of his most popular numbers.

Despite the new-found political enthusiasm that accompanied the campaign to open the Second Front, times were hard at Goldington Street. The first production of 1943 came from outside as a 'filler' and comprised two short pieces: the first was Arthur Arent's Living Newspaper *One Third of a Nation*, adapted to wartime conditions using mass observation techniques by Margaret Leona, who had worked closely with Unity in the 1930s, and by the director and teacher Suria Magito, a Unity supporter to whom Michael Saint-Denis was married. The second was Thornton Wilder's comedy *The Happy Journey to Trenton and Camden* directed by Marion Watson. Billed as part of a drama festival, both were performed by the Toynbee Players, who were based in the East End of London, and the effects of the war on Unity were shown by the quality of the programme which was a single roneoed sheet.

After the general call-up, which included women, all the usual problems of running the theatre in wartime were exacerbated further. Government restrictions meant that communication with members was difficult and most members were dispersed far away from North London anyway. Unity's active membership reached its lowest wartime level and, along with scarcity of people and material, the rigours of internal politics took their toll too. Plays became harder to find and more difficult to present and promote. Notwithstanding Hitler's defeats in North Africa and at Stalingrad, the general mood was far from optimistic and Unity faced one of its most testing periods in which its very existence was threatened. Nevertheless, the difficult times revealed a tenacity that not only kept the theatre open but saw it grow to a position of new influence.

Notes

1. New interviews/correspondence for this chapter: Edith Capon, Doris Clive (Levenson), David Kossoff, Frank Lesser, Henry Marshall, Gwen Molloy (Bennett), Ted Willis.
2. See John Attfield and Stephen Williams, *1939: the Communist Party and the War*, Lawrence and Wishart 1984.
3. Una Brandon-Jones provided me with most of the material from *Sandbag Follies* and *Turn Up the Lights*, which has been deposited in the British Theatre Association library along with items that were published or taken from other sources. Cecil Woolf sent me copies of Barnet Woolf's work.
4. Peter Noble, *British Theatre*, British Yearbooks 1946, says there were three editions of *Sandbag Follies*.
5. See Hetty Bower in *1939: the Communist Party and the War*.
6. See note 3.
7. Unity was not alone in providing war entertainment. The Artists' International Association exhibited in Charing Cross tube station, for example, and other left-wing groups, such as the Workers' Circle, performed a similar role to Unity although on a much reduced scale. Professionals were organised by such bodies as the Entertainments National Service Association (ENSA), which began by entertaining troops only but from the middle of the war on performed to civilians too, for example in factories. Theatres were even built for some workers, like single conscripted women living in hostels.
8. Published by the Workers' Music Association and available in the British Theatre Association library, as is all the quoted Outside Show Group/Mobile group material that I collected.
9. See T.H. Hawkins and L.J.F. Brimble *Adult Education:The Record of*

the British Army, Macmillan 1947; *Other Theatres*; Watson thesis.
10. Available in Lord Chamberlain's collection, British Library. It was licensed for a public performance in Hoxton Hall, East London, in October 1946.
11. First published only by London Macmillan in 1940, then in a revised version in *Collected Plays*, Vol. VII, 1949, from which the quotations are taken.
12. See David Krause (ed.), *The Letters of Sean O'Casey*, Vol. 1, 1910-1941, Cassell 1975. See also Heinz Kosok, 'Unity Theatre and *The Star Turns Red*', *The Sean O'Casey Review*, Vol. 4, 1980.
13. Quoted in Eileen O'Casey, *Sean*, Macmillan 1971.
14. Griffith's version was published by the Pushkin Press in 1941.
15. In some later programmes Caron Rock's name was misspelled Karen because, according to Berkeley Fase, Unity was suffering an attack of gentility. It was her script of *The Match Girls* that Unity used in 1947 when she urged the play's revival. Mitchell's script was lost when his house was bombed and he moved to Chiswick, West London.
16. Shaw's biographer Michael Holroyd did not know of the addition of the scene (or the donation of money for the Goldington Street lighting) but says both stories are 'highly characteristic' of him.
17. Script published by the Workers' Music Association, available in the British Theatre Association library.
18. Michael Redgrave, *In My Mind's Eye*, Weidenfeld and Nicolson 1983, contains reference to this episode in his life but not entirely as Unity survivors remember it.
19. Emigrés from many countries had their own cultural organisations. The most active in the theatre were the Austrians, who ran the Lantern Theatre, and the Germans, who began as a collective called Four and Twenty Black Sheep which soon disbanded and joined the Little Theatre, which was run by the Free German League of Culture. (See Lisa Appignanesi, *Cabaret*, Studio Vista 1975, which does not, however, mention Unity.) Members of such organisations worked with Unity, for example in *We Fight On* (see p.87), but I have not come across any information that suggests Unity played for groups other than the Free German League of Culture. Allan Merson, in *Communist Resistance in Nazi Germany*, Lawrence and Wishart 1985, refers briefly to the League, as does Josef Schleifstein in *Hans Fladung:Erfahrungen*, Roderberg-Verlag 1986, but neither gives much information. The Free French also used Goldington Street.
20. Some of Willis's left-wing activity until the time of the People's Convention is referred to in his autobiography, *Whatever Happened to Tom Mix*, Cassell 1970.
21. The translator is not given. A version by Honour Arundel of the poem, under the title 'The Soldier's Wife', appeared in *Our Time*, Vol. 2 No. 4, July 1942 but was not used by Unity.
22. Material from *Get Cracking* provided by Una Brandon-Jones and available in the British Theatre Association library.

7

People's War

War affected all theatres badly – 'Is Your Journey Really Necessary?' ran one government slogan – but the situation was especially hard for Unity.[1] Along with the disruption of transport, of normal publicity channels and of communications in general, the decline in traditional political activity undermined the block booking system upon which Unity relied. Also, as an amateur theatre, Unity depended on people who had a collective knack of improvising with few resources. War accentuated the difficulty of recruitment and the scarcity of materials. Nevertheless, Unity did manage to flourish, against a wider backdrop of renewed cultural activity in the face of acute dislocation and the constant presence or threat of death.

Building on the left-inspired culture of the 1930s, there arose a popular wartime culture in which a new self-confidence and self-expression was revealed.[2] People found pleasure in art forms that were previously unknown to them or beyond their reach; professional opera, ballet, classical music and theatre all reached new audiences and, because of the changed social context, the unusual venues and unconventional conditions in which much of this cultural activity took place, barriers were broken down between performers and the public and a new awareness was created concerning the relationship between art and society. This movement was reflected in the cinema, on radio and in publishing too.[3] The war years also witnessed regular state support for the arts for the first time. People set up their own artistic organisations, became involved in artistic activity and took part in unprecedented numbers in debate about the culture in which they lived (whether in the Forces Parliaments or in the kinds of topical discussions organised by the London Fire Service, which could involve 15,000 people a week).

Against such a background, it is still remarkable, though less surprising, that Unity not only survived but grew, and it is indicative that, without its regular audiences and actors, Unity kept returning to first principles and often drew its strength from mobile work.

For much of the time, the driving force of the mobile work was female, and, although only in leading positions briefly, it was women who kept Goldington Street going too. The only men who remained were those who were too young or too old for the forces, who were thrown out or invalided out, or those who were working in restricted or 'reserved' jobs. Many women were evacuated or volunteered, and after December 1941, those aged between 20 and 31 were eligible for call up. By Unity estimates in 1942, 1943 (the peak of Britain's war-effort mobilization) and 1944, there were roughly ten women to every man involved in the theatre's work.[4]

In 1942 Unity elected its first woman president, Ann Davies, who, in 1943, became its secretary when Vernon Beste left to work on the magazine *Our Time*. She had worked for the League of Nations and at a home for refugee Basque children. She had brought drama to the unemployed in Wales, had joined Unity in 1937 when she was a shop assistant at Harrods and soon became one of Unity's most popular figures, remaining part of the theatre's leadership throughout the war. A terrific athlete, she was an energetic and conscientious administrator and very powerful on stage, notably as Robin in *Babes in the Wood*. She was the secretary and general manager of Fore Publications, a member of the British Drama League's council and of the arts committee of the National Council of Social Services. She married Jack Lindsay during the war and died of cancer in 1954 at the age of 40.[5]

One of the few paid workers at the time was Helen Dibley, working in the office during the day and as stage manager in the evening (a job that she was to undertake in the professional theatre). Alongside her in the office was Mary Wren, a voluntary helper, who led the play committee. Rose Moser had taken over the electrics. Una Brandon-Jones, later a professional, can remember others that kept the theatre functioning – herself, Trudy Blunk, Elsie Chisnell, Audrey Hale and Sheila Conchie – who

> might be performing in the main theatre, or we might be journeying through the blitz to perform in a shelter. We might be sitting on committees, or sitting in the office typing scripts. We would hurry to the theatre night after night, after a hard days' work in an office, getting more and more tired and more and more frustrated at trying to be in ten places at once.

She also recalls two stalwarts of the Outside Show Group: Doris Levenson, 'the only one of us who had a voice strong enough to sing in the tubes while trains were perpetually thundering through the station', and Doreen Davies, 'a beautiful contralto'.

The Amazons

The preponderance of women led to an interesting if short-lived development in 1943, the year that the National Council for the Defence of Women and Children hired Unity for an all-women show, which included orchestral items, poetry, music hall, lullabies, a short play and a Living Newspaper on women and the war; the Outside Show Group performed *Salute to the Gentle Sex* and a compilation show, *A Stitch in Time*. Bill Owen returned to Unity, having been invalided out of the army, and became Mobile Group organiser on £5 a week. He was joined by an optician's clerk and self-taught musician Benny Norris as musical director. Una Brandon-Jones, who was then in charge of personnel, says of Bill Owen that he

> aspired to a high professional standard and was ever cautious of introducing new talent which might not stand up to the rigours of the sort of work we were doing. Gradually I found myself with a growing number of would-be actresses whom nobody wished to use. Just from taking auditions I knew that there was a certain amount of talent there, although most of the girls were inexperienced. The extent of the talent I didn't know – but I have always disliked wastage of it.

The idea arose of setting up a women's company within the Mobile Group. Una Brandon-Jones had already written one all-women number 'Women in Industry' ('We're turning out tanks for Russia') and began writing some more. She called a meeting of women in what was now the headquarters of the Mobile Group in Great Newport Street and began a workshop for improvisation, voice and movement exercises, and some songs and monologues that she had asked the participants to bring. Out of these supposedly 'uncastable' women was born the Amazons group, taking their name from a mythological race of female warriors.

It had not been a conscious feminist decision but emerged from a strong sense that women were being undervalued. This had always been – and was always to be – the case at Unity, where women were consistently active but constantly under-represented on the highest committees and in the leading positions of the theatre.

Production of the Amazons' first show was aided by Benny Norris at piano, Ted Willis, who by this time was putting his energy into Unity, and Herbert Lom, who was soon to be lost to the film industry. The show comprised seven sketches and songs and a short play by Willis, *George Comes Home*, about a young woman expecting her husband back from the forces after a long time away. The first number, 'It's A Girl', became the Amazons' theme song and was written by Una Brandon-Jones:

> For many hundred years there was a superstition,
> It carried on so long it was almost a tradition
> That women were inferior to men.
> But now the most hard boiled of you can hardly fail to see
> That girls can pull their weight like men wherever girls are free,
> And if you're still in any doubt, just take a look at me ...[6]

The repertoire included songs about life as a woman in different situations – as a fire guard, in a factory, in a queue and as a mother-in-law. The mother-in-law song ended with all the men in the family either ill or in difficulty:

> But if now we try to help them
> We're called interfering folk,
> For they're married men, while
> We are just a vaudeville joke![7]

Mimi Maxwell used to perform a special 'Carmen Miranda' number – she was a peace-loving, irrepressible figure who had lost her looks but not her vitality 'dodging bombs in Camden Town'.

The Amazons played in the usual Mobile Group venues and achieved particular popularity in hospitals treating the war wounded, such as that at Mill Hill for nervous diseases and breakdowns. At the height of the group's fame it had performed at the Scala Theatre as part of the Mobile Group's entertainment *Shop Window*, and when a fill-in show was required at Goldington Street it was called *Shop Window No. 2* and consisted of a double bill; Bill Owen's Mobile artistes partnered by the 'rejected' performers of the Amazons. Una Brandon-Jones remembers the excitement and the apprehension. They need not have worried; the Amazons turned out to be the hit of the evening and its members were quickly absorbed into the main-stream of Unity's work, having 'proved' themselves through their own efforts and a confidence that had been gained from working on their own. The group faded as a separate entity in early autumn 1944 after the run of a show called *One More Mile*. 'A revue in the true Unity tradition', it looked forward to victory and opened in the wake of the Normandy landings as the RAF stepped up its bombing of Germany and London suffered V-bomb attacks. It was directed by Bernard Sarron (one of the Dames in *Babes in the Wood*) and Herbert de Wilde, a refugee from Holland who had helped the Amazons with some of their revue material.

Ted Willis and 'Buster'

It was at this point in the war that Unity was being transformed under the leadership of Ted Willis who sought support for his ideas inside and outside the Communist Party and, with considerable backing, became the dominant figure in the theatre for the next five years. His decision to devote his time to drama and to Unity had such formidable supporters as the Communist MP Willie Gallacher and the playwright, novelist and broadcaster J.B. Priestley, who helped Willis financially. Willis became the theatre critic of the *Daily Worker*, which angered some because he was criticising other playwrights while writing plays himself. His subsequent career, from scripting the first episode of *Mrs Dale's Diary* on radio to creating the long-running television series *Dixon of Dock Green*, developed from the film *The Blue Lamp* which Willis co-authored, made him a pioneer of the British soap opera.[8] He was responsible for at least a dozen series, was a founder member and first chairman of the Writers Guild and, with his many stage and screen credits, he became one of the country's best known popular writers. Willis's creation of Dixon, the comforting Cockney cop, turned many at Unity against him. But for some this dislike had begun earlier with his running of the theatre and reached full pitch in 1963 when he was made a life peer, 21 years after the staging of *Sabotage!*, his first full-length play. When he had seen the production of *Sabotage!* he had been the first to recognise that the Play Department's criticisms had been right but the experience of having his play produced had in his words, given him 'the bug'. He returned to Unity with another play, a naturalistic story of contemporary Cockney life called *Buster*. This was a better effort than *Sabotage!* but clearly needed much work to make it playable. Vernon Beste again steered the play through the necessary committees and oversaw its rewriting under the guidance of the Play Department. The reshaping continued after *Buster* opened, up to and even beyond the point of publication after its transfer to the Arts Theatre in July 1943.

Buster is set in the kitchen-scullery-living room of the King family in the East End of London and opens in 1937 with Mr King unable to find work. Buster, his street-wise, cheeky son, interrupts his reminiscences of serving as a local Labour councillor:

> BUSTER: Whatcher ...
> MRS KING: Where you been?
> BUSTER: Out.
> MRS KING: None of your bloody lip. Where you been all day?
> MR KING: (*chiming in*): What time do you call this?
> BUSTER: Half-past six.
> MR KING: And have you got yourself a job?
> BUSTER: Not yet. Have you?
> MRS KING: That's enough from you. Look at the state of you! Wash yourself and get your tea.[9]

He gives himself a cat's lick at the sink and then from under his coat produces for his sister Mary a pair of silk stockings, which Mrs King believes he has stolen. The local policeman arrives and Buster is taken away for questioning. Buster remains a loner, spurning help from a social worker in favour of living off his own wits, yet he redeems himself later by helping to rescue people during an air raid in the blitz. Buster, nevertheless, is turned down by the RAF because of his record. The social worker intervenes and wins him a place in the Air Training Corps. Buster dreams of being an air ace, still seeing life only in personal terms. This brings him into an argument with Mary's fiancé, Joe, who smashed his leg fighting in Spain:

BUSTER: People ain't like you, Joe. They're like me. Out for themselves.
JOE: You'll change. So will the others. Already they're saying it ...
MARY: They're saying that after this lot, we'll never go back to the old way.
BUSTER: Mm. I don't know. I ain't so sure. You stick up for Russia, don't you, Joe?
JOE: I believe in what she's trying to do.
BUSTER: You want to make it like Russia, here?
JOE: I want to make it the country it ought to be.

Joe is proved right and Buster, who receives the George Medal for bravery, undergoes a transformation, and becomes a sergeant in the ATC. He learns from the local policeman that his best friend has been killed in the war and this triggers his frustration at not being called up. The next morning, however, as the papers carry news of the Nazi invasion of the Soviet Union, Buster gets his long-awaited letter from the RAF. He is exhilarated but Mrs King, who has kept the family going through the depression of the 1930s and the hardships of war in the 1940s, is frightened for him.

BUSTER: Don't cry, Mum. I know it's come as a shock to you. But I got a worse shock last night when I heard about Tommy ... You know, Mum, he wasn't just Tommy. Not just my mate. He was everybody's Tommy. He was quiet, and steady, A good mate ... he was everything. People are like that, Mum ... the ordinary people. They're like Tommy. He was the people. And that's who we're fighting for [...] LOOK OUT, HITLER, HERE I COME. (*As he says the last words he takes a flying leap frog over Mr King's back.*)

Buster is sentimental and warm-hearted, though imbued with a keen if generalised sense of how society thwarts its members who nevertheless fight back. It carries an emotional punch and deals with its characters without condescension, but it lacks the deeply etched anger and individual precision of Clifford Odets. Willis's seemingly natural and spontaneous public domesticity, a forerunner of much 'kitchen sink' drama more than a decade later, shares the mood, if not the politics, of some popular films and magazine journalism of the day in its celebration of an anti-Hitler consensus. Although it is the war effort that has given Buster his opportunity, his father a job and the family a place and purpose in society, which they felt they lacked in the 1930s, the play firmly rejects militarism as well as a return to the awful conditions of the pre-war period. When working-class characters were still strangers to the commercial theatre and the war was by no means going 'our' way, *Buster* struck a chord and offered a humorous, touching and uplifting night out through a robust play with a lively vernacular dialogue that was relatively easy for left-wing theatre groups to perform.

Directed by Eric Capon, *Buster* brought new life to Unity. The play was taken up by other Unity theatres around the country and toured to British and US forces stationed in the UK.

Colloquially written, by Unity's own working-class writer, about an immediately recognisable family living through familiar times, *Buster* suited Unity's needs and fitted its wartime slogan 'Theatre is a weapon against fascism.' As with the theatre's most successful productions, its popularity lay in the rapport with the audience, in this case created mainly by Alfie Bass as the Cockney lad. The two casts played four nights a week for three months and, thanks to an agent Rita Cave, who signed up Ted Willis, the Unity production was presented at the Arts Theatre for a week. In September that year, Alfie Bass began his professional career, taking over from another Unity actor, Harry Ross, as Private Cohen in James Bridie's *Mr Bolfry*. Later in 1945, Alfie Bass joined the Liverpool Old Vic Company at the Playhouse which was run then by Eric Capon.

Capon had been invalided out of the army and for the first three-quarters of 1943 was seen as Unity's artistic director. He restarted the Unity Theatre School of Drama under London County Council auspices at the Marylebone Institute and, by directing two acclaimed productions, *Buster* and *Spanish Village*, helped Unity through this uncertain period which saw the emergence of Willis as the key figure in the theatre's future. It seems, however, as though Capon was undervalued at Unity and did not have the right kind of temperament for the theatre's internal battles (and some recall with acidity that he had the wrong accent for the Unity leadership).

The year 1943 had begun with a visiting group, the Toynbee Players, in a double bill, *One Third of a Nation* and *The Happy Journey*. Despite the success of the following production, which had been *Buster*, Unity then had to rely on another visiting company for its next show – Cambridge Progressive Players with

The One and the Many, which deals with German resistance to the Nazis in Berlin in the winter of 1941-42, written by a young man in the army, Owen Rutherford. A Unity double bill came next, with the stark *India Speaks*, a Living Newspaper in poem-play form written by Mulk Raj Anand, and Randall Swingler's *The Sword of the Spirit*, which had been broadcast recently on radio. *India Speaks* was written, says Anand, 'out of the agony from the recurrent news coming then, during the middle of the war, about the famine in Eastern India, particularly in Bengal, caused by Imperial neglect and the greed of the merchants'. Communist leaders Palme Dutt and Pollitt and Krishna Menon, a local Labour councillor, secretary of the India League and future Indian Foreign Secretary, suggested giving the poem-play a special performance to raise money for the suffering peoples of Bengal. The moving spirit in producing it at Unity was Ann Davies, who had been working with Anand at *Our Time* magazine along with others involved in Unity, such as Honor Arundel, Arnold Rattenbury and Vernon Beste. (There was much cross-fertilisation between Unity, *Our Time* and its publishers Fore Publications, which issued *Buster*.)[10] Anand remembers a cast of some three dozen people taking part, including several Indians, and an enthusiastic response from the audience who donated £2,500 after the performance following a speech by Menon. Accompanied by Menon, Unity took *India Speaks* to the East End of London for a special showing to Indian seamen and to Birmingham, Leeds and Cardiff as part of the India League's campaign on the famine and the need for Indian independence. Anand had already written about life under British rule, and was to write the play *Famine* for the Army Bureau of Current Affairs Play Unit, which began life after *India Speaks* as a Living Newspaper project for Unity.

In the other half of the Unity bill, *The Sword of the Spirit* was written by Randall Swingler, poet, musician, a *Daily Worker* literary editor and leading Communist Party writer and speaker on culture who was well known at Unity as part of a trio along with two sisters Mary Peppin and Geraldine, to whom he was married.[11]

Swingler's play, directed by Unity and Rebel Players veteran Ruby Bendas, tells of a Dutch bishop who decides that he must speak out from his pulpit against the occupying Nazis although this will mean his certain imprisonment and possibly death. It, too, was toured.

Spanish Village, which followed the double bill, was Unity's first classical production, and marked not only a revival of fortune for the theatre but the start of Willis's campaign to forge a new national movement through London Unity. There was much discussion about whether or not to stage the play by Lope de Vega, a contemporary of Shakespeare's, in which a peasant community rises up against its tyrannical and lascivious lord who has raped one of the villagers and has himself rebelled against the king in a conflict over the royal succession. Arguments against mounting the production ranged from the pragmatic (beyond Unity's reach) and patronising (Unity audiences would not understand it) to the ideological (Unity audiences would not want to see a play about rape), all of which were mixed with a residual resistance to the very idea of staging a 'classic' as being politically irrelevant. Counter arguments harked back to the Left Book Club Theatre Guild days, to the debate on embracing and transforming the cultural heritage, and to the often disastrous experiences of left-wing theatres, such as the New York Group Theater, that had concentrated solely on new plays which were always hard to find. The decision to stage *Spanish Village* was seen finally as a progression from the presentation of a play like *The Star Turns Red* which had helped lift the amateur theatre movement as a whole.

After a feverish search in the British Museum for the original *Fuente Ovejuna*, the play was translated by Stanley Harrison, using the pen-name John Greene, later chief sub-editor on the *Morning Star* and during the war working in London as a Spanish monitor for the BBC. Capon mistakenly believed Unity's production to be the first in English, but in fact the Theatre Union had staged a version called *The Sheepwell* during the early months of the Spanish Civil War.[12]

Even though Unity's new general manager George Finch reported that the theatre had had to drop the two-cast system and there was an evident gap between the performances of many newcomers and the few with more experience (led by Vernon Beste as the cruel nobleman), the production earned considerable praise, particularly for the twenty-year old Maxine Audley as the violated Laurencia who stirs both the village council and the women to rebel and kill the unjust overlord. Designed by Eric Capon's brother Kenneth and Bernard Sarron (and constructed largely out of hessian as the only available material) *Spanish Village* was given a spread in *Picture Post* and a Board of Trade commendation for the costumes. Excerpts were broadcast by the BBC Overseas Service, along with a talk by Stanley Harrison. A special performance was given (with other items) for Solomon Mikhoels, the leading actor and head of the Moscow State Jewish Theatre, and Colonel Itzik Feffer, a notable Russian Jewish poet. During its run, Herbert Hodge, Unity's taxi driver playwright, made another radio programme about the theatre which helped put it back on the map. *Spanish Village* seems to have united the theatre's administration, stage staff and performers and brought new energy and new blood to Unity, in spite of a £10 fine and six guineas costs awarded against both the theatre and its general manager for presenting the new translation without either acknowledging the club rules or getting the Lord Chamberlain's permission.[13] Two inspectors from the Lord Chamberlain's office had gained admission to the theatre without being asked if they were members. Unity pleaded that this was an error caused by staff shortages and treated the fine as a minor irritation rather than allowing it to dent the new enthusiasm which was expressed in the reopening of the drama school, a membership drive and the launch of an internal bulletin the *Call*, which ran for eleven issues until August 1945 when it was superseded that December by a revived *New Theatre* magazine.

The production of *Spanish Village* also saw the end of another era, which, in retrospect, may look more momentous than it did at the time. For the first time the names of the actors were published in Unity's programme, signalling the end of that element in Unity's history that derived from an ideology of an oppositional culture in which the individual was submerged in the collective. This change was not identified as such then, and the *Spanish Village* programme did not draw attention to the new practice. The decision came as a result of the changed political situation and the gradual re-assessment since the end of the 1930s of the distinction between the amateur and the professional.

New Talent

As the war progressed, successive victories over the Nazis and the campaign to 'Open The Second Front Now' had raised spirits.

Communist Party membership reached its peak in 1942, the Comintern was dissolved the following year and the party reapplied for affiliation to the Labour Party. Even though this was lost at the 1943 conference, the resolution secured 26 per cent of the votes – the closest result ever on this issue – the TUC withdrew its 1934 so-called 'black' circular of proscribed organisations, and even the Labour Party turned on Churchill for his indifference to the recommendations of the Beveridge Report which were to form the basis of the Labour government's post-war social legislation.

At Unity, new members were being attracted on a broader basis than before, both because its political line now supported the war effort and was less aggressively polemical than previously, and because Unity was one of the few amateur theatres to function throughout the war. It was not surprising that, in such a context, the proportion of members who were not particularly politically aware rose sharply. Unity opened its doors to anyone, other than fascists or racists. (People were refused membership in late 1943 for their attitude to racism and audiences were asked to sign a petition in protest at the release from gaol of the British fascist leader Oswald Mosley.) For many, Unity continued to be what it had always been – and was to be, even in its leanest years – a kind of 'open university' for those with little or no access to cultural expression, let alone to any artistic activity with political relevance. It enjoyed a full programme that offered opportunities in all branches of theatre and continued to provide a social and political world that changed many people's lives. Unity sometimes opened up new avenues for its members, albeit unwittingly, such as a career in the theatre or films or a change of direction, for example, into teaching. (In the case of Paul Scott, author of *The Jewel in the Crown*, a reading of his first play in 1943 did not lead to a production, nor to him becoming a playwright but, according to his biographer, did stimulate him to continue writing and thus helped the emergence of a respected novelist.)

The war had brought full employment to artists and had given many people unprecedented opportunities to earn their living as cultural workers – something unthinkable in the pre-war days of mass unemployment. The creation at the beginning of the war of the Council for the Encouragement of Music and the Arts and the Entertainments National Service Association had provided an organisational focus for this situation and their emphasis on the professional was reflected in the ideas of the new Unity leadership. Most Unity members had no desire to join the professional theatre but in the war more and more people were being drawn to Unity because of its potential as a training ground for a career in theatre. Unity's leadership had shifted position on this issue; the Kingsway project has focused new ideas that were cut short by the war which then broke the barrier itself with its new opportunities and a number of Unity stalwarts becoming professionals (even though they had not planned it this way.)[14]

During the war, over a decade before theatrical fashion changed in favour of a working-class style, it was possible to see Unity as a stepping stone to a professional career; it was possible to gain experience there in a repertoire and method of acting not to be found at drama schools or most reps, and there was a chance of being seen by agents on the look-out for new talent. A few people probably joined with this in mind; for others it happened by lucky chance. Maxine Audley, who had already appeared professionally before being cast in *Spanish Village* and who was committed politically to Unity, says that Unity had a very high standard that was no different from that to be found in many commercial productions and better than in any rep that she knew. Of the wartime newcomers to Unity who did turn professional, and there were many, several were to make singular contributions: for instance, Ted Willis, the actors David Kossoff and Warren Mitchell, and, as a theatre administrator, Hazel Vincent Wallace, who founded the Thorndike Theatre, Leatherhead (named after an ardent Unity supporter).

Unity's fate at this point lay very much in the hands of the general purposes committee, which, having taken over the function of the old executive committee, met weekly and reported to the monthly meetings of the management committee. The general purposes committee was usually five-strong, with a three-person core of Willis, Ann Davies and George Finch. It was on this committee that the detailed plans were worked out to put Unity on a firmer artistic and organisational basis in order for the theatre to recover and then sustain its position as the pre-eminent amateur company in Britain. Though he was still finding his feet and made several false starts, Willis emerged as the driving force. His experience in the 1930s in organisations such as the Spanish Youth Foodship Committee and the British Youth Peace

Association inclined him to broaden Unity's approach and appeal.

He thought that it was, once again in Unity's history, a case of expand to survive or go bust. He believed that the tasks of the first phase of Unity's existence – the establishment and securing of a workers' theatre in a hostile climate – had been completed and that the time had come to move on to a second phase which was appropriate to the new and more favourable political climate following the Soviet entry into the war. He was antagonistic to those on the left who harked back nostalgically to the 1930s which he saw as a decade of danger and misery when the majority of the population were denied access to culture. As the war progressed, he increasingly embraced the term 'People's Theatre' in clear distinction to the earlier 'Workers' Theatre' because he felt that the cultural explosions of the 1930s had been instigated and defined by a necessarily oppositional left, whereas in the 1940s the whole people were as one against fascism and the breadth of cultural interest was national and not partial. It had been shown that the people would respond to the 'best' and it was Unity's duty to provide it. This meant radical changes.

Willis was a man whose organisational skills, persuasive powers and ambition were all considerable. His artistic self-confidence was less keen at this point, and while developing as a writer he concentrated at Unity on structural changes that would affect the artistic profile. The grand scheme was to build a new national society that would be a bridge between the amateur and the professional theatre worlds, something akin to the Left Book Club Theatre Guild but more effectively run. As part of this expansion, negotiations were opened with the Co-operative movement's People's Entertainment Society on the possibility of a merger, with Unity as the amateur wing. The dynamo of the scheme was to be a strengthened London Unity, which was to be run separately from the national society. Willis was looking for premises away from Goldington Street to house the society's offices and for a larger theatre to accommodate what was hoped to be a revamped London Unity. (It was the utmost sacrilege to many who had given their all to build the 'First Workers' Theatre' to even hint at moving out of Goldington Street, which had acquired an almost religious status as a building because of the struggles to create it. Willis did negotiate to take over the Arts Theatre off Leicester Square, and even approached businessman Charles Clore for the money, but a rival bid for the theatre from the actor-director Alec Clunes won the day.) A fund was launched in October 1943 to raise £2,000 to help finance the expansion scheme and the necessary reorganisation was set in motion.

'Winkles and Champagne'

Following *Spanish Village*, an artistic council under Eric Capon was established to advise the management committee and general purposes committee and a five-company system was introduced: three for 'straight' plays, one for variety (absorbing the Mobile Group which was to be disbanded for being too independent of Goldington Street) and one for new members (working on short pieces, sketches and readings). The idea was to allow a higher turnover in production than in the previous two years and to create a distinct 'house' style within an ensemble that would go some way towards realising the anti-commercial ideas of Stanislavsky, whose methods, with the plays of Gorky, represented the model of socialist realism that was to be emulated. Unity had never been able to support the kind of permanent company that was necessary for such an ideal to be achieved, and this time both the artistic council and the five-company system failed too. The 'straight' play-variety differentiation did take hold, however, and was first in evidence in the next production, which fortuitously confirmed the new spirit of confidence and enterprise that was abroad in Unity. Appropriately, it arose from the mobile work and represented the coming together of the aspirations of the Goldington Street leadership and those taking shows to outside venues.

The show was called *Winkles and Champagne* and became a Unity standard for years to come, being revived twice, broadcast live on BBC television from Alexandra Palace and spawning eight more Unity productions and countless mobile shows of similar material but different name. Subtitled 'The Story of the Halls', it was written by Terry Newman and Bill Owen, who had just made his first West End appearance, taking over the part of Private Cohen in *Mr Bolfry* from Alfie Bass.

Many Unity players, especially those in the Mobile Group, had long been interested in music hall – not (as they saw it) in the magpie way of Auden, Isherwood and Eliot, but seeing it as the popular entertainment of their own class. Unity members frequented the nearby music halls – the Met, Collins, Holborn Empire, the Kilburn Empire, the Bedford – and music halls numbers were always included in shelter shows. A group of Unity performers had put together music hall entertainments for their own relaxation and had presented them at Brittania Street in the late summer of 1940 as *The Gay '90s*.[15] This was repeated – to raise money for the Communist Party – after the Sunday matinées of *The Match Girls*, with free beer and sausages for the audience. Following its success, in November that year, an Old Time Music Hall – known then as Old World Music Hall – had been staged at the main theatre, and had drawn crowds that were bigger than the theatre could hold. During research for this show, Bill Owen had come across M. Wilson Disher's book *Winkles and Champagne*, a history of the music halls, and straightaway had wanted to turn it into a full-scale production. It was not until he was out of the army and able to drawn on the help of his Mobile team that he was able to do so. Doris Levenson, Benny Norris and Bernard Sarron carried out research in order to create the period of each item as accurately as possible. Sarron designed the sets and, with Levenson, the costumes too.

The show opens with a burletta unearthed in the British Museum, written in 1790 by Henry Fielding (whose attack on the then Prime Minister brought about the introduction of modern censorship). The next scene in the historical progression shows a Regency romp in a pleasure garden (1825), and then comes a beer hall scene in a Victorian song and supper room (1870). Finally there is a full-blown Edwardian music hall (1900), complete with chairman. The show is framed by a man from the past and a man of the present (these generalisations were always defined as male). The man from the past acts as commentator throughout, taking the audience back from the present to the different historical scenes, and handing over at the end to the Modern Man, who contemplates the names of contemporary artistes. 'Perhaps they could be as good as the old timers,' he muses.[16] 'Damn it, they *are* as good,' he proclaims. 'They don't talk Mayfair. They still speak the language of the people and so long as they do that Music Hall has got a grand future.'

Winkles and Champagne was lovingly created as a lively piece of archaeology. Its politics lay in revealing a popular tradition not in any analysis of that history. As Audrey Hale says in the January

1944 edition of the *Call*, the show 'appeals ... to the working-class audiences, and that is the test of success for us'. M. Wilson Disher in a programme note reinforces the point:

> They [the authors] are not reviving a lot of Victorian songs simply to create the Christmas party, good though that is in itself. They have borrowed something from the theatre as well as something from vaudeville, and something of radio and film techniques ... The right purpose of these experiments with time is to make the past part of the present, and for showing how this can be done the music-hall songs have given us a lot to be thankful for. They are both past and present. They enrich our lives.

With only one cast (though requiring replacements), *Winkles and Champagne* ran for two-and-a-half months to full houses and boosted the fund for Willis's grand plan.

Winkles and Champagne, which was well and widely reviewed, gaining another *Picture Post* spread, was instrumental in helping the revival of music hall in Britain. Leading Unity performers appeared at the Players, which had reopened in 1937 as a song-and-supper theatre and under Leonard Sachs increased its popularity to the point in 1953 at which it launched Sandy Wilson's *The Boy Friend*, directed by the former Unity player Vida Hope. By the early 1960s, Old time Music Hall returned briefly to the West End and was popular on television in The Good Old Days with Sachs wielding the gavel.

The popularity and financial success of *Winkles and Champagne*, coming on the heels of the artistic success of *Spanish Village*, helped the Goldington Street leadership to push through the changes needed to form a national society against fierce dissent from the non-London groups that were to form the other constituent members of the new society.

A National Society

In February 1944, with *Winkles and Champagne* still running, London Unity called a conference to discuss the establishment of a national society. The idea for such a body had been put forward in different forms since the beginning of the war when the Left Book Club Theatre Guild, *New Theatre*, the bulletins and other means of communication between left theatres had collapsed.

Sheffield Left Theatre had originally volunteered to act as a national co-ordinating centre but this had proved impossible, leaving London Unity to assume the role with little organisational back-up beyond a few conferences. The first was called in December 1940 – to tackle the problems of working in wartime – and subsequent gatherings in Leeds, Glasgow and London heard mainly the repeated call for greater and closer collaboration between the groups. Several had survived the war and some, such as Glasgow, grew in strength and influence to equal if not surpass the standard of London.[17]

Glasgow Unity had been formed in January 1941 by five companies – Glasgow Workers' Theatre Group, Clarion Players, Glasgow Players, Transport Players and the Jewish Institute Players – which had been brought together by the necessities of war. The first production was Odets's *Awake and Sing*, which was followed by Afinogenov's *Distant Point* and subsequently two more of Odets's plays (*Golden Boy* and *Till the Day I Die*), O'Casey's *Juno and the Paycock*, Vishnevsky's *Optimistic Tragedy* and three new Scottish plays – *Major Operation* and *The Night of the Blitz* by James Barke, a novelist and Glasgow Unity's first chair, and *Song of Tomorrow* by John Kincaid. Another group within Glasgow Unity toured sketches, revue material and short pieces.

Merseyside Left Theatre had broken through the black-out in late 1939 with an Odets programme of *I Can't Sleep* and *Till the Day I Die* (which the Lord Chamberlain had refused to licence earlier in July because of its references to the Nazis but changed his mind once Britain was at war). Then followed a daring show, Auden and Isherwood's *The Dog Beneath the Skin*, a revue reworked from material sent by Herbert Hodge called *Strike Me Red* which played with Toller's *Requiem*, Brecht's *The Informer* (from *Fear and Misery in the Third Reich*), a chronicle of the years from 1920 to 1940 called *20 Years, Plant in the Sun* and *Awake and Sing*. The bombs came in the late summer of 1941 and from then until 1944 the group performed sketches, short plays, revues and song scenes in factory hostels, camp sites, garrison theatres and public meetings, as well as presenting with the Co-op in 1944 an ambitious centenary pageant.

The towns of Oxford and Cambridge both had left-wing theatres – Oxford Unity staging *Spanish Village* in 1944, for example, and the Cambridge Progressive Players performing several shows,

Katayev's comedy *Squaring the Circle, The One and the Many*, which came to Goldington Street, Elmer Rice's *The Adding Machine* and Willis's *Buster*, which also visited London Unity after a local tour that included playing to segregated audiences in US camps. *Buster* was one of Bristol Unity Players' proud productions, and it played as part of a drama festival at the old Bristol Theatre Royal. The Bristol group was in full swing when war broke; it then offered play readings to the Co-op guilds which led to what was probably the first production in Britain of the American anti-fascist play *The Revolt of the Beavers* by Lantz Saul, in April 1940, involving more than 100 local children. When Bristol was bombed after the fall of France in May many of the regular members had to disperse and a new day-time group sprang up, known as the housewives' section, which was genuinely collective and kept Bristol Unity alive through the war. (Its wardrobe mistress was Renée Short who was to become a notable Labour MP.) *Distant Point* was produced in July 1942 with the Workers Educational Association Players, as was Robert Ardrey's *Thunder Rock*, which Aberdeen Unity also presented. Bristol Unity combined with five other groups to perform *Landmarks of Liberty*, which became a major attraction of the Stay-at-Home Holidays in the local parks. In 1943 a 'spotlight commentary', *Over to You*, became a popular travelling show and the following year the group staged its most influential production, *Now is the Day!*, a pageant of local labour history from 1864 to the present. *Over to You* was a reworking in the Bristol context of a pageant that had been performed by the Co-operative Society in 1942 in the Empress Stadium, Wembley, London's largest open-air arena. Originally called *An Agreement of the People*, the words were written by Montagu Slater and the music by Benjamin Britten, who had earlier collaborated together in Left Theatre and were to do so again on the opera *Peter Grimes*. The pageant presented the theme of real national unity in the face of the common enemy, fascism, as the People's Convention had done, and it announced that this spirit would survive beyond the war because it was imbued with a desire for a better future.

Manchester's Theatre Union, run by Ewan MacColl (known as Jimmy Miller before the war) and Joan Littlewood, disbanded in 1940 and former members and supporters formed a Unity Theatre to continue the work, though with only partial success. Leeds

Unity, which had close ties with Theatre Union and later its successor Theatre Workshop, had a remarkable war record of activity. There was a choir, a school, a children's theatre, an outside touring group and a full programme at its 100-seat theatre in premises which it shared with the Leeds Left Book Club Forum. Borrowing costumes from the London production, Leeds Unity staged *The Star Turns Red* in November 1940; according to several accounts, it matched the standard of the original production and some say that it was better. *Comrade Enemy*, written by local Unity writers Kate Penty and Alec Baron, was performed by the group at the Leeds Civic Theatre, followed by *Distant Point* and J.B. Priestley's *They Came to a City*. The group's strength seems to have lain in drama documentary (one of its Living Newspaper productions during the Soviet-Finnish war asked why the *Daily Worker* had been refused permission to send a reporter to cover the conflict) and in revues – *It's Possible, Off the Record, We're on the Way, You've Had It, Let's Be Offensive* – songs from which would appear (sometimes without permission) in other group's shows, including London Unity productions.

These and other groups came with some skepticism but a lot of hope, to the conference in February 1944 called by London Unity, which by this time had managed to move its offices from Goldington Street to Great Newport Street. The proposal was put that London Unity should transform itself into a national body, with each member group transferring all its assets to the national centre and having a representative on a new national management committee. The national membership would be divided into regions and would give 2.5 per cent of any takings to the national centre. Individual members would hold a common membership card and pay subscriptions to the national body, which would send each group whichever was the greater of 6d or 5.5 per cent of the annual subscriptions for every renewed subscription of every member resident in the region in which the group operated. The proposal suggested that the new Unity Theatre Society Ltd would then be in a position to become the amateur wing of the People's Entertainment Society, which could draw on the vast potential of the Co-operative movement.

The groups present were Aberdeen, Cardiff, Merseyside, Edinburgh, Glasgow, Leeds, Reigate and Redhill, Mid-Rhondda and London. London wanted the plan (which was a form of the

Communist Party's system of democratic centralism) endorsed by each of the group's members before the AGM in April, but there were many problems. One was the complicated nature of the proposed national body, but overriding all was the issue of independence. The general feeling – London apart – was a fear of being swallowed up by London and that the merger with the People's Entertainment Society would lead to a lowering of standards and a loss of artistic control.

Ann Davies reported on the role a new national Unity might play within the British Drama League and on the activities of the People's Entertainment Society. Unity saw itself as a catalyst for the amateur movement, helping to spread left-wing ideas to ever-growing numbers of people. The British Drama League in 1943 had set up at Unity's prompting a Play Encouragement Committee to excite interest in the production of topical pieces that could be used in the war effort. In one year, 158 were submitted and several were circulated to affiliated groups. The need was great, as was shown by an Arts Theatre play competition which attracted 500 entries in 1943, none of which were judged to be of merit. On the organisational front, the People's Entertainment Society offered great opportunity in terms of national scope and resources. As with Unity, its main concern was to create an alternative production network under democratic control. All Unity's members were urged to buy the minimum £1 share in this kindred co-operative society which had been formed in 1942 with the aim of presenting plays and popular entertainment of every type as well as joining together people around Britain both as playgoers and amateur play-makers.[18] It had established a non-profit company, People's Plays Ltd, which was responsible for presenting shows in the West End, including *They Came to a City*. It owned a rep theatre in Huddersfield and variety theatres in Chatham and New Cross, and built a theatre in Guildford. The People's Entertainment Society liaised with Co-operative groups, financed and promoted plays with the Council for the Encouragement of Music and the Arts (the forerunner of the Arts Council) and presented a mobile Unity production of *Winkles and Champagne*. Willis was invited to its board meetings at the end of 1943 and when Ann Davies went to work there as its organiser in 1944, she set up a professional company that undertook a Co-operative centenary tour of *The Rochdale Pioneers* (also known as *Men of Rochdale*), which included a visit to Unity sponsored by the London Co-operative Society political committee. The arguments in favour of a merger between Unity and the People's Entertainment Society were attractive but the anxieties went deep and the groups returned to their respective towns to consult their members before the proposed AGM of that year which was to ratify – or not – the creation of the new society.

In the meantime, London Unity staged the first full-length play by a young civil servant, Leonard Peck, called *Green and Pleasant Land* in a production by Eva Lorm-Schaffer. Peck had contributed to some literary magazines and had written two short plays for the Left Book Club Theatre Guild – *Means Test Trifle*, on family conflict resulting from Tory social legislation, which won a Welwyn Garden Festival prize, and *East End* about fascist marches. After *Green and Pleasant Land*, he wrote eight more plays, seven of which were performed by London or Merseyside Unity theatres or other left-wing companies. London staged three more of his plays – *The Townshends* in 1948, *The Shadow of a Swastika* in 1954 and *Puerto Franco* in 1959. Peck had served in Unity's play department before being drafted to Liverpool in the war where he made contact with Merseyside Left Theatre, which gave *Green and Pleasant Land* its first reading. It is a romantic drama set in 1839, in which the dissatisfied wife of a Whig MP, horrified at his attitude to his workers, falls in love with a Chartist leader and has to choose between the comfort and safety of her stultifying bourgois existence and the life-enhancing danger of living with her radical lover. Agents provocateurs cause an uprising and the Chartist is forced to flee. The MP tries to shoot him but is beaten in a fist fight, defeated politically and personally.

The production was postponed because the play was not seen to be vital to the Communist Party's immediate goals and was criticised for its preoccupation with the middle class (according to Peck). Peck disagreed with tying theatre to immediate political ends and felt that Unity had tended to do this since 1938 and was often naïve in its ideas of revolutionary drama. He clashed with Willis, and the management committee interfered with the production, introducing Herbert Marshall as assistant director. The play was also cut without his knowledge, which led to more bitter correspondence, but he did rewrite it and the production went ahead. Peck always felt that Merseyside was better for writers because its Marxist view of art was less crude than London's and there seemed to be less of a gap there between the two theatre's similar aims and their different practice. In fact, London's production of *Green and Pleasant Land* was almost called off, but for reasons which had nothing to do with politics. The air raids on London had restarted the month before, and on the eve of the first night, the theatre was hit by a dozen fire bombs. Those working inside, particularly a backstage member Leslie Wynard, achieved miracles in saving the theatre and extinguishing the fires. The dressing rooms, bar, general office, backstage area and auditorium were all affected.

In the new mood of enthusiasm, the programme for *Green and Pleasant Land*, which carried the Chartists' six main demands, published the results of the first phase of the membership drive – 5,000 individual and 200 affiliated organisations. Unfortunately, the new mood did not prevail at the AGM, which was the most acrimonious that many could remember, although these meetings were always high drama in their own right. It opened at a disadvantage as the date for it had already been put back because of difficulties in producing a balance sheet and the state of negotiations with the People's Entertainment Society. By the time the AGM did take place, in April, the misgivings of the February meeting had hardened. A vote was taken merely to continue talks with the People's Entertainment Society (which later petered out) but the row over the formation of the national body, led by Leeds and Reigate and Redhill, produced a rebuff for the proposed transfer of all assets to the national society and – an unprecedented occurrence – the adjournment of the AGM until June.

Negotiations continued during the six weeks before the reconvened meeting while a 'filler' had to be found for Goldington Street (which resulted in a Mobile Group compendium show *Shop Window No.2* that included the Amazons). Despite continuing resistance on the details of the national body a compromise was agreed which led to the formation of the Unity Theatre Society Ltd, comprising individual Unity groups affiliated on a voluntary basis, each with representation on a national management committee. This was first elected at the following AGM in 1945 when a national play selection committee also was formed. Aberdeen (the first group to become legally associated with the new society), Birmingham, Cardiff, Manchester, Merseyside and

Oxford which had transferred their memberships to the society before the reconvened AGM, became with London the founder members, although the society was not formally ratified under the relevant Act until 25 September 1945. Willis became its president.

By the end of 1944, UTS Ltd had ten affiliated groups, a national organiser from Aberdeen Unity (a former stock clerk, labourer and civil defence organiser Bill Ramsay, who was based in London) and a drama school once more. It had been reopened with Michel Saint-Denis teaching stage production and Joan Oakham teaching voice. In March 1945, London comprised 92 per cent of the national society's membership and provided 95 per cent of its running costs, though this was balanced that month when Glasgow joined, bringing with it 3,000 members. By the end of 1945, the number of affiliated groups had risen to 36, including thirteen in London and its surrounding area which were organised by a London Unity committee set up in the summer of 1944 as separate from the committee that ran Goldington Street. As well as continuing with affiliations to bodies such as the British Drama League and the Workers' Music Association, the new society also forged links abroad with organisations like the New Theatre League in Australia, the Greek underground theatre United Artists of Lyricon and the Indian People's Theatre.[19]

Divisions over the national society were not the only rows at the 1944 AGM but on one contentious issue, which only affected London, Willis won approval without any modifications. Following the failure of the artistic council, Willis believed that Unity needed an artistic director for the five-company system to work and to create a distinctive Unity style based on socialist realism. He did not have the expertise and had approached Herbert Marshall, who had agreed to take on the job under certain conditions. These included full responsibility for artistic matters (subject to the broad policy line of the enlarged management committee), the final say on methods of acting, production, technical work and training, release from all administrative duties, and twelve months in which to make his changes. The AGM accepted the proposal against severe opposition, both to Marshall and to the notion of an individual holding such power when Unity's record and existence had always depended on collective effort.

Marshall's appointment coincided with the sacking of two staff to save money, a wage cut for the rest and the end to advertisements in tube stations. By September, two more staff had been sacked and the post of artistic director had been abolished due to Marshall's outside activities, notably his work subtitling Soviet films. (His work with the Soviets included writing the official English-language version of the Soviet national anthem.) He did direct two productions that year, however. The first, *All Change Here*, written by Ted Willis, was playing appropriately enough when the reconvened AGM was held to debate Willis's national strategy.

The play, set just before the second front was launched, looks at wartime life and attitudes through characters who work for a bus company and who are in dispute with the directors over long hours and poor conditions. A repatriated prisoner returns home to find that not only has his wife become a bus conductor, which he had been, but she has also taken his place as secretary of the trade union branch and is urging the members to strike. He is offered a management job and finally accepts as he believes that everyone has to be on the same side against fascism and behind the war effort. He prevents the strike and the play ends with an implied, and rather forced, labour and domestic consensus. Willis chose a naturalistic format with which to debate important everyday issues – the workers' desire to provide a service, the company's exploitation of that sense of duty, the opening of the Second Front, strikes in wartime (which the play argues against), the relations of men and women at work and in the home and the different outlooks of different generations. Like *Buster*, it is a cosy, family drama that takes place mainly in a front living room and which touches on key topics without exploring them in any complexity – a prototype of the television 'soap'. Its support for a 'no strike' position in the interests of the war effort, which was taken to be the line of the Communist Party, albeit in highly simplified form, ran contrary to Unity's past history and for many Unity activists, particularly those from the pre-war days, it highlighted the unease that they were feeling at the direction Unity was taking. The show opened just after D-Day when spirits had been lifted, but had the misfortune within the week to suffer Hitler's new flying bomb offensive. The theatre was damaged, Unity was forced to return to weekend-only shows and nearly closed because audiences were kept away by the VI bombs. Not only was it physically difficult to keep the theatre open, the rapidly changing war situation frustrated attempts to mount a topical repertoire.

Marshall's second show, in November, followed the revue *One More Mile* and a visit by the People's Entertainment Society with *Rochdale Pioneers*. The play he mounted was a Soviet thriller, *Comrade Detective* (also known as *Face to Face*), and was the only one of his proposed repertoire to reach the stage (his list included a new version of John Gay's *The Beggar's Opera* and *Spirochette*, a Living Newspaper by Arnold Sundgaard on venereal disease). *Comrade Detective* by the brothers Tour and L. Sheynin was suggested to Marshall by Mrs Maisky, the wife of the Soviet ambassador whom Marshall knew through his work for the embassy, as a change from the more familiar socialist realist Soviet plays that Unity favoured. Marshall not only directed the play, he translated and designed it, with help from the brilliant German photomontage artist John Heartfield who was living in exile in London. Moreover, because the lead actor fell ill, Marshall ended up playing the lead part. *Tribune* found his performance as dull as the piece itself, but *Russia Today* hailed the play.

Marshall's departure opened the way for Willis to assume more artistic control than he had enjoyed previously, especially after immediate efforts were not carried through to establish an artistic advisory council comprising Unity figures and leading personalities from the professional theatre, such as Beatrix Lehmann, Peter Ustinov and Ronald Frankau, who had agreed to participate. Instead, Willis began his most controversial journey – toward the founding of Unity's first, and last, professional company. In November 1944, the general purposes committee agreed the establishment of a permanent Repertory Company that would hire people on a yearly contract and would start work in January 1945, with Willis as artistic director. The plan met stiff internal resistance and took more than a year to be realised, when it was boosted by the euphoria of victory in the war and in the polling booths. The internal dissent was becoming focused on the Mobile or variety group, which saw itself as the vital link with Unity's pre-war 'golden years' and felt that it was as responsible as any other group for the theatre's survival thus far. There was resentment that it was not considered by Willis to be part of the mainstream of Unity, which, to some extent, had been the result of Bill Owen's leadership, but this had been aggravated by Willis's attitude and his disbanding of the Mobile group. The success of *Winkles and Champagne*, which boosted Willis's plans for expansion, had not been consolidated at Goldington Street and when the mobile performers – as the Variety group – presented there the revue *One More Mile*, they felt like visitors improvising in a difficult situation. (Eighteen women and eight men performed two versions of this show which looked forward to an Allied Victory and included two numbers from a Leeds Unity revue – 'Grievous Gremlins' and 'Plan with the Planets' – and two from the influential American revue *Pins and Needles*, 'Doing the Reactionary' and 'A Song of Social Significance', a favourite of the mobile entertainments.)

1945

Many of the same team appeared in the show following *Comrade Detective*, Jack Lindsay's *Robin of England*, with music sent by Berkeley Fase from his RAF camp. Directed by Derek Birch – an actor and BBC announcer who also directed *The Rochdale Pioneers* – it is a poetic exposition of the Robin Hood legend, complete with fourteenth-century Minstrel as commentator. Robin is seen not just as a national hero but as a people's hero, too. At first he appears as a knight, Sir Robert Huntingdon, who loses his land and wealth to a greedy abbot and as a result joins a band of serfs and outlaws in Sherwood Forest, who live in a communal but anarchic way. As Robin, he unites them and becomes their leader. In the process of preparing to resist unjust and draconian laws, which are designed to protect the new-won property of various barons, Robin learns from the 'merry men' the meaning of solidarity and comradeship – a microcosm of how they hope England will be transformed one day.

Lindsay came to Unity to lecture on folk history and fertility rights as background information for the production, which the publicity describes as 'very English … full of traditional material and true in its historical picture. For that very reason it is extremely relevant to our struggles today.' Little did Unity know that a general election would shortly be called and put its ideas to the test. *Robin of England* was quite different to the type of play that Willis promoted and to his own work, which was demonstrated by the next production, a play by Willis called *The*

LEEDS UNITY THEATRE

LEEDS UNITY THEATRE

— presents —

"IT'S POSSIBLE!"

(A POLITICAL EXTRAVAGANZA)

— Commencing —

Sunday, August 25th, 1940, at 7-30 p.m.

LEEDS UNITY THEATRE, 113, Park Lane, LEEDS, 1.
(Opposite Rate Offices)

Performances every Sunday night, 7-30 p.m. ***Admission 1/- (inc. tax)***

Admission restricted to Members, Associates and Friends. — New Members welcome.

Booking Office open daily from 8-0 p.m. to 10-30 p.m. Telephone 278171.

Next production **"THE STAR TURNS RED"** *by Sean O'Casey.*

Publicity postcard for wartime Leeds Unity revue

Yellow Star, with which he made his directorial debut imitating Marshall's Stanislavsky approach.

The Yellow Star is set in the late autumn of 1942 as the Nazis are moving rapidly towards Stalingrad. A Nazi commission arrives in a small Polish town charged with organising the extermination of the Jewish population. The choice for the Jewish population is stark but simple – resist or die. The dilemma is a real one and it is explored through the central figure of the Rabbi, whose religious duty forbids him to kill and who takes some time to understand fully what the Nazis are planning. His request for children to be saved is granted by the commandant's son, Ernst, but soon it is revealed as a trick – the 'torture of hope':

> RABBI: We will show them we know how to die.
>
> DAVID (a young Jewish worker): No, Rabbi, no. They know how we can die. We must show them how we can live. Look ... there are over five thousand of us ... fifteen hundred men ... we must fight ... block the ghetto entrance, barricade the streets ... we must fight.
>
> RABBI: Be calm ... with what shall we fight?
>
> DAVID: With our hands, with clubs, with knives, with stones, with anything ... David shall beat Goliath again [...]
>
> RUTH (a young Polish nurse): Rabbi. Do you know what they have at the station? Do you know? A sleeping car, they call it ... the Jews Bedroom. A gas-chamber ... they are going to pass every Jew left in the place through it like dogs ... Do you understand?
>
> RABBI: Against this ... what can we do? It is a punishment.
>
> DAVID: If it is, it is a punishment for cowardice, and a punishment for humility. We've tried too often to walk the humble way. Now the day has come to be proud. Now the day has come to lift our heads to the sun and the stars and shout! YES. I AM A JEW AND I AM PROUD OF MY PEOPLE. Lift your head to the sun and fight!
>
> RABBI: I beg you ... please ... do not make things worse.
>
> JESSICA (a Jewish woman): Could they be worse? Is there anything they can do to us after death? Have the Nazis occupied the next world, too?[20]

One of the Nazi commission, a Russian prince, offers to sell the Rabbi some passes. He thinks of accepting in order to let others escape (in contrast to a member of the Board of Jewish Deputies who wants passes for himself). The prince flaunts his deeds in a pogrom in Kiev, which turns out to be the rabbi's home town, and treats the persecution of the Jews as a game. The rabbi stabs him to death, invoking God and cursing the fascists:

Director Bill Owen shows Hilda Fenemore how to use a blood swab for the 1947 revival of Robert Mitchell's *The Match Girls*, the story of an historic strike by women workers

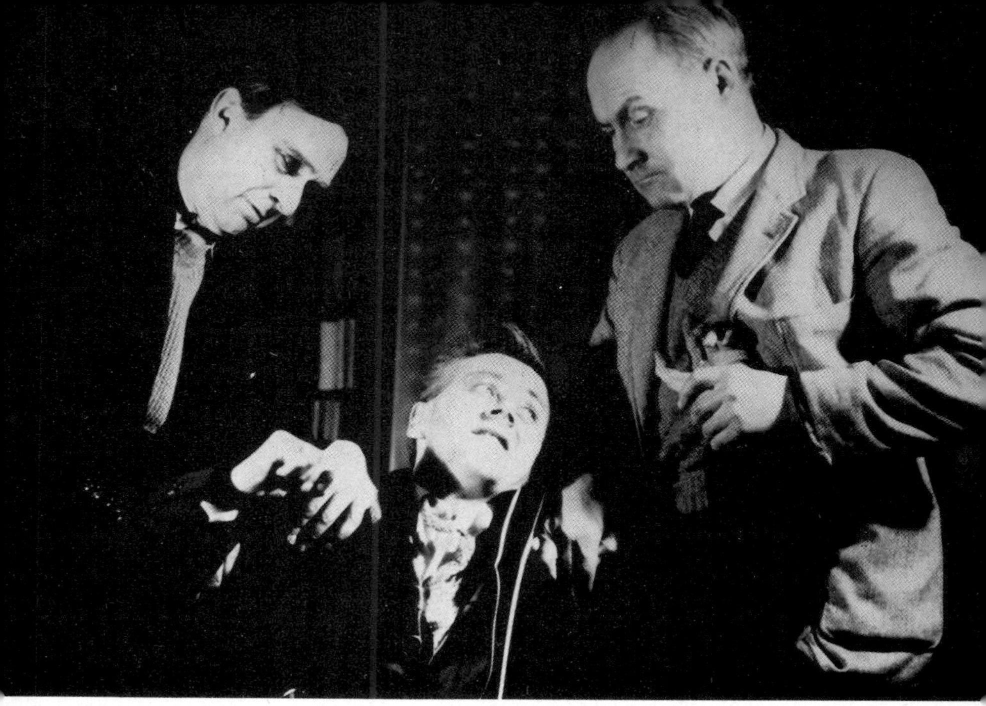

Unity theatres were active outside London; two of the most successful were Merseyside, presenting (*above*) Leonard Peck's anti-witch hunt play *The Big Screen*, and Glasgow, performing (*below*) Ena Lamont Stewart's popular *Men Should Weep*

Expostulating melodramatically on the evils of gin and trade unionism, Ted Willis's Victorian comedy *God Bless the Guv'nor* was a popular Christmas show in 1945 and later revived three times

John Collier's 1947 touring show, *Black Magic*, performed by the professional company, was sponsored by the Ministry of Fuel and Power

A special set was built at Alexandra Palace for Unity's live television performance of *Winkles and Champagne*, the theatre's very popular story of the music hall

Labour ministers Bevin and Attlee, lampooned in a sketch called 'Oklahokum' in the 1948 revue *What's Left?*, pull out their guns at the mention of the word 'socerlism'

Unity's adaptation of Robert Tressell's *The Ragged Trousered Philanthropists* ran for over five months and was well supported by trade unions; it was also one of the most successful mobile shows

Arguing about the revolution leads to trouble aboard a US tanker docked in Iran in Herb Tank's hard-hitting and realistic *Longitude 49*

Have coach, will travel: Unity's touring work flowered in the late 1940s and early 1950s, carrying on a tradition that went back through the wartime outside shows to the 1930s and the Workers' Theatre Movement

Unity looks abroad with two French plays: (*above*) Jean-Paul Sartre's *Nekrassov*, given its British première, ridicules the red scare diet of the popular press and (*below*) the fate of the Paris Commune is told in the world première of Arthur Adamov's *Spring '71*

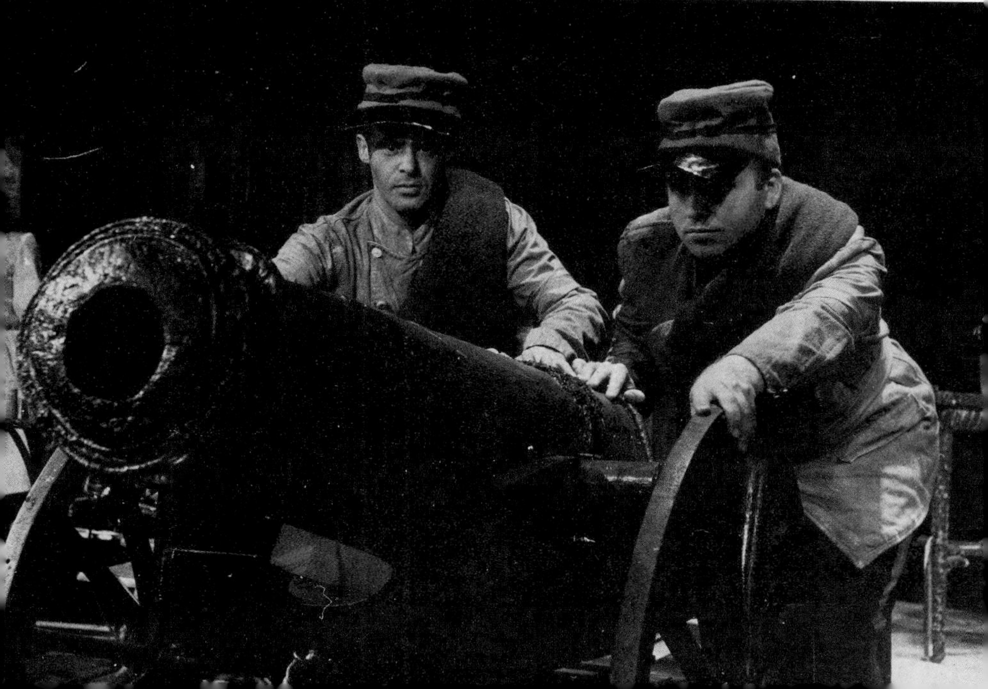

The James Joyce of the Dublin streets is brought to life in Bloomsday, Allan McClelland's adaptation from the novel *Ulysses*: the set was designed and painted by one of the leading designers of the period, Sean Kenny

> The Lord pardon them never; the wrath and fury of the Lord burn upon these men and bring them all the curses which are written in the Laws. Blot out their name under Heaven. Let no man speak to them; no man write to them; no man show them any kindness; no man stay under the same roof with them, no man come nigh unto them. SEE THEM APART FOR DESTRUCTION, O JEHOVAH!

The murder leads to the threat of 200 hostages being executed in retaliation. The rabbi confesses and is shot with the innocent Jessica while the conscience-stricken commandant receives his posting to 'Stalingrad, I think!'

Willis wants to show both the nature of fascism and the journey of its victims from fatalism to resistance. The individual courage of the rabbi symbolises the necessity and the human cost of such resistance, seen in the knowledge that fascism will be defeated by morally superior forces (the reference to Stalingrad). The play is better controlled but less authentic than *Buster* and gains what tension it has from a clash of attitudes rather than an exploration of deeper complexities. The publicity material for *The Yellow Star* quotes Ibsen on the function of a play, which is 'to tell a story of human fate and human beings' rather than to be a political thesis. Willis based his play on a newspaper story about a rabbi in the Warsaw ghetto uprising and a special performance was given in aid of a Warsaw fund. *The Yellow Star* was also performed at the Grand Palais, Whitechapel, the home of Yiddish theatre for nearly two decades. (Willis also entered the play for a Jewish writing competition, which he won – the prize was taken back when the organisers discovered that he was not Jewish but they then decided to return to him half the prize money.) The play was a success, particularly for its lead, David Kossoff, who was drafted in after the original choice had been dismissed for misconduct. Kossoff had trained at architecture school and during the war worked in a protected job as a specialized draughtsman. He really wanted to act, however, and remembers 'coming alive' at Unity. Like everyone else, he did a little of everything, as writer, director and performer in the Mobile Group, and he recalls acting in front of scenery that he had designed, built and painted. He first appeared at Unity in *Spanish Village* and became popular as the chairman in *Winkles and Champagne*. He stayed for three years before turning professional to become a household name through television in the 1960s.

The Yellow Star was playing when Victory in Europe was declared after the surrender of the Nazis. Labour left the coalition government and prepared for the forthcoming general election, in which, for the first time members of the armed forces could vote. Unity's contribution at Goldington Street was a political fantasia, *Alice in Thunderland*, which opened during the election campaign in June 1945. The variety group formed the core of the team behind this show, the title of which echoed Tom Thomas's *Malice in Plunderland* skit of 1929. Bill Owen was the author, Bernard Sarron directed, music was by Benny Norris, and designs were by Rivka Black with masks made by Unity's veteran back-stage wizard and documentary film-maker Tris Stack.

The show opens with Alice and Bunny, two factory war workers, taking their lunch break and having a 'lover's row' over Bunny leaving for a union meeting. Alice falls asleep and awakes to find herself in Thunderland which she is shown around by a rabbit who looks remarkably like Bunny. She sees a soup kitchen, encounters familiar bureaucracy and then finds a Duchess mishandling a baby:

ALICE: Poor little thing, you're liable to choke it …

DUCHESS: How dare you, give it to me … he belongs to us … don't you dear (*crooning to the child … who promptly lets out a wail and is duly banged over the head with a frying pan*).

ALICE: Does he belong to you?

DUCHESS, COOK, CAT: Yes.

BUNNY: No.

DUCHESS: I beg your pardon.

BUNNY: He doesn't belong to you and you know it.

DUCHESS: We've had charge of this child for a long time … and we don't intend to give him up now …

ALICE: What's his name?

BUNNY: He's the future and rightfully belongs to us.[21]

A cricket match to determine who shall have the child is held between the workers of Thunderland and the Old Gang (Mad Hatter, Doormouse, Marsh Hare – all resembling Tory politicians). It is held in the royal gardens where the gardeners are afraid that their heads will be cut off for growing red roses. The Old Gang plays with a blue pad, as does the King. Doormouse is umpire and the Old Gang cheat to win the future. Alice is furious and calls for justice. Amid jokes about housing schemes and different types of 'politically affiliated' tea – Co-op, Indian, Russian, blue or red label – the workers interrupt the Mad Tea Party and arrest the Old Gang for unfair play. [29]

Alice agrees to be the prosecuting counsel but gets hijacked on her way to the court by Delilah Dope, who tells her fortune offering her attractive but empty promises:

> I can promise you easy living,
> No more taking, no more giving,
> I can promise you fox and sable.
> Lovely gowns with a Paris label.

Counsel for the Old Gang is Not-so-simple Simon, who presents his credentials which on one side carry a swastika and on the other the word 'cartels'. Alice, who has managed to turn the tables on Delilah, arrives at court singing:

> No more sleeping, no more dreaming
> No more capitalistic scheming
> No more war with profits high
> No more cartels, no ICI.

The two sides argue over the future in an operetta which culminates in a crescendo as the battle is carried on in musical form and ends with a blackout. Alice is woken by the real Bunny returning from the union meeting, expecting Alice to be cross. Instead, Alice now understands the importance of unions and collective action and agrees with Bunny that the 'future is even more important than the past'.

Alice in Thunderland, which closes with a song called 'Marching Forward', continues Unity's political pantomime tradition although it carries no detailed commentary on the election, only a deep-seated anti-Toryism and the double-edged metaphor of the crooked cricket match in which victory is to be resolved through appeals to justice. To some degree, this approach can be traced to the Communist Party's campaign for an electoral unity within the labour movement to face each Tory candidate with a single opponent, an idea that was only narrowly rejected by the Labour Party conference of 1945. But, as important, the show was not written originally for the election and had to be revised accordingly, and quite a few people believed that Churchill would lead the Tories back to power again.

Japan's defeat and the final surrender of the remaining Axis powers saw Labour, with its far-reaching social programme, returned in July with a landslide majority, and the election of two Communist MPs. A new era seemed to be dawning in which Unity wanted to play a positive part. Willis pushed on toward the culmination of his grand plan, the creation of a professional Unity company based in London which was to be the flagship for building the Unity society throughout Britain. He was clear on the task ahead. He had spelled this out already in the May 1945 edition of Unity's bulletin *Theatre Call*, following the AGM at which his national strategy was consolidated; 'Our task is to win thousands of people – hundreds of thousands – for the idea that the inspiration of theatre, which proved essential in war, is no less essential for the peace.'

Notes

1. New interviews/correspondence for this chapter: David Amias (Yehuda/Tree), Joan Amias (Biske), Mulk Raj Anand, Maxine Audley, Alexander Baron (Bernstein), Zelda Curtis (Brown), Peter Dorrell, Sheila Dorrell (Conchie), Eveline Garratt, Stanley Harrison, Harry Landis, Oscar Lewenstein, Gwen Molloy (Bennett), Gwendy Peck, Arnold Rattenbury, Charles Warren, Elsie Warren (Chisnell), Margaret Woddis.
2. There is a strong tradition on the left of workers' self-expression, in the habit of self-teaching, the labour education movement and organisations such as Unity and the Workers' Music Association. In the 1970s, when small publishing ventures flourished, it took on a national characteristic in the Federation of Worker Writers and Community Publishers. It has always been particularly strong in the Communist movement and during the war *Seven* magazine, published by Fore Publications, was a forum for people's writings as was *People and Poetry* and its successor *Our Time* (see this chapter note 10). In the 1950s, the Communist Party's magazine *World News* carried a supplement of people's writings called *Daylight*. The tradition was carried on through the *Daily Worker*, the *Morning Star* and various Communist publications.
3. Both *Other Theatres* and the Watson thesis identify the currents of this wartime culture. See Jack Lindsay, *British Achievement in Art and Music*, Pilot Press 1945, and his *After the Thirties*; Ann Lindsay, *The Theatre*, Bodley Head 1948; Janet Minihan, *The Nationalization of Culture*, Hamish Hamilton 1977; *Our Time*. For general background, see Angus Clader, *The People's War*, Panther 1971 and Paul Addison, *The Road to 1945: British Politics and the Second World War*, Cape 1975. For comment on Communist culture, including Unity, see Raphael Samuel, *New Left Review*, Nos 154, 156 and 165.

4. Figures and references for Unity activities come from the usual variety of sources, including bulletins called the *Call* and the *Activist*.
5. She wrote a survey of contemporary drama in 1948 called *The Theatre*, which refers briefly to the national Unity movement and to *New Theatre* magazine. The Communist Party Writers Group published a commemorative pamphlet on her death in 1954 called *Nothing is Lost*, which was edited by Edgell Rickword and, among the many tributes, included recollections by Montagu Slater and Geoffrey Parsons.
6. Given to me by Una Brandon-Jones and deposited in the British Theatre Association.
7. See note 6.
8. He wrote the first episode of *Mrs Dale's Diary* (later *The Dales*), which was broadcast on 5 January 1948, under his Unity pen-name of John Bishop but later changed to Willis.
9. *Buster*, Fore Publications 1943.
10. The Communist-led Fore Publications was one of the centres of the Communist cultural effort during the war. Ann Davies was its secretary and general manager and Jack Lindsay became its chief director. It published Key Books (fiction, biography, history, science), *Seven, Theatre Today* and *Our Time*, of which Ted Willis was an associate editor and Vernon Beste editor. (Other editors included Honor Arundel, Edgell Rickword, Montagu Slater and Randall Swingler.) According to Slater, in the Ann Davies tribute *Nothing is Lost, Our Time* circulation reached 15,000 in the later war years, *Seven* 30 to 40,000 or more, and *Theatre Today* 20,000.
11. For an introduction to Swingler and some of his poems, see John Lucas (ed.), *The 1930s: A Challenge to Orthodoxy*, Harvester Press 1978, which also includes a useful antidote to prevailing views of Communist creativity in the 1930s and 40s in Arnold Rattenbury's 'Total Attainder and the Helots', as well as poems and *Stay Down Miner* by Montagu Slater.
12. The adaptation of *Spanish Village* is wrongly attributed in some Unity publications to Ted Willis. The version used by Theatre Union appeared in John Garrett Underhill, *Four Plays of Lope De Vega*, Scribners 1936.
13. Unity was not alone in being prosecuted for breaking club rules; the same fate befell the Arts Theatre, for instance.
14. Unity actors can be seen in documentary films of the period, many of which were sponsored by the government at a time when it was politic for working-class people to feature as the subjects of 'official' propaganda.
15. In the 1970s the Aba Daba Company performed music hall at The Pindar of Wakefield, the local pub for Unitarians when they were at Britannia Street and a Rebel Players venue. Used by Marx and Lenin, it also gave its name to the innovative theatre group Wakefield Tricycle, which was founded in 1972 and out of which came the Tricycle Theatre, Kilburn.
16. *Winkles and Champagne*, New Theatre Publications 1946.
17. See John Hill, 'Towards a Scottish People's Theatre: The Rise and

Fall of Glasgow Unity Theatre', *Theatre Quarterly*, Vol. 7 No. 27 Autumn 1977; Dawson; Tuckett; correspondence with Renée Short MP (Bristol); see also Chapter 3 note 9.

18. At the time of the Unity negotiations, the PES claimed a membership of 432 individuals and 147 affiliated societies. Its chairman was the Rev. G.S. Woods and its president was Alfred Barnes MP. Some accounts give its founding date as 1941.

19. There were personnel links between some of the groups around the world, the strongest for London being with Australia. The New Theatre was formed there in 1932 in Sydney, inspired by the American New Theater League, and then the Sydney group was joined by those in Melbourne, Brisbane, Perth, Adelaide and Newcastle to form a national organisation. In an anniversary pamphlet, *New Theatre: 15 Years of Productions*, published in 1948, the plays that it shared with Unity were *Waiting for Lefty, Bury the Dead, Plant in the Sun, Private Hicks, The Secret, Where's That Bomb?, Cannibal Carnival, Colony, The Match Girls, The Star Turns Red, Sabotage!, God Bless the Guv'nor, What Happens to Love?, All Change Here* and a Rebel Players show *Slickers Ltd*. (attributed to Unity).

20. Acting script of *Yellow Star* given to me and deposited in the British Theatre Association library.

21. Acting script of *Alice in Thunderland* given to me and deposited in the British Theatre Association library.

22. Unity's revues/pantomimes often contained food and drink metaphors; e.g. 'salade Françoise washed down with Vichy water', 'sweet cabinet pudding or congress tart' or 'all the time there was lovely Russian caviare on the sideboard and yet nobody noticed it'.

8

A New Jerusalem

Victory over fascism and the spectacular affirmation of socialist ideas embodied in Labour's overwhelming General Election triumph of 1945 heralded for many the coming of the new Jerusalem. A few Communists believed that, having made its invaluable contribution, the time had come for the party to disband. The majority disagreed, stayed put and party membership reached 45,000. Party influence was strong; the two Communist MPs were supplemented by some 200 local councillors and a co-operative was launched to own the *Daily Worker* in its specially commissioned premises just off Fleet Street. Unity bought shares in the venture and when the first edition was published from the new building the audience attending a special Unity All Star event joined the celebration rally.

Nevertheless despite the Soviet Union's decisive role in defeating Hitler, anti-Communism was quickly mobilised and the United States launched its bid for post-war dominance over its allies who happily picked up the pre-war policy of isolating and confining the Soviet Union. The first atom bombs were dropped by the Americans in August 1945, by which time Churchill was already using in private the 'iron curtain' metaphor borrowed from Goebbels. The phrase was to enter the language and set the tone for post-war politics following the rejected premier's Cold War speech in Fulton, Missouri the next spring.

Unity celebrated Labour's triumph and the return of activists from the armed forces with a topical revue, *Swinging to the Left*, which was produced in only three weeks.[1] Devised by Bill Owen and Frank Godwin, directed by Bernard Sarron, it involved many of the Mobile and Variety team which had presented *Alice in Thunderland*. *Swinging to the Left* was well but not widely reviewed and was noted for its zest and musicality. Its popularity helped make the summer musical become a regular feature of Unity life.

Unity's leadership under Ted Willis was enthused with the nation's optimism and issued bold statements of intent despite facing an uphill task in turning grand plans into reality. Estimates vary, but individual membership seems to have stood at 2,000, yet this figure was way above the number of active people. The society's bulletin, the *Call*, did not appear from November 1944 to April 1945 when it was relaunched under a voluntary editor working from home who could not find enough material for the July 1945 issue. He resigned after publishing the August 1945 edition, which was the last. The summer school, however, had been revived at Netherfield, Hastings, and was in the capable hands of Glasgow Unity's well respected director Robert Mitchell. The school coincided with the bombing of Hiroshima and Nagasaki, which left those attending stunned and without any immediate political line on the events.

In Unity's expansion plan, building the national society became synonymous with strengthening London Unity, and the fate of the two was inextricably intertwined for the next couple of years. An early practical consequence was a year in which half the productions came from guest visits. Unity turned this necessity of bolstering London's flagging programme into the virtue of a welcoming hand to Unity groups from around the country. The Windsor Theatre Guild came in January 1945 with *Juno and the Paycock*, the Civil Service Clerical Association played *Late Extra* in March and Glasgow Unity offered its own triumph to match the July election with a legendary production of *The Lower Depths*. In August, which was designated the guest month, the Kane Players brought *Citizen Kane*, the Cambridge Progressive Players, having toured 1,500 miles and given some fifty performances, presented *Buster*, and Croydon Unity *They Came to a City*. As a policy, the guest visits were not properly thought through. The following year Stepney Unity (which had achieved some notoriety by rehearsing on the plinth in Trafalgar Square) performed *Awake and Sing*, and North-West London Unity, which had 100 members and variety, music and drama sections, staged George Leeson's *This Trampled Earth*. It was the last such visit in this period – a sign of the practical and economic problems of the policy as well as of differences within the society which gave way to a looser federation in 1947.

Going Professional

A catalyst for this disintegration was the achievement and failure of Willis's major ambition for Unity, the establishment of a professional company, which earlier in Unity's history had only been thwarted by the outbreak of war. It was called the Unity Repertory Company and, although it was the national society's group and was ostensibly drawn from the best performers of the constituent Unity theatres around Britain, it was London-based and London-biased. Willis pushed through its establishment against bitter opposition, staking his by then considerable personal standing on the outcome and using to good effect the machinery of democratic centralism, which favours those already holding power and calls heavily on members' loyalty and trust. It took him over a year to succeed and he had many arguments to win. In this he was helped by new recruits to Unity's leadership who supported his broad approach. Some of them were old associates of his, such as Oscar Lewenstein and Alec Bernstein, both of whom he had worked with in the Labour League of Youth.

Lewenstein became manager at Goldington Street, general secretary of the national society, business manager of Glasgow Unity when it went professional and editor of *New Theatre* magazine in its last months. He became general manager and artistic director of the Royal Court Theatre, first when it was a club and then as the home of the English Stage Company, of whose film company, Woodfall, he became a director. He earned a reputation as a tough but adventurous impressario, presenting in the West End among other shows, *Cock a Doodle Dandy, Nekrassov* (first performed by Unity), Theatre Workshop's *A Taste of Honey* and *The Hostage*, and plays by John Osborne, Charles Wood and Joe Orton. Bernstein had been an assistant editor of *Tribune* and had joined the Young Communist League with Willis. He became chair of Unity, assistant editor of *New Theatre* and producer of Unity's short-lived film company, Crescent Films. As Alexander Baron, he became a successful novelist and television writer, known especially for adaptations such as *Oliver Twist* and *Vanity Fair*. Willis oversaw the publication in December 1945 of a Unity pamphlet, *People's Theatre*, that argued for a professional groupand praised Willis highly. It was written by one of his lieutenants John Collier, a former wood finisher, electrician and political organiser. *New Theatre* magazine was revived also that month and supported his proposals, and he enlarged the Unity general council, adding John Allen, Arthur Askey (a Liverpool Corporation employee before becoming an entertainer), the actor Ronald Frankau, London Trades Councils secretary Julius Jacobs, the actress Beatrix Lehmann (president of her union), the playwright MP Benn Levy, J.B. Priestley, Michael Redgrave, British Drama League Secretary and founder Geoffrey Whitworth, and himself. Willis formed a smaller group chosen from the council to be directors of the professional company – Allen (who dropped out almost immediately), Jacobs, Levy, Phyllis Morris from Actors' Equity, and from Unity Bernard Sarron (a former architect and later art director of Pathé Pictures who designed the films of *Sparrers Can't Sing* and *Poor Cow*), Richard Polling, John Collier and himself.

The battles within Unity intensified as pre-war veterans were demobbed; threatened prestige, the burden of previous sacrifice and genuine political and artistic disagreement came together in opposition to Willis's plan and spilled over into conflicts concerning the running of Goldington Street. When Willis, for example, directed *Juno and the Paycock*, a strong body of opinion felt that it was too pessimistic, showing the working class as divided and weak just after winning the most important war of modern times that had put socialism on the agenda across Europe. Willis made his position clear: 'a great play,' he said, 'can never be untimely', or 'out of date'[2] and, with reference to the professional company:

> we do not intend to repay the Labour movement and the working class for their support by putting on plays which make propaganda for their point of view, in a narrow sense, or which portray the working class as a class of angels ... We believe ... [quoting Shaw] that the theatre is a cathedral of the spirit, devoted to the exultation of men, and not a department store in which you commercialise lust.[3]

For his next production, however, he looked to the sentimental Victorian writer, Mrs Henry Wood, and adapted from her work a Christmas show called *God Bless the Guv'nor* for which he brought in the popular radio announcer Lionel Gamlin as director.

The show is a Victorian melodrama on the twin evils of trade unionism and strong drink in which the boss of a family business proposes on Christmas Eve to the daughter of one of his workers. The villain of the piece forces the woman's father to form a union under threat of revealing that his daughter is a foundling. The 'guv'nor' breaks the union with ease when it calls a strike after a drunken worker is sacked and the union has no funds because the villain has used the dues to pay for his gin. The workers return to work but at reduced rates of pay, and the foundling daughter turns out to be the offspring of a Duke. Willis's broad comedy, published by Unity's recently founded New Theatre Publications, proved so popular that it was revived in 1959, 1965 and 1979, and happened to be the last production at Goldington Street before the arrival of the professional company.

In preparing for the professional company, the details changed from time to time and estimates varied as to how much it would cost and how many people could be afforded. At first, it was to consist of twenty men and twenty women, with those from London who were not chosen destined to work with the suburban Unity theatres. The company was intended to be self-supporting on an initial capital outlay of £3,000. Total estimated expenditure was £10,858, with an £8,000 wages bill, yet even the most optimistic income at the box office was £8,750, based on average takings in the year 1944-45 of £25 per performance and assuming fifty weeks playing seven nights a week. (Expenditure for the year 1944-45 had been £3,883 while income had only been £3,500.)

In December 1945 John Collier announced that the company would comprise a dozen actors (to be paid at different rates), the minimum of technical staff and one director. It would present a repertory of one play a month at Goldington Street as well as performing in the West End and on tour. Building on attempts to revive training, which had included lectures during the previous winter by eminent persons such as James Agate, Ralph Richardson, Esther McCracken and John Burrell, it was announced also that there would be a new school with sections devoted to writing, acting and technical production. It would be the only school in Britain linked to a living theatre, boasted Unity. The aim, said Willis, was not merely to present plays with a professional cast, but to train a cadre of actors, according to a particular style and method, and to present vital and new contemporary plays and the classics. That style was to be a working-class realism and the method was to be based on Stanislavsky's teachings with lengthy group and individual analysis of the plays and their characters during rehearsal. Unity amateur activities were to become a tributary for the professional theatre, aimed at a mythical 'Mr Smith and Jones' (no Mrs or Misses). 'When the man who makes his living in industry, agriculture etc., wishes to utilise his hard earned and very short moments of leisure ... there ought to be some organisation to make it easier for him.'[3] Willis said the model was the theatre workshops of America and the Soviet Union, and he did introduce an apprentice system offering employment and training to those who aspired from Unity's amateur groups.[5]

Announcement of the scheme was met by the expected outrage. Opponents accused those responsible, and primarily Willis, of many sins, from secrecy and autocracy to placing personal ambition before the good of the theatre. Willis was indeed nothing if not determined and his prestige was increasing, having broken into broadcasting and cinema as well as being the *Daily Worker* drama critic and member of the Army Bureau of Current Affairs Play Unit which had enjoyed a successful run in the Arts Theatre. He had won backing for the professional company from John Gielgud, Sybil Thorndike, Edith Evans, Miles Malleson and Llewellyn Rees at the newly established Arts Council. Willis recalls also winning the support of Communist Party general secretary Harry Pollitt (reinstated in his post after the Soviet Union entered the war) and that of the powerful London district secretary Ted Bramley, before addressing a huge 'aggregate' meeting of all Communists at Unity, called to discuss the issue.

At the meeting Willis argued that Unity had more than fulfilled both its earlier role and its dreams and had therefore gone as far as it could as an amateur theatre. The labour movement had entered the cultural sphere collectively and as individuals and this represented the first historic challenge to the dominance of the arts by the ruling class. There was now a different situation in which the conflict that marked the 1930s had been replaced by the task of building the future in a mass movement alongside, and not in opposition to, the popular Labour government. The amateur theatre should acknowledge and be proud of its role as the springboard of the professional theatre and Unity's aim should be to make more of this. It should establish a new team across the amateur-professional divide and, by example, change the idea of what a professional company should and could be; Unity's would be democratically run, with everyone having a chance to discuss the plays and their part in the process of making theatre. Willis argued against a simple relationship between theatre and politics and did not see the new company as being a party channel. The three guiding principles were to be social purpose, proper artistic method to suit that purpose and a mass audience, the first and third of which were part of the labour movement and the second a matter of study and hard work[6]

Willis's opponents, however, were not themselves united. Some disagreed more with his artistic ideas than his organisational ones, believing that his populism was no more than a passive reflection of working-class life and therefore consolidated that class in its attitudes without expressing any visionary dimension for qualitative change. Seductive it may have been while the class was in the ascendant, but they feared a future degeneration when political conditions altered. Others argued against the idea of a professional company on principle, seeing it as a betrayal of Unity's ideals which they believed had already been compromised. Among this group were both those who had opposed the 1939 Kingsway plan and others who felt that there had been within Unity a wider consensus behind the 1939 plan than the current one because Unity was then sharp-edged and internationally known thanks to *Babes in the Wood* and that the Kingsway project had grown naturally out the theatre's progress. The timing and the details of the current plan were thought to be wrong, particularly as it was being proposed as a solution to a problem rather than the outcome of growth. Those who had already turned professional were highly sceptical of the plan's viability.

There was also the argument, which was supported by the Communist Party's education organiser Emile Burns, that Unity should not back the Labour government unreservedly but should create another political revue, pointing up the Attlee government's weaknesses. Mostly there was the fear that the plan would detach Unity from the labour movement and leave it nowhere to go but out of existence.

Willis claimed the backing of the party and, with the authority of the platform, won the day. Many, like Bill Owen, made good their threat to leave Unity if the professional company were established. Willis became its director and chose an initial eighteen performers from the 750 that were said to have been auditioned. (The full-timers were offered a two-year contract, while the apprentices were offered employment for a year). The personnel changed later and non-professionals were used too. There were no automatic places in the national society's professional company, yet the apparently egalitarian principle behind forcing everyone to audition led to a feeling of humiliation for many who had given long service and helped build Unity to the point where it could turn professional. It also gave rise to accusations that, in breaking the privilege expected by veterans, Willis was replacing it with patronage of his own favourites. The bitterness was fuelled when stalwarts received the standard letter of rejection without even the courtesy of a personal message. In fact, Willis did keep some places for Unity pioneers from the 1930s who were being demobbed, but they were often the first to be laid off when times were hard.

At Unity's tenth anniversary reception, held on the eve of the professional company's appearance, Willis outlined a further expansion for a nationwide network of democratically run professional theatres, with the actors receiving higher rates of pay than laid down by the union, a family allowance, two weeks' paid holiday, at least one month rehearsal and a voice in the affairs of the company. Nothing came of these proposals.

Unity Repertory Company, which was to have paved the way for these developments, gave its first performance on 19 February 1946 – ten years after the opening of Britannia Street – and it lasted just under fourteen months, until April 1947. Original plans, which included Lorca's *Blood Wedding* and Jonson's *Volpone*, had to be altered and the company began its short life with Eugene O'Neill's 1924 pioneering portrait of love across the racial divide, *All God's Chillun' Got Wings*. Willis directed and the lead parts were played by Louie Bradley and Robert Adams, who had been seen in *Colony* – anonymously – as the workers' leader. (It was not seen as peculiar by the white actors to 'black' up, which was necessary as Unity's cast contained only two black actors, Adams and Ida Shepley. Inner truth was considered more important than external effect, just as when Paul Robeson had played a 'white' character in *Plant in the Sun*.) Willis appears to have opted for a naturalistic approach which did not suit the starkness of O'Neill's six scenes which are juxtaposed to heighten the accumulating anguish. While Adams received some good reviews, it was pointed out that the play centres on two characters and was not, therefore, a good choice to display ensemble skill.

Willis stayed with American plays for his second choice, a British première of *Casey Jones* by Robert Ardrey, author of the popular *Thunder Rock*, which had been made into a successful film with Michael Redgrave. By focusing on one of capitalisms's archetypal inventions – the steam engine – Ardrey questions the values of the social system. The reward for the railway engineer when he starts to go blind after 30 years' devotion to a machine and its masters is demotion to the telegraph office of a small country station. Jones finds liberation not through dedication to the rail company but by leaving to start a new life. The Stanislavsky approach was taken a little too far on one occasion when the ailing engineer of folklore fame (played by Joe Sterne, with an 'e' added to his name for his professional work) punched Jeb, the fireman, so hard on the nose that he broke it. In the best theatrical tradition, Bill Richardson, who usually rode the punch, carried on, holding a handkerchief to his bleeding face. The reviews were cool, but the publicity about Richardson's broken nose increased box office takings.

The third play was a more interesting, if highly controversial, choice – *The Shepherd and the Hunter* by the writer David Martin, who was literary editor of *Reynolds News*. Set in Palestine in the 1940s, where Martin had worked on a kibbutz, the play made a plea for Arab-Jewish friendship and mutual understanding, picking up the theme of the O'Neill piece in a more overtly political context. The British, who ruled Palestine under a United Nations mandate, have imprisoned members of the Irgun Zvai Leumi who are fighting to establish the state of Israel and are sympathetically portrayed. A small group is allowed to escape in order to lead the British to one of their most wanted leaders. The play, Martin's first, was topical but was criticised in the *Daily Worker* and at Communist Party branch meetings in the East End for being pro-Zionist. Irgun supporters visited the theatre during its run, which enraged many at Unity as the Irgun were seen as terrorists (and a month after the end of the play's run the group undertook its most notorious exploit, the blowing up of the British military headquarters in the King David Hotel). Some critics felt that it was too neat and not wholly convincing but the production received a picture feature in *Illustrated* magazine and brought Unity publicity, though this time not a great increase in audience numbers.

A lighter touch, and slightly better box office takings, came with the next production, which was another American offering, a satire on the Hollywood entertainment industry and its values called *Boy Meets Girl* by Sam and Bella Spewack. Willis followed this with *The Star Turns Red* which O'Casey has been persuaded to let Unity revive with some reluctance as he was not a supporter of Willis. (Tension over the production between O'Casey and Willis prevented a planned presentation of *Cock-a-Doodle Dandy*.) Unity applied to the Lord Chamberlain for a licence to perform *The Star Turns Red*, not because the club needed it but because the play had been banned and the theatre wanted to make a point. A licence was granted, which was hailed as an important blow for free speech, and the reasons for the earlier ban were printed in the programme. The play's strident and uncompromising Communist message was a curious choice for Willis, who was campaigning against what he saw as sectarian opposition to his broad approach. Ironically, the production achieved the highest audience figures for the professional company, though without being able to avert the serious financial trouble that the company found itself in.

Financial Problems

Opposition to the company had continued inside Unity, with the creation of a powerful dissident faction that wanted the theatre to revert to its former, exclusively non-professional, activities. Willis was forced to admit to many of the professional company's problems, and he agreed in future to seek sponsorship production by production as well as to close the school. Backing for a tour of Odets's *Golden Boy* came from the South Wales miners' welfare and the Arts Council, which offered a £500 advance against losses. The company gave one performance in London at the Holborn Hall as a send-off in September and then was able to play 65 one-night stands in South Wales, followed by three days in Wolverhampton, three in Worcester and ten in South-East London at Lewisham Town Hall with support from the local arts council. The production was directed by Ellis Solomon.

While the professional company was on tour and Willis was seeking backing for its next show, the 'dissidents', who were centred on the musical and variety team, presented a new show at Goldington Street. It was a musical comedy set in a holiday camp, written by Bill Owen (using an idea of Frank Godwin's) based on his own experience as a camp entertainer. It was called *Gold is Where You Find It* and had music by Arnold Clayton and design by Helen Biggar from Glasgow Unity. It seems to have revived flagging spirits and to have been popular among the squatters who were then involved in the most pressing domestic issue – housing – a campaign in which the Communist Party was particularly active.

Two days after the show opened, the London Communist Party organised a mass squat of empty Kensington flats involving some 400 homeless families and made national news. Five of the leaders were arrested, prosecuted and found guilty of conspiracy. A special show was performed for squatters, which marked a return to making links with the audience and with current social and political struggles. An amateur company was being revived, which mounted a rehearsed reading of George Thomson's version of *Prometheus*, and laid plans for the future after what by now was the inevitable collapse of the professional group.

Goldington Street played host to Stepney Unity in *Awake and Sing* and North West London Unity in *This Trampled Earth*, a play about contemporary Spain and its political prisoners written by George Leeson who had fought in the International Brigade. They were followed by more screenings by the Unity Film Society, which had begun showing films that June with an introduction by the film-maker Alberto Cavalcanti. At the Grand Palais, Stepney, there was a three-week Unity season of plays, films, variety and music, and for Christmas, the musical group formed itself into a variety and cabaret company to present – during an extremely cold winter and a fuel crisis – a frolic written at short notice to fill a gap called *Pardon My Greek*. It was based on *Women in Parliament* or the *Ecclesiazusae* by Aristophanes and used a translation by Benjamin Rogers, to whom apologies were made in the programme. The show was written by Geoffrey Parsons and its director and designer Bernard Sarron, who had designed most of the professional company's shows. Apart from forcing performers in a freezing theatre to wear diaphanous costumes (made out of cerecloth, the only available material allowed without rationing coupons), the show brought together for the first time since the war song-writers Geoffrey Parsons and Berkley Fase, aided by Roger Woddis, and saw the return of Vida Hope giving a helping hand. The show, which opened on Boxing Day, used mock Roman names to poke fun at contemporary politicians – Bevanus, Bevines, Winstones. The opening and closing chorus of gods, who comment bitterly on the warlike nature of the human race, sums up the tone:

> Here in Olympus we've no time for mirth
> Man is forever running wild
> Man is creation's problem child
> Oh, why in heaven did we ever create the earth.[7]

Fase had to play the piano in a muffler, overcoat and hat because of the cold, which was accentuated by the failure of the theatre's heating system, and in such wintry conditions the audiences found it difficult to reach the theatre, even if they had been inclined to venture away from home. Vida Hope later sang two songs from the show – 'Maintenance', which she wrote, and 'The Peace Song' – in Leonard Sachs's Players' Theatre Revue and in Binnie Hales's revue *Four, Five, Six!* at the Duke of York's Theatre in the West End. *Pardon My Greek* also saw the start of a five-month series of exhibitions in the theatre's foyer of work by members of the Artists' International Association as well as a display of photographs from Unity Studios, its own photographic company.

For all its problems and short run, *Pardon My Greek* is referred to by many of Willis's opponents as the beginning of the next, post-Willis, phase of Unity's life. As if to confirm the failure of the professional company, they point also to the fact that the year's biggest success turned out to be a celebration of Unity's past ten years called *Star Parade* at the Adelphi Theatre. The first half comprised excerpts from earlier triumphs, including *Lefty, Busmen, Plant in the Sun, Babes, The Star Turns Red, Spanish Village* and a duet from *Winkles and Champagne* performed by Hattie Jacques and David Kossoff. The second half, compered by the comedian Ronald Frankau, consisted of songs, dances, music and an extract from Konstantin Simonov's *The Russians*.

The professional company's final show coupled Unity's habitual concern for political comment and its new interest in 'classic' writers. It comprised a Living Newspaper play on the power crisis, *Black Magic*, with either Lorca's *The Shoemaker's Wife*, in a new translation by George Leeson, or Synge's *The Tinker's Wedding*, both directed by Dorothea Alexander, a respected drama teacher and inspirer of many theatre luminaries. The idea for *Black Magic*, (or *Coal*, as it was once known) originated in a letter written by Willis to the recruiting director of the new Ministry of Fuel and Power, Noel Newsome, in which Willis suggested the ministry should support a Unity play that put the case for coal. The 1946-47 winter crisis threatened Labour's post-war position because of a massive failure of coal supplies, which intensified in early 1947. The fall in energy reserves and labour power problems had been predicted and yet there was a lack of any proper industrial and consumption strategy. Willis, who had recently worked on similar plays for the Army Bureau of Current Affairs, was not proposing a critique but a propaganda exercise – and probably the Ministry's acceptance marks the first and only time the government directly funded an avowedly left-wing theatre group. Willis wrote the documentary play with John Collier and called it *The Precious Stone*.

The minister, Manny Shinwell, liked the play but Collier and Willis were unhappy with it. Willis withdrew because of other work commitments and Collier wrote a second version, *Black Magic*, which was to be toured after a run in London to Manchester, Birmingham, Glasgow and other industrial centres as recruiting propaganda. In the play, people are shown needing and demanding coal, such as a factory owner, a council official and a woman who wants the furnaces to start 'to make steel to make the fittings to make my new house'. A representative from the fuel ministry and a miner explain the difficulties in their own terms and, as a vivid illustration of the price of coal, a stretcher is brought on stage accompanied by a weeping widow. The *Times* called it 'a series of stage posters' whereas *Theatre Newsletter* described it as 'the slickest documentary drama yet written for the English Stage'.

The opening night on 30 January 1947 proved to be a gala occasion and occurred in the month that the Coal Industry Nationalisation Act came into effect, although the extremely cold winter of power cuts and below freezing temperatures was worsening and two days later severe fuel restrictions were introduced by the government.

Shinwell, Newsome, and others from the ministry were present with George Wigg, Shinwell's parliamentary private secretary, members of the newly created National Coal Board, including its chair Lord Hyndley and former TUC general secretary Lord Citrine, now director of welfare and training at the NCB. Also in attendance were the general secretary of the two-year old National Union of Mineworkers, the Communist Arthur Horner, and Will Lawther, its president. Other Labour and Communist leaders were present – Board of Trade president Stafford Cripps, Health Minister Aneurin Bevan and Communist Party leader Harry Pollitt. Special guests were eight miners who had been picked by their workmates in individual collieries to come to London as a reward for their example.

Joe Sterne, who played the leading miner, recalls that on tour the reception among miners was mixed. One problem was that Willis kept altering the script. Some houses were packed, says Sterne, others were very sparse. In Chorlton-cum-Hardy, near Manchester, there were only six in the audience. 'We took a vote as to whether we should perform or give the audience their money back,' remembers Sterne. Willis urged the former, the cast agreed and the performance went ahead.

In an attempt to begin the revival of the amateur Unity, Vernon Beste returned to direct the next production, Willis's most formally experimental play, called *What Happens to Love*? in which he applied Living Newspaper techniques to an examination of personal relationships. In short, quick scenes, cutting cinematically from one to another with the aid of a commentator, Willis contrasts the stereotyped view of a marriage breaking up as might be found in romantic novels, newspapers or films, with real causes such as poor housing or over-work. The first half is set in an upper-middle-class milieu, with commentary provided by the cleaner, an MP and a psychiatrist, and the audience learns that the actors playing the man and wife are married but are seeking a divorce. The second half shows the disintegration of their relationship. Discussion after the show was led by J.B. Priestley, a return to a practice that Unity had dropped during the war years but which was not to survive this production.

Despite enthusiastic reception by the South Wales miners, the professional touring production of *Golden Boy* lost a lot of money (expenses were heavy on tour) and it was recalled to play at

Goldington Street next. The professional company then collapsed and the tour of *Black Magic* had to be cut short, which hurt Willis badly as he saw in that production a vindication of his plans for Unity and, in contrast to the oppositional Living Newspapers of the 1930s, a fine example of the new role of the theatre in helping to build the peace.

There was much relief as well as despair when the end finally came. The immediate task of clearing the deficit of more than £3,000 was achieved swiftly as if the fulfilment of what everyone had been anticipating had released hidden reserves of energy. An internal inquiry dominated by Willis's critics was set up to investigate the disaster of the Unity Repertory Company, which found that Willis had badly planned and organised the venture and had taken Unity away from the labour movement toward being just another, non-political, rep.

Financially, the warning signs had come early but were not heeded: *All God's Chillun* took £990 14s 2d (54 block bookings), dropping to £778 0s 4d for *Casey Jones*, £600 18s 3d for *The Shepherd and the Hunter* and £817 1s 9d for *Boy Meets Girl*, but rising for *The Star Turns Red* to £1,181 3s 7d with 75 block bookings. Goldington Street's seating capacity was too small ever to have been able to earn enough money at the box office to sustain a professional company. If there had been full houses, Willis could at least have taken this as an endorsement of the company and argued the need to move to larger premises, but the overall losses for 1946 amounted to £3,228 11s 9d, of which the professional company was responsible for £2,724.

Artistically, the company was not good enough, and the Unity reputation not strong enough to overcome that. The Unity audience did not respond to the broad choice of plays nor, on this occasion, did it tolerate the insufficient levels of skill on display. However effective Unity performers might have been in a non-professional context (playing to their own audiences in their own theatre or at the audiences' own venues), they were not able to meet the expectations raised by a professional company that had to compete with the commercial theatre and the experimental club theatres that had sprung up since the war. Willis, who had directed all the full-length plays except the touring *Golden Boy*, was also not skilled enough. His application of Stanislavsky's methods seems to have been pedestrian and in the end he could not justify the change from collective to individual leadership with a right to hire and fire. (There had been no interview for the job of artistic director, though it is arguable that it might have been difficult to fill because sympathetic professionals would probably not have interrupted their own careers to take it on. Its lack, however, rankled as an important departure from accepted principle). For the few amateur actors who had given up secure jobs to join the company the personal disaster was profound, having lost their livelihood and in some cases related benefits such as occupational pensions. A few had supported the company through great personal sacrifice, even to the point of ploughing in a percentage of their earnings from other acting work.

Willis later admitted the artistic failure and economic madness of the project but maintained, with some justification, that the idea behind it was correct. For him it proved, sadly, that Unity's strength could only lie in the achievements of small-scale political work based on limited resources but he believed still that the time for such activity had passed. To advance further, as he had intended, required not just a larger auditorium but new sources of funding, which could only be achieved by the state or the labour movement, and neither was ready to provide. Notwithstanding the support for Unity of the Co-operative movement and individual unions, the labour movement as a whole was not ideologically or organisationally predisposed to aid the arts, and the state, in the guise of the newly formed Arts Council, which did not fund amateur theatre, was already locked into a pattern of subsidy that excluded the likes of Unity's professional company on a regular basis.

National Impact

The failure of the professional company was a blow to both London Unity and to the national society, which on paper looked quite healthy and which, in terms of many individual initiatives, was still active and influential. Fortunately, other activities had not ceased because of the professional company; the particular post-war proclivity for 'thinking big', combined with the left's more general, and seemingly bottomless, optimism and belief in its ability to overcome any obstacle in any field of endeavour, helped keep Unity afloat and flourishing both in London and nationally.

A Unity-organised conference in March 1946 on 'Theatre and the People' was addressed by a wide range of representatives – from the Arts Council, Actors' Equity, the British Drama League, and the Co-operative Drama Association – and by leading performers such as Sybil Thorndike, Claire Luce, Edith Evans and Herbert Lom. Julius Jacobs said that trade unions would be interested in theatre if theatre were interested in trade unions and the conference spoke for many in its hopes for a post-war cultural renovation continuing the upsurge in interest and activity of the war years.

The conference argued for increased direct state funding at local and central level, cultural education at all levels from primary school to university, and the establishment of a network of local repertory theatres that could exchange visits, and it stressed the role of the amateur theatre in stimulating new and experimental work (much of this predating developments in the Arts Council that took off under the first Arts Minister Jennie Lee and recommendations of the later Arts Council-sponsored Cork Report in the 1980s). The gathering helped raise membership of Unity's national society in May 1946 to just under 7,000, with 190 affiliated organisations and 36 branches, two of which, in London and Glasgow, were professional.

The 1946 AGM summed up the achievements of the war and focused on education and, in the spirit of the Left Book Club Theatre Guild, offered advice on how to start amateur groups, which were seen as seed-beds for the professional theatre. The report was critical of the chasm that still existed between amateurs and professionals – there 'was still too much giving to the people and not enough drawing them within the orbit so that they can also give their contribution' – and made the clear distinction between the situation of the 1930s, when Unity represented an opposition trend, and the post-war position of the whole people hungry for the arts and eager to engage in creative activity. Unity, however, was denied membership of the Little Theatre Guild, formed in 1946, because it was not an 'independent play-producing organisation' and certainly could not claim to be 'non-political'.

That summer, Willis, Oscar Lewenstein and Alec Bernstein changed the format of *New Theatre* magazine, which had been founded originally by the Goldington Street branch before being taken over nationally, and launched a membership campaign aimed at winning 3,000 new members, 250,000 affiliates, twenty new branches and £5,000 capital. There were also two summer schools – one in Hastings, one in Clitheroe. By the annual national conference in November which was attended by 113 delegates, ten new branches had been formed, a budget for the national office of £250,000 had been agreed and the principle of being a 'theatre for the labour movement as a whole' with a complementary responsibility to develop theatre in the communities had been accepted. This approach included continued backing for the British Drama League, the next conference of which was galvanised by militant resolutions from London and Merseyside Unity Theatres on support for drama education at all ages and levels, and support for an extension of state aid for drama through the Arts Council and local authorities.

By May 1947, just after the professional company had collapsed, membership of the national society peaked at 10,000 (about 2,000 of whom were active), more than 3,000,000 affiliates and 50 branches. Recently affiliated bodies included the London, Glasgow, Cardiff and Birmingham Trades Councils, the London, Royal Arsenal, Liverpool and Birmingham Co-ops, the William Morris Club, the Walthamstow Labour Party and the Wimbledon Labour League of Youth. A leaflet of the time names other affiliates: the Civil Service Clerical Association, the shopworkers' union USDAW and the Student Labour Federation.

Unity's influence was channelled mainly through *New Theatre* which had grown in prestige since the change of format under Elkan Allan, the editor for the first two issues. Ted Willis took over with Alec Bernstein as his assistant, who acquired more and more responsibility as Willis's other work absorbed his time. By the end of 1946 the magazine claimed a circulation of 15,000 with a good subscriptions list and sales in several West End theatre foyers. Its editorial policy was the same as that of Unity, but Unity was only mentioned when its activities merited attention, and differences regarding productions or attitudes could be aired. For example, in 1947, Unity general council member, the playwright Benn Levy MP, praised Unity's separation of art and politics, and in the next issue Unity general manager Gerry Sharp rebuffed him, alleging this to be an attack on the theatre and a distortion of its approach.

One of the forerunners of the magazine *Encore* a decade later,

New Theatre was an attractively produced and illustrated forum for thoughtful and polemical debate on a wide range of topics, with reviews and letters as well. Its list of contributors reads like a roll call of theatre's leading lights: apart from regulars and those long associated with Unity, Bertolt Brecht, Peter Brook, Jean Cocteau, Basil Dean, George Devine, Edith Evans, John Gielgud, Hugh Hunt, Emile Littler, Arthur Miller and Val Parnell all contributed. Peter Ustinov was once its theatre critic and the last chair of its board.

Publicity material expressed the confidence of the moment – Oscar Lewenstein's well produced pamphlet *Unity Theatre Presents*, illustrated by James Friell (the *Daily Worker*'s cartoonist Gabriel), for example, or *Hurrah for Unity* by Sybil Thorndike and Lewis Casson. In 1947, the same confidence led to the extension to three weeks of the summer school which was held in Edinburgh to coincide with the international festival. The school was under the direction of Robert Mitchell, who had led Glasgow Unity to turn professional and to win an outstanding reputation that surpassed momentarily the standing of its London counterpart.

Glasgow Unity, which had affiliated to Unity's national society in March 1945, had brought 3,000 members with it. That same year, it had achieved some measure of stability and was able to secure for a season a permanent base, at the Athenaeum, to open club rooms and appoint Mitchell its full-time director.[8] The first production of this season was Gorky's *The Lower Depths*, adapted and directed by Mitchell, an electrical engineer by trade and during the war a convenor in one of Scotland's largest factories. The group's commitment to 'a theatre indigenous to the people of Glasgow in particular and Scotland in general' was reflected in this production which was performed in the idiom of the actors without any attempt by them to become 'Russian'. After a visit to London Unity with *The Lower Depths*, the season continued with Bernard McGinn's *Remembered for Ever*, a play by the novelist James Barke, *When the Boys Come Home*, and later *Starched Aprons*, the first play by Ena Lamont Stewart who went on to write one of Glasgow Unity's greatest successes, *Men Should Weep*. Glasgow Unity's casts included Stanley Baxter and other future professional actors Russell Hunter, Roddy McMillan, Andrew Keir, Ida Schuster and Archie Duncan.

In April 1946, two months after London Unity's first professional production, Glasgow launched its 'full-time' company with O'Casey's *Purple Dust*. The company was drawn entirely from its own members, unlike Glasgow's Citizens' Theatre which had looked south when it had been formed. An amateur wing continued under Donald McBean. In May 1946 Glasgow Unity won Arts Council sponsorship and later that year achieved its greatest success with *The Gorbals Story* by Robert McLeish, a cartoonist on a Glasgow newspaper. The play is centred on a day in a slum kitchen shared by eight families and tackles a pressing contemporary issue by attacking the desperate housing situation. A natural successor to Gorky's *The Lower Depths, The Gorbals Story* represents a notable example of native socialist realism that in production appears to have surpassed any equivalent attempts made by London Unity. The Glasgow opening at the Queen's Theatre (not the Athenaeum, which the group had been forced to leave by what the historian John Hill calls a 'perverse and probably political decision' of the governors) saw the civic and literary leadership of the town lectured from the stage before curtain-up by a representative of local squatters who were the group's guests of honour. *The Gorbals Story* came off after five weeks of full houses only because the theatre had a prior commitment to its pantomime, but the show stayed in Unity's repertoire until the end of its days. By April 1947 it had been seen by more than 100,000 people; it was taken to West Hartlepool and then to London at the Garrick Theatre, the first Scottish repertory company to perform a Scottish play in the West End. *The Gorbals Story* was released as a film in 1950 but in no way captured the spirit of the original. Glasgow Unity also presented Robert McClellan's *Torwatletie*, George Munro's *Gold in His Boots* and Benedict Scott's *The Lambs of God* (also known as *This Walking Shadow*), a pioneering play about homosexuality in a 1930s slum. The amateur wing performed the British première of Paschoral Carlos Magnos's *Tomorrow will be Different* and Ena Lamont Stewart's female 'version' of *The Gorbals Story, Men Should Weep*. *Gold in His Boots, Men Should Weep* and *In Time o' Strife* were revived in the 1980s by 7:84 Scotland.

Glasgow Unity initiated the 'fringe' at the Edinburgh Festival but it cost the group its Arts Council support. Six months before the festival, Unity had argued for Scottish representation – not necessarily from Unity – yet when it became clear that no Scots company was to be invited, on the grounds that none had achieved sufficiently high standards, Unity decided to make an appearance. At the next festival, the Scottish presence was acknowledged through the Citizens' Theatre's official production of *The Three Estates* and the 'fringe' appearance of Unity and four other Scottish groups.

The amateur wing continued to present Scottish plays in Glasgow and the professional company transferred from the Garrick to the Embassy Theatre where it slowly became cut off from its roots despite staging some sucessful shows. Under the Glasgow Unity banner, Robert Mitchell directed Siobhan McKenna, Frederick Valk and Beatrix Lehmann in Ibsen's *Ghosts* at the Embassy in 1951, the year that the company folded. This was soon followed by the collapse of the amateur group. Individual Unity members formed a professional company called Envoy Productions, which mounted shows at the Embassy – a link with that theatre which continued up until the mid-1950s even when there was no longer any formal relationship with Unity. The Embassy connection, which went back to the 1930s and André van Gyseghem, saw the coming together of Glasgow and London Unitarians who had turned professional, such as Eveline Garratt, Betty Henderson, Marjorie Thomson, Alfie Bass, David Kossoff, Warren Misel (Mitchell) and Oscar Lewenstein, who had been Glasgow's general manager; it also brought them into contact with others who were to become well-known performers, like Renée Goddard, Miriam Karlin and Harry Towb.

Within the Unity society, the desire for independence always clashed with the recognised advantages of a nationally co-ordinated organisation. The September-October 1947 issue of *Unity News* carried rule changes that allowed the society to revert to its earlier London status, freeing London Unity from the entanglements of a national body and permitting it and the other Unity groups to become autonomous again within a new Unity Theatre Federation. It held its first conference in April 1948.

This relaxation of organisational links coincided with what Willis saw as the high point of Unity's influence on the theatre world, the British Theatre Conference of February 1948, which continued the debate of the 1946 conference on 'The Theatre and the People'. The idea for the gathering had been mentioned first by J.B. Priestley in another magazine, the fortnightly *Theatre Newsletter*. *New Theatre* ran an editorial on the role of the theatre in building the peace (what Willis called the 'second Battle of Britain') and supported the convening of such a conference. The editors of the two magazines formed an organising committee and were helped by another publication, *Theatre Today*, an occasional miscellany edited by the Communists Montagu Slater and Arnold Rattenbury (whose view of theatre differed from that of Willis, which caused some tension). The arts magazine *Our Time* also supported, and reported, the conference, which was chaired by Priestley. It was attended by 471 delegates and was denounced by the theatre managers as a red front, although some individual managers did visit as observers. Conference passed a dazzling number of resolutions, backing the building of a National Theatre, the new Arts Council and UNESCO, and calling for various changes in drama education, amateur theatre, professional training, entry to the acting profession, censorship, theatre regulations, entertainment tax, rent and cost of theatres and, on Unity's initiative, local authority responsibilities and rights to run civic theatres.[9]

Previous discussion on this last point had already helped formulate an historic porposal on the levying of a rate for municipal entertainment that was put to the House of Commons to coincide with the conference. The minister responsible, Aneurin Bevan, pledged to include such a regulation in the final Bill, which marked the first such legislation in Britain. Sir Stafford Cripps, Chancellor of the Exchequer and Unity general council member, addressed the conference and promised to take its proposals back to Cabinet but Labour's priorities were to lie elsewhere (although he did halve the Entertainments Tax on live theatre and abolish it for places with small populations and auditoria seating less than 200 people).

As the Cold War bit harder, and the enthusiasm of the protagonists changed direction, the standing committee that was charged with organising a follow-up national theatre conference went into recess after several meetings for six months and then faded away, just like *New Theatre* magazine (in 1949) and Unity's new federation.

Disagreements continued within the Unity groups and within the federation. Federation secretary V.J. Hearn from Blackpool announced in 1948, as *Unity News* went quarterly, that the number of affiliated groups had dropped to 23. In 1949 the society could still manage a summer school, which, under the direction of Mark Clifford, who had played Agate in the first Unity production of *Waiting for Lefty*, was held at Malvern to coincide with the first post-war revival of the festival there. The school's main speakers were Patricia Burke and Michel Saint-Denis. At the 1949 national conference, the secretary of the Kensington (West London) branch, Frank Marcus, became the focus of the habitual argument on what constitutes 'a Unity play', and, going beyond that, the nature of Unity's political leanings. Marcus, later to become known as a critic and author, had just directed, designed and acted in Peter Ustinov's *House of Regrets* at the Torch Theatre and Goldoni's *Servant of Two Masters* at the Twentieth Century Theatre (in which other cast members included the painter Frank Auerbach, the novelist Patrick O'Connor, and the journalist Harold Jackson). Reviews had been good. Nevertheless, Oscar Lewenstein – according to Marcus – attacked the branch for its 'muddled, liberal, and humanitarian' policy. Marcus and others were angry at the management committee's refusal to admit to its Communist affiliation and his branch proposed that 'there should be no such thing as a Unity play'. (It subsequently left the federation, adopted another name and became the nucleus of a professional, experimental company, the International Theatre Group.)

Willis, Lewenstein, Bernstein and others, who had given total commitment to Unity, were now pursuing their own careers elsewhere and it proved difficult fill the vacuum left at Goldington Street. By 1950 the number of groups in the Federation had fallen to seventeen. Cardiff Unity, a lively group that had presented the British première of Ostrovsky's *Even a Wise Man Errs*, protested that discussion at the conference that year had been abruptly curtailed to avoid further challenge to the notion that federation policy should be the policy for each group. The debate centred again on what was – or was not – a Unity play and to what extent a Unity theatre should – or could – be a theatre of the labour movement as distinct from a theatre of the community. The tortuous nature of the discussion is underlined by Cardiff's case, where the various communities in which Unity was playing were overwhelmingly working-class and the majority were those of the culturally conscious miners.

Ideological differences within Unity were now irreconcilable. Mid-Rhondda Unity changed its name to secure new premises and dropped out of the federation. Brighton Unity collapsed after being attacked in a local newspaper as a Communist group for producing Shaw's *Arms and the Man*. In the face of this falling apart, the management committee's statement to the 1951 conference called on Unity to 'ally itself even more closely with the progressive working-class movement in the struggle against the right-wing Labour policy of subservience to the ruling class of America and its replacement by a policy for peace and socialism'. Labour lost the election that year. In March 1952 the Unity federation was wound up. London Unity was on the verge of collapse and an even more loosely organised federation was proposed, with individual groups taking on different responsibilities.

Jerry Dawson of Merseyside Unity, which was charged with distributing the minutes of the 1955 conference, describes them as 'close to an obituary'. A few groups carried on, and as late as 1963 there was an attempt to set up a Northern Unity operating in Manchester, Leeds and Merseyside (the carpenter and chairman of which was Eric Heffer MP). By the 1970s only Merseyside and London were left and, after the fire that reduced Goldington Street to a shell in 1975, only Merseyside remained. It too closed finally – on its fiftieth anniversary in 1987.

In the five years since the war, the Unity national society, once described by Tyrone Guthrie as expressing 'the thoughts, aspirations and hopes of many of the ordinary people of today', had risen to the challenge of history and then had fallen, unable to meet those stringent demands. There had been grounds for optimism – the cultural upsurge from the war, the Old Vic tours, the emergence of a regional theatre movement, the founding of Theatre Workshop, the work of Glasgow Unity, the new Arts Council, the experimental theatre clubs, the myriad activities of the Unity movement – yet, in a matter of a few years, the situation looked bleak. For the left, however, it was not simply a retreat to pre-war days, as the political climate actually became worse in many ways.

Glasgow Unity's decline in the 1950s foreshadowed the fate of kindred ventures, such as Theatre Workshop, brought down by the economics of commercial production which hit hard a company trying to create an ensemble identity and especially those concerned with establishing a close relationship to the audience. Yet

Glasgow's achievements, notably its promotion of a Scottish national drama, still offer a good example of the extraordinary cultural energy that did emerge from the war. The work of the Unity movement as a whole is a tribute to that impetus, which has been undervalued both in general and by the left. It is a missing element in the creation of a participatory welfare state instead of the alienated bureaucracy imposed from above that it became, in the arts as elsewhere. The culture gap, that kept theatre the preserve of 'them' and not 'us', had been broken down, albeit briefly, and this did help lay the basis for future arts policies that would create the national companies and begin to give theatre back to the people.

The post-war movement, however, was unable at the time to prevent the Arts Council mandarins from establishing an elitist policy of 'Few But Roses' (borrowed from a classical motto designed for a patrician nursery), which replaced the wartime slogan of 'The Best For Most'. Regional arts offices were closed down and the creation of a National Theatre was postponed for another three decades. Although the Unity theatres were undertaking just those tasks that the Arts Council's pronouncements said a theatre should, they and others who were attempting to sustain in peace time the advances of the war and to stimulate people's own creative activities were denied subsidy (with the occasional exception early on), as if striving to be popular and aiming at excellence were now mutually exclusive. The battle was lost on the direction and nature of state funding and various ventures – Theatre '46, (backed by the engineering union), the People's Entertainment Society (supported by the Co-ops), *Our Time, New Theatre* and the two Unity professional groups – folded one by one.

The left's difficulty in adjusting to the new Cold War climate affected Unity, which had its own general council members, Stafford Cripps and George Strauss, as members of the new establishment. The utopian zeal of pre-war opposition could not as easily be turned into a positive passion, particularly as Labour's compromises under American pressure soon soured and then abruptly ended the post-war honeymoon. Inside the Communist Party, the beginnings of a new political strategy, 'The British Road to Socialism', were being debated, but the role of culture, despite the important work of Communists in this area, did not figure centrally. There was discussion on culture and new ideas were abroad, for example, in the magazine *Our Time* or, more particularly in Jack Lindsay's 1945 paper, which he gave to a party conference, on culture as a productive force in its own right rather than as a mere reflection of reality. The theoretical life of the party, however, was still overshadowed by a restrictive interpretation of Marxism which had its effect on Unity where the visionary force of the 1930s had been dulled.[10] Unity had promoted an all-embracing notion of People's Theatre, which, politically, saw an identity between the labour movement and the working class and between the working class and the nation and, aesthetically, valued and projected a common-sense view of working-class experience onto all culture. At the centre of this notion lay the noble, comforting but unrealistic claim of 'serving the whole labour movement', although, even at its height, Unity never played to or represented anything other than a small if dynamic and vital section of the movement. In the enormous post-war expansion of Unity's membership and activities, and with a majority Labour government in power, it is easy to see how the conflation between movement, class and nation was made and wrongly judged, overlooking the important contradictions within and between all three, but as the Cold War progressed the weaknesses of the analysis, which Unity shared with that part of the left that it represented, proved increasingly harmful.[11] The accompanying overestimation of the entry of the labour movement and working class into the cultural sphere soon revealed that the tasks of the 1930s had not been completed and that there was no linear progression to the next stage; the political ground had to be won all over again, which, in the theatre, required different strategies because the intellectual climate was quite different from the 1930s.

For many artists, the commitment of that decade had been replaced by scepticism and a drift away from – or antagonism towards – politics, with the Communist Party discredited in their eyes and the horrors of the Nazi holocaust and the atom bomb rendering them ideologically agnostic. This was reflected in the crisis of traditional theatre which was epitomised by the dearth of challenging new plays. The failure of the people's theatre idea was the failure of Labour to transform post-war society, and, at Unity, the collapse of the professional company as the standard-bearer of this conception allowed narrow thinking back in, with a simplified view of the working class, its composition and homogeneity.

Paradoxically, the approach that sustained this view, which was often belied by the plays Unity presented, contained a spirited doggedness that was necessary for Unity to survive and yet, by its inability to provide growth and development, bore the seeds of its own destruction.

London's role in the decline of the national movement is contradictory. It was both the driving and the destructive force. Those who had opposed Willis on the issue of the professional company saw it as the nadir and not the zenith of Unity's existence and felt that its failure had destroyed the possibility of any other expansion. Instead of invigorating other groups, Goldington Street had drained them of their vitality. Its leaders were in no position to guide the national society, their main concern and contribution being to rescue London Unity in the aftermath of the professional company's debacle, in which task they proved highly successful.

Mobile Plays

The Mobile Group had been re-established and certain London activities had survived; Unity Studios – run by Leo Kruks and Cyril Bernard – had been established in 1946 as a photographic service for Unity as well as the labour movement and amateur drama societies. It was formed as a separate company in order to protect it financially; New Theatre Publications had a strong catalogue that included Alec Guinness's adaptation of *Great Expectations*, Gorky's *The Enemies* and Montagu Slater's *Out of Liverpool*;[12] the orchestra and cabaret group flourished – Unity dances were a popular feature of the social calendar on the left – and the Unity film society was presenting interesting foreign films on alternate Mondays when no play was being produced. A programme of lectures was organised, including a one-off performance of Shaw's *Overruled* complete with preface, and poetry readings were held which attracted notable poets such as Edith Sitwell, David Gascoyne, Hugh MacDiarmid, Ann Ridler, Jack Lindsay and Dylan Thomas (who caught a BBC producer's eye). A script service was established and a library of dialect records made available for hire. The first 'buy-a-brick' drive was launched to raise money for an extension to the front of the theatre which would provide room for rehearsals and a bar that Unity hoped would be licensed. The aim was £350 or 7,000 bricks at 1 shilling each which donors were invited to come and lay. It was hoped that this would lead to the building of a new theatre on the same site with the help of the landlords and local council – the first of several ill-fated attempts to tackle the problem of the inadequacies of the building. When Unity had to give up Britannia Street to the Royal National Throat, Nose and Ear Hospital in 1947, Dick Polling built a new scenery dock and workshop in nearby Aldenham Street. Polling, a member of Unity's leadership before, during and after the war, was noted for many things, including the tails he wore when front-of-house manager and another building exploit, affectionately known as Polling's folly – an outside toilet on the path linking the auditorium to the backstage area and constructed because there was none behind the stage. A conscientious objector, Polling was also one of the regular commuters with Laurence Olivier on the famous last train at night from Victoria Station to Brighton, where he had a Regency flat. If Polling had to miss the train, he would sleep in one of the dressing rooms at Unity, ready to serve the theatre the next morning.

One activity that did not survive was the Unity film unit, Crescent Films, ambitiously planned to be a counterpart of the professional theatre company. It made one film, *Century of Song*, based on *Winkles and Champagne*, which the film's producer, Alec Bernstein, also wrote. Directed by Fritz Weiss (who had to break union rules to make the film), it was shot at Britannia Street by a good cameraman, Joseph Amber, and was funded by a Wardour Street producer whom Willis had persuaded to part with £1,000. The backer decided to reclaim his money and there is no record of the film ever having been shown. Props and film equipment were found at Britannia Street when the premises were taken over.

Unity kept active at the London level; it helped establish the St Pancras Borough Arts Club and adopted a local youth theatre to aid its members in their own theatrical activities.[13] A Theatre Guild was formed to encourage members to participate in Unity's work, especially in criticising productions. An annual One-Act Play Festival (short-lived) was introduced with a Challenge Cup going to the winner. London groups, with the newly created Goldington Street Theatre Workshop, performed at the Free German League of Culture in Priestley's *Music at Night, The Golden Fleece*, Willis's *The Bells are Ringing* and an original revue called *The Academy of Arts*. The London regional committee, which ran an internal bulletin *Unity News* that changed its name to *Active Member* in June 1948, mounted a series of weekend events at the Hampstead Little Theatre. This included a performance of Beaumont and Fletcher's *The Knight of the Burning Pestle*, in a shortened version, and Synge's *Riders to the Sea* by students of the Unity drama school who had also performed Dekker's *The Shoemaker's Holiday*. Among the 'graduates' from these activities was Harvey Unna, who was to become a distinguished literary agent.

There were brief attempts to organise alternative ventures to the Willis-dominated Unity – such as Theatre '46 at the Scala Theatre, which had union backing and involved Jack Lindsay, Ann Davies, Montague Slater and Bernard Miles. (Willis was highly critical of its main production, *A Century for George*, written by Slater to mark the centenary of the Amalgamated Engineering Union. One of its other shows was a dramatisation of the fight for the nationalisation of the mines, *The Face of Coal* by Lindsay and B.L. Coombes, which predated Unity's own *Black Magic*. Unity had discussed the AEU centenary but did not take part in the celebrations, which included an exhibition organised by the Artists' International Association, a film by Ralph Bond, *We Who Make the Tools*, and a history of the union by James B. Jefferys, *The Story of the Engineers*.)

The majority of those opposed to the professional company, however, believed that the battle had to be won inside Unity. Anything else, they felt, would be beyond both their means and ambitions, would suffer from competition from other theatres as the professional company did, and could not win the support of the unions and Co-ops on a continuing basis. (The failure of Theatre '46 after the engineers pulled out could not have encouraged other unions to sponsor drama.) At its height this backing had only been able to sustain a theatre the size of the Goldington Street auditorium and had never been able to provide the security for moving to larger premises. The way ahead was seen as lying along the traditional Unity path – to revitalise the links with the labour movement, to raise artistic standards back to the levels achieved when the war broke out and to revive the Mobile group, which had been a victim of the Willis plan.

It was the demand for shows from squatters' groups during the late summer and autumn of 1946 that raised the idea of relaunching the Mobile Group as a propaganda arm of Unity which also allowed people to make a regular commitment of a couple of nights a week instead of the frantic six or eight-week involvement required by shows at Goldington Street. The revival seems to have coincided with the resolving of personal differences concerning Joe MacColum, a director of the Left Theatre in Ireland who became a central figure at Unity in the immediate post-war years and again in the late 1950s. He was put in charge of the new 'shock group' – a phrase taken from the days of the Workers' Theatre Movement – and it was dedicated to fighting fascism and anti-semitism on its 'home ground'. In fact, the early repertoire was quite varied. It mixed immediate political comment, in plays such as Gadfan Morris's *Bikini Fable* set at Bikini Lagoon during the atom-bomb tests, with more general pieces like O'Casey's *Pound on Demand* or a Unity revival like *Who are the English?* by Jack Lindsay. Lindsay wrote a new mass declamation, *Cry of Greece*, during the civil war there, which played alongside versions of or extracts from Goldington Street shows, such as Leonard Peck's *The Townshends,* Leonard Irwin's *The Circling Dove*, the revue *What's Left?* and *Winkles and Champagne*. Old Time Music Hall featured prominently in the Mobile programme and later a specialist group called the Unity Mobile Solo Artists offered this entertainment exclusively.

In 1947 the Mobile Group presented a documentary by John Collier on how the rates were spent, called *Your Money and Your Life*, which was performed at the St Pancras Arts and Civic Week. *Oh Priceless Heritage* by Peter Collingwood was a 30-minute comedy satirising a cross-section of Londoners and their attitudes to freedom and democracy – a popular Unity theme that was linked to an abiding anti-American feeling. This was represented by a ten-minute sketch from the USA, *The Investigators* by Lewis Allen, and another American play, Mordecai Gorelik's *Gravy Train* concerning the post-war 'red-baiting' which the author began directing on a trip to Britain before returning and leaving the production to Herbert Marshall. Anti-Americanism was not an attack on everything American – Unity owed many of its successes to plays from the USA – but a profound dislike of the prevailing values, as shown in another Mobile show *The Menace of the Comics*, which echoed an especially strident drive led by teachers in a Communist campaign against the US infiltration of and influence on British culture. [14] Complementary attacks on the

Cold War were focused on the most urgent of all topics – peace – and audiences were in no doubt that Unity placed the blame for the arms race squarely on the Americans.

American forces had never really left Britain after the war, although the first formal offer of a presence came in July 1948 following acceptance of the Marshall Aid plan that April and the need to launch the Berlin airlift. Three RAF bases were handed over to the USAF as a 'temporary' measure. With the first atom-bomb carriers installed, the presence became permanent in August 1948. The North Atlantic Treaty Organisation was founded in 1949, the year that the Soviet Union exploded its atom bomb and sponsored the first World Peace Congress. British government visa restrictions forced the second congress to be switched from Sheffield to Warsaw but the peace movement gathered pace and collected millions of signatures for the international peace petition, a campaign to which Unity contributed with its mobile items *A Piece About Peace* by Jack Lindsay and *We Want Peace* (or *A Plea for Peace*) – a programme of poetry and prose with a commentary by the 'Red' Dean of Canterbury, Dr Hewlett Johnson. In the Living Newspaper tradition, Eric Paice's *Focus on Peace* joined the repertoire, along with its companion, *Focus on Germany*, written at the time of the fight against German rearmament.

After the loss of Britannia Street, the almost nightly rehearsals of the Mobile Group had to move to different venues, such as the Garibaldi Restaurant off Rosebery Avenue or rooms above pubs. The group would play mostly at weekends, travelling in a converted ex-army radio van, and when the van was no longer usuable, Sheila Dorrell organised a drive to raise £300 for a 26-seat, second-hand Bedford coach. The group operated within a 30-mile radius of London but sometimes ventured further at weekends, especially for labour movement events at which it would perform one of its trade union plays, such as Ted Willis's *The Jolly George* about the Royal Albert dockers who refused to load a ship that was to sail with munitions for use against the young Soviet republic. The group, for example, went to Birmingham when three branches of the engineering union combined to invite Unity and to Sheffield for a fire brigade union conference.

This kind of play, along with Old Time Music Hall, formed the backbone of the mobile work and usually was a variation of a show that had been or subsequently was presented at Goldington Street, like *The Match Girls* or *The Rochdale Pioneers* (which did not take off). Another, *The Dockers' Tanner*, which tells the story of the 1889 dock strike, played against a background of important contemporary dock strikes. In 1948 a local dispute flared up, troops were sent in and a State of Emergency declared; in 1949 a battle over the registering of stevedores was followed by solidarity action for striking Canadian seamen, a lock-out, more troops being sent in and another State of Emergency; and in 1951 seven dockers' leaders were discharged from the Old Bailey having been arrested for conspiracy to contravene a wartime regulation banning strike action. This legislation, known as Order 1305, had been used by the Labour government in its attempts to control industrial militancy but it was forced to abandon the order in the wake of the dockers' victory. The play was also taken to Dover for the Kent miners' day. In similar vein, *Six Men of Dorset* was performed in a marquee in Tolpuddle for the annual celebration of the trade union pioneers, playing one year to 1,000 people on two occasions on the same day against the noise of band music and heavy rain. On another trip, which took the play to a West London factory, 40 people joined their trade union after seeing the show.

The Ragged Trousered Philanthropists, adapted by Frank Rhodes from Bill Owen's version (which was adapted from the original play by Tom Thomas) was presented to an agricultural workers' meeting in Weymouth and proved to be the group's most popular piece during the Cold War years. Just as the group had visited the docks in preparation for *The Dockers' Tanner*, its members had been taught necessary skills by building trade unionists for this show and the attention to detail must have paid off. During six months of 1950, for example, its bookings included Southwark Trades Council at the local baths, a Unity presentation at Ilford Town Hall, Peckham Electricians' Union at the local Co-op Hall, Tunbridge Wells Labour Party, the Surrey Federation of Trades Councils at Wimbledon Town Hall, the Derbyshire Miners Welfare Holiday Camp at Skegness and the Nottingham Trades Council and Labour Party at the Notts Co-op Hall. In 1951-52, it was sponsored by Unity in almost twenty London suburbs for two performances each. The lead, a gas fitter called Harry Johnson, also drove the bus and briefly ran the Mobile Group which developed a terrific camaraderie.

Under Bill Wardman's direction, the Mobile Group presented a musical in 1950 and, in 1951, a humourous and critical observation on the Festival of Britain called *Exhibition 51*. When the coach needed overhauling in 1953, the roof was mended with a tarpaulin 'borrowed' from British Rail and a quickly applied coat of paint spruced up the bodywork. By the end of 1954 the coach was beyond repair and Unity could not afford a replacement. Full-length plays were dropped and, following the intervention of the then general manager, George Leeson, the Mobile Group soon became defunct with a few, sporadic, exceptions. It was revived in the late 1950s, performing music hall, folk and skiffle, and had an intermittent life thereafter, often being invoked as the true soul of all that Unity should stand for, despite the fact that since the outbreak of the war those most actively involved in its work frequently felt like second-class citizens in comparison with those performing at Goldington Street.

The labour movement emphasis of the Mobile Group, with particular attention being paid to the Co-ops, was shared by the Goldington Street adminstration which was still firmly Communist-led; it sought close liaison with the party in trying to resuscitate Unity after the collapse of the professional company and scripts were regularly discussed with the party centre. The team was led by general manager Gerry Sharp, an accountant, and production manager David Tree from the Cambridge Progressive Players. Bill Owen, establishing himself as a professional actor and moving into films, played a key artistic role between 1947 and 1949, as did others – notably Alfie Bass – who had moved on from Unity to the professional theatre but who would return whenever they could to help.

Goldington Street recovered remarkably quickly from the collapse of the professional company. After two guest 'fillers' – Euston Unity in *An Italian Love Story* by Colin Morris and *Out of the Dust* by Horace Morgan from the Welsh pit village of Ystradgynlais – the first play to be presented by London's new company (much at the insistence of Caron Rock) was *The Match Girls*, which was so popular that it was revived again a few months later. This choice emphasised continuity with Unity's past and the importance of the labour movement. The cast visited the Bryant and May factory and new scenes were added by Roger Woddis and Bill Owen, who directed. Bessie Braddock MP wrote an introduc-

UNITY THEATRE

Presents

The Enemies was one of five Gorky plays staged by Unity; the programme carries Unity's logo of the period - an alliance of drama and industry

tion for the programme. Lucien Amaral, a scenic artist with Associated Pictures and one of Unity's most gifted designers, created a realistic set with real mouldings and a kerb and lantern for the pub. The audience cheered the cast on the first night and an original 'match girl', Elizabeth Morrison, was invited on stage. Unity veteran of the 1930s Hilda Fenemore played Kate, the leading 'match girl', and was approached by Rank afterwards. She became a successful television performer.

This production provided the fillip that Unity needed and was followed by a tribute to Gorky in what Unity believed to be the first English performance of his 1907 play *The Enemies*, which had been banned by the tsarist censor and had not been seen in the Soviet Union until 1933. In a special translation for Unity by Tom Jay Bell, the production was directed rather unhappily by Joe MacColum, who was replaced by Kate and Lucien Amaral. The leading woman, Miriam Brickman, was later to influence British acting styles through her casting work at the Royal Court and with Woodfall Films.

Unity's reason for choosing Gorky's story of textile factory workers fighting for better conditions and unknowingly laying the ground for events in the 1905 Revolution, is made clear from the publicity material, which picks out two quotes. Factory Owner: 'The question is: who is going to be master – you and I or the workers?' and Factory worker: 'We've got to stand by each other like links in the chain!' The programme carried a message from the Soviet ambassador, saying that the production would help relations between Britain and the Soviet Union. Again, continuity with Unity's past was being stressed – Goldington Street had opened with a Soviet play and during the war had presented *Distant Point, Dostigaeff and Others* and *Comrade Detective*.

The Match Girls and *The Enemies* signalled two of Unity's main preoccupations (the labour movement and solidarity with the socialist world) and the next production, *Dragnet* by Roger Woddis, represented yet another, Unity's anti-Americanism, which proved out of the three themes to offer the deepest source of creative energy. It was as if opposition once more released a productive drive that had been muted in the attempts to build the peace after the war. Anti-Americanism provided a clear consensus between audience and performer and the target was both easily identifiable and easily attacked.

Programme · **Sixpence**

THE WHOLE WORLD OVER

by

KONSTANTIN SIMONOV

UNITY THEATRE

GOLDINGTON STREET, N.W.1 Box Office : EUS. 5391

Unity showed its solidarity with the Soviet bloc throughout the Cold War; this comedy was presented in 1948

In *Dragnet*, directed by Ted Willis against Lucien and Kate Amaral's vivid backcloth of the Four Horsemen of the Apocalypse, Woddis satirises the 'manhunt' thriller formula to expose the existence of two Americas; the anti-black, anti-labour, anti-Communist America built on the values of Wall Street, and the America of the decent, ordinary person symbolised by Joe Demos, a demobbed GI on the run for assaulting a policeman in defence of a black person. He is also being chased by his English sweetheart and a Soviet journalist. The key motif for Unity of attacking the lack of democracy in the so-called land of freedom is summed up in *Dragnet* when the Statue of Liberty sings 'Strange Fruit', the haunting American song about lynching that Unity performers had sung to black and to white audiences during the war.

This line of attack was continued with an American play – the world première of Jay Bennett's *Lion's After Slumber* – and more successfully with a Soviet play, *The Russian Question* by Konstantin Simonov, which blames the 'west' for inventing the iron curtain. This had appeared in two parts in an English language news publication issued by the Soviet Embassy and also had been turned into what one cinema historian called the first Soviet film of the Cold War. An American journalist is sent by his press baron boss to the Soviet Union to report on how the Soviet people are preparing for war, but he finds the opposite and files 'unacceptable' copy that leads to personal and professional ruin. The US authorities protested when the play was performed in the Soviet zone in Germany. Bill Owen directed the production for Unity celebrating the thirtieth anniversary of the October Revolution, and the first night audience included the ambassadors of Bulgaria, Hungary, Norway, Poland, Romania and Yugoslavia, and representatives from the Soviet embassy. The production earned a picture spread feature in *Illustrated* magazine. Six months later, Bill Owen directed another Simonov play, *The Whole World Over*, an affectionate comedy of Soviet demobilisation in which everyone has suffered a loss but works harder for a better future.[15]

In the New Year of 1948, Frank Godwin, who went on to become a television producer, revived *Winkles and Champagne*, extracts of which were broadcast live on television from Alexandra Palace with Eric Robinson's orchestra. A series of playreadings was organised, including Ted Willis's adaptation of Gorky's

Mother with Sybil Thorndike. *Six Men of Dorset* by Miles Malleson and H. Brooks was then mounted to mark the ninetieth anniversary of the TUC, which had originally commissioned the play in 1934 to commemmorate the martyrs' centenary. The celebration was marked by a march that went from Trafalgar Square to the theatre, with the cast in costume and accompanied by the banners of the agricultural workers' union.[16] The march tried to follow as closely as possible, though in reverse, the route taken by the huge demonstration of 1834 from Whitehall to the then Copenhagen Fields behind King's Cross which was called in protest at the transportation of the Dorset workers, some of whose descendants were in the Unity audience along with twenty MPs. With the exception of *Winkles and Champagne, Six Men of Dorset* had the best block bookings and audience figures of the year. It was directed by Derek Birch, who resigned during rehearsals and Bill Owen took over.

The next month, May 1948, an Audience Building Conference held at St Pancras Town Hall confirmed the view that London Unity had recovered from its initial postwar setback. The conference, organised by David Tree and chaired by Leah Manning MP, was the culmination of months of preparation through leaflets, booklets, speakers addressing meetings and the mobile 'flying squad'. It was attended by professional theatre people such as Peggy Ashcroft, Bessie Love and Herbert Lom. The official figures give an overall figure of 1,200 delegates attending from 600 organisations representing some three million members, half coming from the Co-ops, two-fifths from unions and the rest from left-wing political bodies. Those who applied too late were invited to an overflow conference in June. A 28 member trade union advisory committee was set up which functioned well for a few years and was revived periodically during the next decade and a half.

'What's Left?'

Unity's immediate revival reached a high point that August when the theatre's accommodation with the Labour government had completely disappeared. Following the historic welfare measures, the energy crisis had exposed Labour's weaknesses on the home front and had led to austerity measures, including a wage freeze.

Internationally, Britain was keeping Europe at arm's length, especially in trade, while identifying its main interests with those of the Americans as its own empire waned with the loss of India, Ceylon and Burma in quick succession. Anti-Communist Foreign Secretary Ernest Bevin continued Churchill's line on Greece, Germany, and Palestine. While the Soviet Union was helping install Communists in power in central and eastern Europe, Bevin was accepting the American Marshall Plan that, in the complexities of the emerging Cold War which Stalin fuelled with his own sectarianism, helped remove them from government in Italy, France and Belgium. At the same time as the Berlin airlift, Unity members heard a member of the Communist Party's executive committee explain the reasons for Tito's expulsion from the newly formed Cominform, the successor to the Comintern. International trade union unity was being broken, which led later to the TUC leaving the World Federation of Trades Unions and the founding in London of the International Confederation of Free Trade Unions in opposition to WFTU.

Prime Minister Attlee had attacked the Communists at the 1946 TUC, the year the Labour Party changed its rules to prevent further Communist Party attempts to affiliate. He had then continued his own 'witch-hunt', expelling 'fellow-travelling' MPs from the Labour Party, supporting an employers' and trades union prohibition of 'red' left-wingers, and, in imitation of the US legislature, introducing in March 1948 a catch-all Act which banned Communists from being employed by the state in positions of national security. Labour also failed to repeal the wartime Order 1305 banning strikes, which meant that the 10,000 strikes that occurred between 1945 and 1951 were all illegal and many took place in an atmosphere of 'red-baiting'.

This was the background to Unity's great summer success, the political revue *What's Left?* which opened a few months after Attlee's Act had become law. The show may have acknowledged that the peace had been lost but it was not going to give it up without a fight. It was written by Geoffrey Parsons and Berkeley Fase, with supplementary material from Roger Woddis, Bernard Black, John Spag (Bill Owen), Sean Rafferty and Stan Edwards. The opening number 'Step Up and Sigh' comments on Britain's parlous economic state and its reliance on America:

Step Up don't buy
It's for export only [...]
For though the pound note
May be quite a sound note
If you've got no dollars to spend
Step up and sigh.[17]

Sketches such as Churchill leading an underground opposition of Free Britons after three years of socialist tyranny and jokes about Attlee's witch-hunt made their mark, but the real punch, as ever, came in the songs. They ranged wide, exposing the housing shortage, lampooning the fashion for duffle coats, attacking Hollywood 'sexploitation' (with 'nobody asked me to act' the refrain from the abused actress) and lamenting the decline of the Liberals.

Life's not much fun for a Liberal today ...
The public's lost interest in the middle way.

The 'Last of the Romanovs' has Washington desperately looking for a dynastic heir to 'chase from the Kremlin that Communist gremlin' while 'The Crowned Heads of Europe' celebrates the passing of monarchs who are

[...] part of the export drive.
Our people still thwart us
They won't re-import us,
No matter how hard we strive.

The fighting finale shows a 'housewife' driving Mars the god of war from the stage followed by the refrain:

Break it up boys, break it up
The world is ours, don't shake it up
For one man sitting on his bum
Could blow us all to kingdom come

This song was published by the Workers' Music Association, along with three others from the show, a solo 'My Man from MI5' and the two big numbers, one of which closed the first half. This was 'The Gradual', a parody of 'The Lambeth Walk' that stopped the show:

The tune we use is Ernie Bevin's choice
By kind permission of His Marshall's Voice …
Doing the Gradual
The dance is old though the title's new
The steps aren't bold and the tune is blue …
You drift along in a Fabian groove
You can't go wrong for you scarcely move …
You put your right leg out to show you can begin well
Do a roundabout, be sure you shake your shin well
Keep your left leg trailing at the back
You've done it all before in the Ramsay Mac …

The other big show-stopper was 'Oklaholum', the penultimate item, a skilful parody of *Oklahoma* which was then running at Drury Lane. 'Oklahokum' was vetted by Chappels, the publishers of the original music, for breach of copyright, but although the tunes were instantly recognisable, Fase's pastiche was so successful that he could not be sued for plagiarism. The scene is a Cabinet meeting, the day after its members have been to see *Oklahoma*. The time is 'any beautiful morning' and the characters bear an uncanny resemblance to leading Labour politicians. Aunt Eller (Bevin) is disclosed in her rocking chair alongside a churn marked 'United Prairies'. Curly (Attlee) and the First Farmer (Gaitskell) join her in:

Oh what a beautiful mornin'
What if the outlook is grey?
We gotta beautiful feelin'
Dollars are comin' our way.

The farmer says that Slimm (Cripps) has changed his 'toon'. 'Why I kin remember – he war in ther wilderness – when most evry word that came outer his mouth was sumpin' ter do with socerlism?' Curly reacts, struggling to draw his gun from his holster:

Don't breathe that word in here
Who knows who's listening
Shinwell's eyes are glistening
People will say we've gone red.

After Eller has confessed that he cannot say 'Boo to a goose' unless it is red, the second Farmer (Morrison) enters looking for 're-yud skins'. He is not taking any chances and brings on a 'sanitary posse from thur Morgan Phillips ranch' (Morgan Phillips was Labour's general secretary). The action is watched by a 'redskin' who has entered unseen. A trio from Labour's headquarters enter, wearing 'secretarial' costume – spectacles, note-books, pencils – but also with cowboy hats. To what sounds like the tune of 'Surrey with a Fringe on Top' they sing:

> Those left wing rebels give me the pip
> They'd better do as we tell 'em
> Or else the executive'll crack the whip
> And have 'em up and expel 'em.

The hat-waving finale drives the point home:

> Um-m-m-m-m-Mister Marshall
> May we have our orders for today.
> If you think we've erred just breathe the word
> And we'll agree with anything you say.

Directed by Bill Owen (protecting his career with the pen-name John Spag while advertising it by arriving in a Rolls Royce courtesy of Rank), *What's Left?* was such a success that its run was extended. It played five nights a week (from Wednesday to Sunday) for 114 performances, and attracted some 400 block bookings of more than 25 people and many more of under that figure. The *Times* critic said Parsons was 'delicately satirical' and the *Daily Mail* that the show was 'two hours' of rollicking entertainment and devastating satire.' Tory MP Beverly Baxter, the *Evening Standard*'s critic, wrote that it was the wittiest revue in town, and in the House of Commons, during a debate on censorship, recalled that he had done his utmost to ensure that the theatre had been packed for months. In a letter to Unity concerning possible public performances at which club rules did not apply, the censor had insisted on the removal of the song 'The Crowned Heads of Europe' and that in 'Oklahokum' there 'must be no offensive representation of living persons'. 'Oklahokum' did appear in the second edition of the West End revue *Sauce Tartare* by Parsons and Fase and was printed in the magazine *Our Time*, using the names of the impersonated politicians.

A party to celebrate the hundredth performance of *What's Left*? was attended by a host of personalities such as Tom Driberg, Willie Gallacher, Kingsley Martin and John Platts-Mills MP, whose expulsion from the Labour Party by Attlee had figured in the 'Oklahokum' sketch. MPs Bessie Braddock and Leah Manning went on stage after the show and performed in short sketches.

What's Left? had been in the news for another reason in October when one of the cast, Beryl Lund, who had worked in the civil service for eight years, was 'purged' from her job as a clerical officer in the contracts department at the Ministry of Supply (the Minister of which was Unity general council member George Strauss). She refused to attend the tribunal that was due to investigate her case and was transferred to the Ministry of Education.

Her appearance in the revue was construed as proving her association with the Communist Party in a way that cast doubt on her reliability. Ironically, one of her numbers in 'Oklahokum' attacks the government's purge:

> Cryptos and their friends'd better look out,
> Morgan Phillips's got his little black book out.

In another song, performed by Noreen Callaghan, called 'The Real Thing' and then renamed 'My Man from MI5', new lyrics were added to the serenade of an off-stage spy:

> It's entirely due to him,
> He saved us from the peril
> Of Unity's red Beryl.

The BBC broadcast an excerpt of Renée Houston singing the song in the revue *Sauce Tartare* – though Parsons and Fase remember her draining all the politics from the song – and the *Evening Standard* published a Low cartoon sympathetic to Unity which stayed pinned up in the theatre for some time. The paper said that she was the fifth member of the CCSA, the civil service union, to be accused of Communist activities and, although hers was the most publicised case, she was not alone in suffering for her association with Unity. Leonard Peck, fourteen years in the civil service, was also suspended from the Ministry of Supply on the same grounds as Lund. He had never been a member of any political party but had been active as a playwright with Merseyside and London Unity theatres. He too refused to attend the tribunal and was transferred to the Ministry of Labour as a wages clerk. He wrote of this experience in a play called *The Big Screen*, which was performed by Merseyside Unity in 1958, and in his novel, *It's a Free Country*, which he wrote using the pen-name Leonard Brain. The following year, Robert F. Gorley, who had been an actor with Unity twelve years previously, was prevented from emigrating to Canada although he had a job there. Not only had he not been a member of any party, he had not ever been a member of a trade union. His case was taken up by the campaign then running to limit the secret powers of the police. Some former Unity members found that, because of past links with the theatre, they could not obtain work in America, or even a visa for a visit; as is often the practice in these cases, such infringements of civil liberties happened 'unofficially' and were not subject to open challenge or publicity. It was in this kind of atmosphere – Britain's own and little recorded McCarthyism – that the Liverpool City Council went so far as to ban Merseyside Unity from the use of its halls. It was not surprising or necessarily an unfounded paranoia that led some people to adopt pseudonyms to protect themselves, though even this could have its amusing side; Elsie Chisnell, a teacher who appeared in *Winkles and Champagne* on television, did not want the *Radio Times* to print her real name. When the director was telephoned by the magazine for the cast list and he came to her name, he hesitated, looked around and, seeing a box of matches, decided to call her May Bryant which then appeared in the listings through a mishearing or a misprint as May Brian.

'The Ragged Trousered Philanthropists'

What's Left? made way for a double bill of pre-war standards, *Where's That Bomb?* and *Plant in the Sun*, as if to underline the point in the new combative mood of beleagured entrenchment that the old Unity values had not been buried and were very much alive. The sentiment was reinforced by a visit from Paul Robeson to see *Plant in the Sun*, the show in which he had so happily appeared. The double-bill did not work too well, although Rita Webb as the landlady in *Where's That Bomb?* went on to a successful professional career and Robeson's return gave everyone a boost. Looking to the past, however, could not answer the two main problems facing Unity – personnel and repertoire. The turnover of activists was high and despite a continuing commitment to new work, few writers had emerged to provide

Unity with the type of plays that it wanted. *New Theatre* had held a play competition in 1947 that attracted 355 entries, but the winner, Alison Macleod with *Keep the Gallows*, was refused a production – despite this being a condition of coming first – because the theatre's management committee did not agree with her treatment of the subject, capital punishment.

Vernon Beste recognised the personnel and dramatic problems and tried to tackle both at once. He offered Unity his comedy, *Cousin Elwyn*, which followed *Where's That Bomb?* and *Plant in the Sun*, and promised a new play for production at Goldington Street after that, to be staged with new members of the Unity evening school which had restarted under London County Council auspices at the Marylebone Institute. *Cousin Elwyn*, which was mistaken, the author recalls, for an attack on the Marshall Plan, is an openly boulevard play in which a successful American businessman visits his English cousin who runs a 200-year-old shoe firm. Elwyn transforms the middle-class English home with a range of gadgets and is finally sent back home to the states, having disrupted the household but also having taught the shoe-maker how to introduce a few useful improvements. It was directed by Bill Owen with Warren Mitchell in the lead. Mitchell was then known as Warren Misel and was learning little at the Royal Academy of Dramatic Art during the day, he says, but a lot in the evening at Unity – which he calls 'my alma mater'. Vernon Beste's student company, named after backstage wizard Tris Stack, presented as its new play a second Leonard Peck piece, *The Townshends*, which had already been produced by Merseyside Unity. Based on his own childhood experiences, the play is set in the slums of west London in 1913 where, in his own words, 'The back streets were tough, and the pubs were open all day, and my father was mostly in them.'[18] Peck recalls his early diet of ginger beer and arrowroot biscuits, eaten on the pub steps, and his mother's 'interminable industry on a Singer sewing machine' (when she was an outworker to the cheap tailoring trade) for which he discovered plausible explanations in the works of Marx and Engels. The play recreates this childhood context in a straightforward, naturalistic way, and was written – after Peck's mother had died – as an answer to the Tory 'Ask Your Mum' campaign, which sought to exploit nostalgia for 'the good old days'. Peck was determined to show how hard it had been to lead a decent life.

The 1949 AGM recorded a loss of £1,000 for the previous six months. Unity was particularly pleased, therefore, with the popularity of the next production, an adaptation of Robert Tressell's labour movement classic, *The Ragged Trousered Philanthropists*, which became one of Unity's best loved shows. It was directed by Bill Owen, as John Spag again, who seemed to be a furnace of activity and it earned Unity another spread in *Picture Post*. The play's depiction of '12 months in hell by one of the damned', was said by the magazine to be 'an experience unique on the London stage. Fresh and wholly unstagey – this is the real thing.' It was what Unity did best – authentic working-class experience, using natural, working-class voices in an ensemble production without stars. The show was seen by more than 25,000 people and ran for 130 performances, six nights a week from May to November, a run which Unity claimed was the longest for a straight play by an amateur company anywhere in the world. It attracted 241 block bookings, including eighteen for the entire auditorium by the Transport and General Workers' Union – a Unity record. So successful was the show that Unity needed its double cast system to keep it going and a feasibility study for a professional tour was carried out but it was decided that Unity could not undertake such a venture. The script by Bill Owen was published with a foreword by Sir John Stephenson and Richard Coppock, president and general secretary respectively of the building workers' union.

Actors in the cast remember especially the spontaneous responses from the audiences – one night plumbers, another electricians or another a women's Co-op guild; they might call out, 'Look how he's holding that hammer,' or, in response to a line about poverty, 'Remember what the royal family gets.' A favourite scene for audience interruptions was that in which the socialist Owen gives his lunchtime lecture on the meaning of capitalist exploitation using a loaf of bread. During one performance in front of building workers, the actors replied from the stage and began an impromptu debate. Prominent German Communist Gerhard Eisler also visited early in the run, on his way back to what was soon to become the new German Democractic Republic where he later became head of state broadcasting. He had been held in Brixton Prison, after being removed from a Polish ship off Southampton at the request of the US authorities because he had jumped bail pending an appeal against convictions for contempt of Congress and for visa irregularities. Unity members took part in a demonstration at the prison and he was released the day that *The Ragged Trousered Philanthropists* opened.

A benefit performance of *The Ragged Trousered Philanthropists* was held in the summer of 1949 at which a specially commissioned series of panels was unveiled. A major redecoration scheme had been planned the year before but only the designs for the foyer were executed. This resulted in a series of murals depicting the history of drama painted by Anthony Dorrell, with assistance from George Poole and, briefly, Ern Brooks. Dorrell, who became Unity's chair, remembers the impulse to return to a public form of art in the wake of Labour's victory, inspired by the art of the Russian revolution and Mexican muralists. A booklet was published to accompany the unveiling, which was performed by Bessie Love, a great supporter of Unity who often helped out front-of-house and who was in London appearing in *Death of a Salesman*. Richard Coppock spoke from the stage on behalf of his union, for which the benefit was given. All the Unity characters shown in the murals were present – Geoffrey Parsons, Berkeley Fase, the theatre's manager Dick Polling, Gerry Solomons on lighting, Ada Corkery at the bar, Beryl Lund on stage, and Harry Newton, the carpenter. Dorrell showed the murals to Krishna Menon, then the Indian High Commissioner, beginning with the first panel which depicts primitive ritual dance as conveyed in neolithic cave paintings. The second represented the classic Greek drama. 'Big jump,' commented Menon.

The year ended with a pre-election revue *What Next!* that obviously took its cue from the successful *What's Left?*? but did not have Parsons and Fase contributing. Attacks on the Marshall Plan, Bevin and dollar domination were not fresh enough to have the same bite as the earlier show and *What Next!* suffered from repetition of the same themes. Much of the material seemed like the afterthoughts of its predecessor, although sometimes the imitation almost worked as well. 'The Old Vic at Westminster' (or 'Labour's Lost Love') took over where 'Oklahokum' had left off, though not with quite the same panache. The Cabinet realises that Shakespeare is a great British export to hard currency regions and decides to muscle in on the act by removing the middle men like Donald Wolfit and Laurence Olivier. The politicians play the

Bard's roles themselves, with full supporting cast. The scene is a blasted heath in SWI (Parliament's postal district). Three witches circle a cauldron labelled Fleet Street. They are powerful newspaper proprietors Beaverbrook, Astor and Kemsley:

Thrice the *Daily Herald* mewed
Thrice the *Daily Mirror* whined [...]
Double, double, toil and trouble
Don't let the *Worker* burst our bubble.[19]

Deputy Prime Minister Herbert Morrison as Lady Macbeth cries 'Out damned Red' and the sketch switches to *A Midsummer Night's Dream*, with Cripps as Titania, Strachey as Ophelia, and MI5 as Puck, parodying *The Tempest*, who intones

Where a Red works, there lurk I
And on civil servants spy.

Churchill then comes on as Hamlet and naturally enough he is preoccupied with the central theme –

To win or not to win,
That is the question.

The finale, however, shows Unity at a loss for any strategic challenge to Labour's decline. The chorus can only take refuge in hope for the future, relying on the common sense of the people:

DUET: Fellow voters gather round
Hear our words of greeting
DISILLUSIONED CROWD: We're sick and tired of all this sputing
Of all this propaganda shouting [...]
Let's leave it all to the politicians
Let them clear the mess up on their own
DANCERS (*answering*): But this is not the time to lose your nerve
You only get the rulers you deserve
CHORUS: What next?
Our daily bread
Is getting dearer
What next?
Before we're through
We hope to clarify the view
And leave the final answer up to you.

The Cold War had truly set in yet Labour's compliance with American policy did not rescue it at the polls. Attlee's parliamentary majority was reduced to five in 1950 and both Communist MPs lost their seats.

Internal disputes at Unity were growing increasingly bitter again, mainly over personalities rather than politics, and the decade ended with general manager Gerry Sharp resigning. Choice of casting would figure often in the arguments, as would choice of play or whether Unity should be Communist-run or an autonomous co-operative. The loss of the Willis group and the professional commitments of many veterans left a problem of continuity and leadership. A group would emerge that would invest its energy in running Unity and would do so for a while with unflagging commitment, but, when the long-term process of decline again became evident and the first group had become exhausted, another would arise to blame the theatre's ills on the now-ailing group. The new leaders would take over and the pattern would be repeated.

The peaks and troughs of Unity's life became more marked and further apart. The management committee was riven with factional wrangling and the general council had faded without formal abolition. When J.B. Priestley was expelled from it in 1951 for being critical of the Soviet Union and announcing in a journal his rejection of socialism, he said that he did not know that he was still a member.

Despite being in the depths of the Cold War, Unity not only survived, though at great cost, it also made a number of startling recoveries with several outstanding productions. Under a new general manager, Mick Manning, a businessman who had been Unity's press officer, and the stablising influence of Dick Polling, who was a link with the pre-war years, Unity still offered a rare chance to learn and practice theatre skills in an atmosphere of increasingly unfashionable left-wing commitment that isolated it in a Britain which was beginning to see ahead a degree of affluence unknown since the deprivations of war.

The 1950s were not going to be easy.

Notes

1. New interviews/correspondence for this chapter: Kate Amaral, Anthony Dorrell, David Gascoyne, Joe MacColum, Frank Marcus, Warren Mitchell (Misel), Patricia O'Gorman, Bill Richardson, Frank Singuineau.
2. *New Theatre*, No 1, December 1945.
3. Programme note for *All God's Chillun Got Wings*.
4. Quoted in the annual report to the 1946 AGM of Unity Theatre Society.
5. Norman Marshall in *The Other Theatre* compares Unity's apprentice system favourably with the training offered by the Royal Academy of Dramatic Art, particularly in Unity's offering of education alongside practical stage experience before a public audience.
6. Willis' arguments are developed in 'The Labour Movement's Challenge', *New Theatre*, Vol. 3 No. 2, July 1946.
7. Words provided by Geoffrey Parsons.
8. See John Hill for fuller account of Glasgow Unity and *Clydebuilt* souvenir programme of season of Scottish popular theatre from the 1920s and 1930s, 7:84 Theatre Company Scotland, 1982. The programme notes were written by Linda McKenney whose book *Scottish Popular Drama 1900-1950* awaits publication. *The Gorbals Story* and *Men Should Weep* were published by 7:84 along with plays, poems and theatre writings of Joe Corrie.
9. Of several accounts of the conference, see *New Theatre*, Vol. 4 No. 9, March 1948 and *Our Time*, Vol. 7 No. 6, March 1948.
10. Theoretical work by the Communist Party can be seen in *Communist Review, Modern Quarterly*, in various publications such as *The Communist Answer to the Challenge of Our Time*, Thames 1947 (lectures given in response to BBC broadcasts), a Marxism Today series issued between 1943 and 1950 through Fore Publications, books published by Lawrence and Wishart, articles in party or party-related journals and the *Daily Worker*. There was a renaissance of specialist groups within the party, for example a new cultural committee, a writers' group and a history group (for which see Eric Hobsbawm in Maurice Cornforth (ed.), *Rebels and their Causes: Essays in Honour of A.L. Morton*, Lawrence and Wishart 1978, and Harvey Kaye, *British Marxist Historians*, Polity 1984). I have put in the Communist Party archive a copy of Lindsay's unpublished paper 'Marxist Theory of Culture' (to which he refers in *Life Rarely Tells*). The central ideas of this paper reappear in Lindsay's *The Crisis of Marxism*, Moonraker Press 1981.
11. This is a complex issue touching on the relationship between analysis, ideology and cultural practice which needs more investigation (e.g. how people at Unity could see the working class in different ways at the same time and express these contradictions depending on context and how certain of these definitions were more influential than others. Unity's published material often accepted and projected the white, manual, male image of the working class which was dominant on the left yet in its varied

repertoire it often belied this).
12. New Theatre Publications also issued, among other titles, Ted Willis's *What Happens to Love*, Colin Morris's *An Italian Love Story*, George Thomson's translation of Aeschylus's *Prometheus*, George Leeson's *This Trampled Earth* and Gadfan Morris's *Bikini Fable*. All but eight of the complete run of plays are held in the Merseyside Left/Unity Theatre Archive, Merseyside Museum of Labour History, Box 13.2.
13. Unity's files at the British Theatre Association include a press cutting that says after the war Leslie Seyd was asked by Unity to produce plays for the Junior Socialist Fellowship, which then won two festival awards. I have not been able to find out anything about this, except that Leslie Seyd later set up a theatre group in the Unity neighbourhood (in Crowndale Road) called Young Playmakers.
14. See Sam Aaronovitch *et al.*, *The American Threat to British Culture*, Arena n.d., and, from a different point of view, Martin Barker, *A Haunt of Fears: The Strange History of the British Horror Comics Campaign*, Pluto 1984.
15. Peter Cotes, *No Star Nonsense*, Rockcliff 1949, which contains illustrations of *The Whole World Over* and *The Match Girls*, describes these two productions as 'the two finest amateur productions of my experience'. In *A Handbook for the Amateur Theatre*, Oldbourne Press 1957, he adds *Winkles and Champagne* to the list (though he also makes some errors in relation to Unity's history).
16. The programme for a conference in 1963 called 'Unity Theatre and the Unions' says that *Six Men of Dorset* appeared on television. Presumably this was in newsreel as no one I spoke to could remember the production being filmed or televised.
17. Acting script of *What's Left?* deposited in the British Theatre Association library.
18. Programme note for Peck's *Puerto Franco*, which Unity performed in 1959.
19. Script of *What Next!* given to me and deposited in the British Theatre Association library.

9

Out in the Cold

Half-way through the twentieth century, Unity still had a surprising amount of life left in it.[1] Although the theatre recorded a financial deficit in the year 1950, it offered a full programme, undertook necessary repairs (such as mending the roof) and revealed a pattern of interests that sustained it for some time to come. Musical shows and the occasional comedy were balanced by serious plays which tended to deal with three main topics – the history of the English working class, the fight for peace against the domination and corruption of America, and the complementary problem of building new societies – whether in central and eastern Europe or through colonial liberation struggles.

Following a stop-gap revival of Ted Willis's *Buster*, Herbert Marshall returned with grand plans as productions manager to direct two British premières, both of them sturdy parables: *How I Wonder*, a play of ideas written by Donald Ogden Stewart, a highly successful Hollywood figure and former President of the League of American Writers who had left America after receiving a subpoena to appear before the House UnAmerican Activities Committee; and *Hell is What You Make It*, a morality play written by Ewan MacColl in 1939 which had been performed already in Prague.

Ogden Stewart's play was one of the first written by an American author to tackle issues thrown up by the atom bomb. It shows an astronomer facing removal from his laboratory because the military want it for atomic research and he is considered too dangerous to be kept on. A Faust-like battle develops between his sense of truth and his sense of survival, which is personified in characters that argue to a conclusion that sides with political action – scientific analysis of far-off planets does not remove the need to tackle immediate problems on earth. The professor decides to stay, refusing to accept the presidency of another university, and discovers a new star – a symbol of hope for the future of liberty in this world. Ogden Stewart was well known as the writer of scripts for films such as *The Barretts of Wimpole Street, The Philadelphia Story* and *Edward, My Son. How I Wonder* played in the Fortune Theatre but came off after a short run.

Marshall's second production was a rescue operation: MacColl's play was highly ambitious and the original director needed help. Captain Charon, stranded in limbo because of a strike in the shipping industry, forces his passengers to work their passage to hell. They include

> a toolmaker who couldn't tell a turbine from a marlin spike. A shipping director incapable of directing anything except food into his mouth and money into his pocket. A man with a genius for making others work. A general, who, if his passport tells the truth, has burned more towns than there are villages in Hell. Also a murderer, a scribbler, a harridan and a harlot.[2]

They sail to hell and meet Lucifer and Faustus, among others, and the parable begins of how ordinary people who work hard and struggle for a better life can turn the darkest of places into paradise.

Another première followed – *The Circling Dove* by Leonard Irwin, who had worked for the Co-operative Society in Manchester, had become the youngest manager of one of its large stores, and, after the war, had worked for the civil service in London. Irwin's mother was a music-hall singer and his father was a bricklayer from Ireland. Like Leonard Peck, another working-class socialist, Irwin loved writing and used conventional, naturalistic styles to convey unconventional messages. Also like Peck, he was encouraged by Merseyside Unity, which had first performed *The Circling Dove* and had helped the play receive subsequent productions, including several abroad. In this play, set in the future, a hospital matron is ordered by a colonel to move out her patients to make room for the war wounded. She is about to agree but then changes her mind and, as a consequence, is suspended. Patients, visitors and staff demonstrate on her behalf and finally the colonel withdraws. Nevertheless, the matron feels like leaving. However, she is persuaded to stay and fight for what she believes in: 'The things that I can do here,' she concludes, 'are the things that can be done for peace everywhere – in homes, in factories, in offices – wherever ordinary men and women can make their stand against unnecessary war.'[3]

A revival of *Winkles and Champagne* filled another gap before the opening of what turned out to be one of Unity's most successful productions of a socialist realist play in the post-war period, *Longitude 49*. Herb Tank, the author had been refused work in 1946 after sailing tankers in the war, had become an official of the US Maritime Union and, with Howard Fast and Michael Gold, had founded New Playwrights Incorporated. Its first production was this highly charged account of life one night on board a tanker docked in Iran on longitude 49 and latitude 30. There is an argument among the crew on different forms of revolutionary activity and it leads to a fight in which a black seaman is shot by the ship's Mate. When the seaman dies, the crew stand firm together and refuse to work the ship until the Mate is arrested and charged with murder. The captain agrees and, as the Mate's gun is thrown out of a porthole, the author's message is made clear. He rejects the role of individual action, symbolised by the gun, in favour of united action and class solidarity across racial divides. Tank came to Britain to direct a strong cast on one of carpenter Harry Newton's memorable sets. It was designed by architect Michael Cain and was as authentic as possible, down to its rivets. An excellent cast included Errol Hill, who was to become one of the foremost influences in the development of Caribbean drama. (He played the part originally performed by Sidney Poitier.) *The Candy Story* by Barnard Rubin, which examines the life of a New York store owner and was presented by Unity in 1952, also came from New Playwrights Inc.

UnAmerican Activities

Spirits were lifted even higher by *Here Goes!* which opened in the New Year of 1951 and saw the return of Parsons and Fase in a production by Alfie Bass and Vida Hope which coincided with the Korean War. The show not only exploited the anti-American theme with renewed gusto, it also managed to promote the peace cause with great effect, too. A sharp international issue and the resurgence of the Tories seems to have put Unity back on its mettle.

In 'Camp Followers of England', the government's surrender to American military interests is satirised in a sexual metaphor. Four women welcome back the US Air Force:

After all, we're only human,
It's our way of thanking Truman,
We do it for democracy.
For the North Atlantic Pact is
Only preaching what we practise
When we open our defences to the Yanks.[4]

There were the familiar parodies of popular tunes – 'There's No Tories Like Young Tories' and 'Truman's Bustin' Out All Over' – sketches on the housing problem for immigrants and televising the House of Commons, a Lysistrata up-date 'Nothin' Doin' Tonight' and a fantasy 'AD 2051' of a world in which people are taught to create instead of kill. In the chilling 'Military Objective', three North Koreans are 'liberated' by Uncle Sam's bombs, and in 'Smothercraft' TGWU general secretary Arthur Deakin is seen as Nanny Deakin rocking a cradle labelled TUC and singing: 'And if, unofficially, you strike for more, your old nanny Deakin will give you what for.' (Troops had been used that year in a dock dispute that did not win Deakin's backing, though it helped force the repeal of the wartime Order 1305 banning strikes.) A brilliant monologue, 'Brush Up Your Economics' delivered by Unity veteran Bill Ward, explains the ins-and-outs of currency and could have been used without alteration (or embarrassment) in the satire boom of the 1960s: the dollar 'is easily recognised by the long strings which are always attached to it' and the English pound 'answers to the name of nine and fourpence'. T.S. Elliot's *The Cocktail Party* and Christopher Fry's *Venus Observed* are lampooned in 'Cocktails in Camberwell' or 'The Proletariat Observed' which reveals that

Happiness exists in not
Fighting to improve your lot,
Happiness consists in just
knowing that what must be, must.

In 'Entertainment à la Mode', the attack switches from esoteric art to commercial culture: a commissionaire outside a London theatre offers the crowd the prospect of nudes from Paris. Alongside, a barker in front of Unity Theatre shouts, 'Apart from politics we're never naughty.' Unity loses the crowd to the nude show and decides to present its own stripper, Winston Churchill, dressed as peace, who, by the end of his act, has revealed himself as war. He looks forward to the election later that year, singing 'Invitation to a Party':

Change the government to Tory
And I promise you the ballon will soon go up.

One of the show's best songs was 'Civilisation', which summed up the fears of a nuclear war and was sung by Doris Levenson (now married and called Abrahams), a stalwart of the wartime entertainments and Old Time Music Hall:

Civilisation
Work out a civilised plan
It's mend your ways now
Or end your days now
And exit civilised man.

Civilised nations
Why don't you learn to combine
You're on the slide now
To suicide now
Just like the Gadarene swine.
It's up to us to make the choice
This earth on which we dwell
Can be a place to make the heart rejoice
Or a radio-active hell.[5]

The big set-piece sketch was a parody of *The Mikado* by Gilbert and Sullivan, an extravaganza called 'The Secretary of State' or 'On the Shores of Lake Distress'. Set in the future at a UN meeting, the US politician enters to the tune of 'He is the Lord High Executioner'. A trio of delegates sing:

Three little states to rule are we
Take us as we ask on bended knee
You are the boss we all agree
Three little states to rule.

A US Senator insists they undergo a loyalty check because he is 'making up a list' of all those he considers dangerous.

> There's the man who says that coloured folk are just as good as white
> Or think the ten in Hollywood should be allowed to write [...]
> All people who say Coco-Cola isn't nice to drink
> And those who say the working class should be allowed to think [...]
> If I add 'em to my list – If I add 'em to my list –
> Then they must be Communist – Yes that makes 'em Communist!

Her Britannic Majesty's Secretary of State for War, the former left-winger John Strachey, reminisces on his past in 'Fellow Traveller' ('Ah me! Ah me! I was a fellow traveller then ... Ah me! I must have changed a lot since then.') The sketch ends with America offering the other states protection and a song which describes the Korean War as an invasion by the US under UN disguise. The show's finale makes an international plea for peace ('over the Atlantic there are decent folk as well') based on a belief in the ability of the human race to take control of its destiny for a better future:

> We are ordinary people leading ordinary lives,
> Ordinary husbands, ordinary wives,
> Our heads are not up in the clouds, our feet are on the ground,
> We're the ordinary people who make the world go round [...]
> So why despair? The outlook's fair
> The world is what we make it.
> Stand on your feet, life can be sweet,
> Life can be happy and brave and gay
> All put together now for where there's a will there's a way.

It is the same up-beat message of defiant optimism regardless of the political situation that had been the core of Unity shows from the 1930s onward and *Here Goes!* ran for sixteen weeks at the height of the Cold War. It was widely and positively reviewed; the *Times* commented on its 'cleverness and vivacity', the *Stage* noted 'novel ideas [and] vitality of presentation', the *Observer* remarked on the 'flashing technique of Parsons' lyrics' while the *Daily Worker* called it a 'rip roaring success' and 'wickedly witty'. *Arts News and Review* commented on the show's 'close relationship to real life ... *Here Goes!* deals freshly with the things one reads about every day in newspapers.' Little did its critic realise that *Here Goes!* was itself to become news when 'real life' intervened too closely and the theatre was taken to court in what became a sequel to the harassment suffered during *What's Left?*[6]

Agents provocateurs had for some time been trying unsuccessfully to break Unity's club rules and buy tickets for the same evening's performance without being members or waiting the statutory time after membership had been taken out. The *Daily Worker* reported visits by people who said that they were associated with the US embassy and who tried to get in to see *Here Goes!* in this way. Their questioning of a Unity member was made public in the *Daily Worker* after a stenographer took shorthand notes of the conversation through a hole bored in the wall (the incident took place before tape-recorders became cheaply and generally available). The visitors were interested in biographical details of Unity members and their friends and why *Here Goes!* attacked Americans. The *Daily Worker* also reported visits to the theatre by CID and Special Branch officers and again denounced the line of questioning they pursued as political intimidation. Understandably, when two policemen and two officials from the Lord Chamberlain's office, who had failed to gain admission on a previous occasion, were able to buy a ticket from a Fire Brigades Union officials, who was offering a spare from his block booking to the queue instead of returning it to the box office, the resulting prosecution was seen by Unity as an example of covert pressure from the US embassy. This fitted with personal experience and in the case of Alfie Bass confirmed what he thought had happened in 1947 to the musical *Finian's Rainbow*, in which he had starred. (He believed the show was closed prematurely at the behest of the embassy because of its political overtones: it attacks the lynch mentality and the idle rich and at one point the white protagonist turns black and a magic crock of gold planted in America grants the poor sharecroppers' wishes.)

Although the incident with the union official was not the theatre's fault, Unity, its general manager Mick Manning and the two directors of *Here Goes!*, Alfie Bass and Vida Hope, were charged under the 1843 Theatres Act (which, ironically, had been introduced to help free theatres from Charles II's restrictive patent laws). At first they were issued with two summonses but the number finally rose to twelve, all related in various ways to the unlicensed presentation of a new play. Unity claimed that this was the first such prosecution under the Act, curiously overlooking its own fine in 1943 during the run of *Spanish Village*. The case turned out to have more than local significance because it revealed that, strictly speaking, it was an offence for any theatre to present a play without a licence if it were deemed to be 'for hire', which could mean simply selling alcohol or paying someone connected with the production. For more than a century, the Lord Chamberlain obligingly had ignored the exact provisions of the Act, but Unity's prosecution showed that a loophole existed that could be used in an oppressive manner if the authorities desired.

The court hearings were almost as funny as the revue, with Alfie Bass using Yiddish to swear at the bench, much to the delight of those in the gallery, and Vida Hope assuming her simpering posture of innocence and insisting on calling the magistrate 'Me Lud'. They were both successful professional artists unpaid by Unity but charged because the wording of the Act names the 'producer', which in the nineteenth century did not mean the director as it subsequently came to.

The Director of Public Prosecution asked for eight of the twelve charges to be withdrawn but the magistrate refused. He was most concerned at the notion of Unity's affiliated membership, which he said stretched the theatre's definition as 'private' too far because thousands could arrive to claim entry to a show. The charges against Vida Hope, however, were dismissed while Unity was fined £12 plus 10 guineas costs; Manning also received a £12 fine and Bass was fined £20. Bass's conviction was quashed on appeal because the prosecution had not proved that he was the same Alfie Bass that was quoted in the programme nor that he had taken part in presenting the show on the two nights that the policemen had observed the theatre. The magistrate also wanted to close Unity down, but even the prosecution had to point out that such a move was beyond his powers.

Recognising the threat that was posed to all private theatres, a meeting had been held immediately at Unity to rally support on the widest possible basis. Sybil Thorndike, Lewis Casson and Miles Malleson led a fourteen-strong committee that took a resolution to Unity's local Labour MP, raised more money than was needed to pay the fines and gained Unity much valuable publicity. The campaign was backed by 110 organisations, including the National Council for Civil Liberties and many prominent theatre figures as well as the Arts Council's drama director and two Labour MPs.

Here Goes! closed an era. It proved to be the last show that Parsons and Fase wrote for Unity, partly because they felt that the theatre had lost its energy, and partly because changes in musical taste were making their revue style redundant.

Unity musicals were never the same again, though the baton was picked up by subsequent writers, often following the pattern of the Parsons and Fase pantomimes and revues.

Mother Goose by Eric Paice and Alfie Bass later that year, which played after the Tory victory in the October election on a minority vote, also focused on the American threat and the struggle for peace. (The lead role was played by an excellent Music Hall artist Will Stampe, who was the Unity stalwart Bernie Cohen.) Mother Goose is in deep trouble; she cannot pay her grocery bills and the Squire wants to evict her because the Americans are carrying out secret research under her cottage and they want to test their new weapon, SCUM, which can wipe out the earth's population seventeen times in thirteen seconds. The scientists need to test this wicked broth on a living creature and they choose the goose. GIs capture the animal but the villagers, helped by the Good Fairy, win it back. The magic word 'peace' is spoken and the goose lays a golden egg. Mother Goose can now pay her debts and open a co-operative grocery that will put the monopolistic grocer out of business.

Paice wrote a great deal for Unity in the 1950s. He had left school at thirteen-and-a-half and had returned to his job as a printer's machine minder after serving in the Royal Navy during the war. He joined Unity in 1949 and worked on the lighting side, wrote two mobile shows, *Focus on Peace* and *Focus on Germany*, and in 1951 became Unity's nightwatchman, living in a room at the back of the building. He later wrote many television series, including *The Avengers*, and became president of the Writers' Guild. He was also one of the 300 British delegates to the third World Youth Festival in Berlin in August 1951, which became the centre of an international scandal when his group was turned back in the US zone of Austria and taken under armed guard to Innsbruck. The group made a second attempt to reach Berlin but was stopped again in the US zone, this time at Saalfelden, and was forced back to Innsbruck. News of this blockade reached Britain and a protest campaign was mounted that ended with the delegates finally getting to Berlin, suitably late and harassed.

Paice wrote a documentary play on the events called *Barrier Across Europe* with a cast of 40 including the black playwright Errol John and John Bluthal, who went on to a successful career on stage and in television. Paice took his information from the files of the British Youth Festival committee, the published evidence of an inquiry held by the National Council for Civil Liberties, newspaper and Hansard reports, and from sworn personal statements of the group's leader and other delegates. It was a successful production by Dave Dawson and Unity extended the run of the play. The show's exciting lighting effects, such as car headlights sweeping across the auditorium, were designed by Walter Lassally who was to become a leading international film cameraman whose credits include *A Taste of Honey, Tom Jones* and *Zorba the Greek*, for which he won an Oscar.

The World Youth Festival offered a stark contrast to the euphoria surrounding the Festival of Britain which was held in the same year. As a counter to the official rhetoric on the state of the nation – and in answer to Unity's call for an examination of native working-class history – Unity entered the Festival's play competition with Charles Poulsen's *The Word of a King*, adapted from his book *English Episode*. An article in *Unity News* encouraged groups to look at their own roots as a way of serving the current labour movement, especially when contemporary political strategy was weak. Unity had already begun to explore an indigenous radical tradition with shows as diverse as *Who are the English?*, *Busmen, The Match Girls, Robin Hood* and *Six Men of Dorset*. Poulsen, a taxi driver, added to this body of work by reaching back to Wat Tyler, John Ball and Jack Straw in the Peasants' Revolt of 1381 when Kent serfs rose up against grave injustices such as the poll tax. Poulsen wanted to show that revolutionary ideas were not foreign to Britain and cited one of Ball's speeches as the first in Europe to propound a socialist and egalitarian vision of society. *The Word of a King* was taken by the Mobile Group to Tolpuddle for Unity's third visit to the annual celebrations.

'The Cradle Will Rock'

Even more ambitious than *The Word of a King*, with its 50-strong cast, was Unity's next show which returned to the American radical theatre of the 1930s. Bill Owen had been playing Touchstone in *As You Like It* in New York and had managed to obtain the British rights to *The Cradle Will Rock* by Marc Blitztein. Owen rehearsed the cast for months, paying particular attention to the difficult score with the help of the musical director, Maria Pouschka, and the pianists Jimmy Gibb and Mary Peppin. It was a considerable feat for an amateur company to stage this piece, which had never been seen in Britain but had entered theatrical legend because of its first performance in 1937. The Federal Theater Project administration had withdrawn its support for the production by Orson Welles and John Houseman, which meant that the musicians and performers were unable to participate. On the opening night, the company and a huge audience that had queued to see the show walked twenty blocks to an empty theatre where Blitztein played the piano alone on stage without scenery, props or costumes, while the cast sang their parts from wherever they were in the auditorium.

The Cradle Will Rock is set in Steeltown USA, which is run by the all-powerful Mr Mister who controls the industry, the police, the courts, the media and the schools. Mrs Mister is the guiding spirit on the social, religious and cultural fronts. Blitztein uses a mixture of forms – jazz, swing, blues, ballad – to satirise those who act on behalf of America's rulers. The police mistakenly arrest the town's Liberty Committee (a parody of a league set up by business interests opposed to Roosevelt's New Deal) who are protesting against a union drive. Its members are revealed as hypocritical and corrupt in contrast to the archetypal union activist, Larry Foreman, an ordinary, decent, honest American worker fighting for basic rights. Blitztein follows the Popular Front notion of alliance based on the organised working class in presenting the union as a symbol of the true America. The show is a didactic piece taking the 'cradle' as a metaphor for the comfortable, complacent ruling circles which will be rocked by united struggle. At the end, workers from different trades are marching to the court in which the Liberty Committee and Larry are being held.

LARRY: (*Joins in with the song and music*)
That's thunder, that's lightning,
And it's going to surround you!
No wonder those stormbirds
Seem to circle around you [...]

> Well, you can't climb down, and you can't sit still;
> That's a storm that's going to last until
> The final wind blows ... and when the wind blows ...
> The cradle will rock![7]

Unity was clearly in fighting mood at the height of the Cold War although the political climate had made it extremely difficult to sustain audiences through the block booking system. Unity stood by the Soviet Union and staged a number of plays from the new 'People's Democracies'. The first was *The Germans* by the Polish novelist and playwright Leon Kruckowski, which had won prizes, had been performed in six countries and had been made into a film. The play moves from occupied Poland, France and Norway in 1943 to a professor's home that same year. Kruckowski shows the different responses to wartime situations of several Germans, each of whom is linked to the professor celebrating 30 years of scientific work. He thinks that he represents the 'real' Germany. He hates Hitler and does not believe that the Nazis are using his cell transplant techniques on Jews, though they are. His son is a cruel Nazi, who after the war is released early by a lenient West German government instead of serving his 30 years in prison.

It is the professor's daughter, a musician, who forces him to face himself when she hides an old colleague of his, an escaped Jew seeking refuge in his house. The professor turns on his friend for endangering the life of his daughter and for threatening his own seclusion from politics, which he considers necessary in order to continue his research. The daughter confesses to the police and later dies in Ravensbruck concentration camp. In the epilogue set in 1950, the professor is asked to resign from his university post because he is corresponding with Leipzig in the East. He spurns his son, who comes home singing the Nazi Horst Wessel song, and does resign, 'but not from life ... I draw it [my philosophy] from humanity – for it is humanity whom it must serve'.[8]

The production – directed by Hilda Manning and designed by Bernard Sarron (both professionals) – was broadcast on Polish radio and had a 'celebrity' first night, attended by MPs, leading figures on the left and 40 representatives from the embassies of the Communist-led countries. A play from the Ukraine followed immediately, a comedy about an old miner by Alexander Korneichuk called *The Hawthorn Grove*,[9] and after that, in 1953, another prize-winning play in a British première, *The Bridge of Life*, by Hungary's eminent playwright Julius Hay, whose message to the world was the last to be broadcast from the central Budapest radio station in November 1956 before the Red Army arrived. Hay's rather two-dimensional heroic play is set just after the retreating Nazis have blown up all the bridges across the Danube, which cuts the country in two. A precondition of any future reconstruction of the society is the building of a new bridge before the winter ice freezes, which is achieved despite low morale and poor materials.

In the following year came *Timid People*, a comedy of village life set in China in 1949, the year of the Chinese revolution, in which a young man and woman decide to marry against the wishes of their parents. It was written by one of China's most popular authors, Chau Shu Li and presented at Unity in a version by George Leeson. In 1955, Unity staged *The Road to Life*, the story of the Soviet educationalist Anton Makarenko, based on his three-volume 'epic' about how he organised a school for juvenile delinquents and turned them into good citizens. In 1956, Unity presented its last play from the Communist-led camp for nearly a decade, *Hold the Line* by the Soviety writers K. Iskayev and A. Galitz, in a production that was visited by members of the Berliner Ensemble who were performing in London. The play is a farce set in a Moscow hotel room where identities are confused as one of the guests waits for an important trunk telephone call.

Unity was sent such plays by people who had been abroad or by the embassies, which, in turn, looked to Unity to provide suitable plays for production in their countries. This kind of exchange involved several visits by Unitarians to the Soviet bloc, notably during the international youth festivals in Bucharest in 1953 and Warsaw in 1955 as well as Berlin in 1951. Eric Paice recalls that the mime he created for the Romanian event purported to tell the history of the British working class. It was set to music and produced by Joan Clarke who had to overcome severe rehearsal difficulties caused by the inaccessibility of the only tape recorder in Bucharest that could be provided for the group. To use the machine, a German model owned by the capital's radio station, the group had to be driven daily in a large black Zim through heavily guarded gates to the appropriate ministry where everyone would have to wait an hour or so for a special pass to be stamped which they then took under escort to the radio station for a wait of another couple of hours before the machine would be produced. The contingent that went to Poland performed O'Casey's *The End of the Beginning*, excerpts from *Twelfth Night* and Old Time Music Hall (including Lionel Bart singing 'Any Old Iron' to cap his interpretation of Sir Andrew Aguecheek).

As well as maintaining its international solidarity, Unity also stood firm to other commitments regardless of the serious consequences at the box office. It staged plays about liberation struggles and continued to promote new writing, despite great difficulty in finding suitable material. From the kindred New Theatre movement in Australia came two liberation plays: first, Mona Bland's *Strangers in the Land*, presented in 1952, which was banned from public performance by the Lord Chamberlain because of its portrait of life among the planters in Malaya at a time when British troops were leading the jungle war there against the Communist-led guerrillas. The play attacks the merciless grip the planters have on the country and was conceived as a riposte to a pro-colonial film *The Planter's Wife*; the second was Nan Macmillan's *The Christmas Bridge*, a plea to end the Korean war. In similar spirit, Lillian Hellman's version of *Montserrat* by Emmanuel Roblès, written during the Nazi occupation of France, was a reminder that the struggle for national freedom was centuries old. The play offers a stirring account of a Spanish officer, serving in what was to become Venezuela, who is loyal to the revolutionary Simon Bolivar and who has to weigh the lives of six people against the damage he would cause by betraying Bolivar's hide-out.

Leonard Irwin's second play for London Unity, *The Wages of Eve*, was staged in 1952, directed by Una Brandon-Jones and Anne Dyson, a long-standing Unity activist and accomplished professional performer. The play is a comedy about equal pay, in which a female charge-hand is sacked for demanding the same wage as her male predecessor. The boss tells her: '...justice, conscience, equality and all the other slush doesn't *exist* in business, only in books.'[10] She wins back her job after a go-slow affects production and then prepares to fight for her claim, not alone this time, but with the support of her workmates. As the works manager declares:

> You'll get what you want when you re-unite – and you can't unite except in a union – and when you galvanise your union into action. It

won't be glamorous; it won't be personal; it'll be SOCIAL – some of the men'll resent your bid for their rate of pay so you'll have to educate them and the women too ... You don't want martyrs; you want justice, and the power to get it is women's voices, women's energy, and women's courage.

In *Land of the Living*, staged at Unity in 1954, Irwin turns to an uneconomically small farm and the problems of making a livelihood. A woman is at the heart of the play again, this time challenging the fatalistic farmworkers who do not belong to a union because they believe that nothing can be changed. They let their landlord run the village through the local council, which is controlled by his land agent. The woman comes from a town – she became a 'Land Girl' in the war and never went back – and now she is trying to open a social centre to bring some life back to the community:

> You men can go shootin' or fishin' ... or to town for cattle-market, but the women have nothin', for there's miles between woman and woman, and what's in the village? A pub, and a dirty ugly dump it is. Did your mother ever go *anywhere* with your father? [...] The centre *I* mean is a place where folks could meet at nights and weekends. A small hall with a piano and a little canteen. Maybe we could have a film show in it sometimes, and concerts. A place for folks to go instead of frowstin' by the fire at nights, or sitting solitary. Tables and chairs for the old folks. Oh, there's all sorts of things we could do with it![11]

She falls in love with a farmer's son but agrees to marry him only if he helps her in her fight for better conditions, notably for piped water and electricity, which he finally does in the face of his traditional allegiances. In private, he rehearses a speech in front of her: 'I've called this meeting to say that village and estate need wakin' up. These are modern times, these are, but we all go on livin' the same way they did far back.' *Land of the Living*, which had already been seen at the Manchester Library Theatre and had been broadcast on radio, won Irwin the Atlantic Award and was published by the Unity New Play Service.

In lighter vein, Dennis Gleeson from St Helens – yet another writer passing through Merseyside Unity – provided London Unity with much sought after comedies of contemporary working-class life: *No!*, staged in 1953, is set during a crucial by-election that hinges on the peace issue, and *Russian for Yes*, presented in 1955, deals with Anglo-Soviet relations. Both were written under the name Tom Cobley. *No!* included a memorable line from a *Daily Worker* journalist, who is helping the new anti-bomb Labour parliamentary candidate and is asked to invent a campaign slogan quickly because the old pro-bomb candidate has only just been replaced. 'Give me a minute,' says the reporter. 'I'm a Communist – I'm not used to these sudden changes of policy.'[12] It usually brought the house down, according to the show's director Sheila Dorrell, but was the target of some on the management committee who wanted it cut.

Unity had to wait until 1955 for a 'straight' new play to make a profit – the first since *Longitude 49*. It was Leonard Peck's third to be staged at Goldington Street and was called *The Shadow of the Swastika*. Like most of his work, it is written in a conventional form – such as domestic drama, thriller, melodrama – but given unconventional content. In this case, it is a 'who-dunnit' that explores the resurgence of Nazism in post-war West Germany as the country rearms and it questions the responsibility of respectable Germans for their country's past crimes. The production had to be staged at three-and-a-half weeks' notice because of Sean O'Casey's abrupt cancellation of *Red Roses for Me*, which was already in rehearsal but clashed with a proposed professional performance. Nevertheless, *The Shadow of the Swastika*, directed by Frank Rhodes, took 72 block bookings. It was also mounted under the title *Double Cross* by the professional Repertory Players at the Strand Theatre and in many Soviet cities as well as in Belgium. With yet another title, *The Worn Shoe*, it won top marks in a play competition organised by the leading amateur theatre Questors.

Box office trouble was not the only problem facing Unity, but it was the most serious. A profit was recorded in 1951, thanks mainly to *Here Goes!*, but in 1952 the theatre came near to closure. A conference was held at the end of that year on the difficulties facing Unity and was addressed by, among others, Konstantin Simonov. The general tone was highly critical of Unity's performance yet the proposed solution – to draw from life and mount classics if they reflected peoples' struggles – was of little practical use. Unity almost closed again the following year. Takings had dropped by £1,713. The theatre had lost £273, the Mobile Group £88 and the Grays Inn Road premises of the society a lot more. The management committee decided to vacate them that year. The best business since *Here Goes!* had been registered by *Mother Goose* with 150 block bookings and £1,606 at the box office. *The Christmas Bridge* had only attracted 33 block bookings, all but one from Communist Party bodies, and dissatisfaction with this production led to an explosive management committee meeting as well as a series of internal tussles that ended in a change of leadership and the general manager Mick Manning going. Puppet shows (under puppetmaster Bob Smith) and children's and bazaar entertainments were suspended in 1952 and film shows were presented in the winter.

Unity was saved in 1953 by another revue, called *Turn It Up!*, which built on the success of *Mother Goose* by using many of the same team. The title refers to the opening number which mocks the irrelevance of Shaftesbury Avenue entertainment. Three young men and women in evening dress with cigarette holders are singing 'a witty, satirical, cowardly brew' when they are interrupted by a Unity cast shouting 'Turn it up' or 'what a crew'.[13] They continue:

> Political things
> are critical things to do!
> West End revue
> Is ready for dumping
> Time we had something new.

The show lampoons moral rearmament, a trades union official in the House of Lords and the Coronation:

> We've got Coronation flags and Coronation bells,
> Coronation chlorophyl for Coronation smells.

There were skits on Boadicea, on an ex-Nazi German industrialist singing 'I see eye-to-eye with ICI', on Japanese businessmen praising democracy because it helps them exploit their workers, and, in a fairy tale, on Chiang Kai Shek (the deposed Chinese leader) – 'once upon a time lived a little man with a great big past and a tiny future'.

A Parsons and Fase number, 'My Man from MI5', had been updated to 'My Guy from the FBI' and their spoofs were copied in another Gilbert and Sullivan parody based on *Iolanthe*. It is called 'Nyebevanthe' or 'The Budget Opera' and satirises figures from the 1951 election, in which the Tories used the slogan 'Red meat and eggs'. The show's finale reproduces Unity's habitual good cheer, with its chorus 'Great things are happening now', and ends in a tableau showing the Soviet Union and People's Democracies as heroic symbols of a brave new world. Unity's message, however distant from the real international situation, found favour among those who wanted to hear. People queued at weekends to get into *Turn It Up!*, which was lavish and full of speed under Alfie Bass's direction, and had a strong cast that included Bill Ward, Will Stampe, Una Brandon-Jones and Julian Glover. *Tribune*'s critic Richard Findlater attacked the politics but praised the 'dynamic energy' and the 'hard-working company with plenty of talent'.

The show had seven authors credited to it, including Eric Paice, who had written *Mother Goose* with Alfie Bass, Bob Halfin (one of the authors of the popular song 'I'm a Pink Toothbrush, You're a Blue Toothbrush') and a new group of friends who had come together on *The Wages of Eve* and hatched the original idea for *Turn It Up!*; they were John Gold, Jack Grossman, who became a film writer, director and producer and was co-author of the revue *The Lord Chamberlain Regrets* which played in the West End in 1961, and the composer Lionel Bart, who had been an understudy for *The Wages of Eve* and had designed its poster and painted the scenery. This was the start of Bart's career in the theatre, having swapped his own name of Begleiter for that of the famous London hospital. He was nurtured by many people at Unity and he contributed to three more Unity shows before collaborating with Frank Norman at the Theatre Royal Stratford East, via Unity contacts, on *Fings Ain't Wot They Used T' Be*, a show that ran for two years in the West End with several Unity actors in the cast. The Unity shows provided Bart with the basis for songs that were to make him a celebrity. He went on to write the lyrics for *Lock Up Your Daughters!*, the opening production of the new Mermaid Theatre, the internationally successful *Oliver!* and *Blitz* (with story by Bart and Joan Clarke, known as Maitland, costumes by Bernard Sarron and Unity people in the cast too). He also wrote or contributed to several other musicals, including *Maggie May*, and wrote film scores for Tommy Steele, the title song of a James Bond film and the Cliff Richard hit 'Living Doll'.

Despite the popularity of *Turn It Up!*, internal strife threatened the theatre's future. A 'filler' had to be found – three short O'Casey plays – followed by the comedy *No!* while the wrangling became nastier and accusations flew in all directions as to who was responsible for Unity's plight.

There was no local audience to replace those missing from the fall in block bookings, which, with the slump in public political activity and the drop in Communist Party membership, were becoming ever harder to organise.

In the climate of the Cold War many national affiliations were lost and the Clerical and Administrative Workers Union even proscribed Unity in 1952. (This decision, however, was reversed a year later.) Local affiliations, nevertheless, increased and a record number of constituency Labour Parties joined, presumably in reaction to Labour's loss of government. The figures give a generous picture of Unity's activity. The Communist Party's weekly magazine *World News and Views* says (in its 13 June 1953 issue) that Unity had 350 active members, 3,000 individual members and 2,000,000 affiliates through 375 organisations. By 1954, figures were given in a leaflet, 'A Theatre of Your Own', aimed at the London labour movement, of 212 organisations affiliated, including 115 at national, district and local level from 28 different unions. In that year, four staff had to be dismissed, leaving only three, and the theatre was reduced to playing Friday, Saturday and Sundays only. Anne Dyson, working then as the theatre's secretary, remembers discussions on mutual co-operation with Joan Littlewood, whom she had known from Theatre of Action days in Manchester, but despite good and friendly relations at a personal level between several members of Theatre Workshop and Unity, there was no chance of any more formal contact between the two theatres.[14]

Unity was still an important social focus for the left-wing and, whether in its productions, at its dances, on its rambles or propping up its bar, it brought together all kinds of people from different backgrounds and with different interests. You might have met there, for instance, Harry Landis, just turned professional and coming back, as he would time and again, to help out; or a young Johnny Speight, eager to defend Shaw against all detractors and ready with sketches that he wanted to try out, before writing *Till Death Us Do Part* for Unity graduate Warren Mitchell; or David Winnick, working backstage prior to national service and election as a Labour MP; or you might have seen Stephen Moore, who appeared in *The Germans*, little knowing then, but dreaming perhaps, that he would become a leading actor with the National Theatre and the Royal Shakespeare Company. Mostly, as ever, you would find those whose names are not recorded here but without whom Unity would not have existed.

In spite of its attractions, however, people were passing through Unity rapidly and the theatre was having to rely on a diminishing number of activists to maintain it. There was little enthusiasm for committee work and, after the annual trawl to find enough bodies to serve on the management committee, attendances quickly fell. In Unity's isolation, feuding over minor issues became more frequent, bitterness developed against those who were considered not to be pulling their weight and an even more inflated sense of importance among some in the leadership reinforced certain conservative tendencies in attitudes to life, politics and aesthetics. Mick Manning was blamed for the theatre's decline and was kicked out after exhausting himself in Unity's service. He was replaced in the autumn of 1953 by the Communist Party's choice of former seaman, party organiser and teacher George Leeson, whom many came to see as an authoritarian figure and who was recalled more fondly for his collection of Flamenco records and love of Spain where he had fought against the Franco forces, had been captured and sentenced to death. Leeson had travelled widely but did not know the theatre very well. He soon disbanded the trade union advisory committee that used to meet after the first night of a production and he also dissolved the Mobile Group. He was supported in running the theatre by a committed group, including Eric Paice, Anne Dyson and Dick Polling.

A Sartre Première

Leeson took over as general manager at a difficult moment and under his leadership, which lasted until the summer of 1956, the most noteworthy artistic event was the staging, through his contacts, of the British première of Jean-Paul Sartre's *Nekrassov*.

The first immediate problem that faced him, however, was the poor state of the building. Its fabric had not been properly maintained and, from this point on, the consequences of that neglect absorbed more and more of Unity's time and money. In late 1953 the London County Council ordered new building work to be carried out and the management launched a building fund to meet the costs. The century-old drains had to be made good and the whole building rewired. By the end of 1955, doors had been rehung to be self-closing and had been covered with asbestos to make them fireproof, the wardrobe and backstage workshops had been cleared, fire escapes had been built from the dressing rooms, all the wood panelling had been made fireproof with asbestos, a brick wall had been built to seal off the stage from the dressing rooms, emergency lights had been installed, steps from the foyer to the theatre had been constructed, a fire-resisting glass panel had been put on the lighting box, the loft had been cleared, sealed and fitted with a ventilation shaft, the ceiling backstage had been stripped and covered with plasterboard, and the gas fires had been removed from the wardrobe and dressing rooms. (Installation of a new drainage system was begun but shelved through lack of funds.) When this work had been completed, the management committee was able to take the decision to let the theatre to visiting groups as a matter of policy – a tacit admission of its own difficulty in mounting a full repertoire, although the move was primarily and publicly aimed at raising money.

The first production under Leeson's reign was another drama documentary play from Eric Paice, *The Rosenbergs*, based on the trial of Ethel and Julius Rosenberg and written in the wake of the international solidarity campaign organised in horror at their death sentence. A rough version of a play had been brought into Unity by William Bland. Paice, with his experience of documentary writing, agreed to help improve it. Bland soon dropped out and Paice continued alone, reading as source material letters, which were published with a foreword by Canon Collins, the official US documents and the verbatim court account of the fourteen-day trial (reproduced in abridged form in the play).

The couple had been arrested for passing to the Soviet Union during the Korean war secrets concerning the atom bomb and use of the bomb in the conflict had become a serious option for the US. Newspapers recklessly indulged the already prevalent anti-Communist witch-hunt mentality, prejudging the case with bloodthirsty glee. The Rosenbergs were found guilty, though they protested their innocence to the end, and were the first people in peacetime to be sentenced to the electric chair for spying. Their lawyer fought for two years for a retrial, during which time many Rosenberg defence committees sprung up around the world and pleas for clemency were heard from political, religious and intellectual leaders of many nations, including the French President and Pope Pius XI. Each plea was rejected and the Rosenbergs were executed on 9 June 1953.

Spy mania had also gripped Britain, notably through the cases of Fuchs, Pontecorvo and Nunn May, the distinguished physicist who was sentenced in 1950 for passing nuclear secrets to the Soviet Union. In addition, the Burgess and Maclean saga, that was to sell newspapers for years to come, had already been launched when they left the country in 1951. In such a climate, Paice was therefore concerned to be as accurate as possible. His problem was that he had come to believe that the Rosenbergs had passed on some sketches of a trigger mechanism but felt that they were right to have done so. He argued with the management committee that if Soviet possession of the bomb were necessary to guarantee peace, then the Rosenbergs were morally right to have helped create the nuclear balance. He thought that the dramatic point of the play should be the savagery of the American response to their actions and to world opinion. He was overruled, he says, and even went to the Communist Party to put his case, but, again, was told to insist on their innocence. Much to his later regret, he did. The production broke Unity's own record for block bookings for a 'straight' play and the Dean of Canterbury paid a visit.

The year ended with a pantomime, *Cinderella*, from the same group that had created *Turn It Up!*: Lionel Bart appeared as an Ugly Sister and wrote the lyrics with Jack Grossman; Una Brandon-Jones, John Gold and Roger Woddis wrote the story and the musical director was one of Unity's many unsung mainstays, Arnold Clayton. *Turn It Up!* is set in the Kingdom of Pandemonia, 'today or yesterday', and once again mines the theme of the Americans taking over Britain. Old pantomime characters such as Cinders, Buttons and Prince Charming are joined by new ones – the Fairy Pressmother (an echo of *Babes in the Wood*), Charley Chutney, Senator McAbre, ZigZag Ree, and Baron Bull, who stands for the Tory establishment. Inevitably such shows can be compared unfavourably to the earlier Parsons and Fase successes and the main difficulty of this later work is the absence of a sufficiently strong idea at its centre, despite some individually effective items. *Peacemeal* in 1955, for example, was just what the title suggests – lacking overall coherence – yet it contained some excellent songs and sketches. Bart and Paice's 'Hassanthony' was a skilful skit on *Kismet* and, coming before Suez, poked fun at the British in Egypt. Bart's 'Newmarket Nightmare' was a witty response to the Soviet Union's victories at Henley Royal Regatta on its first visit there in 1954 which were repeated in 1955 just before *Peacemeal* opened. Bart transferred the rowing successes to the racecourse but this gave rise to a long discussion at Unity on whether or not a Soviet horse could be called For a Lasting Peace, For a People's Democracy because it was an irreverent reference to an international Communist journal. This debate was a classic example of the damaging petty rifts that were continually breaking out at Unity and which in *Peacemeal* saw two camps emerge – one wanting the revue to become more overtly political and the other less so. The professional actor Heinz Bernard, who was working at Unity, was called in to referee and he directed a compromise production with Joan Clarke.

These kinds of arguments occur in all theatres and, like most of Unity's difficulties, will be familiar to anyone who has been involved in drama, either professionally or otherwise. Unity, however, proved more resilient than many theatres, although survival brought its own problems. Unity, for instance, managed to maintain its serious attitude to both its work and its internal democracy, yet its repertoire choices followed the track laid down at the end of the war and took Unity further into a cul-de-sac and the theatre's committee structure, from the management committee at the top to the cast committees elected by each company, often proved cumbersome and counter-productive in the face of practical needs.

The staging of more 'classics with a message' alongside 'slice-of-life' plays, documentaries, music hall, pantomimes and revues seemed to vindicate the broad approach associated with the earlier period of the much-criticised Ted Willis, but it also revealed inherent weaknesses. Just as there was a crisis in professional playwriting, Unity was finding it difficult to stimulate new plays and had no source of material or model that was the equivalent to the role played by the early Soviet theatre, the German workers' theatre movement or the progressive American writers in previous times. Unity's borrowings from abroad, such as the socialist realist plays from the Soviet bloc, can be seen as having more of a solidarity function than a challenging aesthetic one, and Unity's lack of innovation contrasts sharply with the work of Theatre Workshop and its playwright Ewan MacColl. Most of Unity's writers were, in a theatrical sense, formally conservative and relied on content to make their point – a convention that suited the naturalistic acting that Unity had encouraged alongside its expertise in comic and musical performance. The state of aesthetic debate on the left and in the Communist Party in particular could not provide much stimulation either, being locked largely into unchanging models of the relationship between culture, politics and economics or being too literary and remote for the needs of Unity. The crisis was shown in the increasing recourse to Old Time Music Hall, the very popularity of which was the root cause of its degeneration. Familiarity, ease of presentation and of rehearsal, and a simple, direct appeal made music hall the first refuge in repertoire difficulties. The motto seemed to become 'if in doubt, put on a music hall', and the result (with honourable exceptions) became ever more remote from either the original enthusiasm that informed it or the working-class audience for whom it was supposed to be a sure winner. Not that it did not remain popular but it contained no means for renewal or development and took no account of changes in the composition and taste of the working class. Arguments raged inside Unity on the subject, with one strand convinced that music hall was the 'bread and butter' of the people, while others countered that its ascendancy represented only a very short period in English cultural history – and one that had passed – and that politically too much reliance on it fed nostalgia rather than innovation or an ability to confront the future.

Renewed interested in the classics led to Joe MacColum presenting what he thought was the first London performance since 1926 of Ibsen's *Pillars of the Community*, a radical play dealing with the position of women in society and the dubious morality of powerful men. Merseyside Unity brought *Widower's Houses*, a production in honour of Shaw's centenary and the first full-length play that Goldington Street had seen of his (in fact his first play, attacking slum landlords and a society based on profit), and, for three nights, Unity performed *Women of Troy* by Euripides in a production that had won the first St Pancras Drama Festival competition. The British première of Brecht's *The*

Exception and the Rule, a parable on class ideology, with music by Frank Wagland, lyrics adapted by Bill Norton and text translation by Eric Bentley, was played with Lorca's short comedy *The Shoemaker's Wife* (previously mounted by the professional company) as a conscious re-examination of the classic tradition as well as an attempt to revive the double-bill format. The production also coincided with the first visit to Britain of the Berliner Ensemble, an event which was to have enormous influence on the direction and style of British theatre in the decades to follow.

Some classics were chosen because they were thought to have a direct relationship to Unity's interests, such as Dekker's *The Shoemaker's Holiday*, written in 1599 and presented in 1954 as a Londoners' 'knees up' that offered a glimpse of Unity's forebears, or John Gay's *Polly,* his banned sequel to *The Beggar's Opera*. It attacks merchants and slave-owners and was seen by Leeson 200 years later as a musical 'taken from the lips of Cockneys'.

Union shows were still popular and two in 1954 breathed new life into Unity for a while. The first, from the New Theatre movement in Australia, was Dick Diamond's *Reedy River*, a musical on sheep shearers and trades unionism that celebrates a great shearers' strike of 1892 and was described by Unity as 'the working man's *Oklahoma*'. Complete with bush orchestra, it drew on the folk world for its cast and helped stimulate a wider interest in the folk revival. It was directed by Ivor Pinkus and musical direction was by John Hasted. The second union show was *The Docker's Tanner*, which attracted 85 block bookings, the highest of the year but still well below the expected level and the figure necessary for a healthy bank balance.

Specially written for Unity by Leslie Martin and enlarged from its mobile version, the play tells of the six-week strike in 1889 against a cruel system whereby starving men would fight each day at the docks for a few hours work, paid at 5d an hour. The work was contracted and then sub-contracted, thereby giving many middle-men a profit before the dockers received their miserly coppers. The strikers survived on funds raised by public collection in a wave of unprecendented national and international solidarity. They won the 'tanner' – 6d per hour – the end to the worst excesses of the 'call-on' system and the recognition of the union, which marked the entry of unskilled and unorganised labour into the huge general unions. The play opened at Goldington Street during a dock strike against compulsory overtime that brought accusations from labour leaders like Arthur Deakin of a 'red' plot to cripple the economy. This was eagerly picked up by a local North London newspaper which accused Unity of being part of the plot, not realising that the play had been in the touring repertoire for some considerable time.

The union connection was also present in special events, such as the tribute to the legendary American militant Joe Hill, staged in conjunction with the Workers' Music Association in 1955 to commemorate the fortieth anniversary of his death.

The greatest coup during Leeson's time was his acquisition, with the help of the French Communist Party, of Jean-Paul Sartre's *Nekrassov*, which Unity presented in 1956 for the first time in Britain only six months after its première in France. It was written just after the People's Peace Congress in Vienna in 1952, which was organised by the World Peace Council and which issued an appeal to writers. Sartre was among the signatories and was at his closest then to the Communist movement. Set in contemporary France, the story concerns a con-man who masquerades as a defecting Soviet minister and fools a right-wing newspaper with his sensational revelations which prove useful just before a by-election. Sartre attacks the anti-communism of the reactionary mass-circulation press and the values of a society that allows the swindler to thrive and be admired.

Unity's production ran for four months and became the hit of London's theatreland. Harold Hobson in the *Sunday Times* called it a 'high-spirited, satirical, journalistic and political extravaganza', Kenneth Tynan in the *Observer* 'the best political comedy we have seen since Shaw's perihelion [...] the only play in London which takes the Western dilemma seriously enough to laugh at it'. Richard Findlater in *Tribune* said 'the new year has begun with a miracle [...] it is a pleasure to see how the hard-working amateurs of Goldington Crescent have risen to the occasion of this theatrical scoop.' Some people inside Unity were less happy than the critics with the director Margery Shaw, a professional performer associated with Unity since the war when she appeared in *The Match Girls* and who had been brought in after much internal squabbling.

The show made £475 profit (though the theatre's total deficit still stood at £947) and the Unity version by George and Sylvia Leeson was taken up by George Devine for the English Stage Company. It was the first production of Devine's new company to be staged at the Edinburgh Festival and was also seen at its own theatre, the Royal Court.[15] However, the play did not work as well as at Unity, due to a miscast Robert Helpmann and awkward political timing; Krushchev's denunciation of Stalin in his 'secret' speech and the Red Army invasion of Hungary had turned sour the play's general tone and its references to choosing freedom. Unity managed not to make much money from the play's broadcast and professional production, although Sartre had given Unity the British rights. Internal rows on the finances of *Nekrassov* continued for months, over who had said what and to whom and with whose authority, while the theatre faced its next crisis. Leeson knew that he was not popular and resigned. Shortly after, he left the Communist Party having had a letter published in the *Daily Worker* suggesting that the party dissolve and enter the Labour Party.

In September 1956 a special general meeting was called to discuss the poor financial situation, a threatened Compulsory Purchase Order from the London County Council, which was worried about the delapidated state of the building despite the renovations, and Leeson's resignation. There were no nominations for the post. Membership subscriptions were raised and it was agreed to undertake further work on the theatre to stave off the LCC – otherwise Unity would have been forced to move to new premises. It had only just renewed the lease, for a further ten years at a cost of £400 per annum. Heinz Bernard, whose tuberculosis made it difficult for him to pursue a career as a professional actor, later agreed to act as general manager. He was interviewed by a Communist Party official, although he was not a member of the party himself, and on 2 October the management committee agreed his appointment. He took up the job on 5 November and on 23 November a watershed production of a Living Newspaper on Suez and Hungary took place.

'World on Edge'

World on Edge, or Living Newspaper No. 5, began when the management committee approached Eric Paice and Roger Woddis to write a documentary on Suez. They replied that the show had to include events in Hungary, which in their view would not have happened without the 'West' having offered the example in Egypt of 'settling' differences by invasion. The well-respected André van Gyseghem, Unity's first president who had returned to Unity in 1954 to take acting classes, agreed to direct and Unity's proposed Christmas production, *Burlesque*, was postponed despite the potential loss of revenue and the theatre's huge debt, which now stood at £1,700. Advertisements and letters were placed in the press – from *Stage and Television Today* to the *Daily Worker* and *Peace News* – asking for material (songs, sketches, lyrics) from those in the labour movement and those without political affiliation who wanted to contribute to the theme that 'only by making the UN work can the sovereignty of small nations be assured and peace for all be maintained'. According to *Peace News, World on Edge* took twelve days to write. In its method of production *World on Edge* bore many similarities to previous Unity Living Newspapers; it was created while it was being rehearsed, it was updated as events occurred (and new endings were tried)[16] and it involved a lot of people contributing collectively – from BBC drama producer and long-standing Unity supporter Reggie Smith (the basis for Guy Pringle in Olivia Manning's Balkan and Levant trilogies) to Howard Goorney of Theatre Workshop and a young director, Charles Marowitz, newly arrived from America. It had important differences, too, and it was inconceivable that it could have been presented by Unity previously. It was not a single-issue show and it did not present a consensus view. Most markedly, it contained criticisms of the Soviet Union and asked audiences to make up their own minds. The ironic sub-title was 'All Your Answers Questioned'.

To the noise of war sounds, a woman refugee from Eastern Europe walks on stage with a bundle. She looks around for a moment, stunned. From the opposite side, another refugee, a man from Egypt, also walks on. They meet.

1st REFUGEE: Which way?
2nd REFUGEE: I don't know.
1st REFUGEE: Is it bad there?
2nd REFUGEE: I can't describe it.
1st REFUGEE: There must be some place.
2nd REFUGEE: Where?
1st REFUGEE: Where, where ...
(*They walk off together. Editor of Living Newspaper enters.*)

EDITOR: Where? Where are any of us going? I don't know. Do you? (*to audience*) But I do know this. We've got to find out, and find out quickly. We must be honest with you, we don't know all the answers, but we know that if this crisis is to be solved at all it must be solved by reason and clear thinking. And that goes for everybody.[17]

Two war correspondents report from Suez and Budapest. Their accounts are intercut and interchangeable. The two refugees from the beginning of the play return. They sit down. Without looking at each other one takes out a crust of bread and breaks off half to give to the other. They chew almost mechanically, staring dumbly out into the auditorium. A Communist defends the Red Army, a Tory defends Sir Anthony Eden. A second Communist, of 20 years' standing, disagrees with the first and slowly tears up a party card. A second Tory screws up a copy of the *Times*. Reports come through of the French Communist newspaper *L'Humanité* being attacked by a large crowd. Three Communists are beaten to death, and over the speaker comes the chant of a crowd, rising and dying away – 'Soviet A-ssa-ssins! Soviet A-ssa-ssins!' A middle-aged working-class woman protects a solitary Red Army man from baying crowds. She speaks to him as though the others were not there:

> Are you surprised! After what you've done? Oh yes, I suppose you can justify it – find reasons – or will you turn around tomorrow and say it was all a 'terrible mistake?' I never thought I'd say this to you, but I'll say it to you now – I'M ASHAMED OF YOU – MUCH ASHAMED! When the other side does what you did I expect it – but YOU – somebody I – I – (*she falters, unable to go on*) I brought up my kids to believe in you – you were something to love and live up to – what are you now? Don't you see? They don't believe in you anymore. All the wonderful things you've done – 40 years of – of – splendour – blown away overnight. Well, I'm not going to take away their hopes, I'm not going to let them forget – what you were and what you CAN be! I'll NEVER let them forget – however hard you make it for me!

She hits him hard round the face and the crowd goes mad but she whips around on them and cries out: '*No*! I am the only one that's got the right to hit him!'

World on Edge was packed every night. Performances were sometimes interrupted by hecklers and scuffles broke out.

EMERGENCY EDITION!

Living Newspaper

*** London – Fifth Edition Price 6d.

WORLD ON EDGE!!

Armoured Divisions Go In.
Refugees Crowd Roads

U.N. IN SESSION
Call for Big 4 Talks.

THOUSANDS KILLED

FIRES

AMBUS
TO KILL

UNITY THEATRE
1956

****

****

City Notes:-
Steel Hardens

POLICE CHARGE
DEMONSTRATORS

Scientists Warn of H-Bomb Peril.

"NAKED AGGRESSION"
SAYS NEHRU

Arrests

3 HANGED

WEATHER

DUKE VISITS
NEW GUINEA.

Handbill for the Living Newspaper in which Unity broke ranks with the Communist Party by linking Suez and Hungary

Discussions were held after the show at first on Saturdays only but then, by public demand, following every performance and were led by a different person on each occasion, such as Sidney Silverman MP, Kingsley Martin or James Cameron, who was reported as saying 'Thank goodness that there is somewhere in the London theatre where actualities are being taken seriously.' According to those who ran Unity, the Communist Party leadership was furious with the theatre and, it was believed, operated an unofficial boycott of the show. Certainly official Communist Party speakers could not be found and it seemed as if the party's wayward child had finally overstepped the mark.[18] The *Daily Worker* reviewer applauded the theatre for tackling the issue, but added: 'We can accept the fact of a Communist tearing up his card, for that is news. But we cannot take the Unity Theatre Company beating its breast in public.' Other critics echoed this complaint, that 'we are left without any editorial decision.' It is not boring, said the *Daily Worker*, but it should not 'abdicate responsibility'.

Eric Paice recalls:

> We took a Newtonian view, that every action had an opposite and equal reaction. Everyone was in turmoil. Quakers refused to fight. Krushchev's revelations followed by Hungary had caused tremendous upset. Everyone seemed clear on Suez but not on Hungary. There was a great deal of discussion on whether or not to include the crowds outside the Soviet embassy shouting 'Assassins' and the scene of tearing up Communist Party membership cards.

Woddis says, 'It was a great challenge but it was also great fun. With all its faults, we were right to do it.'

The *Stage* said that *World on Edge* showed a 'remarkable degree of open-mindedness', was very well presented but contained 'much with which one must disagree.' *Tribune*'s critic thought that it blurred the truth to equate Suez and Hungary with 'such energy and passion' yet recognised that this was the link that had touched the conscience of the Communists. 'Perhaps ... this amateur theatre ... may now justify its claim to be a theatre speaking for the Labour movement,' he said. The *London Diary* commented that 'how deeply the Russian massacre of Hungarian workers has lacerated the minds and hearts of British Communists is best shown by the present revue at Unity ... It pulls no punches.' Yet it was just at this moment of openness which seemed to be fully in the spirit of the Communist Party's programme 'The British Road to Socialism' that the Communist Party declined to support Unity, although the anger was never publically acknowledged and, with whatever differences, never led to a complete break. The year 1956, however, did represent a decisive break-point for the Communist Party in other ways, since it had not been able to recover properly from the hostility turned against it by the Labour Party in government. The Communist Party faced its own crisis in the face of the widespread dissent that had been sparked off by what were to Communists the devastating revelations about Stalin that had been made in secret by Nikita Krushchev at the Soviet party's 20th Congress, and this opened the way for the rise of the New Left. One third of the British party membership resigned or was forced out, including some Communists at Unity.

World on Edge died with the events that it was portraying. Unity was never to be the same again. As the theatre entered its twenty-first year, it looked as if it might have come of age, but this new maturity also brought with it obligations that were not always easy to fulfil.

Notes

1. New interviews/correspondence for this chapter: Maurice Bardiger, Lionel Bart, Heinz Bernard, Nettie Bernard, George Brandt, Anne Dyson, Stanley Forman, Pat Fyrth, Jack Grossman, Ewan MacColl, Charles Marowitz, Eric Paice, Frank Wagland.
2. Script given me and deposited in the British Theatre Association library.
3. Script in Merseyside Museum of Labour History, Merseyside Left Theatre/Merseyside Unity Theatre Archive, Box 22.1.
4. Script given me and deposited in the British Theatre Association. Fase recalls a 'pale, over-dressed travesty' of 'Camp Followers' being performed at a London dinner-and-dance club called Ciro's and this finally convinced him and Parsons that there was no point in letting Unity material be presented commercially.
5. 'Civilisation' was published by the Workers Music Association.
6. The *Daily Worker* covered the whole story and other papers picked it up when it came to the court case. There is a reference to it in Richard Findlater, *Banned! A Review of Theatrical Censorship in Britain*, MacGibbon and Kee 1967.
7. *The Cradle Will Rock*, Random House 1937. For accounts of its opening, see Chapter 1 footnote 16; John Houseman, *Run-Through*, Allen Lane 1973 and *Unfinished Business*, Chatto and Windus 1986.

8. Script in the British Theatre Association library.
9. In a pamphlet called *Man Conquers Nature: the new Soviet construction schemes*, published by the Society for Cultural relations with the USSR in 1952, one piece contains reference to Unity (and was brought to my attention by Steve Parsons). It is by Eleanor Fox, based on conversations with the Soviet novelist Boris Polevoi for whom she acted as interpreter during his visit to Britain in 1951. She writes: 'During Polevoi's stay he saw the London Unity Theatre production of Korneichuk's *Hawthorn Grove* and he was asked whether such people as Amanda – painted, self-centred, on tottering high heels and in clothes unsuitable for any kind of work – really existed in the Soviet Union today. He laughed and said, "Of course".'
10. See note 3.
11. See note 8.
12. Script in private hands.
13. Script given me and deposited in the British Theatre Association library.
14. Differences between Theatre Workshop and Unity can be traced back to the 1930s, particularly in the emphases they placed on experiment and the relationship between art, politics and the labour movement. They were trying to achieve different aims and established different types of organisation for their different purposes (e.g. the Willis project apart, Unity prided itself on its labour movement links, its amateur status and its 'open university' approach whereas Theatre Workshop was a relatively small band of full-timers shaped more forcefully by the vision of particular individuals. This changed in the mid-1950s when increasing ambition and success led to a necessary opening out from the core group). Doris Lessing says that in *The Four-Gated City*, MacGibbon and Kee 1969, the Red Cockerel theatre is based more on Theatre Workshop than Unity.
15. Books on the Royal Court tend to omit Unity's role in bringing *Nekrassov* to light, even describing the Devine production as the British première. An honourable exception is Irving Wardle in *The Theatres of George Devine*, Cape 1978.
16. The ending was changed during the run. At first it involved the screening of an excerpt from Paul Rotha's *The World is Rich* with an appeal for support for the UN Food and Agricultural Organisation. (The film had been made in 1948 for the Central Office of Information and had been scripted by Arthur Calder-Marshall.). It was replaced by a mythical 'man in the street' figure, Fred, getting the Soviet Union, the USA, France and Britain back to the negotiating table as the only hope for the future.
17. Script given me and deposited in the British Theatre Association library.
18. There are brief references to *World on Edge* and its independence from the Communist Party line in Mervyn Jones, 'Days of Tragedy and Farce', *Socialist Register 76*, Merlin Press 1976, and in Neal Wood, *Communism and British Intellectuals*, Gollancz 1959.

10

The Final Years

In the period after 1956, Unity lacked the internal cohesion and external political support that it needed to reverse its decline.[1] Finally, it was not able to survive at all. The weakening influence of Communist politics formed the backdrop to the weakening of Unity's relationship to its audience, with a consequent decline in block bookings and an inability to mount a satisfactory repertoire. Warring factions engaged in endless democratic procedures and relentless introspection alienated more and more members. Higher and faster turnover of people lowered the general standard of the shows and lack of technique came increasingly to outweigh interest in the content of the plays. The financial burden of insufficient box office income and the taxing cost of maintaining the building proved crippling. Unity, nevertheless, did continue to support new writing, to provide a platform for challenging work from abroad and to play its role as 'open university'. It was still capable of enlisting to its aid a surprisingly wide range of sympathisers and even the most intense and self-destructive disputes did not prevent moments of extraordinary theatrical energy from lighting up what had become a dowdy curiosity of a building.

The debates were often presented in crude terms of 'revolution' versus 'reform' but at their heart lay the complex issue of the relationship between art and politics. The apparent simplicities of earlier years would no longer hold true and, even though some still clung to old certainties and fixed attitudes were to resurface with a vengeance in the 1960s, the mood at Unity just after the shattering events of 1956 favoured a more questioning approach.

In February 1957, Unity published a booklet, *Here is Drama*, that aimed to restore stability by fixing the past in print for those trying to grapple with the present and the future. Sub-titled 'Behind the scenes at Unity Theatre', it carried accounts of Unity's history, biographies of Unitarians and articles by Unity stalwarts as well as descriptions of how the theatre functioned. It was compiled by Malcolm Hulke, who was to write for television series like *The Avengers* and *Dr Who*. In what was clearly a post-1956 foreword, the playwright Benn Levy MP, a member of Unity's now defunct general council, asked what it meant to be a committed theatre:

> A dramatist, like any other artist, will do less than his best if, like a politician, he suppresses what tells against his propagandist case. He must tell the truth as he sees it even though it leads him whither he would rather not go. Though this may happen, it is unusual because, if he is as engaged as he should be in the life about him, he will have contracted an astigmatism to left or right which will govern his view of the truth and therefore his statement of it.
>
> Even so, however, he will surprise himself every so often and infuriate his political colleagues with exhibitions of disloyalty. But let him not distress himself. He must stick to his treacheries. And Unity, if it understand its job, will swallow them.[2]

This represented, more or less, the views Levy had propounded in the late 1940s in *New Theatre* which had been rebuffed then by Unity's general manager as a travesty of the theatre's position. Now, a decade later, Levy was introducing an official Unity publication with these same views on the occasion of the theatre's 21st birthday. The introduction, however, was only a general statement of principle. It did not reflect what was to be Unity's practice and its inability to keep pace with changing times. All 500 copies of the booklet, produced on the theatre's duplicator, were sold within two months of publication. A second, letterpress, edition of 3,000 copies was produced in 1961, Unity's silver jubilee year, with financial help from Unity veterans who had become successful in show business; a third edition, this time with a foreword by Ted Willis, was issued in 1963 (the year that Willis entered the House of Lords). He was writing after the founding of Centre 42, which took its name from the number of a TUC resolution on the arts. Under its director Arnold Wesker, it sought to mobilise the trade union movement in support of cultural activities around Britain. Despite the changes that had taken place in the theatre since Unity's heyday, Willis saw the need for Unity's continued existence:

> This [i.e. Unity] is a theatre which grew out of the Labour Movement. It was not the creation of well-meaning outsiders, it was not imposed from above upon a suspicious movement. If this had been the case, it would have collapsed under the weight of its difficulties a long time ago. It has survived, it has out-faced disaster time and time again, because its roots go deep.
>
> The historians of the 20th century theatre might well spend a little time over this. I believe, for instance, that this little theatre has had an enormous and subtle influence on British drama as a whole. It was the work of Unity, especially in the pre-war years and during the war, which helped to prepare the theatrical climate of today. Fifteen or twenty years ago dramatists like Wesker and Osborne, for instance, would have turned naturally to Unity as the only outlet for their plays. Now they have other opportunities: and for this they owe something, a part at least, to the pioneer work done by Unity. But as Wesker himself has recognised by his valiant efforts with Centre 42, the victory is a small one, on a very limited front. The theatre is still, to a large extent, a thing which remains outside the life of the working class.
>
> So the need for Unity remains. It is important to strengthen it, so that the path-finding, the pioneering can go on, so that from within the Labour Movement new talent may find a centre from which it may develop and extend.[3]

Wesker, whose mother was a Unity supporter, would probably have agreed with the final sentiment; but Willis continued, 'on a personal note', to hope that Centre 42 might decide to merge with Unity – something to which Wesker would never have agreed given his commitment to a professional organisation and his own distance from the Communist left.

Changing Times

As Britain continued to recover from the war, with an end to rationing, the further development of new housing and civic building programmes, and an expansion in education, the media and consumer goods, Unity found itself overtaken by the very advances that it had helped to pioneer. In some ways, its demise became a tribute to its earlier success.

'Kitchen sink' drama had become the fashion as had working-class accents, and the naturalism of television, to be seen to impressive effect in Armchair Theatre and serials such as *Z*

Cars, was to outstrip Unity on its own territory. Soon, even the political satire and the Living Newspaper drama documentary approach that Unity had championed were to become acceptable and popular on television and in the West End. Theatre Workshop at Stratford East, which was seen at Unity as belonging to the same world as itself, had come to national prominence and was challenging, among other things, conventional ideas of play-making in ways that had grown from the same roots as Unity's in the collective creations of the 1930s. Theatre Workshop arrived in the West End in 1956 and stayed there until 1964. In a different way, Unity was overtaken by the English Stage Company at the Royal Court, which Unity saw as belonging to a different, if sympathetic, world (and one in which many Unity members were active as professionals). Unity had no Shelagh Delaney, Brendan Behan or Arnold Wesker, nor was it part of the 'new wave' of British theatre that dates from 1956.[4] Instead of building on the substantial contribution that it had already made to the theatre, with many of its aims coming to fruition in the professional world, Unity turned inwards and failed either to find a new role or to renew with sufficient vigour its traditional one.

In 1957, Unity claimed a membership of 650 activists, 6,000 associates and 218 affiliates yet it faced its largest ever deficit of nearly £4,000 and during the year it used up its reserves. In September, it called a trade union conference to try and boost support and it revived its trade union advisory committee.[5] The print union NATSOPA and cine technicians' ACTT affiliated at a national level, and there were modest increases in audience figures. Immediately following the conference, however, the highest number of block bookings still only reached 47 – for Arthur Miller's *The Crucible*, which opened the St Pancras Arts Festival – and the highest box office takings were recorded for the pantomime, *Robin Hood and his Merry Men*. Runs became shorter, more productions were staged (at a budget of between £20 and £30), visiting groups came more frequently, and 50 people on a Saturday night was considered respectable.

The difficulty of attracting audiences, and at the same time helping them to understand and enjoy the new and the challenging, was starkly demonstrated by the poor reception given to Lionel Bart's provocative and original musical, *Wally Pone*. Based on Jonson's *Volpone*, Bart set his story in the contemporary world of the Soho vice barons and satirised the fashionable coffee-bar culture which preceded the Swinging Sixties. According to an internal bulletin, *Wally Pone* played to practically empty houses for ten weeks and the report commented that all the audiences seemed to want was Old Time Music Hall.

In spite of the problems, Unity remained open and offered mainly a familiar repertoire mix of new plays, classic revivals, political revues and pantomimes. Old Time Music Hall was sustained, as popular, vernacular theatre, in shows such as *Tripe and Onions*. They often included new revivals of Victorian melodramas, like *Temptation*, written in 1875 and unearthed by Tom Mercer for the show *Beer and Skittles*. The Victorian period became a rich source of exploitation before it was fashionable in the West End, from *Sweeney Todd*, revealed as a fictional character who was not the legendary nineteenth-century Englishman but a fourteenth-century Frenchman, to two vigorous adaptations by Arnold Hinchliffe, teacher, BBC script reader, radio playwright and translator who was then a leading figure at Unity. The first was *The Misadventures of Mr Pickwick*, a musical which appeared the same year as *Oliver!* and which was revived as part of the Dickens centenary celebrations; and the second was *The Life of Kaggs*, featuring a con-man who turns the hypocrisy of the age against itself to his own advantage. It was drawn from the writings about the London poor of Henry Mayhew and had won second prize in a Granada Television play competition.

Unity was naturally interested in the militant past too. It revived *The Ragged Trousered Philanthropists*, as if like a talisman, and *The Match Girls*, with new music and lyrics that reflected on women's role in society. Unity also staged James Plunkett's *The Risen People*, a stirring account of the Dublin general strike of 1913-14.

Ireland figured again both in Patrick Galvin's first play, a savage commentary on the Republic called *And Him Stretched*, which was seen at Unity before being presented in Dublin, and in *Bloomsday*, an adaptation by the Irish actor and writer Allan McClelland of part of James Joyce's *Ulysses*. McClelland, who had appeared in the original cast of *The Mousetrap*, had played the Narrator in an adaptation of another part of the novel, *Nighttown*, which had been staged at the Arts Theatre the year before. *Bloomsday* had been heard on radio and seen in Oxford but not in

London, and the professional companies that could have coped with the play's demands had turned it down. Unity was not sure whether to present the play or not. The problem was not its cast size but its sexual content. After a hard-fought internal battle, a production was agreed which was promoted as representing a proletarian Joyce, the Joyce of the Dublin streets, and it turned out to be one of Unity's successes.

Sets and lighting were designed and executed by McClelland's friend Sean Kenny, one of the most influential post-war stage designers who had designed the Oxford production. Cast members of *Bloomsday* recall that Kenny came to the first rehearsal and then was not seen again until the night before the dress rehearsal when he brought with him an assistant and several bottles of whisky. Kenny painted Dublin on Unity's back wall that night but it is a vision that was sadly lost a few productions later when it was painted over for another show.

Directed by McClelland himself, the production had Joe MacColum as Bloom, Helen Gold as Molly, Denys Hawthorn as Stephen Daedelus and, as Buck Mulligan, an apprentice engineer called Michael Gambon who was to become one of the leading stage and television actors of his day. Gambon had played as a child in the streets outside Unity and later, when, as an aspiring actor, he saw its advertisement in *Amateur Stage* ('Actors and Actresses always wanted for productions played under near-professional conditions') he decided to return to his old neighbourhood. At first he helped build the sets, but, as Unity was constantly short of performers, he was soon asked if he would like to act, which is what he had really wanted from the start. His half-dozen shows there assured him that he really did wish to turn professional and gave him the confidence to go ahead and do so.

Bloomsday showed Unity's interest in presenting classics that could be seen to have 'relevance', as did its productions of *The Crucible*, for example, or Shaw's *Heartbreak House*. Even Giles Cooper's *Everything in the Garden*, an apparently 'bourgeois' play, was staged to expose the morality that is required to succeed in capitalist society. Most of this classic repertoire was drawn from what was to become the standard fare of the two nationally subsidised theatre companies, the Royal Shakespeare Company and the National Theatre, which were being established during this period. Unity performed Farquhar's *The Recruiting Officer*, in the wake of the Berliner Ensemble's production in London of Brecht's *Trumpets and Drums*, which is based on the Farquhar play, and two years before the National's much acclaimed revival. Unity also presented the rarely seen *School for Wives* by Molière, Ibsen's *Hedda Gabler* and *A Doll's House*, Gorky's *The Lower Depths* (directed by a visiting Bulgarian, Levcho Zdravchev), a centenary Chekhov, *The Seagull*, and another Shaw, *Androcles and the Lion*, with a specially written fantasy prologue by Tom Mercer. *The Glass Menagerie* by Tennessee Williams was given a production without décor.

Unity's international concern, however, only led to one play from the Soviet bloc being performed at this time, Valentin Katayev's 1928 comedy about the Moscow housing shortage, *Squaring the Circle*, although Unity's interest in Brecht might be placed in this category as he had settled in the German Democratic Republic.

Brecht and Adamov

In 1958, Heinz Bernard directed the London English-language première of Brecht's *Mother Courage and her Children*, deliberately following the Berliner Ensemble's production, which had been seen in London two years before. Unity borrowed the costumes from Theatre Workshop, which had already presented the play in Barnstaple, although, unlike Unity, without a full orchestral score. Arnold Clayton was the musical director and Robert Dyson the designer. The production was only made possible by a donation from Donald Ogden Stewart for the one unavoidable expense, the cart, which was specially hired from a South London firm that made market barrows.

The most daring of Unity's eight Brecht productions was the British première in 1961 of *The Visions of Simone Machard*, which he wrote with Leon Feuchtwanger and is set in central France in 1940 during the Nazi advance. Simone Machard, a young woman in her teens, identifies with Joan of Arc in dream sequences through which, in spite of strong local opposition, she feels moved to oppose the Nazis. She prevents food and transport from leaving the town, aids refugees and blows up the town's petrol tanks so that the Germans cannot use the fuel. She is caught finally but by this time she has already become an inspiration to others to resist.

Unity used its own version by Arnold Hinchliffe, which was later performed by the Citizens' Theatre, Glasgow, and the play was directed by Heinz Bernard. Its strengths seem to have been a gritty authenticity, which overcame any lack of technique, and Hanns Eisler's music. This was played by a quartet from Morley College and sung by the Morley choir conducted by Peter Racine Fricker under the overall musical direction of Jack Wellgarth. The critic Harold Hobson came on three successive nights and the production was reviewed favourably in the European press. People queued round the block to see *The Visions of Simone Machard* and it did the best business of that financial year. (It was typical of Unity that a prominent theatre practitioner like George Devine, a friend of Unity over many years, was left to take his chance for a ticket with everyone else, receiving no preferential treatment, and typical of Devine that this was what he expected.)

Having been refused the rights to present Brecht's *Trumpets and Drums*, Unity followed *The Visions of Simone Machard* in 1964 with two of his most performed plays, *The Good Woman of Szechwan* (for which the director removed Unity's proscenium arch) and *The Caucasian Chalk Circle* (which the theatre said was coloured with the working-class humanity that was Unity's special contribution to contemporary drama). Then came two more British Brecht premières, the rarely-revived *Antigone* in 1967 accompanied by a documentary on Brecht called *Change the World, It Needs It* and, after much negotiation with the Brecht estate, *The Mother* in 1969. Unity this time could not manage all the demands of Eisler's music and Frank Wagland had to re-score the show for a smaller ensemble. The production was mounted with the help of the London Co-operative Society's education committee and opened on the anniversary of the Russian Revolution.

Unity's links with Brecht's work go back to 1938 when it staged *Señora Carrar's Rifles*, the first Brecht play to be seen in Britain. There was a gap until 1956, when Unity played *The Exception and the Rule*. This time lapse, while reflecting a somewhat uneven interest in aesthetic theory, can also be explained by the difficulty of obtaining English translations and, as an amateur company, the rights to perform the plays. Unity and its members, nevertheless, played an important part in introducing Brecht's work to Britain and in spreading his influence. For instance, along with the

productions, five of which were British premières. Unity's magazine *New Theatre* carried (in March 1949) an article on 'A New Technique of Acting' by Brecht, and replies to it in subsequent issues by John Gielgud, Alec Guinness and Frederick Valk; Heinz Bernard wrote informatively about Brecht in *Prompt* magazine and so, in *Encore*, did Eric Capon, who in 1955 had directed the first open reading in Britain of *Mother Courage and her Children* before Joan Littlewood's production for Theatre Workshop.[6]

Following on from the presentation of Sartre's *Nekrassov* and the Brecht plays, Unity's desire to help break down Britain's self-imposed isolation from Continental drama was highlighted even more sharply by its two world premières of plays by Arthur Adamov, the Russian-born French writer who had renounced his earlier involvement with the Theatre of the Absurd in order to embrace an imaginative and iconoclastic socialist realism.[7]

In the first, *Spring '71*, secured for Unity with the help of the French Communist Party, Adamov uses 21 realistic scenes interspersed with eight symbolic grand guignol interludes to dramatise the Paris Commune both as an historical event and as a series of episodes in the lives of the people. He shows a cross-section of the Paris population – workers, priests, councillors, soldiers – slightly out of step with each other and with the course of events, reacting differently to the fate of commune. (One character says that everything will be all right because Montmartre has not been taken when the audience knows already that Montmartre has fallen. An old woman comes to realise that the workers have become her masters instead of the landlord, who then ceases to be a figure of terror, yet, after the Commune's defeat, she turns as rapidly against the Commune as she had come to support it.) In contrast, the commenting interludes, inspired by Daumier's cartoons, depict the history symbolically, personifying the Bank of France and the Commune as well as key people like Bismarck and Thiers.

Designer Ian Mooney opened up the whole stage to create there the streets of Paris, and the stage management team under Elaine Pransky rose to meet the considerable demands of the play, which, with its 40-strong cast, were for the most part beyond Unity's means. The translation by Arnold Hinchliffe and Jim Sluszny was necessarily rushed. The original, which had been published in

1960, would have run for more than four hours. Unity had to cut it down and Adamov kept losing the translations that were sent to him. Hinchliffe and Sluszny divided the play up to work on and Hinchliffe edited the final version. The director Michael Almaz, who produced Adamov's *Paolo Paoli* at the Tower Theatre, turned out to be the wrong choice mainly, it seems, because he was unable to cope with the pressures of the production and was not used to Unity's working method. The first night was a disaster and the production never quite became the success that it might have been.

Nevertheless, the ambitious production did reveal, in Adamov's words printed in the programme, how 'three little months of joy, effort and error' and 'of truth born before its time' had changed history and changed the people who lived through a rare range of experiences. Adamov enjoyed his time at Unity and spoke from the stage on the first night to denounce the France of de Gaulle which had not then seen his play because, he said, it was still the France that had murdered the Communards.

Adamov was sufficiently pleased to let Unity mount the world première of *The Scavengers (La Politique des restes)* in a translation by Tom Vaughan, which was preceded by Max Frisch's *The Fury of Phillip Hotz* played on a composite set designed by Adrian Vaux. Heinz Bernard directed Adamov's trial play which exposes the paranoia of a racist industrialist. He believes that he will be forced to eat refuse, which he indentifies with black people, and has therefore killed a black employee in self defence. Through flash-backs, the play shows the individual's neurosis and prejudices to be rooted in the wrongs of society. (Unity used back projections to illustrate this approach but Adamov disapproved). The Frisch play, directed by Clive Barker with future arts impressario Michael Kustow in the lead, satirises the breakdown of a marriage. In 1970, the year Adamov died of an overdose, probably a suicide, Unity presented his *Professor Taranne*, the one dream play that he did not reject because it had helped him become free of his nightmare obsessions to develop a less personalised view of the world.

It was not just Continental Europe that provided Unity with plays from abroad; in 1958 the theatre staged *The Ganze Macher* (His Friend at Court) by the humourist Ephraim Kishon in what Unity believed to be the first production in Britain of an Israeli play.

Originally presented by the Habimah Theatre in Tel-Aviv, *The Ganze Macher* satirises the bureaucracy of the Israeli government. It was followed later by another British première of a Kishon comedy, *The Licence*. In 1960, to celebrate one of the founders of modern Yiddish drama, Unity staged an anniversary production – albeit a year late! – of the popular play *The Big Win* by Sholem Aleichem whose comic tales of Tevye the Milkman formed the basis of the musical *Fiddler on the Roof*.[8]

From America, as well as *The Crucible*, came *The Biggest Thief in Town*, a satire based on the funeral business. It had been seen in the West End and was written by Dalton Trumbo, one of the 'Hollywood Ten'. Also from America there was Burt Marnik's *Cyanamide*, set amid the dangerous world of chemical manufacture in which trade union struggle and safety requirements conflict with promotion and domestic bliss. However, it was the least political American import, *Burlesque*, that proved to be the most popular. This was the show that had been postponed to make way for *World on Edge*, and derived from Bill Owen's visit to the United States. He omitted the nudity but added a little social comment and managed to capture in the production something of Unity's earlier energy. *Burlesque* – pronounced 'burley-cue' – travelled back in time to the prohibition era of the roaring 1920s when the combined resolve of the Daughters of the Revolution and the state authorities drove this type of entertainment underground into illegal dives.

Outside the theatre, Keystone Cops, Hallelujah evangelists and belligerent 'hoboes' urged the audience not to enter, while 'molls' and 'floozies' did all they could to entice the patrons. A sign read 'No guns or binoculars'. Once inside, hot dog and popcorn at the ready, the audience watched silent movies, including a short Chaplin (when the projector was working). Miss 'Tootsie' Brown and various 'lovely ladies' performed to catcalls and whistles, and under the gaze of a rough, tough, cigar-chewing proprietor, the melodrama of 'The Shooting of Dan McGrew' was played out.

Burlesque included the newly-formed Smoky City Skiffle Group, which was part of the resurgence of interest in folk songs. Unity Folk Club's regular Wednesday evening sessions run by Jack Firestein, who was responsible for the bookstall, attracted the leading names on the folk revival circuit as well as major visiting artists, like Pete Seeger. As well as providing a social meeting place for people of different backgrounds and interests, the sessions offered a chance for anyone and everyone to sing in turn, regardless of talent or reputation. At times, this area of activity became more lively than the theatre productions. It spawned a group offering children's entertainment, including Punch and Judy, and was largely responsible for the Unity contingent on the first CND Easter Aldermaston march in 1958. At this and subsequent Aldermaston marches Unitarians could be seen carrying such slogans as 'Justice to the Toilers' or 'He who would be free must strike the blows' alongside the red and gold Unity banner which read 'The Theatre of the Labour Movement'.

Another play from America, Eugene O'Neill's *Anna Christie*, was performed by a visiting company of particular interest that had links with Unity. It was the West Indian Drama Group, formed in 1956 by Joan Clarke, a Unity activist who was then in charge of Unity's training and a close associate of Lionel Bart, with whom she later fell out. For Unity she co-directed *Peacemeal* and directed *Russian for Yes*, and for the British Council she directed *The Insect Play* and *Thunder Rock* with all-black casts. The West Indian Drama Group was based at the West Indian Students' Union and presented the *Time of Your Life* by William Saroyan, Jules Romain's *Dr Knock* and Shaw's *Androcles and the Lion*. Its all-black Caribbean *Anna Christie* in 1959 may have been a world first. An exhibition was held in Unity's foyer, using material related to the play. This included photographs of past productions and of Paul Robeson in two other O'Neill pieces, *All God's Chillun Got Wings* and *The Emperor Jones*. In the cast of *Anna Christie* was Carmen Munroe, who was to become an important figure in the development of black theatre in Britain and who had appeared already in the Unity revue *Take It As Red*.

Anna Christie continued the links that Unity had established with black actors from the pre-war days of Paul Robeson and Robert Adams, who had founded the London Negro Repertory Theatre with another Unity member Peter Noble. Unity's first president André van Gyseghem had worked at the Embassy Theatre with Robeson and Adams before they came to Unity and with other black performers as well as with black casts in South Africa. During the war, Unity had staged *India Speaks* with performers from India who were living in Britain and after the war black performers such as Adams, Ida Shepley, Frank Singuineau and Errol Hill appeared at Unity both in plays that touched on racism, such as *Dragnet* or *Longitude 49*, and others that did not, like *Barrier Across Europe*. Black performers from other generations also came to Unity (including, for example, Rudolph Walker, Mark Heath and Anton Phillips) before black theatre began to take root more strongly in Britain. Another Unity link to this largely unreported area of theatre history was the founding in 1961 of the Ira Aldridge Players, named after the nineteenth-century black tragedian, by Unity director Herbert Marshall, with the aim of establishing a permanent black theatre company. The Players presented an all-black musical at the Theatre Royal Stratford East called *Do Somethin' Addy Man!*, a reworking of the Alcestis story in contemporary Camden Town. After this the group seems to have folded. Unity also played host to the local Greek Cypriot community theatre and in 1961 Theatro Technis presented at Goldington Street two plays in Greek: Lorca's *The Shoemaker's Wife* translated by K.P. Rossides, and his own *The Tree of Idleness*, dealing with Cypriot peasant life. Theatro Technis (or, in English, Greek Art Theatre) presented several shows at Unity, and when Unity lost its building the roles were reversed and Unity played at Theatro Technis, which was in the same neighbourhood.[9]

Attempts were made to revive political revue with *Six Away, Take It As Red* (which included a sketch on Mosley and the Notting Hill riots) and *People Like Us*, and Eric Paice returned to devise *Circus,* a series of political sketches set in a tent and designed by the painter Brian Phelan. Paice had also compiled the Unity pantomime *Aladdin*, written, in the best Unity traditions, in two weeks by half-a-dozen unnamed television writers. It adhered to the Unity pantomime formula and showed Lord Foam (pronounced 'Fume' to rhyme with Lord Home, then Foreign Secretary) seeking, with the Queen of All the Old Chinas, a mountain to name after a commoner who had married the princess. They get mixed up in the Imperial Atomic Fallout Shelter with Aladdin and his nuclear lamp, Fairy Fallout, and a two-faced horse comprising the Prime Minister Harold Macmillan at one end and the Labour leader Hugh Gaitskell at the other.

Taking a leaf out of Theatre Workshop's book, Unity approached Charles Chilton to write a musicl documentary. His radio programme on First World War songs had been the inspiration for Theatre Workshop's huge success, *Oh, What a Lovely War!*, and it turned out that he had been born next door to Unity. He devised a show, using voice, slides and music, on the slave trade and black history in America called *Oh! Freedom*, which was directed by Roger Hudson, had a multi-racial cast and employed the skills of the Unity Folk Group. It played with Arthur Miller's examination of the monotony of the work routine in a car spares warehouse called *A Memory of Two Mondays*, which was directed by Michael Kaye.

Unity also turned a Theatre Workshop play *You Can't Always Be On Top*, into a musical. Written by Henry Chapman, its portrayal of life on a building site had lent itself to colloquial embellishment at Stratford East, where members of the company were prosecuted because of the florid ad-libbing that necessarily had been unlicensed. (The case led to the establishment of a Censorship Reform Committee which paved the way for the campaign to abolish the Lord Chamberlain's censorship powers.) The Unity version carried a programme note by the general secretary of the Amalgamated Union of Building Trade Workers, George Lowthian, who became chair of the TUC in 1963. He noted that building workers were unpaid actors, industrial nomads constantly being observed by the public in the paradoxical activity of creating permanent features of the social landscape while knowing that their own work would be finished when the particular job was completed and that they would be moved on.

You Can't Always Be On Top was another example of the connection between Unity and Theatre Workshop that operated at the informal level of co-operation between individuals such as Oscar Lewenstein, Lionel Bart, Howard Goorney, Tony Leah or Tony Eatwell, for example, and had been seen in productions like *World on Edge* or *Mother Courage and her Children*. It was continued in Unity's training programme under Amelia Bayntum, who played in *Fings Ain't Wot They Used T'Be* and *Sparrers Can't Sing* at Stratford East, and later under Clive Barker and Brian Murphy, who both appeared in *Oh, What a Lovely War!* and other Theatre workshop productions. Barker, who was also festival director of Centre 42, directed the Frisch play and, with Elaine Pransky, *The Good Woman of Szechwan* for Unity. Murphy, later to star in the television series *Man About the House* and *George and Mildred*, directed *School for Wives* and *There's a Megabutton on My Living Room Floor.*

Actor training had undergone frequent changes of leadership and direction. Efforts had been made to re-establish the group idea and to overhaul Unity's method of work. Charles Marowitz, later to become an internationally known avant-garde theatre director, remembers two special meetings at which these issues were discussed. He had joined Unity on arriving from America in the autumn of 1956, thinking by mistake that he was coming to the home of Auden and Isherwood. He was asked to take over from the previous head of training, Joan Clarke, to implement the new policy and he used rooms in a local pub to run Unity's training school. In 1958 Marowitz presented at Goldington Street his first London production, his own adaptation of Gogol's *Marriage*, performed by actors from the school using the name The Method Workshop. (He left Unity to become a freelance director and worked with the Royal Shakespeare Company in the early 1960s on its Theatre of Cruelty experiments before founding his own theatre in London, the Open Space, in 1968.)

Joe MacColum then ran the Unity Training Group, which presented *Heartbreak House*, and under Dorothea Alexander, who had directed a short play for Unity's professional company, Unity experimented with improvisations. She brought her explorations to Goldington Street in a show called *Drama in the Making*, which comprised three short pieces: *Milk and Honey, Homecoming* and *I Like Eddy*. They were performed by her Experimental Theatre Group that met at the St John's Wood branch of the Marylebone Institute in north London. Later, improvisation work was carried on under the guidance of Reg and Pat Wagland.

New Writing

Throughout this period, the other major element in Unity's repertoire was new writing and Unity continued to encourage new plays even when this cost it dear at the box office. It supported writers from within its own ranks, such as Margery Shaw with *Mind the Baby*, a farce about a mother's fight to open a day nursery that has been closed by the mayor. From its own writers' group there was Ruth Messinger with *Call Me Not Naomi*, which explores the generation gap in a Jewish family when the daughter has a chance to get married and leave her aged parents, one of whom is retired and the other is bedridden. Unity also presented another play by Leonard Peck, *Puerto Franco*, a thriller set in a Central American republic in which pro-imperialists seize power from the indigenous population's democratically elected government at the behest of a US corporation. A reign of terror follows, and the play shows three people looking for a woman on the run from a local hard man. Based on events in Guatemala, which suffered a US-backed counter-revolution in 1954 after the United Fruit Company had been expropriated, the play won the St Pancras Drama Festival. It was perhaps symptomatic of Unity's generally parlous state that no one from the theatre turned up to receive the cup.

Unity staged several first plays; for example, *The Affluent Athenian*, an attack on advertising and big business by sociologist Derek Hall, who had worked in America and had turned his experience into a satire of its society in which the vital ingredient of a popular drink is found to be poisonous; or *The Deviates*, by Don Mathews, an actor and television script writer, in which four young people who refuse to conform to the expected behaviour of contemporary society discover that refusal alone is no answer and must be translated into positive action. Unity also backed another discovery, a lively satire called *The High Jinks of Bishop Saull* by Vic Jones which attacks politicians and various forms of moral corruption in a mad world on the verge of its own nuclear destruction. (Britain had signed an agreement with the US in 1958 on missile bases and the first US nuclear submarines arrived in 1961.) The Bishop, who baptises a bomb with Coca Cola and Holy Lock water as Pax Leukemia, is made a Minister of Morals and intones:

> Hermaphroditic earthworms live pure and wholesome lives,
> And manage to have babies without the aid of wives,
> Then why must English gamekeepers (and English *ladies* too!)
> Have to stoop to practices you'd blush at in the zoo?[10]

An 'everyman' figure refuses to launch a rocket attack and is shot but refuses to die. The play closes with a sentiment that was to stand out as Unity's major commitment to topical politics at the time: 'let's try to keep the earth going round'. Peace was the contemporary issue above all others to which Unity most actively responded, much as Spain had been the catalyst in the 1930s. It generated much of Unity's new work. Alongside the Mobile shows on peace, Unity presented *A Rocket for the Governor*, a comedy attacking the nuclear arms race, written by A. Garson and G. Kelly of Manchester Unity. It was designed by Charles Wood, who had been a scene painter for Theatre Workshop and was to become a prominent playwright noted for his treatment of war and the military, including the television play about the Falklands War, *Tumbledown*, and the film *The Charge of the Light Brigade*. In *There's a Megabutton on My Living Room Floor*, the first stage play by television writer Stuart Douglass, the manager of a police truncheon factory, Harold Freeman, wakes one morning to find that the means to explode the bomb has arrived in his home. The play was designed to involve the audience, posing the same question to them as that which confronted Harold Freeman; democracy runs amok and everyone takes it in turns to exercise power over life and death. Marghanita Laski's *The Offshore Island* showed a British family surviving nuclear war and facing conflicts that were both new and familiar. It was written in 1953 before CND was set up, and broadcast on television a year before Unity's production. Unity also showed Peter Watkins's anti-nuclear film *The War Game*, which had been commissioned and then banned by the BBC.

Despite the commitment to providing a platform for new work, the theatre was not always able to keep pace with the changes in playmaking and producing that were beginning to influence mainstream theatre. A certain conservatism was sometimes evident, bred of an abiding fear either of missing out on a new talent such as Arnold Wesker or of becoming too middle class and 'arty'. One attempt to encourage young writers was the introduction in 1962 of a series of productions 'without décor', an idea that had served the Royal Court well. For example Unity mounted an evening of three short new plays with no set – *A Displaced Milkmaid* by Ian Hamilton Finlay, *Room for Adjustment* by Nathan Field and *The Reluctant Prodigy* by Harvey Schneider – and two full-length plays, the second from Ruth Messinger called *The Rotter*, and *Earoles* by Michael Feld.

There was also an arrangement made with a commercial producer, Michael Codron, that would have helped promote new plays, but this fell through almost immediately it had been set up.

Codron had sent Unity four plays and had told the theatre that he would guarantee a number of ticket sales if it staged one of them. The chosen play, however, was taken away from Unity by its author after a week of rehearsals and nothing more came of the deal.[11]

A general worry at the lack of political bite in the repertoire stimulated the late-night revue on Vietnam and Dominica, *All the Way with Elbie Jay*, devised and directed by Tom Vaughan, which was later played in an evening 'slot'. Vaughan was also responsible for what turned out to be a brief appearance of a new play by Frank Marcus, *The Man Who Bought a Battlefield*, loosely based on the life of George Dawson, an ex-scrap metal merchant who had become a millionaire through arms dealing. It was another mammoth play – with 45 characters and 21 scenes – which had been rejected by many other managements before Arnold Hinchliffe, then in charge of Unity's Play Department, accepted it. Unfortunately, at the dress rehearsal, Unity's secretary Cliff Fenn threatened to close the theatre if the production went ahead. Various objections were raised including the unfounded accusation that the play was 'anti-Jewish', but in the end, the anarchic satire was given three performances. Ironically, the *Daily Worker* gave a favourable review and yet, following the emergency management committee meeting that decided, for political and aesthetic reasons, to end the play's run, the paper also managed to congratulate the theatre on having had the courage to take it off. Despite Vaughan's probably wrong-headed idea to turn the play into a musical, it did help to encourage Marcus to write another play, *Formation Dancers*, which played in the West End the following year; this in turn led to his biggest success, *The Killing of Sister George*, the year after.

There was nothing new in this kind of political intervention. Unity was a political theatre and, not surprisingly, from the earliest days plays had been excluded from the repertoire for political reasons. Mayakovsky's *The Bath House*, which satirises the survival of bourgeois ideas in the Soviet Union, was given a reading but did not receive a production, apparently because of unease at the political implications of the play. Such matters of choice, however, were usually handled properly within the procedures of the society. Tensions rose more sharply when interference came peremptorily from individuals on the management committee who had appointed themselves as political commissars; trouble would often occur at a dress rehearsal when senior Unitarians, who had not been present during rehearsals, would see a production for the first time. For example, an emotional and personal speech at the close of *The Word of a King*, concerning the death of a peasant who is killed when he goes to see Richard II, was cut after the dress rehearsal and had to be replaced on the first night by a new speech that emphasised more the need for political struggle. The necessity for political correctness led to many wrangles – *The High Jinks of Bishop Saull*, for instance, could only proceed when the title had been changed from 'Canon' to 'Bishop' to avoid offending the sympathetic Canon Collins. A participant in the show also recalls that a scene concerning two Labour Party central office bureaucrats was removed because it was thought to attack the Labour Party too harshly and there were fears that a senior politican, George Brown, might sue.

The problems of 'shop-floor' democracy in the theatre were also evident during the run of this production. The author wanted to cut the last act after agreeing with the reviews that generally praised the first two acts but criticised the last one. A meeting was called in the auditorium at which those most affected argued vehemently against the proposal on personal, not artistic, grounds. The author offered to write in another scene to accommodate those who would be disappointed at the loss of the third act and a vote was taken which only just went in favour of the playwright's suggestion. He was more fortunate than another writer who came to his first night to discover that the actors had abandoned the masks that were to be worn as an integral part of the style of the play. They had decided that the audience should see their faces, had voted on the issue and proceeded to perform maskless regardless of the playwright's intentions and protests.

Management was put under severe strain in the years after 1956 as the turnover of people became faster. A letter from the Unity management to the London district committee of the Communist Party in 1959, asking for help in finding people who might become active at Unity, said that 75 per cent of Unity members joined to act, 20 per cent because they were lonely and only 5 per cent because they saw theatre as a political instrument. In such a situation, it became increasingly difficult to sustain the breadth, quality and continuity of leadership. Heinz Bernard resigned as general manager in 1958 because he wanted to devote more time to directing than to administration. It was a great loss; he had guided Unity through the aftermath of *World on Edge* and was a steadying influence amid the stormy debates. He did stay, however, to become the first organiser of the major appeal that was launched in the 1960s as well as to continue directing. Professional actor Bernard Goldman, known for his performance in Wolf Mankowitz's *Make Me an Offer*, took over from Bernard in 1959 but he resigned within a year because of outside acting commitments and the new chair that year, trade unionist Ray Dowell, also lasted only a year.

Problems of leadership, which had always been tense, now became fraught. In an article in *Reynold's News*, Ted Willis is quoted as saying that Unity needed a big personality to save it, like a Joan Littlewood or a Bernard Miles. Heinz Bernard, however, disagreed and said that Unity's strength lay in its openness to collective activity and not in the leadership of a single, dominating figure. This was true, but the openness had led to chaos. Takeovers were always being planned by people who had written off Unity and saw it as ripe for picking.

The rows were exarcerbated by the appalling financial situation, which was made steadily worse by many members not holding a fully paid-up share. Unity was always underfinanced and its leadership had never provided for the future, either because they could not afford to or because they did not think about it. Money had never been invested for maintenance, for instance, and the constant need to repair and improve the building was having a serious effect. There was an added problem in that the building was not insured because the management committee had not been able to find a company that did not find the undertaking too great a risk. Also, the electricity board always seemed to be calling to cut off supplies, followed by London County Council officials with a compulsory purchase order and fistfuls of notices enforcing fire regulations or safety and sanitary requirements. The theatre had no reserves and a lottery, known as Lottie, was introduced to raise the one full-time wage that remained. (This paid Molly Sole, the treasurer, who, in 1961, was awarded Unity's Stanislavsky badge for her valuable services; among her many contributions to the adminstration of drama, she was clerk to the governors of the Old

Vic.) The bar had become licensed, and boasted a fridge bought on HP, but even this facility did not alter the financial fortunes of the theatre significantly, although it did make for a popular meeting place and centre of much argumentation and politicking.

Fund-raising inevitably came to occupy more time, and one of the many emergency appeals of the period was launched at the end of 1957 after Unity had received an especially heavy electricity bill and rates demand. Legal proceedings were also imminent on a number of debts, the theatre was carrying a huge deficit and there was no money available to tide Unity over. The appeal raised £780, kept the theatre open and won Unity a five-minute spot on BBC radio's popular 'Town and Country' programme, which featured actor John Slater talking about his time at Unity. Five MPs (including a Tory) signed the appeal along with one peer and several leading theatre people, from long-standing supporters like Sybil Thorndike to new ones like Wolf Mankowitz. Unity also directly approached the Labour-run local authority, overcoming its fear of losing its independence, and St Pancras Borough Council agreed to reduce the rates because of Unity's educational aims. It offered the theatre a £300 grant too, which was then blocked by the Tory-run central government. This mean-spirited move backfired, however, because Unity won more much-needed publicity, including another mention on 'Town and Country', and, after a row in the House of Commons, the grant was awarded by putting it through under different legislation. The money helped Unity cover its expenses for the first three months of 1958, which was a welcome reprieve but only temporary. A second emergency appeal, aimed at a target of £1,250, was issued in January 1959 along with an announcement of the theatre's intended closure in a fortnight's time. In response to this crisis, Ted Willis gave Unity the rights of *God Bless the Guv'nor*, which the theatre presented that March, and again in 1965. Through the commitment of the theatre's activists and its supporters, Unity stayed open and staved off collapse.

Silver Jubilee Appeal

Despite the problems, Unity could claim on its 25th birthday in 1961 that individual shareholders numbered 430, associates 1,500 and affiliated members 750,000. The Mobile Group had been reformed, offering *The Ragged Trousered Philanthropists, God Bless the Guv'nor* and Old Time Music Hall, which continued to dominate its programme. The Folk Group was thriving and spawned Unity Singers, there was a Unity All-Star Soccer team, but the puppets, children's theatre, film group, writers' group and training scheme had been abandoned (though at different times and in different ways, all of these were to re-appear in the years to come). No. 1 Goldington Street had acquired a new entrance with gates, a lick of paint to its exterior and new seats, bought for 4 shillings each, from Collins Music Hall, Islington, when it was demolished in 1960 after a fire. The money was raised by Unity members and the seats were installed by voluntary labour. The theatre was still scruffy, however; some members felt that this was a necessary antidote to the false comfort induced by the age of 'you never had it so good' while others believed that it was simply off-putting. Worst of all, the management could not get rid of the theatre's notorious musty smell, a mixture of odours that came from poor sanitation and the forest of funghi growing apace beneath the stage. (When one director suggested destroying the funghi he was sent packing because the only solution meant destroying the stage too and the stage was sacrosanct. It was still the 1937 original and, therefore, the scene of many heroic stories.) A policy of hiring out the theatre during the day – to institutions like the Royal Shakespeare Company for its auditions – brought in some revenue (and the occasional extra interest – for example, when it was used for the dress rehearsal of an Arts Council touring production of *Five Finger Exercise* in which the popular Jessie Matthews was appearing). But the general state of dilapidation made it unattractive to many prospective clients.

However hard the management tried, and seemingly regardless of repertoire decisions, the threat of insolvency never disappeared. At a special meeting held in May 1961 to discuss 'The Problems of Unity and their Solution', the main ideas proposed were more productions and more lettings, but the new chair, Manny Goldstein, put forward a bolder plan – a 25th anniversary appeal to raise £50,000 to buy the theatre's freehold and then build a new Unity on the same site to become the cultural centre that it had always aimed to be. Goldstein, who had helped form a Middlesbrough Unity in the 1930s, had worked for the Young Communist League and the Communist Party and had become a civil servant, joined London Unity as an actor in the mid-1950s. He chaired the management committee from 1961 to 1965 when he resigned and was succeeded by Tom Vaughan. The appeal plan was supported by Unity's secretary Cliff Fenn (an engineer from Liverpool who had become nightwatchman and had lived at the back of the theatre for ten years) and other senior figures such as the business manager Raymond Cross.

The idea of buying the freehold had become a possibility after the owners, Wilkinson Property Investment Trust Ltd, had failed to turn the premises into a telefilm recording studio in 1959 when the London County Council refused planning permission. Unity became keen to buy the freehold in order to protect itself from future threats to its existence at Goldington Street and Wilkinson was happy to sell rather than face lengthy procedures, with an uncertain outcome, to change the use of the site. The sale was helped by the fact that Unity had good relations with its landlords, who gave the theatre its first £50 toward the appeal target.

Evidence existed of a fund of goodwill toward Unity that could be built on in the appeal. When the film producer Sidney Box was asked to become one of the ten guarantors whom the bank had requested for the theatre's overdraft, he is reported to have replied that, as Unity had done so much for the film industry, he would stand the total sum of all ten guarantees on his own. Another example of general support beyond Unity's own world can be found in an article written by Tom Stoppard in *Scene* magazine. Unity was living off its past, he said, and its politics were still equated with 'cloth-capped Socialism', but

> it deserves credit for keeping alive some of its intellectual vigour – and not least for devoting its stage to worthwhile minority ventures like Adamov's *Spring '71*, new playwright Arnold Hinchliffe's *The Life of Kaggs* [...] and others.

However, balanced against these positive signs was the generally poor record of backing for the arts from what Unity saw as its natural support – the trade unions – and the competition from Centre 42 for what little they might give.

The appeal nearly did not get launched at all. It had to be postponed because of a libel case brought against Unity by NATO's Commander of Central Europe's land forces, General Speidel. A film made in the German Democratic Republic exposed his Nazi past and accused him of complicity in the killing of the King of Yugoslavia and of war crimes in the Soviet Union and France.[13] The film, first shown in Britain at the National Film Theatre, had been refused a public certificate but the local authority agreed its showing by one vote and Unity insisted on it being screened at the theatre. The protracted libel case was finally settled out of court – and cost Unity nothing – but meant that while it was in progress, the theatre could not raise any money for fear of its going straight into the general's or the lawyers' pockets. These events contributed to the formulation of a necessary preliminary phase before the launch of the appeal which involved the setting up of a trust. This was established on 24 April 1962 and initially the trustees were the composer Alan Bush, the actor Alfie Bass, the general secretary of the foundry workers' union David Lambert and the barrister John Platts-Mills QC. (Membership of the trust changed in subsequent years.)

The trust, and not the Unity society, was to buy the freehold of the Aldenham Institute, as the theatre was still legally known. By registering as a charity, it could be exempt from paying tax on the money raised in the appeal and it could consolidate the rate reduction already granted by the local council for the theatre's educational work. However, in order to gain charitable status with the Charity Commissioners, the trust had to draw up its deeds in a particular way which upset many people in the society. One management committee member at the time claims that it was done without consulting the society. In the deeds, the trust's aims are identical to those of the Unity Theatre Society Ltd, but this is not spelt out and Unity is not mentioned at this point. It is only cited later as an example of the type of organisation that the trust might support in its use of the newly acquired site. This was considered by some in the society as heresy and it fuelled tensions that were to mount during the appeal campaign. In a deed of variation signed in 1964 two years after the purchase of the freehold, all references to Unity have been removed and the aims of the trust have been changed 'to advance the education of the public in the art of drama and in the co-related arts'. This change further incensed what was by now a large hostile group within the society that was demanding a new leadership and a new direction for Unity.

The setting up of the trust differed from Unity's previous practice of founding legally independent but subsidiary bodies under the Unity umbrella in order to protect the theatre. The trust was completely separate from the society and its management committee. It was not elected and did not owe either its continued existence or its authority to the society. Such a major organisational division was unprecedented and went further than any earlier administrative changes, even those during the days of the professional company and the national society.

This, however, was not just a matter of legal and financial convenience. According to some participants it resulted also from damaging differences within Unity, the inability of the theatre's democratic structures to overcome these differences and the related drift towards self-destruction. As it turned out, the actions of the trust, and of those in the society's leadership who were identified with the trust, became the focus of the most damaging dispute in Unity's history, which foreshadowed similar battles within the Communist Party and the left that were to be just as ruinous.

Paranoia and conspiracy theory flourished at Unity as the clash sharpened between 'church' and 'gospel' – those who saw themselves as defenders of the true faith, based on immutable first principles, and those who saw themselves as equally principled but also as realists and modernisers. By this time the argument did not divide along party lines. With the rise of the 'New Left', there was an influx into Unity of non-Communist Party activists who felt that the theatre was not political enough. They blamed this on the Communist Party, believing, as did some Communists, that the party programme, 'The British Road to Socialism', was a revisionist document and that Unity had gone astray because the party had ceased to be revolutionary. There was a nostalgia for the 1930s, when politics and art seemed to be simpler; and there was a contradictory feeling that the party should both be exerting proper and direct control over Unity, which it would do if it were only to return to the revolutionary path, and that Unity should be an autonomous left theatre free of authoritarian party control.

A significant number of senior Unity people were not members of the party and resentment at Communist influence and at the Communists meeting separately – and some felt secretly – was reinforced in turn by the Communist Party's private irritation at the theatre's squabbles and the continuing sourness arising from its production of *World on Edge*.[14] A small example of how far the breakdown had gone is the fact that in 1957, the year after *World on Edge*, the London district committee of the Communist Party did not find its affiliation fee. Publicly, however, the party remained proud of the theatre and its history, which, along with the *Daily Worker* and its successor the *Morning Star*, were tributes to the party's continuing role and influence, despite its decline in membership. The party still wanted to exercise moral authority over Unity and to have a majority of party members on the management committee in order to guide it through the difficult days ahead. But there was a personnel problem, here as elsewhere in the party's world, and even a numerical majority did not guarantee a united vote as disagreements between party members could be as sharp, if not sharper, than those between members and non-members.

Unity was keen to lose its Communist tag while the party, isolated by the Cold War and embarrassed by the national scandal of Communist leaders of the electricians' union being caught ballot-rigging, had become more sensitive than hitherto about its public rôle in non-party organisations. Links were maintained, nevertheless, between the Unity party group and the party executive, its cultural committee and the London district committee, either through individuals or through party representatives attending Unity party meetings.

Relations between the party and Unity were greatly improved under Manny Goldstein. He recalls that when the party backed Centre 42 he presented Unity's plans for the appeal to the political committee and won agreement for that support to be coupled to backing for Unity as well. What the modernsiers at Unity were trying to achieve struck a chord with those in the party leadership who wanted to adjust to new realities, as they were demonstrating by changing the name and approach of the *Daily Worker* to that of the *Morning Star*.[15]

Unity's appeal to purchase the freehold and build a new theatre was launched on 25 September 1962 at the headquarters of the Arts Council of Great Britain, then in St James Square. The trustees were present along with Herbert Marshall, whose association with Unity went back thirty years, George Elvin, general secretary of the cine technicians' union ACTT, the folk singers Robin Hall and Jimmy McGregor, who appeared at Unity's Folk Club, the ballerina Beryl Grey and Ted Willis, who made a speech in tribute to Unity. Baroness Summerskill, who had opened the first Unity Theatre at Britannia Street in 1936, noticed that the gathering was taking place in what had been Nancy Astor's dining room. Jokingly, she was shocked at Unity's current association with the hostess of the Cliveden set which had been one of the theatre's princpal targets in the 1930s as a centre of fascist sympathy.

The list of the appeal's 46 sponsors was impressive and broadly based, crossing generations and political affiliations in a way that was reminiscent of the Popular Front days. They ranged from the arts and communication worlds, including some of the post-1956 theatrical 'new wave', the trade unions and politics, to old friends and Unity veterans in the professional theatre. Signatories included Lindsay Anderson, James Cameron, Shelagh Delaney, George Devine, Alec Guinness, Joan Littlewood, Hugh MacDiarmid, John Osborne, John Piper, Alan Sillitoe and Ruskin Spear. Heinz Bernard was the appeal organiser.

An appeal leaflet signed by Alfie Bass and Paul Robeson (who by now had become very ill) set the target at £50,000 – £5,500 to buy the freehold and the rest to create a new cultural centre which would cost at least £30,000. Drawings were made by architects Arthur Stewart and Colin Penn, in consultation with Herbert Marshall, which proposed a second auditorium to be built at circle level. Each auditorium would have its own revolve, enabling conversion to theatre-in-the-round, with portable seats upstairs and an orchestra pit downstairs. The upper, more flexible auditorium, would be attractive for hire, particularly for children's theatre and films. 'You could even hold a fashion show,' suggested the publicity. The reduction in capacity for the ground floor auditorium (to between 230 and 270 seats) would be compensated for by more wing space and a deeper stage, which at only 9 inches high, and with a single block of steeply-banked rows of seats, would allow for greater actor-audience contact. New sound and lighting equipment would be installed and, by tunnelling under the entrance, there would be additional rehearsal and meeting rooms. These would also be available for hire, including one with special facilities for dancers, and a fully-equipped workshop. The bar would be extended, and a second bar added which would double as an exhibition room and a venue for folk and jazz music. Management committee members toured Britain looking at theatres of a similar size, returning to Goldington Street to modify the plans in the light of their discoveries.

The appeal adopted the slogan: 'Theatre with a history, theatre with a purpose, theatre with a future'. Its publicity recorded that Unity had staged 179 productions since 1936 – of which 106 had been new scripts, mostly written for Unity, 35 had been British premières of foreign plays, and one-in-three had used specially composed original music. It was an outstanding achievement.

As part of the appeal, a new drive was launched directed at the trade unions, and another labour movement conference was held, in March 1963, at which it was suggested that Friends of Unity groups be set up in trade union branches. A show was provided for the 53 delegates representing 27 unions; there were sketches from revues, excerpts from productions, music hall numbers and the Unity Folk Group in a programme specially devised by Roger Hudson called *Here is Unity*, which was compered by former Unity chair Ray Dowell, an executive member of the London district committee of the white-collar union ASSET. National affiliations came from unions covering printers, tobacco workers, plumbers, builders, construction engineers, and sign makers. London district affiliations included engineers, electricians, train drivers and ASSET.

One of the excerpts that was presented in *Here is Unity* came from the current production, *See A Man Falling* by Jo Joseph, which showed the life of ironfighters, the men who erect the iron girders that form the skeletons of modern buildings. It was Joseph's first stage play and was funded by the Constructional Engineering Union which organised the ironfighters. The union's London district secretary responsible for ironfighters advised on the production and on the building of the set which, naturally enough, was made up of iron girders.

Alongside a 'buy a brick' campaign, borrowed from 1946, there were many fund-raising events and even an appeal song, written by Jack Cooper. Three different Old Time Music Hall shows at the Bishop Park Open Air Theatre reached audiences of between 1,500 and 1,800 each; David Kossoff performed his one-man show; Im Rayevsky, leading actor and director with the Moscow Art Theatre, which was performing in London in the World Theatre Season, gave a lecture demonstration and visited Unity with other company members; Lewis Casson and Sybil Thorndike presented an evening of poetry and drama; a special performance of the review *Six Away* was given at the home of Michael Redgrave and Rachel Kempson; several celebrities, including the playwrights Arnold Wesker and Bernard Kops, attended an appeal garden party at the Sussex home of John Platts-Mills; and a film was started – but not completed because of excessive costs – with survivors of Rebel Players, Unity's forerunners, recreating shows like *Requiem* at Clerkenwell Green as they had performed them thirty years earlier. Footage was also shot of current productions and music hall.

The first major appeal event was held at the Metropolitan Palace of Varieties on 26 May 1963, an historic date as it was the last performance at the theatre that had played host to Sarah Bernhardt and Charlie Chaplin. The next day the contractors moved in to demolish it in order to replace it with a police station. Unity's gala appeal show was presented there by The Variety Artistes' Federation and the Musicians' Union as well as the Unity Trust, thanks to the good offices of its manager, a long-time Unity supporter Sidney Bernstein. The line-up included Cleo Laine and Johnny Dankworth, Dorita y Pepe, Soo Bee Lee, Joan Littlewood and her 'Clowns from Stratford East', Mrs Shufflewick and Billy Russell, as well as Miles Malleson, Lewis Casson, Sybil Thorndike and Unity veterans Alfie Bass, David Kossoff, John Slater and Lionel Bart.

Freda Field, a former shop steward and Communist Party worker who was then employed by the Musicians' Union, was now running the appeal with extraordinary energy and organisational ability. She had taken over from Heinz Bernard's successor, Bessie Bond, who had been forced to relinquish the job after a few months because of ill health. A second huge gala night was held that October at the Adelphi Theatre, courtesy of Jack Hylton, with an even more remarkable cast. It was compered by Johnny Pearn and, as well as artists from the previous show, the line-up included the Manhattan Brothers from South Africa (starring in a West End jazz musical *King Kong*), concert violinist Tessa Robbins, Larry Dann, concert singer Martin Lawrence, folk singer Enoch Kent, David Frost, Dickie Henderson and, top of the bill, Frankie Howerd.

Vanessa Redgrave performed a 'history lesson' on the British empire and for this she used her own props and costume, which was forbidden on Sundays. Members of the Lord's Day Observance Society stopped the show and it only started again after skilful negotiation by Dickie Henderson. Frost, who by then had only just become known as the anchor-man of *That Was The Week That Was*, had been approached after Freda Field had seen him perform at a Soho club. His first response to her telephone call, she remembers, was to ask if he would be playing to an intelligent audience because he would perform for no other. Her reply was that he would be the least intelligent person in the theatre and she put the telephone down. A call came the next day. Frost had accepted, and, according to Freda Field, he gave unstintingly of his time.

At the time of the gala, Unity was closed briefly for repair and redecoration. This had happened both out of necessity and in order to avoid putting off potential supporters who might come to see the theatre they were backing and find it a little dispiriting. The interior was painted, the bar service area was enlarged and a new floor laid, the wall of the staircase to the dressing rooms was resurfaced and strengthened and the guttering was repaired. After much pressure from the London County Council to make the theatre less of a fire hazard, and to prepare it for its new role as a cultural centre with an expected rise in attendance, a new exit was built. The problem of insurance remained, however, although Unity did manage to find a company that was willing to make an offer. Unity thought that the building was worth £85,000 but it was valued at only £42,000 and the best deal that could be reached was temporary cover to the value of £28,000. The Trust paid the premiums and gave the society £75 to install a burglar alarm, a condition of the insurance deal.

The Adelphi show raised £873 after expenses and took the appeal past the £11,000 mark. The freehold was bought and a celebration show was mounted at Unity called *It's Ours*, which attracted a distinguished audience, including Anthony Greenwood, the Labour Party chair – and butt of earlier shows – as well as mayors and senior councillors from four local councils. It was also significant that, as far as Unity activists could remember, John Gollan, the general secretary of the Communist Party, was making his first visit to Unity since the tensions caused by *World on Edge* seven-and-a-half years before.

Success for the appeal brought good media coverage which

reported that Harold Wilson, then Leader of the Opposition, and Lord Snowdon had both donated. A Tory minister made another attempt to veto a council grant, and in the end donations came from fourteen borough councils. A charity performance was given by the English Stage Company at the Queen's Theatre of Brecht's *St Joan and the Stockyards*, with Siobhan McKenna taking over at a week's notice from Vanessa Redgrave, who was ill. An anonymous gift of £1,000 was given to the appeal in recognition of this production and Unity's own production of *The Good Woman of Szechwan*. In another collaboration with the English Stage Company, Unity shared a charity première screening of Ann Jellicoe's *The Knack*. By the close of the appeal, Unity had raised some £20,000.

Within Unity, divisions had soon emerged over the energy that the appeal was consuming and the direction that it was taking. Many felt that the time and money spent on the appeal detracted too much from the running of the theatre and was not worth the return, either in publicity or financially; Unity's own shows were not doing well and a lot of the money raised by the appeal went into paying for the appeal events. Critics contrasted the style and cost of the appeal's smart publicity with Unity's own modest publications. They felt that using entertainers such as Frankie Howerd or Dickie Henderson was compromising with a commercialised culture that Unity had spent its life opposing, and, in a curious way, they seemed to be happier when Unity was poor than when it began to bring in cash. There was also a suspicion that some who supported the appeal never believed that its aims would be achieved and saw the appeal mainly as a catalyst for releasing new energy.

Divisions grew as the appeal gathered momentum and its critics embraced an ever widening circle of support, from the secretary Cliff Fenn to the architects of the proposed new building. Artistic, political and personal conflicts overlapped and reached boiling point when, after much debate over and adjustment to the original plans, it was suggested that Unity move out of Goldington Street to run a new theatre with stronger municipal links, a professional administration and a core of professional artists.[16]

The group running the appeal and the trust had privately been anxious about the cost of the rebuilding scheme and the continuity of Unity's activity during the construction work. Negotiations had been opened with St Pancras council to explore the possibility of Unity moving to a new site and the first formal application to make such a move – to the nearby Bedford Music Hall, which was to be demolished – was submitted in May 1964. The application was made in the name of the appeal organiser and not of the theatre secretary. The idea was now to exchange premises through the council, swopping the Goldington Street site for another elsewhere in the borough. In the belief that this would happen within seven years, the appeal target was lowered.

Great stress began to be placed on Unity's role in the locality and programme notes were carried on local history. A measure of the support that Unity won can be seen by the fact that *The Good Person of Szechwan* was funded by the council to play in the town hall, and when the old borough of St Pancras was abolished in 1965 to be absorbed by the new Camden council, Unity was chosen as the venue to host the first civic reception for the new borough's councillors. The outgoing St Pancras council also recommended to the incoming administration that Unity should be provided with a new site, and a Unity-Camden joint consultative committee was set up to explore this.

There was serious disquiet in Unity at this option and a compromise was reached between those who were for and against whereby the move to a new site was officially dropped and the plans for a new centre were altered to a proposed conversion of the existing premises. In this scheme, the theatre would be wrapped around with foyers, rehearsal rooms, bars and dressing rooms. Tenders were sought for the new scheme in May 1966 by the building sub-committee – an advisory body to the trust set up the year before and chaired by former Communist MP Phil Piratin. They ranged from £59,000 to £69,000, with an additional £15,000 to £18,000 for internal decoration and technical equipment. This contrasted badly with the original Unity estimate of £30,000. The tenders were beyond Unity's reach and suggested a disproportionate investment in a small site for what could be achieved.

Debate had continued, however, on the merits of a move to a new site and the establishment of a new theatre playing a municipal role. A series of productions were mounted to demonstrate Unity's fitness to tackle such an undertaking. Harry Landis, potential artistic director of a new Unity, directed Arnold

Programme for 1965 production of Arnold Wesker's contemporary classic

Wesker's *Chicken Soup with Barley* with Marjorie Mason as Sarah Kahn. It was a natural choice – Unity members had been involved in the early events referred to in the play, stopping Mosley's Blackshirts at Cable Street, and the production was able to draw on the continuing strength of the Jewish component in Unity's make-up, which, although not as decisive as it had been in the 1930s, was still important. Three more 'prestige' productions were staged, and critics within Unity pointed out how expensive they were. Arthur Miller's *Death of a Salesman*, with Shey Gorman as Willy Loman, directed by Harry Landis, was so successful that people were turned away. It was felt to have surpassed the Wesker production and earned a long review in the *Times Literary Supplement* which made many at Unity confident that negotiations with the council could bear fruit. Less successful, however, were Synge's classic, *Playboy of the Western World*, directed by Bathsheba Garnett using actors from the East 15 drama school, and David Bauer's production of *Inherit the Wind*, an American play by Jerome Lawrence and Robert E Lee based on the 1925 'monkey' trial in Tennessee when the defendant was found guilty of teaching Darwinism.

Inherit the Wind turned out to be the last play to be performed at Unity before the theatre had to close. The immediate reasons were financial; there had been closer scrutiny of the books since the founding of the trust. The Registrar of Friendly Societies was having particular difficulty with the bar and lottery audit. Unity was living on a rising overdraft and in the credit squeeze of July 1966, as the theatre's suppliers pressed for payment, the bank foreclosed and Unity became insolvent. Nevertheless, the closure took place in a spirit of optimism because the appeal was being successful and the theatre had to stop performing in any case to allow the rebuilding work to begin. Closure was presented as the necessary prelude to rebirth, yet the mounting costs of the reconstruction added to insufficient funds and the wrangling over the different options for the future led to a series of postponements in the rebuilding programme and finally to the cancellation of all plans amid furious rows and heated recriminations.

The appeal carried on, and to raise money the Mobile group continued to perform its standard fare of Old Time Music Hall as well as O'Casey's *A Pound on Demand*, Wolf Mankowitz's *The*

Bespoke Overcoat and a collage of prose, poetry and reportage called *The Ballad and the Mast*. Unity was run from temporary offices provided by Camden council in Lyndhurst Hall, Wardon Road, Kentish Town, some ten minutes by car from Goldington Street.

Throughout the debates contacts had been maintained with the council and discussions had continued on the Unity-Camden joint consultative committee about the exchange proposal. Unity had bid for the Bedford Music Hall but a more attractive proposition was offered by the council's plan to build an office block on the Euston Road containing a library and theatre. Unity drafted plans for a new type of municipal theatre there, with Unity as the resident company operating under a tenancy agreement that would allow for the use of the theatre at certain times by other organisations such as the council itself or the National Youth Theatre. Unity wanted to maintain its traditions, its independent position in the theatre world and its identification with the labour and progressive movements. Yet, in its plans, Unity recognised

> the need to evolve a new type of theatre related not only to modern artistic developments but to the changing structure in society, catering for the better educated young people of to-day; taking into account the greater leisure opportunities and the broader interests which now prevail among all sections of the community.[16]

Unity also proposed to plan its repertoire in consultation with the education authority and wanted to be able to present classical plays that were beyond the means of many professional companies because of the large cast sizes, by involving a wide group of talented amateur players alongside a professional core. Unity also understood that the new theatre – to be called the Shaw – would not have a workshop or any storage space, and proposed that Goldington Street be used in these capacities as well as for rehearsals, the folk club, training and local children's projects.

Critics of the Shaw Theatre idea were anxious that the council would retain the right to evict Unity and that, therefore, the proposal lacked sufficient guarantees for Unity's future security. Unity had just spent considerable time and energy raising the money to buy the freehold of its premises and it seemed senseless to them to squander that achievement straightaway. In terms reminiscent of the arguments in the 1940s, when Ted Willis had launched the professional Unity company, the critics insisted that Unity's existence depended on its amateur status and 'open university' philosophy. They disliked the increase in the influence of professionals that had already taken place, a process exarcerbated by greater opportunity in the profession, a higher turnover at Unity and a tendency to fill the major ensuing gaps with 'resting' Equity members, some of whom had even asked to be paid, and they saw the proposed role of professionals in reverse proportion to the declining influence of the amateurs. The opponents of the Shaw Theatre deal were also incensed at the suggested use of the Goldington Street building, which they viewed as an ignominious end for an historic theatre that, to them, had the status of a shrine.

The opponents, however, were themselves divided. Some had become leading figures at Unity by dint of longevity rather than through any artistic or political vitality and they feared any change that might challenge their position; some felt that the suggested accommodations with a changed reality were unacceptable compromises; and others were not against the Shaw plan in principle but believed that it would not work in practice. Those supporting the plan, which was formally submitted to the council in December 1966, included several Unitarians who had been vehemently against the Willis scheme for a professional company years before, the people mainly responsible for the appeal, and the trust, with the tacit backing of the Communist Party.

There was strong support for Unity's plan on Camden council. Several past mayors, as well as the current one, were Unity enthusiasts (and a future one, Arthur Soutter, was an activist of long standing). But there was also considerable opposition, motivated often, Unity leaders felt, by anti-Communism. Camden was seen by Unity leaders as a right-wing Labour council and they also saw Britian's first Arts Minister, Jennie Lee, who had given permission for the Shaw Theatre to be built, as being lukewarm toward them. They thought she was more interested in supporting Centre 42, which was also based in the borough and trying to secure a theatre-cum-cultural centre in Camden.

A weakness in Unity's case was the lack of any local audience that might have campaigned on its behalf and carried weight with the council. Unity had always made its appeal to the labour movement as a whole rather than to the neighbourhood, in spite of its recent emphasis on serving the borough (which it had done).[17] Audiences, in general, did not come to Unity because it was their local theatre but because of a political identity of interests.

As Camden was about to make its decision on the Shaw proposal, its opponents at Unity organised a round robin, which was signed by many who were no longer active, and sent it to the council, saying that Unity did not want the Shaw after all. Unity might have lost the vote anyway, although its chances were good, but the exposure of the internal rift made defeat certain and Camden offered the Shaw to the National Youth Theatre and its professional company.

The Shaw episode was symptomatic of the huge rift that existed among Unitarians. The critics of the plan had requisitioned two special general meetings of Unity Theatre Society Ltd to force the Goldington Street premises to be re-opened, fearing that the site might be sold off. At the 1967 AGM, they achieved their aim by removing the old management committee on the grounds of its inactivity, lack of democracy, and failure to re-open the building. The trustees were accused of going beyond their remit, with intent to sabotage Unity, and relations between the society and the Trust were never the same again.

Both, however, had to continue working with each other, and at times efforts were made on both sides to repair the damage, but it was always an uneasy co-existence.

Counter-Culture

With a new management committee in power following the 1967 AGM, Unity left Lyndhurst Hall and moved back to Goldington Street. The theatre needed attention after nine months of neglect; people had come in off the streets to sleep there, stray cats had made it their home and the elements had taken their toll. Repairs and renovation continued for the next few years – the Greater London Council was holding in suspension a dilapidation order on the premises on the understanding that the theatre was to be rebuilt. In 1968, it was rewired, windows were bricked up for greater warmth, a new switchboard was installed and the front of house was repaired. The work took three months to carry out. In 1969, with the help of the London Co-operative Society, further renovations were undertaken in the foyer. The new management committee also had to clear scenery and props from an annexe that the theatre used nearby in Aldenham Street; the previous leadership had given up the premises, owing almost £80 in rent arrears.

The main task of the new regime, however, was to open the theatre with new shows, but that was not easy as the committee was split between the old and the new left across a range of ideologies that embraced Lenin, Trotsky, Stalin and Mao. There had been activity at Goldington Street while the theatre was closed, organised by those pushing for the re-opening. A folk evening had been held in January on Burns Night and song sessions linked to CND, the folk circuit and the burgeoning agitprop movement continued until the opening in April. This was marked by a social evening of Victoriana, with a sausage and mash supper accompanied by lantern slides, ballads, melodrama, monologues and dancing. The management committee was divided on the future direction of Unity. When the theatre re-opened on 28 April 1967 with a double bill advertised as 'Two Protest Plays for Today' and performed by a visiting company, it was not designated as the official re-opening production, which came next. This, by way of contrast, was Wycherley's Restoration comedy, *The Country Wife*, favoured by the traditionalist wing of the new leadership.

'Two Protest Plays for Today' comprised *John D. Muggins is Dead* and *Mr Oligarchy's Circus* presented by Cartoon Archetypal Slogan Theatre (CAST), which had been invited to appear at Unity by management committee member Roger Hudson who had seen the group perform while Unity was closed. CAST was the original 'new wave' political theatre group of the 1960s and, ironically, it had grown out of Unity, in opposition to what Unity had become. Nevertheless, it still looked to Unity as its home until that, too, became impossible.[18] CAST's founders, Roland and Claire Muldoon, had both worked at Unity on the production side and had run a technical course at the theatre in the evenings. They were frustrated at the repertoire Unity was offering, which they saw as falling far short of the popular, political drama the theatre said it was aiming at, and they were also critical of some of the values associated with the appeal campaign. Roland Muldoon was expelled from Unity in 1965 for 'conduct injurious to the society in that he secretly conspired with non-members to overthrow the legally elected management committee' (in the words of the AGM resolution that was passed). He was proposing a new direction for the theatre that embodied a form of political cabaret that later became known as 'new variety'. Having been expelled, Muldoon later that year put into practice what he had been preaching and, with Claire Muldoon, he founded the socialist theatre group CAST, along with two others who had been at Unity, Ray Levine and David Hatton. The historical wheel had come full circle forty years on with anonymous collective creation of flexible, mobile shows in a style that CAST dubbed 'agitpop' rather than 'agitprop'.

CAST was the first of many visiting companies to appear at Unity in what was to be the final phase of its life as a performing theatre. Several troupes of drama students had already played there – a group from RADA in a Büchner double bill of *Woyzeck* and *Leonce and Leona*, for example, or the East 15 Acting School in Genet's *The Balcony* – and other guests included the neighbouring Greek Cypriot theatre Theatro Technis in a modern version of Aristophanes's *Peace*, directed by its founder George Eugeniou. Unity achieved a sort of fame through one visiting group when the transient Dramagraph company presented there the world première of David Halliwell's *Little Malcolm and His Struggle Against the Eunuchs*, directed by Mike Leigh. Then over four hours long, it was slimmed down for the Abbey Theatre, Dublin, later the West End and was turned into a film. Dramagraph was remembered at Unity, however, as much for the £80 rent it owed as for the famous play it performed. Two visiting companies came from abroad: the STG Theatre from Poland with Čapek's *Fabryka Absoltut* (Absolute Standards) and from Paris, le Théâtre de l'Unité, which had been formed in response to London Unity and members of which had attended the first night of Adamov's *Spring '71* at Goldington Street. This group brought Molière's *L'Avare*, a school text, and caused consternation by asking for the front rows of the auditorium to be removed in order to accommodate a huge maypole, which had objects flying around it.

More importantly, with the rise of the alternative theatre movement in the late 1960s and early 1970s, Unity became a London venue for several of the most important of these touring groups. As well as CAST, there was General Will, 7:84 (England), Belt and Braces, Mayday, Rough Theatre, York Shoestring,

Paradise Foundry, Popular Theatre and Kartoon Clowns. Unity had made tentative links with 'fringe' theatres as far back as 1963 when it participated in a theatre perimeter scheme to exchange information and the booking of tickets with other groups and, later, in 1969, it enjoyed collective membership with several small theatres, such as the Ambience, the Arts Laboratory and Hampstead Theatre Club. One theatre group associated with the Communist Party, Stage Left, founded in 1971 and including a Unity stalwart Ron Bevan, wanted to revive Unity's touring tradition. The group, however, found the Goldington Street guardians insistent that everyone should instead share their chief priority of keeping the building open. Stage Left never appeared at Unity.

In these years, politics and culture were coming together with an intensity and on a scale that had not been seen since the 1930s. If the 1956 'new wave' had largely ignored Unity, for the political theatre groups of the 1960s and 1970s its continued existence was also an irrelevance. They saw it as moribund and unable to create new theatrical forms to represent the new politics that were defined by gender and race as well as by class and that were as concerned with ecology and community as with higher wages and more nationalisation.[19]

The new groups ranged across the left and libertarian spectrum, espousing a complete political and cultural break with existing institutions in an echo of the sectarian period of the late 1920s. They were non-aligned in a party political sense and generally hostile to what they saw as two wings of a reformist, male-dominated and white labour movement – a Labour Party, hopelessly compromised by its record in power in the 1960s, and a Stalinist, revisionist Communist Party. Some of the groups made contact with individual unions, not on the organisational scale nor for the duration that Unity had achieved, although often with greater involvement on individual plays, and one, 7:84 Scotland, did build a strong relationship with its national trade union movement. In England, any hope that the trade unions might support a new culture on any widespread or consistent basis had collapsed with the demise of Centre 42. The beacon of progressive drama, Theatre Workshop, had been extinguished by its financial reliance on the West End and the subsidised theatre, for which Unity had fought passionately, had become in the eyes of the new groups a cultural prop of the ruling class. However, after various tussles, the alternative theatre movement itself became part of the subsidised sector, which it renewed with great vigour.

Out of these groups, and from like-minded cultural researchers, came a new interest in the history of political drama, which concentrated mostly on the earlier agitprop movements. Productions were mounted of plays from this militant tradition, such as *Waiting for Lefty* by North-West Spanner and CAST, for example, *Men Should Weep, In Time o' Strife, The Gorbals Story* and George Munro's *Gold in His Boots* by 7:84 Scotland and *Six Men of Dorset* by 7:84 England. Unity's *Where that Bomb?* was given several readings. A Bristol-based group mounted a show about Joan Tuckett, the leading figure of Bristol Unity Players

Unity's management committee was divided on its relationship to the new cultural and political forces. One group was suspicious, if not hostile, to the 'new left' and favoured a traditional approach. The other group had links with the emerging counter-culture and saw Unity as a part of the new ferment, participating alongside and encouraging the new groups. A radical cinema group, Angry Arts, was invited to screen films at Unity and CAST was asked back, in 1968, with John Arden and Margaretta D'Arcy, to present *Harold Muggins is a Martyr*. (Muggins appears in CAST's plays as a homegrown archetype along the lines of 'the good soldier Schweyk'.)

Arden had an international reputation but was dissatisfied with what conventional theatre could offer and was trying new ways of creating a popular political theatre. His collaboration with CAST at Unity was the first time that he had worked with an explicitly socialist theatre group at an explicitly socialist theatre. The play is set in a run-down café, the proprietor of which, Harold Muggins, pays protection money to local gangsters who take over the place and modernise it. The workers revolt against both. The café stands as a metaphor for the Britain of Harold Wilson's Labour government, with the mobsters the hired hands of the White House and the Pentagon.

Arden and D'Arcy's original plan had been to mount a community-based show and some of this intention survived. John Fox, founder of the theatre group Welfare State, was asked to create an environment for the piece and his constructs in the front drive stayed throughout the run while a mini-funfair and processions were organised in and around them. Parties took place at the weekends after the show, involving singers, bands, local youth groups, students from the Bradford College of Art, members of the Unity Folk Group and anyone who turned up to discuss the show, talk politics and have a good time – the 'new variety' in practice that Muldoon had been talking about before his expulsion from Unity. The first weekend saw the actor Peter Bowles conduct a marathon monologue in the yard outside the theatre and one Sunday, a version of the play was improvised for local children. This was very much in keeping with the spirit of the show, which itself was fluid and included various visitors, such as two members of the San Francisco Mime Troupe who were in England at the time. (They formed a group called Bill Stickers which brought children from the local estates into Unity). On the last night, the actors tore down the set, the huge face and hands of a Mr Big, thereby adding their own theatrical finale to an experience at Unity that was nothing if not dramatic.

The show also provided the background to what became the major catalyst for the counter-culture of the next few years. After an initial meeting in Muldoon's front room, a conference was called by CAST at Unity during the preparation of the play that led to the formation of the Agitprop Information Service. This provided and co-ordinated a range of left-wing activities, from a booking agency and a directory of groups to a poster workshop and a library of cultural political publications. It also gave rise to a festival in Trafalgar Square, out of which came the AgitProp Street Players, which turned into Red Ladder, one of the best-known political theatre groups of its day. (Ironically, CAST went its separate way from those associated with the agitprop movement, believing that its work was more political art than artistic politics).

Despite the creative ferment surrounding *Harold Muggins is a Martyr*, the Unity old-guard was not pleased. It did not like the 'hippy' aspect of the weekend activities, for which Unity was not insured, and felt that they might offend the residents. Even the raising of a red flag over the theatre was not a popular move and the influx of local children caused great anxiety. The management committee also took exception to a scene in the play, which brought the production to the verge of cancellation. One of the gangsters introduces a stripper who, without visible emotion, completes her act and elicits the comment from the gangster of 'Is that all?'[20] The management argued against this scene in terms reminiscent of the objections voiced about *Bloomsday* and threatened closure. (In another irony, Roland Muldoon also objected to the scene, though for different reasons.) The authors insisted that if the scene were cut then they would pull out; the point of the scene was to comment both on the commercial exploitation of the naked body and the fashion for sexual liberation that was to be symbolised by the musical *Hair!* and *Oh! Calcutta!*, a revue. The scene stayed in and the show went ahead, although tensions within the company were as fraught, if not more so, than those between Unity and Arden and D'Arcy. *Harold Muggins is a Martyr* recorded the largest box office returns of the year and Unity at one point seriously talked of a West End transfer.[21]

Unity ended 1967 in profit, following *Harold Muggins is a Martyr* with its own 'inaugural' show, *The Country Wife*; a revue called *The Don't Just Sit There Show*, which consisted of two short plays by David Campton separated by a political cabaret that included a black actor who whited up and sang 'There'll Always Be An England'; the British première of Brecht's *Antigone*; and, on the 50th anniversary of the Russian Revolution, an adaptation of John Reed's *Ten Days that Shook the World* and Vsevolod Ivanov's *Armoured Train 14-69*, which deals with an incident during the civil war in Siberia when partisans capture an ammunition train from the Whites and take it to the Red Army. It was presented by Pat and Reg Wagland's group that had been working on improvisation and was called the 67 Group. Attempts were made to revive the mobile work and expand its repertoire beyond folk and music hall. *Ten Days that Shook the World* was mounted, as were Edward Bond's *Passion* for a CND festival in Birmingham, *Robert Owen* for a Co-operative Party congress and the London Co-operative Society, *Storm Warning* for the Society for Anglo-Chinese Understanding, *Viet Review* at the Belgrade Theatre, Coventry, and compilation shows for Communist Party events. *Say Uncle*, about Vietnam draft dodgers, written by Lester Cole, one of the 'Hollywood Ten', was performed during the 1968 sit-in at the London School of Economics and finished with the cast marching through the audience chanting 'Victory to the NLF'

(National Liberation Front). This was a slogan associated by the traditionalist wing of Unity with the ultra-left and the Vietnam Solidarity Campaign, of which the Communist Party was initially suspicious.

Unity now represented a mish-mash of ideas, from the old-fashioned, conservative left to the libertarian and far left, some of which revealed curious overlaps and contrasts between the old and the new schools of socialist drama.[22] The repertoire at Goldington Street could include both heroic plays of Soviet history, such as Shatrov's *The Bolsheviks* (to mark Lenin's centenary) and topical pantomimes like *Cinderella*, in which Cinders falls in love with a pop star Prince Engelberk and is taken to honest Buttons by Demon Tariq Ali. At the same time the panto harks back to earlier Unity themes and approaches in ditties like that of Baron Hard-Up of Huyton – lampooning the Labour Prime Minister Harold Wilson – who enters to the tunes of both 'The Red Flag' and 'A Fine Old English Gentleman':

> If only I can borrer
> A single silver dollar
> I can stave off till tomorrer
> What I know's in store.
> I might borrow half a knicker
> A quarter if they bicker
> While the dust is getting thicker
> On the old Clause 4.[23]

Yet there was still room for rarities, such as the Spanish classic *The Concert at St Ovide* by Antonio Buero Vallejo, which received its British première.

Unity revived its first success, *Waiting for Lefty*, while 7:84 and Belt and Braces offered a new, more polemical, version of another Unity standard, *The Ragged Trousered Philanthropists* (called *The Reign of Terror and the Great Money Trick*). Belt and Braces also presented Farquhar's *The Recruiting Officer*, which Unity had presented in 1961, but turned it into a study of modern military recruitment.

The new left's concern for community politics had its affect on Unity, however belatedly, and in 1973 Goldington Street was opened up for a week at Easter to 83 children, aged between two-and-half and sixteen, from four adventure playgrounds in

Stevenage. Since the Shaw Theatre campaign, local issues had been taken more seriously by Unity and it soon had local councillors serving as president and the two vice-presidents of the society. During the neighbourhood Somers Town Festival of 1974, Unity performed an afternoon open-air history of the area called *The Will Somers Show* and the following month played host at the theatre to the Mayday Theatre Company in *The Tolmers Square Show*, which dealt with the threat of property developers in the borough. Local children staged their own plays at Unity on Saturday mornings in 1975 under the title of the Krowndale Kids Kompany, taking their name from the nearby Crowndale Road.

Theatrically and politically there was a stark difference between the style of the new groups and that of Unity; the former were aggressive, abrasive and used rock music, which Unity regarded as iniquitous, and instead still looked to folk or music hall, as can be seen in a show such as *They Made Me a Present of Mornington Crescent*, the story of the local music halls, which was mounted as part of the Camden Festival. It had a cast some 40 strong and was so popular that it ran for two-and-a-half months (and Roy Hudd liked it so much that he offered to appear in it). The following year, the same team who had created the show – Arnold Hinchliffe, Beryl and George Woods, Tom Mercer and Frank Wagland – reworked it as a history of Islington music hall, called *Up and Down the City Road*. It came after *Rent, or Caught in the Act* at Goldington Street, a show by David Edgar for General Will that used Victorian entertainment for quite different purposes – to explain and challenge the Tory government's housing legislation.

Unity's concern for, and best efforts at, chronicling the past were exemplified in this period by Arnold Hinchliffe's contribution. One of his plays was *Strike*, a measured, detailed account of orderly working-class action in 1926. It was presented with the aid of the education committee of the London Co-operative Society, which supported another production involving Hinchliffe – James Gregson's *Robert Owen*, developed by Hinchliffe to celebrate the bicentenary of the co-operator's birth. Hinchliffe also wrote *Tom Barker of Camden and the World*, the story of a Wobbly – a militant of the American labour movement – who, after an adventurous life in different countries, became mayor of St Pancras. Barker had been an agitator in Australia against conscription during the First World War and, at Lenin's request, had recruited technicians in America to help create the Autonomous Republic of the Kuzbas beyond the Urals in the building up of the Soviet Union's heavy industry.

The clashes of style and taste within the Unity leadership made hard times more difficult to manage, yet, until a fire in 1975 closed the theatre, Unity remained busy with its own productions, visiting companies and an increased number of one-off lets for special occasions. The Folk Club kept active and Albion Music, which specialised in developing the English folk heritage, gave performances; a Poet's Circle met regularly and there was an evening with the Scottish poet Hugh MacDiarmid as well as a Festival of Poets that included docker-poet Jack Dash, the Cockpit Theatre Poets and Third World Poets; the National Council for Civil Liberties celebrated its 40th anniversay with the help of Wakefield Tricycle and Recreation Ground theatre groups; the British-Cuba Association remembered Che Guevara three years after his death; and Unity's heirs, the amateur workers' group Banner from Birmingham, performed *The Collier Laddie*, taken from a radio ballad by Ewan MacColl.

Plans and policies were drawn up to try and solve Unity's crises – for example, there was a proposal for Unity to become a mixed media centre run by a production/administration group with the management committee acting like a board of governors – but such ideas came to nothing. Even artistic directors were tried, although the notion ran counter to the management committee's commitment to collective democracy, which itself took a battering as the promised egalitarian system degenerated into more squabbling and a new generation of politically conscious theatre people were forced to look elsewhere to express their imaginations.

A well publicised meeting in 1970 on 'The Role and Purpose of a Unity Theatre under Modern Conditions' was poorly attended. The 1971 AGM was adjourned over the presentation of the balance sheet and accounts, and the 1974 AGM was postponed over a legal action taken by an angry member. By the end of 1974, the official figures put full Unity membership at 112 individuals, with 452 associate members and 31 affiliated organisations.

Those who did come to Unity were often attracted by its past record, yet a measure of how times had changed can be seen by the historical reversal of Unity staging *Viet Review*, an updated version of the Royal Shakespeare Company's *US*, which was a contemporary adaptation of the living newspaper and drama documentary techniques that Unity had pioneered thirty years before.

Viet Review was directed by one of the Unity movement's outstanding figures, Glasgow's Robert Mitchell, who had come to Goldington Street as artistic director. Mitchell was responsible for Unity productions of *Billy Liar*, the popular comedy by Keith Waterhouse and Willis Hall first seen in the West End in 1960, the première of *The Rent* by the American writer Theodore Roszak, which continued Unity's attacks on the corrupting effects of the American way of life, and the première of another American play, *Say Uncle*. He also directed a modern melodrama *Dirty Work at the Crossroads* and *Epitaph for George Dillon* by John Osborne and Anthony Creighton. The management committee was suspicious of artistic directors and put a great deal of pressure on Mitchell, who finally resigned when a show went into production without his knowledge.

Unity continued with its training work, now under Tess Gorringe, who, using her group Stagecraft, presented Wycherley's comedy *The Way of the World*. Unity also maintained its 'open university' role and offered valuable opportunities: Alfio Bernabei had his first production at Unity of *The Jump*, a kaleidoscope of contemporary political events from the Greek colonels' coup to the death of a left-wing publisher at the hands of the Italian police. It led to him forming the Bite Theatre Group. The National Union of Agricultural and Allied Workers booked the theatre for an evening to see Paul Thompson's first play, *Captain Swing at the Penny Gaff*, set during the farm labourers' uprisings in the 1830s, which resulted in the union commissioning the author to write a piece for a Trafalgar Square rally. Bob Hoskins, to become an internationally famous actor, began his career at Unity where he was spotted by an agent. He was recruited from the bar and first appeared as a radio man reporting the Darwin-teaching trial in *Inherit the Wind*. He made more impact in a new play, *The Feather Pluckers*, which was commissioned by Unity from a Unity activist, John Peter Jones, as an adaptation of a novel he had written based on his experiences reporting juvenile court cases for a South London paper. He decided to write from the accused's point of view and told of three unemployed youths (two white, one black) who get involved in crimes of violence that lead to a victim being kicked to death.

From the re-opening of the theatre in April 1967 to the fire eight-and-a-half years later, Unity sustained a flow of new plays, mounting fifteen premières in full production, several Living Newspaper documentary shows and a series of staged readings and productions without décor as well as revivals of contemporary plays on important topics. They were a mixed bag. Some were biographical, like *Tom Barker of Camden and the World* and *Robert Owen*. Some offered portraits of contemporary Britain, like Alan Plater's *The Tigers Are Coming, OK?*, which traces the life and times of a Hull City football supporter. Others were linked to campaigns, such as *How We Knocked 'Em in the Old Kent Road*, on the struggle of the Bryant Colour Print workers, scripted by Unity stalwart Raymond Cross with the help of the shop stewards, or *In Place of Strife* by Phil Woods, which supported the fight against the Labour government's trade union legislation. A militant 'Everyman' figure, John Mann, is seen on trial before a future National Industrial Relations Court for leading a strike. He calls in his defence his heroes and heroines from the past – the Tolpuddle Martyrs, the Match Girls, the dockers who won the tanner. Paul Tomlinson's *South Africa '70* was shown at the time of the Springbok rugby tour and was presented by Unity with the Stop the 70 Tour organisation and the Anti-Apartheid Movement. Tomlinson, himself a South African, directed the documentary play with a cast that included five Africans, one of whom, the actor and writer Yemi Ajibade, played Nelson Mandela, the gaoled leader of the African National Congress. The Vietnam war featured in *All the Way with Elbie Jay, Viet Review* and in the double bill of *Say Uncle* and *Johnny, I Hardly Knew Ye*, a montage of songs, poems and facts arranged by Roger Hudson. On the first anniversary of the signing of the Paris Peace Agreement, Unity mounted a production called *Vietnam – the 'Postwar' War*, devised by Raymond Cross and others.

Many subjects were tackled: David Caute's *The Demonstration* examined the old and new left through student unrest; John Wilson Haire's *The Diamond, Bone and Hammer and along the Shoughs of Ulster* was concerned with civil rights in Northern Ireland; and Obi Egbuna's *The Agony* drew on his experience of imprisonment in Brixton gaol and was smuggled out of the prison.

A Nigerian writer and author of the novel *The Anthill*, Egbuna was editor of *Black Power Speaks*. His dramatisation of another of his novels, *Wind Versus Polygamy*, had been broadcast on BBC television just before his arrest. He was held without trial for six months and was given a year's suspended sentence. The cast of *The Agony*, which is set in a cell and in a prison hospital consultation room, included Mark Heath and Rudolph Walker, who became well known in the television series *Love Thy Neighbour*. While Unity maintained its commitment to political plays mainly through its new writing, major events were ducked. For example, the invasion of Czechoslovakia did not give rise to any comment from the stage as Hungary and Suez had done in *World on Edge*, although it further disrupted Unity's political affiliations.

Fire

It was a new play, *The Cocoa Party* by Ruth Dunlap Bartlett (another name for Unity activist Helena Stevens), presented to celebrate International Women's Year, that was showing when a fire broke out in the early hours of 8 November 1975. The fire brigade was called at 4 a.m. and, with five pumps and two escape ladders, it took almost two hours to control the blaze. Neighbours were evacuated and the theatre cat, Tabby, burnt its paws. The roof collapsed but the four main walls and structure supporting the circle remained intact. The auditorium, where the fire had started, was destroyed. Some believed that fascists had started the fire but there was no evidence for this – no previous harassment and no 'signature' (as was the case later when the Albany Empire theatre was burnt down). A few thought that local children had begun the fire. Some looked to a group of squatters who had taken over Unity 'in the name of the people', hoping to change the theatre's management, and had been evicted by the police. Others believed that an electrical fault was responsible.

The fire broke out in the early hours of the day that the Actors' Equity union held its AGM and there was an audible murmur when the news was announced from the platform. While many of those present were aware that Unity had lost its place and function in the movement, it was with its physical demise that there came a renewed sense that nothing had replaced it, and probably nothing ever would.

Bill Owen, by now a member of the trust, recalls the sadness at seeing the shell, after the trustees had met in an office above that had not burnt down. 'We went down to the theatre, opened the doors and looked at the four walls and up at the sky. It was a frightening experience. All my memories raced through my mind, full of ghosts. It was my life.'

The theatre was under-insured – for £32,000 – and this sum was to be used to rebuild Unity. A 40th anniversary appeal was launched and fund-raising began all over again. Alan Plater's *The Tigers Are Coming, OK?* was revived at the Hampstead Theatre Club as Unity's first production in exile after the fire and later in 1976 a group of Unity's professional supporters staged Trevor Griffith's *Occupations* at the same theatre. A second fire broke out in the rear of the Goldington Street premises in December 1976 and the trust was thereafter faced with greater problems in keeping the site safe. It was used as a rubbish tip and the cost of maintaining the ruins rose over the years. In February 1977 a proposal was put to Unity's membership that a consortium of socialist-feminist touring theatre groups consider Unity as its London base. STGRU – Socialist Theatre Groups for the Rebuilding of Unity – comprised 7:84 England and Scotland, Foco Novo, Monstrous Regiment, Belt and Braces, The Women's Theatre Group and, for a time, Broadside Mobile Workers Theatre. They were offering up to 30 weeks of performance a year, if required, and a plan to establish similar projects throughout Britain, with theatres around the country playing the same role in the regions as Unity in London. The potential was clear from the work that these groups were already producing and which was seen at Unity just before the fire when 7:84 England played to packed houses with *Lay Off*. Although some people in the STGRU consortium knew Unity from the inside – John McGrath of 7:84 had worked there backstage in the 1960s, for instance – collectively they misjudged the situation. They had their own internal differences and failed both to mobilise sufficient support within Unity and to achieve sufficient cohesion with those Unity members who were sympathetic to carry the day. Their plan to revitalise Unity and to restore it to its former position as the leading venue for working-class and political theatre in Britain was rejected at Unity's AGM by the society's members who mistrusted outsiders even more than they mistrusted each other. What could have been the most important development in political theatre for more than twenty years was dashed and with it any chance of Unity ever rising from the ashes.

After the failure of the STGRU initiative, it became clear that Unity was no longer sustainable in any recognisable form. The trust continued to guard the theatre's interests while the society disintegrated. Its books were badly kept and meetings improperly called. Shows would appear from time to time: a new play, *Mad Tom* by Paul Ryan was presented at the Hampstead Theatre Club, another revival of *The Ragged Trousered Philanthropists* surfaced, and even *Pleasure and Repentance*, originally devised by Terry Hands of the RSC, was produced at the York and Albany pub. A group called Friends of Unity, supportive of the trust but in opposition to the rump of the society, mounted readings of *The Non-Stop Connolly Show* by John Arden and Margaretta D'Arcy. There was no prospect, however, of these occasional and disjointed efforts forming the basis of a regeneration of Unity.

Nevertheless, in 1980 new plans for rebuilding the theatre were drawn up and architects' drawings were displayed in the foyer of the Hampstead Theatre Club during the run of the Unity production of *Mad Tom*. A grand occasion was planned for May 1981 at the Old Town Hall, Haverstock Hill, to 'relaunch the rebuilding of the world famous theatre of the labour movement' (as the publicity said), and to raise £8,000 for the first stage of work. Alfie Bass and Bill Owen appeared, but the venture collapsed. Amid the victories of a Thatcher government bent on neutralising the trade union movement and destroying socialism – a process aided by her cultural counterparts, including those in the theatre – there were no signs of a revival of Unity. The pattern of sporadic, one-off productions continued even more fitfully – with, for example, David Campton's *Then*, George Byatt's *The Clyde is Red*, a revival of *Bikini Fable*, Vic Jones's *Comprehensive Cuts* and more Old Time Music Halls. There were intermittent appeals for money, memorial meetings for Unity veterans, such as Laurence Davies, Arthur Soutter and Bram Bootman, and schemes being mooted to rebuild the theatre or for Unity to be resurrected on another site.

The trust took steps to wind up the society legally, although a handful of survivors from the society fought this and went on planning a revival. Friends of Unity folded and after a decade of attempts to bring Unity back to life, the trust decided to sell the Goldington Street site. After several efforts to conclude a satisfactory deal (one potential buyer was the Magic Circle), the land was bought in 1988 by the St Pancras Housing Association, which aimed to build sheltered housing for local elderly people. The association was keen to retain as much of the remaining shell of the theatre as possible and was happy to agree to the trust's proposal for a commemorative plaque to be erected.

The trust had considered different plans for keeping alive the memory and name of Unity, from entering a trade union backed consortium which put in a bid first for Camden's Roundhouse theatre and then the Mermaid Theatre, to a possible liaison with the 7:84 company. Other ideas that were canvassed included the commissioning of plays and the endowment of drama school scholarships to perpetuate Unity's philosophy through new generations of practitioners. While the longer term aim of helping to build a new socialist cultural centre was never abandoned, the trustees knew that they must support people rather than buildings because that was always where Unity's strength lay.

Unity's legacy went beyond the productions at Britannia Street, in Goldington Street or on tour. Its contribution is embodied in considerable individual achievements, whether at Unity itself, in the theatre movements associated with or coming out of Unity, and in the successes and contributions made by those Unity members who made their mark in the world of theatre and other arts. It can also be found in a wider context, as the collective achievement that it truly is – a pioneering influence on beneficial developments in the theatrical life of Britain and a unique conduit into cultural activity for many people most of whom would otherwise have been excluded from what was regarded as, and to a large extent remained, the preserve of a minority class.

Unity worked for a publicly subsidised theatre accessible to everyone and for drama to be taken seriously at all levels of education as an essential component of local, regional and national cultures. It broke down the isolation of the British theatre by staging innovative plays from abroad. It developed forms of documentary drama that were absorbed into mainstream theatre, created its own style of political pantomime and revue that prefigured the post-war satire boom, and introduced popular, vernacular theatre that influenced the writing and acting of both theatre and cinema.

As Sean O'Casey once said of the Unitarians, it was left to them

> to set about bringing the theatre back to the people, building with much labour and hard going a little theatre to bring colour and a laugh and an occasional tightening of the spine to the common people in the form of play and pantomime.

Notes

1. New interviews/correspondence for this chapter; Clive Barker, Amelia Bayntum, Raymond Cross, Karl Dallas, Cliff Fenn, Freda Field, Jack Firestein, Patrick Galvin, Michael Gambon, Manny Goldstein, P.C. Grimes, Arnold Hinchliffe, Bob Hoskins, Roger Hudson, Vic Jones, Helena Stevens, Roland Muldoon, James Pettifer, Alan Plater, Sara Randall, Paul Ryan, Helena Stevens, Paul Thompson, Tom Vaughan.
2. Quoted from the second edition (1961), a copy of which, along with a copy of the third, was given to me and has been deposited in the British Theatre Association library.
3. *Here is Drama*, third edition 1963.
4. An indication of Unity's isolation – in contrast to its position a decade before – is the paucity of reference to the theatre in the magazine *Encore* which was launched in 1956 and was the 'house' journal of the new movements in British drama. In the March-April issue of 1958, (Vol. 4 No. 4) however, Willis quotes a letter from one of the magazine's editors, Clive Goodwin, which reads 'we've read all the issues of *New Theatre*' (Unity's magazine 1945-49) and that 'we have always tried to be a new sort of *New Theatre*'. Willis' conclusion in the article, which assesses what went wrong after the war, is that 'the organised Labour Movement wasn't interested'. In the same issue, playwright Bernard Kops bemoans the current lack of co-ordination, experiment and adventure. He says 'The unity of the old Unity Theatre should serve as an example.' However, he continues: 'If we had that unity *without political affiliations* [my italics] a vital theatre would be born once again.' In the selection of *Encore* articles published in 1965 (Charles Marowitz *et al.* (eds), *New Theatre Voices of the Fifties and Sixties*, Eyre Methuen) Unity has been forgotten completely. Robert Hewison, whose survey of wartime culture *Under Seige* (Weidenfeld and Nicolson 1977) refers only briefly to Unity, gives Willis and Unity a passing mention in his sequel covering the years 1945-1960 *In Anger* (Weidenfeld and Nicholson 1981). The isolation worked from Unity's side, too, and, according to some sources, Unity rejected Wesker's first play, a short version of *The Kitchen*, Wesker has no memory of this but does not contradict the report.

5. Membership figures given in Peter Cotes, *A Handbook for the Amateur Theatre*.

6. Heinz Bernard, 'Producing Brecht', *Prompt*, No. 1, summer 1962; Eric Capon, 'Brecht in Britain', *Encore*, No. 42, March-April 1963; Nicholas Jacobs and Prudence Ohlsen, *Bertolt Brecht in Britain*, TQ Publications 1977, is useful and contains a chronological list of productions designated professional but including some amateur, e.g. Unity's, productions, although it omits *The Caucasian Chalk Circle*, 1964, and *Antigone*, 1967.

7. To coincide with Unity's first production, Adamov was interviewed by Unity member Roger Hudson in *Prompt*, No. 2, spring 1963. Also in this issue is Heinz Bernard on working-class theatre, including Unity, and Tom Vaughan and Manny Goldstein on 'The Vision of Unity'.

8. Oscar Lewenstein, a former Unity leader, and Wolf Mankowitz presented in 1955 in the West End *The World of Sholom Aleichem* with Unity members Alfie Bass and David Kossoff in the cast; and in 1956 they presented, also in the West End, Brecht and Weill's *The Threepenny Opera* with Bill Owen, Warren Mitchell and George Tovey from Unity in the company. In 1968 Alfie Bass took over the part of Tevye in *Fiddler on the Roof*, which enjoyed one of the longest runs for a musical in London.

9. Aside from these relationships, Unity had always taken a stand on racism, particularly against anti-semitism, and during the war had refused membership on grounds of racial attitude. Black actor Frank Singuineau remembers just after the war how friendly Unity was compared to the West End managements and agents he approached for work. Later, when Britain had become more multi-ethnic after recruiting Commonwealth labour, Unity, like most of the left, remained overwhelmingly white though it continued to be staunchly anti-imperialist. (In 1971, however, a row broke out between Unity management and the Kunapipi – Aboriginal for snake mother – Company, which was involved in the presentation of Rory O'Briain Bell's play *Black Girl*. The dispute concerned cast members, who were mostly black, offering temporary membership to people without, allegedly, following the society's rules.)

10. Script in the British Theatre Association library.

11. Michael Codron has no memory of this arrangement, though he does recall the play and a similar attempt to liaise with the Hampstead Theatre Club.

12. *Scene*, November 1 1962.

13. The film was originally called *Operation Teutonic Sword* but was retitled *General Spiedel – the Archives Testify* as legal action began on its showing in Britain. It was made by Andrew and Annelie Thorndike (relatives of Sybil). The case ran from 1959 to 1963. Stanley Forman of ETV, who was at the centre of the case, has a massive file on the events, with many press cuttings.

14. Eric Paice in *Fiction Magazine*, Vol. 4 No. 5, Autumn 1985 says that the party committee met in secret. Others have denied this.

15. Long-time Unity supporter Dame Sybil Thorndike pressed the button to launch the *Morning Star* in 1966.

16. I was given a copy which is deposited in Unity files held at the British

Theatre Association. Harry Landis, putative artistic director of the new Unity, elaborated on these ideas in the April and May 1967 issues of *Labour Monthly*. The August edition carried criticism of them from Helena Stevens, a writer, performer and Unity activist in the opposing camp, as well as a reply to her from Landis.

17. In 1939 at the time of the planned professional company, Unity proposed the establishment of suburban groups, for example in Hammersmith, west London, and Stratford, east London, but not in the neighbourhood surrounding Goldington Street. This plan floundered with the outbreak of war but was resurrected a few years later when the national society was formed. The existence of the society's professional company allowed a Goldington Street branch to be formed and it acted briefly as a local theatre. With the collapse of the professional company, Goldington Street returned to its national amateur role. As the national function receded, the ever-present London emphasis came more to the fore. (The seventeenth-century play *The Shoemaker's Holiday* was presented as a Cockney revel, for instance.) Unity took part in local events, such as the St Pancras Arts Festival, had many local links (for example, with the local Working Men's College which had a drama club, a library and a canteen, all frequented by Unitarians) and featured regularly in the local press, but it was not until the 1960 and 1970s that the locality and a local audience became important in policy and in choice of repertoire. *The End of the Story: A Souvenir of St Pancras*, produced by the borough in 1965 on its abolition, carries reference to Unity and a photograph of *Plant in the Sun*.

18. Muldoon's account of CAST's origins can be found in 'CAST Revival' in *Plays and Players* January 1977 and in Catherine Itzin, *Stages in the Revolution*, Eyre Methuen 1980. In 1986 he became the director of the Hackney Empire, a music hall in east London fighting for survival as a popular place of entertainment in a culturally deprived area.

19. For example, John McGrath, in *A Good Night Out – Popular Theatre: Audience, Class and Form*, Eyre Methuen 1981, traces a line of political theatre from the Blue Blouse troupes through Theatre Workshop to 7:84 omitting Unity altogether. Similarly, when the Greater London Council published a report in 1986 on its community arts programme, *A Record of Struggle and Achievement*, the authors referred to its work as realising the vision of the Workers' Theatre Movement but made no mention at all of Unity's forty years' of activity. For accounts of the alternative theatre movement see: Peter Ansorge, *Disrupting the Spectacle*; *Five Years of Experimental and Fringe Theatre*, Pitman 1975; Sandy Craig (ed.), *Dreams and Deconstructions Alternative Theatre in Britain*, Amber Lane 1980; Colin Chambers and Mike Prior, *Playwrights Progress: Patterns of Postwar British Drama*, Amber Lane 1987; Davies; Itzin. For arguments on the limits of agitprop in the 1960s and 1970s, see David Edgar, 'Ten Years of Political Theatre 1968-1978' in *The Second Time as Farce: Reflections on the Drama of Mean Times*, Lawrence and Wishart 1988; Colin Chambers 'Socialist Theatre and the Ghetto Mentality' *Marxism Today*, Vol. 22 No. 8, August 1978.

20. Quoted in Albert Hunt, *Arden: A Study of his Plays*, Eyre Methuen 1974.
21. Itzin contains Muldoon's account of the *Harold Muggins* saga and comments by Margaretta D'Arcy and John Arden on his version of events.
22. The upsurges in political theatre in the 1930s and 1960s both followed the failure of Labour governments, the first in a depression, the second in relative affluence. Both produced at first a turn to agitprop because all other drama was seen as part of bourgeois culture and politically hostile. In both periods, agitprop failed to provide a basis for development of political theatre but offered exciting dramatic interventions and schooled a generation of theatre practitioners who continued to work in the theatre in a variety of effective ways. Both were predominantly movements of young people, the 1960s' upsurge, not surprisingly, with a greater preponderance of people who had been through higher education and came from middle-class backgrounds. It was also more diverse than its forerunner, with community-based groups, women's groups, black groups, gay groups, art groups and education groups as well as socialist groups. None came out of the left or labour movement in the way that the Unity and left theatres had in the 1930s. Even though the later groups did not all begin with public subsidy, they saw themselves as 'professional' as opposed to 'amateur' and through campaigning and their own organisations soon won subsidy and professional recognition of their work.
23. Script given me by Malcolm Page and deposited in the British Theatre Association.
24. Quoted in Ronald Ayling (ed.), *Blasts and Benedictions*, Macmillan 1967.

Unity Productions 1936-1983

Part 1: Productions at Unity's two London Theatres

The following chronological list includes guest productions where information has been available, but omits film showings, occasional events, readings and certain one-off performances.

Unless otherwise stated, scripts of Unity productions are available through the British Theatre Association (BTA), London, either in the Unity files held there, the reference library or the borrowing library. Scripts held in the Lord Chamberlain's Plays collection (LCP) can be found in the British Library. The Merseyside Left Theatre/Merseyside Unity Theatre Archive (MLT/MUT Archive) is in the Merseyside Museum of Labour History. If scripts are held in private or cannot be traced, they are designated as not published (np) even if other versions may be available. The above information is not provided for music hall shows, which were compilations of various material and often included a Victorian melodrama, or for guest productions. Translators are given where known.

Code
(A) Première.
(B) English première of a foreign play.
(C) Living Newspaper or documentary drama.
(D) Original pantomime, musical or revue.
(E) Music hall or melodrama.
(F) Revival.

1936-1937

Britannia Street
Unity performed here, in different combinations, mostly short plays, skits and mass declamations until the building of the Goldington Street theatre began in September 1937. After the opening of the new theatre two months later, Britannia Street was used for rehearsals, readings, one-off performances and meetings until it was taken over by the Royal National Throat, Nose and Ear Hospital in 1947. Only the productions in the first period are given, several of which had been performed already by Rebel Players.

Opening 19 February 1936
Private Hicks Albert Maltz (F)
Waiting for Lefty Clifford Odets (F)
Requiem (A Man and a Woman) Ernst Toller (F)
Newsboy adapted collectively from poem by V. J. Jerome (F; np. Manchester Theatre of Action's version appears in *Agitprop to Theatre Workshop*, Manchester University Press 1986)
The People's Court Hubert Griffith (F)
I Can't Sleep Clifford Odets (B)
Where's that Bomb? Roger Gullan (Herbert Hodge) and Buckley Roberts (Robert Buckland) (A)
The Fall of the House of Slusher collectively written (F)
Home of the Brave author unknown (A; np)
Not for Us Norman Levy (Norman Lee) (A; np)
Who are the English? Jack Lindsay (A)
The Secret Ramón Sender (F)
Spain Randall Swingler (A; MLT/MUT Archive, Box 12.2)
On Guard for Spain Jack Lindsay (A)
Cannibal Carnival Herbert Hodge (A; extracts only)

1937-1975

Goldington Street

1937

Opening 25 November
Aristocrats Nikolai Pogodin, translator not credited (B; version by Herbert Marshall held at Southern Illinois University. Version by Anthony Wixley and Robert S. Carr, in *Four Soviet Plays*, Lawrence and Wishart 1937, held in BTA)

1938

Where's that Bomb? (F) with Dance Drama Group or Workers' Propaganda Dance Group
Busmen collectively written (C)
The Case of the Baffled Boss collectively written (D)
Trial of a Judge Stephen Spender (Group Theatre)
Bury the Dead Irwin Shaw (B)
ARP Vance Marshall (C)
Plant in the Sun Ben Bengal (B)
The Rehearsal Albert Maltz (B)
Señora Carrar's Rifles Bertolt Brecht, translated by Keene Wallis (B; *Theatre Workshop* April-June 1938). Played later, also as *Mrs Carrar's Rifles*, in version by Herbert Marshall and Fredda Brilliant (LCP – Stage Plays Submitted But Not In Accordance With The Theatres Act 1843, And For Which A Licence Was Not Therefore Issued, 1938 Vol 9, under title *Señora Carrar's Rifles*)
ARP collectively rewritten (F; np)
Crisis collectively written (C)

Babes in the Wood Robert Mitchell (story), Geoffrey Parsons (lyrics) and Berkeley Fase (music) and others (D)

1939

Harvest in the North James L. Hodson (F)
After the Tempest (F) in double bill with:
Colony (A) both by Geoffrey Trease
Sandbag Follies collectively written (D; extracts only)
Turn Up the Lights collectively written (D; extracts only)

1940

The Star Turns Red Sean O'Casey (A)
Distant Point Alexei Afinogenov, translated by Hubert Griffith (F)
The Match Girls Robert Mitchell (A)
Old World Music Hall (E)
Jack the Giant Killer Peter Quince (Robert Mitchell) (story), Geoffrey Parsons (lyrics) and Berkeley Fase (music) (D)

1941

Dostigaeff and the Others (also known as *And the Others*) Maxim Gorky, translated by G. Gibson-Cowan (B)
Distant Point (F)
This Is Our World: Erna Kremer (had several titles) John Bishop (Ted Willis) (A); *Hop Pickers* Norman Bailey (A); *The People's Court* (F); *According to Plan* Geoffrey Parsons (A)
Till the Day I Die Clifford Odets (F)

1942

Sabotage! John Bishop (Ted Willis) (A)
Get Cracking! several authors (D; extracts only)
Let's Be Offensive several authors (D; extracts only)

1943

One Third of a Nation Arthur Arent, in double bill with:
The Happy Journey to Trenton and Camden Thornton Wilder (both Toynbee Players)
Buster Ted Willis (A)
The One and the Many Owen Rutherford (Cambridge Progressive Players)
India Speaks Mulk Raj Anand (C; np. Anand's *Map of India* – same format, same issues, same period – is held at Southern Illinois University)
The Sword of the Spirit Randall Swingler (A)
Spanish Village Lope de Vega, translated by John Greene (Stanley Harrison) (F; LCP 1944/7)
Winkles and Champagne Terry Newman and Bill Rowbotham (Owen) (D/E)

1944

Green and Pleasant Land Leonard Peck (A; MLT/MUT Archive, Appendix A)

Shop Window No. 2 several authors (D; np)
All Change Here Ted Willis (A)
One More Mile several authors (D; extracts only)
Rochdale Pioneers James Gregson (People's Entertainment Society)
Late Exchange (no firm details, probably revue by visiting company such as the Civil Service Clerical Association)
Comrade Detective Brothers Tour and L. Sheynin, translated by Herbert Marshall (B; LCP 1944/38)

1945
Juno and the Paycock Sean O'Casey (Windsor Theatre Guild)
Robin of England Jack Lindsay (A)
Late Extra Barnet Woolf and van Phillips (Civil Service Clerical Association)
The Yellow Star Ted Willis (A)
Alice in Thunderland Bill Rowbotham (Owen) (story and lyrics), Benny Norris and Rowbotham (music) (D)
The Lower Depths Maxim Gorky (Glasgow Unity)
Buster (Cambridge Progressive Players)
Citizen Kane based on the Orson Welles film (Kane Players)
They Came to a City J.B. Priestley (Croydon Unity)
Swinging to the Left several authors (D; extracts only)
Juno and the Paycock (F)
God Bless the Guv'nor Ted Willis (A/E)

1946
Professional company:
All God's Chillun Got Wings Eugene O'Neill (F)
Casey Jones Robert Ardrey (B; np)
The Shepherd and the Hunter David Martin (A)
Boy Meets Girl Sam and Bella Spewack (F)
The Star Turns Red (F)
Amateur company:
Gold Is Where You Find It Bill Rowbotham (Owen) (story and lyrics), Arnold Clayton (music) (D; np)
Awake and Sing Clifford Odets (Stepney Unity)
This Trampled Earth George Leeson (North-West London Unity)
Pardon My Greek loosely borrowed from *Women in Parliament* (Ecclesiazusae) by Aristophanes, Bernard Sarron (story), Geoffrey Parsons (story and lyrics) and Berkeley Fase (music) (D; np)

1947
Professional company:
Black Magic John Collier (C) in double bill with either:
The Tinker's Wedding J.M. Synge (F) or:
The Shoemaker's Wife Federico García Lorca, translated by George Leeson (F)
Amateur company:

What Happens to Love? Ted Willis (A)
Professional company:
Golden Boy Clifford Odets (F)
An Italian Straw Hat Colin Morris (Euston Unity)
Out of the Dust Horace Morgan (Ystradgynlais Drama Group)
Amateur company:
The Match Girls with new material by Roger Woddis and Bill Rowbotham (Owen) (F)
The Enemies Maxim Gorky, translated by Tom Jay Bell (B; New Theatre Play Service No. 9, MLT/MUT Archive, Box 13.2)
Dragnet Roger Woddis (A; Lord Chamberlain's Plays 1947/24 as *Dragnet for Demos*, credited to the director Joe MacColum.)
The Match Girls (F)
The Russian Question Konstantin Simonov (B; LCP 1947/41)

1948
Winkles and Champagne second version (E)
Six Men of Dorset Miles Malleson and H. Brooks (F)
The Whole World Over Konstantin Simonov, translated by Thelma Schnee (B)
Lions after Slumber Jay Bennett (B; Marx Memorial Library, London)
What's Left? several authors (D)

1949
Plant in the Sun (F) in double bill with:
Where's that Bomb? (F)
Cousin Elwyn R. Vernon Beste (A; LCP 1950/12)
The Townshends Leonard Peck (F; MLT/MUT Archive, Box 22.1)
The Ragged Trousered Philanthropists adapted from Robert Tressell's novel by Bill Rowbotham (Owen) (F)
What Next! several authors (D)
The Jolly George Ted Willis (A; LCP 1949/38)

1950
Buster (F)
How I Wonder Donald Ogden Stewart (B; Southern Illinois University)
Hell Is What You Make It Ewan MacColl (F)
The Circling Dove Leonard Irwin (F; MLT/MUT Archive, Box 22.1)
Winkles and Champagne third edition (E)
Longitude 49 Herb Tank (B)

1951
Here Goes! Geoffrey Parsons (story and lyrics) and Berkeley Fase (music) (D)
The Word of a King Charles Poulsen (A)
The Cradle Will Rock Marc Blitzstein (B; Random House 1937)
The Germans (also known as *The Sonnenbruchs*) Leon Kruckowski, translated by M. Michalowska and J. Rodker (B)

The Hawthorn Grove Alexander Korneichuk, translated by Kathleen Bird (B; np)
Mother Goose Eric Paice and Alfie Bass (story) and David George (music) (D)

1952
The Candy Store Barnard Rubin (B)
The Wages of Eve Leonard Irwin (F; MLT/MUT Archive, Box 22.1)
Barrier Across Europe Eric Paice (C)
Mild and Bitter (including *Lovers' Vows* by Mrs Inchbald) (E)
Christmas Bridge Nancy MacMillan (B; np)
Strangers in the Land Mona Bland (A; Lawrence and Wishart 1954)

1953
The Bridge of Life Julius Hay, translated by Heinz Bernard (B; np)
Turn It Up! several authors (D; extracts only)
Three in a Row: Hall of Healing, Time to Go and *The End of the Beginning* Sean O'Casey (F)
No! Tom Cobley (A; np)
The Rosenbergs Eric Paice and William Bland (C; np)
Cinderella several authors (D; np)

1954
Timid People adapted from a Chau Shu Li story by George Leeson (A; LCP 1945/24)
Land of the Living Leonard Irwin (A)
The Shoemaker's Holiday Thomas Dekker (F)
The Dockers' Tanner Leslie Martin (A; LCP 1953/64)
Montserrat Emmanuel Roblès, adapted by Lillian Hellman (F)
Reedy River Dick Diamond (F)

1955
The Shadow of the Swastika (had other titles) Leonard Peck (F)
Russian for Yes Tom Cobley (A; MLT/MUT Archive, Box 14.2)
Peacemeal several authors (D; np)
The Road to Life adapted from the 'epic' of Anton Makarenko by M. Stehlik, translated and adapted by Frank Rhodes and Heinz Bernard (B; np)
The Trojan Women Euripides, translated by Gilbert Murray (F)
Pillars of Society Henrik Ibsen, translated by Una Ellis-Fermor (F)

1956
Nekrassov Jean-Paul Sartre, translated by Sylvia and George Leeson (B)
Widowers' Houses George Bernard Shaw (Merseyside Unity)
Polly John Gay (F)
Hold the Line (also known as *Hold On!*) K. Iskayev and A. Galitz, translated by Ruth Kisch (B)
The Exception and the Rule Bertolt Brecht, translated by Eric Bentley,

lyrics adapted by Bill Norton, music Frank Wagland (B) in double bill with:
The Shoemaker's Wife (F)
World on Edge Roger Woddis and Eric Paice (C)

1957
Mind the Baby Marjorie Shaw (A; np)
Burlesque devised by Bill Owen without credit (D/E; np)
Cyanamide Burt Marnik (B; np)
The Match Girls with new material by Bill Norton (lyrics) and Frank Wagland (music) (F)
The Biggest Thief in Town Dalton Trumbo (F)
Othello William Shakespeare (Touchstone Theatre Company)

1958
Robin Hood and his Merry Men Tom Kernot (lyrics) and Frank Wagland (music) (D; np)
The Crucible Arthur Miller (F)
Marriage adapted from Nikolai Gogol's comedy by Charles Marowitz (B; np)
The Ganze Macher (His Friend at Court) Ephraim Kishon, translated by Lothian Small (B; np)
Heartbreak House George Bernard Shaw (F)
Wally Pone Lionel Bart, loosely based on Ben Jonson's *Volpone* (D; np)
Tripe and Onions, preceded by *Green-Eyed Monster* by J.R. Planche (E)
Call Me Not Naomi Ruth Messinger (A)
Mother Courage and Her Children Bertolt Brecht, translated by Eric Bentley (F)

1959
Puerto Franco Leonard Peck (A; MLT/MUT Archive, Appendix A)
God Bless the Guv'nor (F)
The Risen People James Plunkett (A)
Take It As Red several authors (D; np)
A Rocket for the Governor A. Garson and G. Kelly (A)
Anna Christie Eugene O'Neill (West Indian Drama Group)

1960
Bloomsday adapted from James Joyce's *Ulysses* by Allan McClelland (F; LCP 1958/45)
The Big Win adapted from Sholem Aleichem by I.D. Berkowitz, translated by Tamara Kahana (B; np)
The Offshore Island Marghanita Laski (A)
Drama in the Making: Milk and Honey, Homecoming and *I Like Eddy* (Experimental Theatre Group)
The Seagull Anton Chekhov, translated by David Magarshack (F)
Shakespeare's Lovers (Company of Eight from RADA)
You Won't Always Be On Top Henry Chapman (F)

Old Time Music Hall and *Lady Audley's Secret* by Elizabeth Braddon (E)
The Ragged Trousered Philanthropists (F)
Androcles and the Lion George Bernard Shaw (F) in double bill with:
L'Après Midi de Mr Shaw Crome Mathers (Tom Mercer) (A; np)
The Misadventures of Mr Pickwick Arnold Hinchliffe (story and lyrics) and Frank Wagland (music), based on Dickens (D; np)

1961
The Lower Depths (F)
The Affluent Athenian Derek Hall (A)
The Shoemaker's Wife translated by K.P. Rossides in double bill with:
The Tree of Idleness by K.P. Rossides (both performed in Greek by Theatro Technis)
The Visions of Simone Machard Bertolt Brecht, translated by Arnold Hinchliffe (B; LCP 1967/7)
Beer and Skittles (E), including *Temptation* author (1875) unknown (E)
The Recruiting Officer George Farquhar (F)
And Him Stretched Patrick Galvin (A; np)

1962
Echo of Thunder Kenneth Ware (A, without décor; np)
Aladdin several authors (D; np)
The Life of Kaggs Arnold Hinchliffe, based on Henry Mayhew's writings (F; np)
Three in One: A Displaced Milkmaid Ian Hamilton Finlay; *Room for Adjustment* Nathan Field; *The Reluctant Prodigy* Harvey Schneider (all A; np)
The High Jinks of Bishop Saull Vic Jones (A)
Spring '71 Arthur Adamov, translated by Arnold Hinchliffe and Jim Sluzny (B)
School for Wives Molière, adapted by Miles Malleson (F)
Ear'oles Michael Feld (A, without décor)
Hedda Gabler Henrik Ibsen (F)
East Lynne Mrs Henry Wood and *Music Hall* (E)

1963
Circus devised by Eric Paice, music Phillip Charles (D; np)
See a Man Falling Jo Joseph (A; np)
Six Away several authors (D; np)
Here is Unity compilation show arranged by Roger Hudson
The Rotter Ruth Messinger (A, without décor; np)
The Deviates Don Mathews (A; np)
The Scavengers Arthur Adamov, translated by Tom Vaughan (A) in double bill with:
The Fury of Phillip Hotz Max Frisch, translated by Michael Bullock (B)
The Man Who Bought a Battlefield Frank Marcus (A; np)
People Like Us several authors (D; np)

A Memory of Two Mondays Arthur Miller (F) in double bill with:
Oh! Freedom Charles Chilton (C; np)
Music Hall (E)
Mandragola Niccolo Machiavelli (Marlowe Society)
A Doll's House Henrik Ibsen (F)

1964
Port and Lemon including *Track in the Snow* dramatised by W.E. Suter (E)
The Good Woman of Szechwan Bertolt Brecht, translated by John Willett (F)
It's Our's (compilation show arranged by Frank Wagland to celebrate the buying of the freehold)
Everything in the Garden Giles Cooper (F)
Woyzeck and *Leonce and Lena* Georg Büchner (RADA Students)
Peace Aristophanes (modern version by Greek Art Theatre/Theatro Technis)
The Licence Ephraim Kishon (B; np)
The Glass Menagerie Tennessee Williams (F, without décor)
The Merchant of Venice William Shakespeare (New Company of Actors)
Squaring the Circle Valentin Katayev, translated by Eugene Lyons and Charles Malamuth (F; Gollancz 1935)
The Pea-Pickers Joyce Goodes, from the novel by Eve Langley (B; np)
The Caucasian Chalk Circle Bertolt Brecht, translated by Eric Bentley (F)

1965
God Bless the Guv'nor (F)
Little Malcolm and his Struggle against the Eunuchs David Halliwell (Dramagraph)
Yegor Bulichov Maxim Gorky (B)
Chicken Soup with Barley Arnold Wesker (F)
All the Way with Elbie Jay devised by Tom Vaughan (D/C; np)
Julius Caesar William Shakespeare (RADA Students)
There's a Megabutton on my Living Room Floor Stuart Douglass (A; np)
Sweeney Todd George Dibdin Pitt and *Music Hall* (E)
Christmas Palace of Varieties arranged by Frank Wagland (E)

1966
Death of a Salesman Arthur Miller (F)
The Balcony Jean Genet (East 15 Acting School)
The Playboy of the Western World J.M. Synge (F)
Inherit the Wind Jerome Lawrence and Robert E. Lee (F)

1967
Opening 28 April
John D. Muggins is Dead and *Mr Oligarchy's Circus* (Cartoon Archetypal Slogan Theatre)
The Country Wife William Wycherley (F; Unity's official re-opening production)

The Don't Just Sit There Show: Soldier from the Wars Returning David Campton (F; J. Garnet Miller 1963); Cabaret; *Getting and Spending* David Campton (F; Studio Theatre 1960)
Antigone Bertolt Brecht, translated by K.L. Porter (B) in double bill with:
Change the World, It Needs It Brecht programme devised by Roger Hudson (C/ np)
The Feather Pluckers John Peter Jones (A; np)
Armoured Train 14-69 Vsevolod Ivanov, translated by G. Gibson-Cowan (F; Martin Lawrence 1933)

1968
Dirty Work at the Crossroads author unknown, adapted by William Johnson (E)
Billy Liar Keith Waterhouse and Willis Hall (F)
Say Uncle Lester Cole (B; np) in double bill with:
Johnny, I Hardly Knew Ye devised by Roger Hudson (C; np)
Harold Muggins is a Martyr John Arden, Margaretta D'Arcy and Cartoon Archetypal Slogan Theatre
Viet Review '68 adapted from Royal Shakespeare Company's *US* (C; Unity version np)
The Rent Theodore Roszak (B; np)

1969
Cinderella several authors (D)
Epitaph for George Dillon John Osborne and Anthony Creighton (F)
Rag to the Bull several authors (D)
Music Hall devised by Frank Wagland (E)
Strike Arnold Hinchliffe (C; np)
The Diamond, Bone and Hammer and Along the Shoughs of Ulster Wilson John Haire (F)
The Frogs and Co...Axed! words and music by Raymond Cross and Bert Bennett, based on Aristophanes (D; np)
The Mother Bertolt Brecht, translated by Lee Baxandall (B; Grove Press 1965)

1970
Jack and the Beanstalk several authors (D)
A Case for Euthanasia John Clarke (A; without décor)
The Agony Ogi Egbuna (A; np)
The Bolsheviks Mikhail Shatrov, translated by Robert Daglish (F)
South Africa '70 Paul Tomlinson (C; np)
Triple Bill: Professor Taranne Arthur Adamov, translated by Peter Meyer (F); *Dock Brief* John Mortimer (F); *The Waiting Room* Ron Champion (A; np)
The Demonstration David Caute (F; Deutsch 1970)
The Misadventures of Mr Pickwick (F)

1971
The Dragon Yevgeny Schwartz, translated by Max Hayward and Harold Shukman (F)
Captain Swing at the Penny Gaff Paul Thompson (A; np)
It's Never Too Late Raymond Cross and Laurence Davies (D; np)
Black Girl Rory O'Briain Bell (A; without décor; np)
They Made Me a Present of Mornington Crescent Arnold Hinchliffe (story) (D/E; np)
Rebellion from Erin to Eureka Rory O'Briain Bell (A; np)
In Place of Strife Phil Woods (A/C)
The Chinese Machine Frank Dux (B; np)
Robert Owen James Gregson, adapted by Arnold Hinchliffe (A)
Henry V William Shakespeare (Kismet Players)

1972
Pins and Needles Harold Rome, revised by Bernard Sarron (F)
Waiting for Lefty (F)
Burlesque devised by Raymond Cross (D/E)
Rent, or Caught in the Act David Edgar (General Will)
Up and Down the City Road Arnold Hinchliffe (story) (D/E; np)
Huis Clos Jean-Paul Sartre, translated by Stuart Gilbert (F) in a double bill with:
A Matter of Convenience Richard Moss (A)
Bull Durham Jeremy Newsome (F; np)
Summerfolk Maxim Gorky, translated by Francis Hanley (F; np)

1973
L'Avare Molière (Théâtre de l'Unité)
How We Knocked 'em in the Old Kent Road Raymond Cross (C; np)
Partitions Michael Cahill (joint production with London Group Productions; A; np)
And Play on the Flutes of their own Vertebrae Bethani Travis, from the poems of Mayakovsky and others (A; np)
Tom Barker of Camden and the World Arnold Hinchliffe (A)
At Enormous Expense devised by Eric Mason (E)
The Way of the World William Congreve (Stagecraft)
The Collier Laddie adapted from Ewan MacColl (Banner Theatre)
The Reign of Terror and the Great Money Trick adapted from *The Ragged Trousered Philanthropists* (7:84 England and Belt and Braces)
One Way Trip Bill Shiers (Shelbourne Youth Theatre)
My Life Noah Elstein (T.P. Productions)
The Concert at St Ovide Antonio Buero Vallejo, translated by Victor Dixon (B; np)

1974
New Positions: Hopscotch and *A New Profession* Norris Harvey (A)
Before Your Very Eyes (E)
Fabryka Absolutu Karel Čapek (STG Theatre,Poland)

The Jump Alfio Bernabei (A)
Vietnam – The 'Postwar' War devised by Raymond Cross and others on the anniversary of Paris Peace Agreement
Number 3 John Grillo and *Self-Accusation* Peter Handke (Garage Theatre)
The Recruiting Officer adapted from George Farquhar (Belt and Braces)
Open House: Dear Janet Rosenberg, Dear Mr Kooning Stanley Eveling and *The Inhabitants* Olwen Wymark (Naoise Theatre Company)
Case for a Rebel Emmanuel Roblès, translated by James and Marie Kilker (B; np)
The Tolmer Square Show Nigel Baldwin (Mayday Theatre Company)
10 Nights in a Bar Room William Pratt (E)
The Police Slavomir Mrozek, translated by Nicholas Bethell (B) in a double bill with:
Saxon Dedwynn Jones (F)
The Tigers Are Coming, OK? Alan Plater (F)
Widowers' Houses George Bernard Shaw (F)

1975
Common Will Against the Giant David Craig and Nigel Gray (D; np)
Echo and *Dreams of Mrs Frazer* Gabriel Josipovici (Paradise Foundry)
The Heart of a Patriot (Rough Theatre)
The Adventures of Jack Boot (Mayday Theatre Company)
The Black and White Miners' Show (York Shoestring Theatre)
Right Turn: The Bridge (B; *Themes in the One-Act Play*, R.D. and Sheila Cox (eds.), McGraw Hill 1971) and *The Dolls No More* both by Mario Fratti (B; np) and *A Smell of Burning* David Campton (F; Studio Theatre 1960)
Fanlights (Theatre 84)
Muggins No Longer (Kartoon Klowns)
The Bureaucracy Show Jack Bingham (D)
Strike 1926 (Popular Theatre)
Lay Off John McGrath (7:84 England)
Stop Press Mikhail Sebastian (A; np)
Family Play (Jester Company)
The Nuns Eduardo Manet, translated by Robert Baldrick (Reaper Productions)
Music Hall
The Cocoa Party Ruth Dunlap Bartlett (Helena Stevens) (A; np)

1976-1983

After the fire on 8 November 1975 performances bearing Unity's name were mounted in various venues. No attempt has been made to list all the music hall shows that were staged in this period. The list of productions stops in 1983. From here on the arguments intensified over who could legitimately represent Unity to such an extent that further additions would have been meaningless.

1976
The Tigers Are Coming, OK? (F; Hampstead Theatre)
Occupations Trevor Griffiths (F; Hampstead Theatre)

1977
Attic Comedy John Henry Jones (A; np; King's Head)
God is Just a Copper in a Long White Beard group-devised (A; np; Oval House)
Unity Theatre Story group-devised (C; np; Jellicoe Hall, London)

1979
The Non-Stop Connolly Show John Arden and Margaretta D'Arcy (F; readings by Friends of Unity at Theatro Technis)
God Bless the Guv'nor (F; Theatro Technis)

1980
God Bless the Guv'nor (F; Hampstead Theatre)
The Ragged Trousered Philanthropists (F; Goldsmiths College and Irish Club)
The Bridge (F; Rhoda McGaw Theatre, Woking)
Pleasure and Repentance devised by Terry Hands (F; York and Albany)
Mad Tom Paul Ryan (A; np; Hampstead Theatre)

1981
Waiting for Lefty (F; reading at British Theatre Association)
Mad Tom (F; Irish Club)
Then David Campton (F; Studio Theatre 1960) and *The Clyde is Red* (joint production with Theatre PKF) (F; np) (Hampstead Theatre)

1982
Then (F) and *Bikini Fable* (F) (British Theatre Association)
New Positions (F; British Theatre Association)
Reminiscences of Unity Theatre Cliff Fenn and Norman Bedow (Crown Tavern, Clerkenwell Green)

1983
Comprehensive Cuts Vic Jones (A; British Theatre Association)
Come Fry With Me group-devised (D; np; Hampstead Theatre)

Part 2: Touring Productions

Plays are listed alphabetically not chronologically because their performance patterns were frequently irregular and impossible to document. Some stayed in the mobile repertoire for long periods in several different productions, while others disappeared quite quickly. For the purpose of this listing, 'touring' is taken in its broadest sense of performing away from the home theatre. Given the very nature of Unity's touring, this list is likely to be incomplete. Authors are not included if already cited in the chronological list of productions.

1936-1939

Up until 1939, it was Unity's policy to tour all its shows where possible. Every performer was expected to tour and, with the exception of a short-lived attempt at creating a special mobile shock troupe, there was no separate group for this purpose. From 1937-1939, Unity was involved in the work of the Left Book Club Theatre Guild but mobile shows that toured under the guild's banner have been omitted.

Agony of China, The Jack Lindsay
Aristocrats
ARP
Babes in the Wood
Bury the Dead
Busmen
Case of the Baffled Boss, The
Crisis
Fall of the House of Usher, The
I Can't Sleep
Newsboy
On Guard for Spain
People's Court, The
Plant in the Sun
Private Hicks
Rehearsal, The
Requiem (A Man and a Woman)
Salute the Soviet Union Jack Lindsay
Secret, The
Señora Carrar's Rifles (Mrs Carrar's Rifles)
Spain
Waiting for Lefty
We Need Russia Jack Lindsay
Where's that Bomb?
Who are the English?

1940-1975

During the war, an Outside Show Group was formed, later renamed the Mobile Group. It functioned strongly,although with some gaps,until the mid-1950s and thereafter intermittently. Omitted from the list are: compilation shows, such as *Shop Window, Grand Review* or *Star Parade*, and music hall or variety shows; some one-off productions, such as *We Fight On* or *Lift the Ban*; Goldington Street productions taken out for special performance, such as *The Yellow Star*; plays performed at other venues after the fire in 1975. These can be found in the chronological list of productions.

According to Plan
Amazons shows
Ballad and the Mast, The
Bespoke Overcoat, The Wolf Mankowitz

Bikini Fable
Black Magic
Change the World, It Needs It
Circling Dove, The
Dockers' Tanner, The
Erna Kremer (various titles)
Exhibition 51 group-devised
Farmworker, The Paul Thompson
Focus on Germany Eric Paice
Focus on Peace Eric Paice
Gabriel Perri Ted Willis
God Bless the Guv'nor
Golden Boy
Gold Is Where You Find It
Gravy Train Mordecai Gorelik
Homage to Vatutin Jack Lindsay
India Speaks
Inherit the Wind
Investigators, The Lewis Allen
Jack the Giant Killer
Jolly George, The
Match Girls, The
Menace of the Comics, The
Oh Priceless Heritage Peter Collingwood
Passion Edward Bond
Piece about Peace, A Jack Lindsay
Playboy of the Western World, The
Pleasure and Repentance
Pound on Demand, A Sean O'Casey
Ragged Trousered Philanthropists, The adapted by Frank Rhodes
Robert Owen
Rochdale Pioneers, The
Russia's Glory: The Red Army group-devised
Salute the Maquis (Man of the Maquis) Jack Lindsay
Salute to the Gentle Sex group-devised
Say Uncle
Shoemaker's Wife, The
Six Men of Dorset
Storm Warning
Sword of the Spirit, The
Taming of the Shrew, The (extracts) William Shakespeare
Ten Days that Shook the World adapted from John Reed by Roger Hudson
Tinker's Wedding, The
Townshends, The
Trip to the Big Store group-devised
Twelfth Night (extracts) William Shakespeare
Viet Review '68
Voice of Greece, The (Cry of Greece) Jack Lindsay

Waiting for George Ted Willis
We Want Peace (A Plea for Peace)
What's Left?
Winkles and Champagne
Word of a King, The
Your Money and Your Life John Collier

Select Bibliography

The select bibliography concentrates on material that is either directly concerned with London Unity and related movements – the Left Book Club Theatre Guild and the national Unity Theatre Society – or material that places them in an important context. It does not include biographies and memoirs; where appropriate, these have been mentioned in notes to chapters, as have other secondary sources. The bibliography does not list Unity's own publications which can be found in the British Theatre Association.

Archives and Collections: (not including personal collections that were made available to me but which are not available to the public)

British Theatre Association (Unity Theatre Society archive and material deposited by author. This archive contains the most complete collection of Unity material that is available, including scripts, programmes, photographs, reviews, leaflets, posters, cuttings, articles, minutes of meetings, accounts, newsletters, bulletins, correspondence and author's research files).

Communist Party Library (miscellaneous).

International Brigade Archive, Marx House.

Marx Memorial Library (miscellaneous).

Merseyside Museum of Labour History (contains catalogued material from Merseyside Left/Unity Theatre, Left Book Club Theatre Guild and national Unity movement collected by Jerry Dawson).

National Museum of Labour History, Manchester (London Unity material collected by Bram Bootman).

Scottish Theatre Archive (Glasgow Unity material).

Southern Illinois University, Carbondale (Unity material held in the Morris Library and collected by Herbert Marshall. Includes documents belonging to other Unitarians. Big collection, notable mainly for detailed information relating to Marshall, much of which is not available elsewhere).

Theatre Museum.

University of Sheffield (Betty Hunt papers).

University of Warwick (Bristol Unity Players archive in the Modern Records Centre; miscellaneous material in the Department of Theatre Studies).

Working Class Movement Library, Manchester.

Newspapers, periodicals: the complete list runs into the hundreds. The main publications consulted are mentioned in the text and in the notes to chapters.

Unpublished Material:

Jones, Len, *The British Workers Theatre 1917-1935* (Leipzig 1964); a small section appeared as 'The Workers Theatre in the Thirties' *Marxism Today*, Vol. 18, No. 9, September 1974. See also 'The Workers' Theatre Movement in the Twenties', *Zeitschrift fur Anglistik und Amerikanistic*, Vol. 3, No. 14, January 1966 (Leipzig) and 'The Workers' Theatre Movement in the Thirties' *Zeitschrift fur Anglistik und Amerikanistic*, Vol. 4, No. 23, January 1975.

Travis, Ron, *The Unity Theatre of Great Britain 1936-1946: A Decade of Production* (Southern Illinois 1968).

Wallis, Mick, *Hodge and the BBC* (draft 1988).

Watson, Don, *British Socialist Theatre 1930-1979: Class,Politics and Dramatic Form* (Hull 1985).

Books, Monographs, Pamphlets, etc.:

Bradby, David and McCormack, John, *People's Theatre*, Croom Helm 1978.

Branson, Noreen and Heinemann, Margot, *Britain in the Nineteen Thirties*, Weidenfeld and Nicolson 1971.

Chambers, Colin and Prior, Mike, *Playwrights' Progress: Patterns of Postwar British Drama*, Amber Lane 1987.

Clark, Jon *et al.* (eds), *Culture and Crisis in Britain in the 30s*, Lawrence and Wishart 1979.

Cotes, Peter, *No Star Nonsense*, Rockcliff 1949.

Cotes, Peter, *A Handbook for the Amateur Theatre*, Olbourne Press 1957.

Craig, Sandy (ed.), *Dreams and Deconstructions: Alternative Theatre in Britain*, Amber Lane 1980.

Cunningham, Valentine, *British Writers of the Thirties*, Oxford University Press 1988.

Darville, Keith, *Unity: Life and Death of a Theatre 1937-75*, BBC Radio 3, 8 August 1978.

Davies, Andrew, *Other Theatres: The Development of Alternative and Experimental Theatre in Britain*, Macmillan 1987.

Dawson, Jerry, *Left Theatre: Merseyside Unity Theatre*, Merseyside Writers 1985.

Findlater, Richard, *The Unholy Trade*, Gollancz 1952.

Fyrth, Jim (ed.), *Britain,Fascism and the Popular Front*, Lawrence and Wishart 1985.

Gloversmith, Frank (ed.), *Class, Culture and Social Change: A New View of the 1930s*, Harvester Press 1980.

Goorney, Howard, *The Theatre Workshop Story*, Eyre Methuen 1981.

Hewison, Robert, *Under Siege: Literary Life in London 1939-45*, Weidenfeld and Nicolson 1977.

Hewison, Robert, *In Anger: Culture in the Cold War 1945-60*, Weidenfeld and Nicolson 1981.

Hodges, Sheila, *Gollancz: The Story of a Publishing House 1928-1978*, Gollancz 1978.

Hogenkamp, Bert, *Deadly Parallels: Film and the Left in Britain 1929-39*, Lawrence and Wishart 1986.

Itzin, Cathy, *Stages in the Revolution: Political Theatre in Britain since 1968*, Eyre Methuen 1980.

Jacobs, Nicholas and Ohlsen, Prudence, *Bertolt Brecht in Britain*, TQ Publications 1977.

Jones, Mervyn, '1956: Days of Tragedy and Farce' in Miliband, Ralph, and Saville, John (eds), *The Socialist Register 1976*, Merlin Press 1976.

Kemp, Harry, Riding, Laura *et al.*, *The Left Heresy in Literature and Life*, Eyre Methuen 1939.

Laing, Stuart, *Representations of Working-Class Life 1957-1964*, Macmillan 1986.

Lehberger, Reiner, *Das sozialistiche Theater in England 1934 bis zum Ausbruch der Zweiten Weltkreigs*, Peter Land (Frankfurt am Main) 1977.

Lehmann, John (ed.), *New Writing in Europe*, Penguin 1940.

Lewis, John, *The Left Book Club: An Historical Record*, Gollancz 1970.

Lindsay, Ann, *The Theatre*, Bodley Head 1949.

Marshall, Norman, *The Other Theatre*, John Lehmann 1947.

Medley, Robert, *Drawn from Life: A Memoir*, Faber & Faber 1983.

Noble, Peter, *The British Theatre*, British Yearbooks 1946.

Osborne, E.A. (ed.), *In Letters of Red*, Michael Joseph 1938.

Rees, Goronwy, 'Politics on the London Stage' in Lehmann, John (ed.), *New Writing*, Hogarth Press 1939.

Rickword, Edgell (ed.), *Nothing is Lost: Ann Lindsay 1914-1954*, Communist Party Writers Group 1954.

Samuel, Raphael, MacColl, Ewan and Cosgrove, Stuart, *Theatres of the Left 1880-1935*, Routledge & Kegan Paul 1985.

Sidnell, Michael, *Dances of Death: The Group Theatre of London in the Thirties*, Faber and Faber 1984.

Stourac, Richard and McCreery, Kathleen, *Theatre as a Weapon: Workers' Theatre in the Soviet Union, Germany and Britain, 1917-1934*, Routledge & Kegan Paul 1986.

Symons, Julian, *The Thirties – A Dream Revolved*, Faber & Faber 1975.

The End of the Story: A Souvenir of St Pancras, St Pancras Borough Council 1965.

The Red Network: The Communist International at Work, Duckworth 1939.

Tuckett, Angela, *The People's Theatre in Bristol 1930-1945*, Our History Pamphlet, No. 72, Communist Party 1980.

Index

Aberdeen Unity, 96, 246, 247, 250, 251
Abrahams, Dave, 198
Academy of Arts, The, 290
According to Plan, 222
Ackland, Rodney, 189
Adam, Ronald, 33
Adamov, Arthur, 18, 355, 356, 369, 385
Adams, Robert, 182, 270, 271, 358
Adding Machine, The, 246
Adelphi Theatre, 220, 274, 375, 376
Adler, Luther, 158
Adler, Stella, 158
Affluent Athenian, The, 362
Afinogenov, Alexander, 209, 211, 267
After the Tempest, 179, 180
Agate, James, 208, 211, 267
agitprop, 21, 61, 63, 80, 164; WTM and, 27-33 *passim*, 43, 44, 140, 145, 176; Unity and, 57n, 139, 140; Left Book Club Theatre Guild and, 95, 98; 1960s political theatre and, 384, 385, 388
Agony, The, 394, 395
Agony of China, The, 82
Agreement of the People, An, 246
Ajibade, Yemi, 394
Albion Music, 392
Alexander, Dorothea, 275, 361
Aladdin, 359
Ali, Tariq, 390
Alice in Thunderland, 257-9, 263
All Change Here, 252
All God's Chillun Got Wings, 33, 187n, 270-1, 277, 358
All One Battle, 87, 90n
All the Way with Elbie Jay, 364
Allen, John, 43, 67-85 *passim*, 91, 94, 97, 100, 102, 106, 108, 109, 113, 114, 131, 137, 138, 140-5 *passim*, 207, 208, 266
Allen, Lewis, 292
Almaz, Michael, 356
Amaral, Kate, 297, 299
Amaral, Lucien, 297, 299
amateur theatre, 28, 47, 79, 100, 101, 118, 148, 190, 207, 208, 228, 237; Workers' Theatre Movement and, 29, 31; Left Theatre and, 34; New Theatre League and, 36; Rebel Players and, 44; Unity and, 17, 20, 50, 91, 118, 158, 167, 183-4, 190, 207, 228, 238, 241, 268-89 *passim*, 308, 381, 382, 392
Amateur Theatre and Playwrights' Journal, 65, 118
Amazons, The, 230-2, 250
Amber, Jospeh, 290
America, United States of: influence of in 1930s, 36, 98, 141, 336; Workers' Theatre Movement and, 27; Unity and, 18, 41, 59, 78, 98, 104, 145, 154, 158, 174, 268, 271, 272, 306, 357, 360; criticism of, 292-3, 297, 299, 301-4 *passim*, 316-24 *passim*, 330, 334, 362, 387, 390
Anand, Mulk Raj, 203, 236
And Him Stretched, 351
Androcles and the Lion, 353, 358
Anderson, Lindsay, 373
Angry Arts, 387
Animal Ideas, 138

Anna Anna, 86
Anna Christie, 358
anonymity (of casts), 14, 18, 48, 57n, 150, 156, 158, 161n, 238, 270
Anti-Apartheid Movement, 394
Antigone, 354, 389
appeasement, 18, 162, 163, 166
Arden, John, 387, 389, 397
Ardrey, Robert, 246, 271
Arent, Arthur, 141, 225
Aristocrats, 86, 134-8
Aristophanes, 78, 273, 385
Armoured Train 14-69, 389
Arms and the Man, 213, 286
Army Bureau of Current Affairs, 146, 203, 236, 268, 275
Army is Born, An, 85
ARP, 97, 145, 149
Artists' International Association, 76, 102, 226n, 274, 291
Arts Council, 203, 248, 268, 272, 278-87 *passim*, 321, 368, 372
Arts Theatre, 233, 235, 241-2, 248, 268, 351
Arundel, Honor, 225, 236, 261n
Ashcroft, Peggy, 300
Askey, Arthur, 266
Attlee, Clement, 269, 301, 303, 304, 311
Auden, W.H., 67, 96, 146, 147, 242, 245, 361
Audley, Maxine, 22, 237, 240
Auerbach, Frank, 285
Avare, L', 385
Awake and Sing, 78, 89n, 161n, 245, 264, 273

Babes in the Wood, 18, 165-79, 182, 183, 186n, 188, 192, 194-8 *passim*, 213-4, 217-8, 229, 232, 269, 274, 335
Bailey, Norman, 221
Baker (Block), Celia, 49
Baker, Fred, 83
Balcony, The, 385
Ballad and the Mast, The, 381
Banner Theatre, 392
Bantu People's Theatre, 33, 54n
Barke, James, 245, 281
Barker, Clive, 356, 360
Baron, Alec, 247
Baron (Bernstein), Alexander, 13, 265, 279, 280, 285, 290
Baron, H., 40
Barr, Margaret, 49, 137
Barrie, J.M., 26
Barrier Across Europe, 323, 359
Bart, Lionel, 22, 327, 331, 335, 336, 350, 358, 360, 375
Bartlett, Ruth Dunlap, *see* Stevens
Bass, Alfie, 22, 125, 126, 157, 158, 174, 185, 189, 192, 193, 200, 235, 242, 283, 295, 316, 320, 321, 322, 331, 370, 375, 397
Bath House, The, 364
Bauer, David, 380
Baxter, Beverley, 304
Baxter, Stanley, 281
Bayntum, Amelia, 360
BBC, 13, 65, 68, 86, 164, 200, 219, 237, 238, 242, 254, 289, 305, 341, 351, 363, 367, 395
Beaumont, Francis, and Fletcher, John, 291
Beaverbrook, Lord, 175, 185, 310
Bedford Music Hall, 108, 243, 378, 381
Beer and Skittles, 351
Before Guernica, 85
Beggar's Opera, The, 253, 338
Bell, Tom Jay, 297
Bells are Ringing, The, 290
Belshazaar (Handel), 102
Belt and Braces, 385, 390, 396
Bendas, Ruby, 236
Bengal, Ben, 99, 154, 158
Bennett, Jay, 299
Bennett, Peter, 111, 113, 168
Bentley, Eric, 338
Berliner Ensemble, 326, 338, 353
Bernabei, Alfio, 393
Bernard, Cyril, 289

Bernard, Heinz, 161n, 336, 340, 353-6 *passim*, 366, 373, 376
Bernstein, Alec, *see* Baron, Alexander
Bernstein, Sidney, 73, 207, 375
Berry, John, *see* van Phillips
Besant, Annie, 213
Bespoke Overcoat, The, 381
Beste, R. Vernon, 85, 111, 126, 178, 194, 208, 212, 222, 228, 229, 233, 237, 276, 307
Bevan, Aneurin, 274, 276, 284
Bevan, Ron, 219, 386
Bevin, Ernest, 141-2, 219, 274, 301, 309
Big Screen, The, 305
Big Win, The, 357
Biggar, Helen, 273
Biggest Thief in Town, The, 357
Bikini Fable, 292, 397
Billy Liar, 393
Birch, Derek, 254, 300
Birmingham Unity, 250
Bishop, John, *see* Willis
Bite Theatre Group, 393
Black, Bernard, 301
Black, Misha, 76
Black, Rivka, 72, 76, 211, 258
Black Magic (Precious Stone/ Coal), 147, 275-7, 291
Blackpool Unity, 284
Blaikie, Derek, 46, 48
Bland, Mona, 327
Bland, William, 334
Bliss, Dave, 173
Bliss (Brenner), Nat, 156
Blitz, 331
Blitztein, Marc, 324
Blood Wedding, 270
Bloomsday, 351-2, 389
Blumenfeld, Simon, 41, 56n, 98
Blunk, Trudie, 229
Bluthal, John, 323
Boland, Bridget, 203
Bolsheviks, The, 390
Bond, Bessie, 376
Bond, Edward, 389
Bond, Ralph, 145, 291
Bootman, Bram, 39, 45, 46, 48, 49, 56n, 57n, 65, 106, 117, 152, 219, 397
Boswell, Bruce, 86, 87
Boswell, James, 217
Boughton, Rutland, 132
Bowen, Elizabeth, 133
Bowles, Peter, 388
Box, Sidney, 369
Boy Meets Girl, 272, 277
Boyfriend, The, 175, 244
Braddock, Bessie, 295, 305
Bradley, Louie, 270
Braham, Maurice, 48, 55n
Braham, Ray, 111
Bramley, Ted, 268
Brandon-Jones, Una, 186n, 192, 223, 229-32 *passim*, 327, 331, 335
Brecht, Bertolt, 18, 21, 85, 86, 90n, 134, 138, 164, 223, 225, 245, 281, 337
Brickman, Miriam, 297
Bridge of Life, The, 326
Brighton Unity, 96, 286
Brilliant, Fredda, 86, 151, 179, 186n
Bristol Unity Players, 36, 98, 246, 387
British Drama League, 36, 66,101, 102, 106, 108, 121n, 134, 154, 157, 167, 203, 207, 229, 248, 251, 266, 279, 2880
British Theatre Conference (1948), 283-4
Britten, Benjamin, 34, 184, 246
Britton, Lionel, 33, 137, 138
Broadside Mobile Workers' Theatre, 396
Brook, Peter, 281
Brooks, Ern, 309
Brooks, H., 98, 300
Brown, F.J., 222
Brown, Isobel, 84
Browne, George, 168, 186n
Browne, Maurice, 107, 122n, 137, 183
Bryant Colour print workers, 394
Büchner, Georg, 385
Buckland, Robert (Buckley

Roberts), 69-74 *passim*
Buero Vallejo, Antonio, 390
building workers, 48, 110, 308, 360, 374
Building Workers' Sports Association, 110
Bull Sees Red, The, 90
Burke, Henry (Edward), 68,86
Burke, Patricia, 189, 285
Burlesque, 341, 357
Burns, Emile, 130, 135, 141, 168, 192, 269
Burrell, John, 267
Bury the Dead, 69, 71, 97, 99, 148-51, 154, 159, 168, 177, 208
Busmen, 18, 77, 140-6, 150, 176, 203, 207, 277, 323
Buster, 211, 233-6, 246, 252, 257, 264, 314
bus workers, 66, 76, 140-5
Bush, Alan, 80, 102, 106, 107, 117, 118, 122n, 137, 138, 143, 207, 370
Bustamante, Alexander, 180
Byatt, George, 397

Cable Street, 92, 380
Cain, Michael, 316
Call Me Not Naomi, 361
Callaghan, Noreen, 305
Cambridge Progressive Players, 235, 245, 264, 295
Cameron, James, 344, 373
Campbell, Andrew, 203
Campbell, J.R., 99
Campton, David, 389, 397
Candy Store, The, 316
Cannibal Carnival, 74-7, 79, 80, 89n, 135
Čapek, Karel, 25, 385
Capitalist Rationalisation, 32
Capon, Eric, 181, 211, 235, 237, 242, 355
Capon, Kenneth, 237
Captain Swing at the Penny Gaff, 393
Carnovsky, Morris, 158
Carr, Mary, 192
Casey Jones, 271, 277
CAST (Cartoon Archetypal Slogan Theatre), 66, 384-9 *passim*
Casson, Lewis, 98, 102, 107, 122n, 185, 281, 321, 374-5
Caucasian Chalk Circle, The, 354
Caudwell, Christopher, 132
Caute, David, 160n, 394
Cavalcanti, Alberto, 273
Cave, Rita, 235
CEMA (Council for the Encouragement of Music and the Arts), 239, 248
censorship, 24, 182, 195, 284, 297; *see also* Lord Chamberlain
Centre 42, 348, 349, 360, 369, 372, 382, 386
Chamberlain, Neville, 162-6 *passim*, 169-76 *passim*, 185, 188-96 *passim*, 209, 220
Chaney, Mark, 48, 57n
Change the World, It Needs It, 354
Chapman, Henry, 360
Charley's Aunt (Brandon Thomas), 138
Chartists, 24, 33, 81, 250
Chau Shu Li, 326
Cheeseman, Peter, 146
Cheharkov, 40
Chekhov, Anton, 25, 353
Chicken Soup with Barley, 380
children's theatre, 22, 330, 358, 368, 388, 391
Chilton, Charles, 359-60
Chisnell, Elsie, 229, 306
Chlumberg, Hans, 33, 148
Christmas Bridge, The, 327, 330
Churchill, Winston, 176, 203, 208, 219, 220, 239, 259, 263, 274, 301, 302, 310, 318
Cinderella, 335 (1953), 390 (1969)
Circling Dove, The, 292, 315-6
Circus, 359
Citizen Kane (play from film), 264
Citizens' Theatre, Glasgow, 211, 282, 283, 354
Civil Service Clerical Association, 264, 280, 305

Clarion movement, 24, 91; Clarion Players, Glasgow, 245
Clarke (Maitland), Joan, 326, 336, 358, 361
Class against Class, 31-2
Clayton, Arnold, 223, 273, 353
Clerical and Administrative Workers' Association, 332
Clifford, Mark, 285
Clogs, 98, 138
Clurman, Harold, 63, 158
Clyde is Red, The, 397
Campaign for Nuclear Disarmament, 358, 363, 384, 389
Cobb, Lee J., 158
Cobley, Tom *see* Gleeson
Cock a Doodle Dandy, 265, 272
Cockpit Theatre Poets, 392
Cocoa Party, The, 395
Cocteau, Jean, 281
Codron, Michael, 363-4, 400
Cold Coal, 98
Cold War, 18, 151, 284, 287, 288, 293, 294, 299, 301, 311, 319, 332, 372
Cole, Lester, 389
collective work, 19, 23, 30, 31, 48, 79, 126, 158, 163, 168, 238, 251, 277, 341
Collier, John, 266, 267, 275, 292
Collier Laddie, The, 392
Collingwood, Peter, 292
Collins, Canon, 334, 365
Collins Music Hall, 48, 108, 243, 368
Colony, 179-82, 185, 195, 211, 270
commercial/West End theatre, 20, 24, 30, 38, 61, 67, 73, 91, 107, 125, 139, 146, 150, 154, 184, 190, 194, 267, 274, 277, 286, 304, 305, 317, 345n, 350, 377, 386; *see also* professional theatre
Communist International (Comintern), 25-6, 31, 35, 53n, 188, 190, 239
Communist Party (French), 202, 339, 342, 355
Communist Party (Great Britain), 14, 19, 21, 25, 26, 35, 121n, 150, 160n, 177, 189, 211, 224, 239, 258, 263, 273, 288, 292, 311, 312n, 332, 337, 340, 368, 371,386; Workers' Theatre Movement and, 29, 30; attraction of in 1930s, 37-9, 54n, 127-8; Left Book Club Theatre Guild and, 101-3, 120-1n; actors' group of, 102, 121n, 137; cultural committee of, 130; 1937 bus strike and, 142-4; Spender and, 146, 147, 160n, 207; appeasement and, 162, 165; Nazi-Soviet pact (1939-41) and, 103, 190, 191, 194, 211, 214, 218-221; Second World War (1941-5) and, 201, 252; London district of, 89n, 130, 131, 150, 199, 268, 273, 365, 372; Unity and: founding, 43, 44, 47-51, 54n; members/supporters, 92, 94, 105, 129-30, 212, 239, 243, 271, 295, 330, 332, 389; relationship between, 130-33, 168, 192, 194, 206, 285, 301, 335, 340, 372, 382; Willis plans, 232, 248, 249, 268, 269; Cold War witch-hunt and, 305-6; Hungary (1956) and, 344-5, 371
Communist Party (Germany), 31
Communist Party (USA), 41, 64
Company of Ten, 207
Comprehensive Cuts, 397
Comrade Detective (Face to Face), 253, 254
Comrade Enemy, 247
Comrade has Died, A, 117
Concert at St Ovide, The, 390
Conchie, Sheila, *see* Dorrell
Constructional Engineering Union, 374
Cooper, Giles, 352
Cooper, Jack, 374
Cooper, Duff, 165
Co-operative Drama Association, 279

Co-operative movement, 19, 30, 33, 44, 65, 92, 94, 96, 102, 105, 119n, 122n, 130, 137, 138, 176, 222, 241, 245-9 *passim*, 278, 280, 287, 291, 294, 295, 300, 308, 354, 383, 389, 391
Coppock, Richard, 308, 309
Corkery, Ada, 309
Corrie, Joe, 25, 98
Council for Proletarian Art, 25
Country Wife, The, 384, 389
Cousin Elwyn, 307
Cradle will Rock, The, 99, 324-5
Creighton, Anthony, 393
Crescent Films (Unity company), 265, 290
Crescent Theatre, Birmingham, 101
Cripps, Sir Stafford, 107, 122n, 176, 207, 276, 284, 287, 303, 310
Crisis (Czechoslovakia), 163-5
Cross, John E., 182
Cross, Raymond, 369, 394
Croydon Unity, 264
Crucible, The, 350, 352, 357
Cry of Greece (The Voice of Greece), 82, 292
Cunard, Nancy, 211, 222
Cyanamide, 357
Czechoslovakia, see *Crisis*

Daily Herald, 136, 157, 195, 224, 310
Daily Worker, 28, 29, 35, 99, 130, 203, 218, 219, 224, 247, 263, 372; Unity and, 49, 50, 92, 93, 102, 111, 118, 135, 152, 166, 168, 171, 192, 206, 209, 213, 218, 223, 232, 236, 263, 268, 281, 310, 320, 329, 340, 341; reviews, 144, 147, 164, 181, 271, 319, 344, 364
dance/drama, 36, 49, 55n, 77, 117, 138, 359
Dance Drama Group, 77
Dankworth, Johnny, 375
Dann, Larry, 375
D'Arcy, Margaretta, 387, 389, 397
Dash, Jack, 392
Davidson, Joy, 169
Davies, Ann, 198, 229, 236, 240, 248, 261n, 291
Davies, Doreen, 230
Davies, Laurence, 397
Dawson, Dave, 213, 323
Dawson, Jerry, 56n, 286
Dawson, Oliver, 109
de la Haye, Ina, 33, 54n
de Wilde, Herbert, 232
Deakin, Arthur, 142, 317, 339
Dean, Basil, 152, 281
Death of a Salesman, 309, 380
Dekker, Thomas, 291, 338
Delaney, Shelagh, 350, 373
Demonstration, The, 394
Deviates, The, 362
Devine, George, 281, 340, 346n, 353, 373
Diamond, Dick, 338
Diamond, Bone and Hammer and Along the Shoughs of Ulster, The, 394
Dibley, Helen, 213, 229
Dirty Work at the Crossroads, 393
Disher, M. Wilson, 243, 244
Displaced Milkmaid, A, 363
Distant Point, 209-2, 221, 245, 246, 247, 297
Dixon of Dock Green, 232
Dmitrov, Georgi, 40, 54n
Do Somethin' Addy Man!, 359
dockers, 213, 293, 294, 338, 339, 394
Dockers' Tanner, The, 294, 338-9
documentary drama, 17, 41, 141, 145-6, 161n, 203, 213, 247, 275, 292, 323, 334, 336, 350, 359, 393, 394, 398; *see also* Living Newspaper
Dog Beneath the Skin, The, 96, 245
Doll's House, A, 353
Dominica (US intervention), 364
Donnelly, Charles, 163
Don't Just Sit There Show, The, 389
Doone, Rupert, 146, 147
Dorita y Pepe, 375
Dorrell, Anthony, 309

Dorrell (Conchie), Sheila, 229, 293, 329
Dostigaeff and Others (And the Others), 220, 297
Douglass, Stewart, 363
Dowell, Ray, 366, 374
Dr Krupps, 40
Dragnet (Dragnet for Demos), 297, 299, 359
Drama Documentary, 203
Drama in the Making, 361
Dramagraph, 385
Draw the Fires, 34
Driberg, Tom, 46, 112, 304
Dublin Left Theatre, 96
Dublin lock-out/general strike, 205, 351
Dukes, Ashley, 207
Duncan, Archie, 281
Duncan, Ronald, 138
Dundee Red Front Troupe, 29
Dutt, R. Palme, 118, 168
Dyson, Anne, 327, 332, 333
Dyson, Robert, 353

Earoles, 363
East 15 Acting School, 380, 385
East End, 249
East End, London, 37-9, 45, 55n, 67, 84, 119n, 125, 200, 212, 225, 233, 236, 249, 271
Easter 1916, 34
Eatwell, Tony, 360
Edgar, David, 391
Edinburgh Festival, 281, 340
Edinburgh Unity, 96, 247
Edwards, Stan, 301
Egbuna, Obi, 394, 395
Eisenstein, Sergei, 33, 134, 152
Eisler, Gerhard, 308
Eisler, Hanns, 223, 354
Eisler, Paul, 97
Elliott, Pauline, 169
Elvin, George, 372
Embassy Theatre, 33, 48, 59, 148, 283, 358
Encore, 280, 355, 399
End of the Beginning, The, 327
Enemies, The, 289, 297
engineers, 167, 287, 291, 374
English Stage Company, 184, 265, 340, 377
Enough of All This, 98
ENSA (Entertainments National Service Association), 202, 226n
Epitaph for George Dillon, 393
Equity, 55n, 266, 279, 395
Erma Kremer of Ebenstadt (several titles), 222
Euripides, 24, 98, 195, 337
Euston Unity, 295
Evans, Edith, 268, 279, 281
Evans, Eynon, 98
Even a Wise Man Errs, 285
Everything in the Garden, 352
Exception and the Rule, The, 338, 354
Exhibition 51, 295
Expedient, The (The Measures Taken), 86

5,000 Years of Poetry, 102
Fabryka Absoltut (Absolute Standards), 385
Fagan, Hymie, 132
Fall of the House of Slusher, The, 41, 79-80, 96, 99, 119n, 140, 164, 176
Famine, 236
Farjeon, Herbert, 175, 218
Farquhar, George, 352, 353, 390
Farren, Nellie, 213
fascism, 17, 34, 43, 44, 55n, 58n, 69, 82, 83, 97, 100, 104, 124, 128, 150, 162, 164, 166, 191, 193, 202, 204, 206, 214, 224, 246, 257, 263, 292
Fase, Berkeley, 167, 168, 174, 177, 182, 185, 192, 196, 197, 213, 214, 223, 225, 226n, 256, 274, 301-5 *passim*, 309, 316, 322, 330, 335, 343n
Fate or – !, 40
Fear and Misery in the Third Reich, 245

Feather Pluckers, The, 393
Federal Theater Project, 88n, 105, 145, 324
Federation of Workers' Film Societies, 94
Feffer, Itzik, 238
Feld, Michael, 363
Fenemore, Hilda, 297
Fenn, Cliff, 364, 369, 377
Fernald, John, 86, 137
Festival of Britain, 295, 323
Feuchtwanger, Leon, 353
Field, Freda, 375, 376
Field, Nathan, 363
Fight Goes On, The, 40
Film and Photo League, 36, 84, 119n
Finch, George, 237, 240
Findlater, Richard, 331, 339
Fings Ain't Wot They Used T' Be, 331, 360
Finians Rainbow, 320
Finlay, Ian Hamilton, 363
Firestein, Jack, 357
Foco Novo, 396
Focus on Germany, 293, 322
Focus on Peace, 293, 322
folk, 295, 338, 357, 384; Unity Folk Club/Group, 22, 357, 360, 368, 372, 374, 384, 388, 392
For Dmitrov, 40
Fore Publications, 229, 236, 261n
Foster, Tommy, 65, 69, 93, 94, 106, 108, 109, 131, 137
Four, Five, Six!, 274
Fox, John, 387
Fox, Ralph, 132
Frankau, Ronald, 118, 253, 266, 274
Free German League of Culture, 87, 222, 226n, 290
Fricker, Peter Racine, 354
Friell, James, *see* Gabriel
Frieze, J.S., 87
Frost, David, 375, 376
Fullard, George, 98, 138
Fury of Phillip Hotz, The, 354
Gabriel (James Friell), 102, 168, 282
Gabriel Perri, 202
Gaitskill, Hugh, 303, 359
Galitz, A., 326
Gallacher, Willie, 30, 162, 232, 304
Galsworthy, John, 98, 100
Galvin, Patrick, 351
Gamble, Roland, 150
Gambon, Michael, 22, 352
Gamlin, Lionel, 266
Ganze Macher, The, 356-7
Garnett, Bathsheba, 380
Garratt, Eveline, 283
Gas, 39
Gascoyne, David, 289
Gay, John, 253, 338
Gay '90s, The, 243
gender, 21, 111, 125, 127, 154, 155, 159n, 229, 232, 312n, 313n, 386
General Election (1931), 30; (1935) 35; (1940, proposed) 98, 178; (1945) 203, 258-9, 263; (1950) 311; (1951) 318, 322, 330
General Will, 385, 391
Genet, Jean, 385
George Comes Home, 231
German War Primer, 164
Germans, The, 325, 332
Germany, 25, 27, 31, 36, 104, 128, 143, 147, 163, 164, 188, 205, 232, 301, 325, 329
Get Cracking, 223-4
Gibb, James, 88n, 168, 192, 324
Gielgud, John, 268, 281, 355
Give Me Liberty, 87
Glaser, Ben, 68, 86, 87
Glasgow Players, 245
Glasgow Unity, 190, 245, 247, 251, 264, 265, 273, 279, 281-3, 286, 287
Glasgow Workers' Theatre Group, 97, 98, 245
Glaspell, Susan, 26
Glass Menagerie, The, 353
Gleeson, Dennis (Tom Cobley), 328-9
Glover, Julian, 331

God Bless the Guv'nor, 266-7, 367, 368
Goddard, Renée, 283
Godwin, Frank, 263, 273, 299
Gogol, Nikolai, 361
Gold, Helen, 352
Gold, John, 331, 335
Gold in His Boots, 282, 387
Gold is Where You Find It, 273
Golden Boy, 158, 165, 245, 272, 276, 277
Golden Fleece, The, 290
Goldman, Bernard, 366
Goldoni, Carlo, 285
Goldstein, Manny, 368-9, 372
Gollan, John, 376
Gollancz, Victor, 93-7 *passim*, 102, 107, 110, 117. 118, 121n, 122n
Good Woman of Szechwan, The, 354, 360, 377, 378
Goorney, Howard, 341, 360
Gorbals Story, The, 282, 387
Gorelik, Mordecai, 292
Gorky, Maxim, 18, 34, 135, 146, 220, 242, 281, 282, 289, 297, 299, 353
Gorley, Robert F., 306
Gorman, Shey, 380
Gorringe, Tess, 137, 393
Goss, John, 107, 127
Gowing, Lawrence, 168, 207
Grand Palais, 200, 273
Gravy Train, 292
Great Expectations, 289
Greece: civil war, 82, 292, 301; colonels' coup, 393
Greek Art Theatre, *see* Theatro Technis
Green and Pleasant Land, 249, 250
Greene, Graham, 218
Greenwood, Arthur, 196, 376
Greenwood, Walter, 171
Gregson, James, 391
Grey, Beryl, 372
Griffith, Hubert, 40, 139, 209
Griffiths, Trevor, 396
Grossman, Jack, 331, 335
Group Theatre (London), 50, 55n, 67, 68, 146-7, 161n
Group Theater (New York), 61, 64, 99, 137, 158, 159, 183, 184, 237
Gullan, Roger *see* Hodge
Guinness, Alec, 289, 355, 373
Guthrie, Tyrone, 50, 73, 106, 107, 122n, 157, 286

Habimah Theatre, 78, 357
Hackney Labour Dramatic Group, 26
Hackney People's Players, 27
Haddy, Harry, 173
Haire, John Wilson, 394
Haldane, J.B.S., 99, 149-50
Hale, Audrey, 229, 243
Hales, Binnie, 175, 274
Halfin, Bob, 331
Hall, Amner, 49, 146
Hall, Derek, 362
Hall, Fernau, 81
Hall, Jimmy, 372
Hall, Jo, 169
Hall, Willis, 393
Halliwell, David, 385
Hamilton, Patrick, 189
Hammer, John, 40
Hampstead Theatre Club, 386, 396, 397
Hands, Terry, 397
Happy Journey to Trenton and Camden, The, 25, 235
Harold Muggins is a Martyr, 387-9
Harris, Bagnall, 48
Harrison, Stanley (John Greene), 237, 238
Harrison, Tom, 145
Harvest in the North, 178, 195
Harvey, Janet, 168
Haslam, George, 168, 179
Hasted, John, 338
Hatton, David, 385
Hawthorn, Denys, 352
Hawthorn Grove, The, 325, 346n
Hay, Julius, 326
Hearn, V.J., 284
Heartbreak House, 352, 361
Heartfield, John, 253

Heath, Mark, 359, 395
Hedda Gabler, 353
Heffer, Eric, 286
Hell is What You Make It, 314
Hellman, Lillian, 327
Helpmann, Robert, 340
Henderson, Betty, 283
Henderson, Dickie, 375, 376, 377
Henshaw, George, 72
Henson, Leslie, 118
Herbert, A.P., 12, 159
Herbert, Joceyln, 112, 137
Here Goes!, 316-22, 329, 330
Here is Drama, 89n, 347-9
Here is Unity, 374
Hewer, Johnny, 219
Hewers of Coal, 98
High Jinks of Bishop Saull, 362, 365
Hill, Errol, 316, 359
Hill, Joe, 88n, 339
Hill, John, 282
Hinchliffe, Arnold, 351, 354, 355, 356, 364, 369, 391
Hobson, Harold, 179, 339, 354
Hodge, Herbert (Roger Gullan), 69-78 *passim*, 88n, 108, 117, 135, 142, 179, 186n, 238, 245
Hodson, James, 138, 178, 179, 183
Hold the Line, 326
Homage to Vatutin, 201
Home of the Brave, 78
Homecoming, 361
Hop Pickers, 221
Hope, Vida, 175, 176, 185, 189, 218, 220, 244, 274, 316, 320, 321
Hoskins, Bob, 22, 393
House of Regrets, 285
Houston, Renée, 305
How I Wonder, 314-5
How We Knocked 'Em in the Old Kent Road, 394
Howerd, Frankie, 375, 377
Hs'Ung, 137
Hudd, Roy, 391
Hudd, Walter, 183, 189
Hudson, Roger, 360, 374, 384, 394
Hughes, Ken, 182
Hulke, Malcolm, 348
Hungary (1956), 21, 340-4, 395
Hunger Marchers, 40
hunger marches, 30, 40, 78, 92
Hunt, Hugh, 281
Hunter, Russell, 281
Hylton, Jack, 375

I Can't Sleep, 78, 165, 245
I Like Eddy, 361
Ibsen, Henrik, 24, 257, 337, 353
Illingworth, Nelson, 97, 135, 136
In Place of Strife, 394
In Time o' Strife, 25, 26, 282, 387
Independent Labour Party, 25, 30, 98
India League, 236
India Speaks, 146, 236, 358
Indian People's Theatre, 251
Informer, The (from *Fear and Misery in the Third Reich*), 245
Inherit the Wind, 380, 393
Insurgents' Aid Committee, 85
International Brigades, 84, 87, 136, 153, 202, 273
International Theatre Group, 285
International Union of Revolutionary Theatres (IURT), 31, 42, 134
International Workers' Dramatic Union (IWDU), 31
Invergordon, 32
Investigators, The, 292
Ira Aldridge Players, 359
Ireland, plays about, 204-6, 351, 352, 394
Irgun, 271
Irwin, Leonard, 292, 315, 327, 328
Isherwood, Christopher, 67, 96, 146, 242, 245, 361
Iskayev, K., 326
Italian Love Story, An, 295
It's a Free Country, 40
It's Ours, 376
It's Possible, 247
Ivanov, Vsevolod, 389

Jack the Giant Killer, 214-20, 224
Jackson, A.T., 115

Jackson, Freda, 189
Jackson, Harold, 285
Jacobs, Juluis, 266, 279
Jacques, Hattie, 274
Jagger, John, 159
Jardine, Robin, 118
Jellicoe, Ann, 377
Jerome, V.J., 41
Jewish culture, 37-9, 55n, 67, 103, 257, 271, 321, 356-7, 380; *see also* Yiddish theatre
Jewish Institute Players, Glasgow, 245
John D. Muggins is Dead, 384
John, Errol, 323
Johnny, I Hardly Knew Ye, 394
Johnson, Harry, 294
Johnson, Hewlett, 293, 335
Jolly George, The, 293
Jones, Bill, 142
Jones, Frank, 95, 97
Jones, Jack, 139
Jones, John Peter, 393
Jones, Vic, 362, 397
Jonson, Ben, 270, 350
Joseph, Jo, 374
Joyce, James, 351, 352
Judgement Day, 98
Jump, The, 393
Juno and the Paycock, 245, 264, 266

Kaiser, Georg, 143
Kane Players, 264
Karlin, Miriam, 283
Kartoon Clowns, 386
Katayev, Valentin, 246, 353
Kazan, Elia, 158
Keep the Gallows, 307
Keir, Andrew, 281
Kempson, Rachel, 219, 375
Kenny, Sean, 352
Kensington Unity, 285
Kent, Enoch, 375
Kincaid, James, 254
Kingsway Theatre, 184, 185, 188, 191, 192, 196, 197, 207, 215, 240, 269
Kino, 36, 49, 89n, 95, 195
Kishon, Ephraim, 356, 357
'Kitchen sink' drama, 179, 234, 349
Klein, E., 87
Klingender, Francis, 132
Knack, The (film), 377
Knight of the Burning Pestle, The, 291
Kops, Bernard, 375, 399n
Korean War, 148, 316, 317, 319, 327, 334
Korneichuk, Alexander, 325, 346n
Kossoff, David, 22, 240, 257, 274, 283, 374, 375
Krowndale Kids Kompany, 391
Kruks, Leo, 289
Kustow, Michael, 256

Labour League of Youth, 222, 265
Labour Party/government: in 1920s-30s, 26, 30, 35, 37, 39, 86, 93, 101, 127, 128, 150, 222; in 1940s-70s, 104, 219, 221, 239, 258, 259, 260, 263, 284, 286, 287, 288, 294, 300, 301, 309, 311, 340, 386; Unity and, 47, 92, 94, 122n, 268, 269, 275, 305, 332; Unity plays and, 196, 215, 218, 301-4 *passim*, 309-10, 359, 365, 387, 390, 394
Labour Stage, 136-7
Laine, Cleo, 375
Lambs of God, The (This Walking Shadow), 282
Lambert, David, 370
Land of the Living, 328
Landis, Harry, 332, 378, 380
Landmarks of Liberty, 246
Lang, George, 111
Laski, Harold, 107, 122n
Laski, Marghanita, 363
Lassally, Walter, 323
Last Edition, 191
Late Extra, 264
Lawrence, Jerome, 380
Lawrence, Martin, 196, 375
Lay Off, 396
Leah, Tony, 360
Lee, Jennie, 279, 382

Lee, Robert E., 380
Lee, Will, 99, 158
Leeds Left Book Club Forum, 247
Leeds Unity, 190, 225, 246, 247, 250, 254
Leeson, George, 87, 89n, 264, 273, 275, 295, 326, 333, 334, 338, 339-40
Leeson, Sylvia 339
Left Book Club, 93, 96, 97, 98, 102, 119n, 120n, 121n, 175, 247; LBC Professional Actors' Group, 102; Scientists' Group, 102; Poetry Group, 102
Left Book Club Theatre Guild, 67, 93-104, 115, 118, 120n, 121n, 131, 140, 145, 149, 159, 165, 203, 237, 241, 244, 249, 279
Left News, 95, 98, 99
Left Review, 50, 52, 65, 80, 83, 84, 100, 121n, 141, 211, 217
Left Theatre, 33-4, 41, 44, 51, 54, 86, 105, 137, 156, 246
Left Theatre (Ireland), 292
Lehmann, Beatrix, 106, 185, 189, 253, 266
Lehmann, John, 208
Leigh, Mike, 385
Leona, Margaret, 68, 83, 137, 225
Leonce and Lena, 385
Lesser, Frank, 206
Let's Be Offensive (Leeds), 247
Let's Be Offensive (London), 223, 225
Levenson (Abrahams, Clive), Doris, 192, 194, 230, 243, 318
Levine, Ray, 385
Levy, Benn, 266, 280, 348
Levy (Lee), Norman, 78
Lewenstein, Oscar, 265, 279, 281, 283, 285, 360
Leyton Unity, 165
Licence, The, 357
Liebknecht, Karl, 39
Life, 174
Life of Kaggs, The, 351, 369
Lift the Ban, 223
Lindsay, Jack, 13, 80-5 *passim*, 102, 109, 202, 203, 229, 254, 261n, 288, 289, 291, 292, 293
Lines, Joseph, 168
Lions After Slumber, 299
Little Malcolm and His Struggle Against the Eunuchs, 385
Little Theatre Guild, 279
Littler, Emile, 281
Littlewood, Joan, 246, 332, 355, 366, 373, 375
Liverpool Playhouse, 86, 211, 235
Living Newspaper, 17-8, 2, 41, 77, 97, 99, 138, 140-146, 149, 161n, 163-5, 191, 201, 203, 225, 230, 236, 247, 253, 275, 276, 277, 293, 340, 341, 350, 393, 394
Lloyd Webber, Andrew, 175
Lom, Herbert, 231, 279, 300
London Co-operative Society, 102, 249, 280, 354, 383, 389, 391
London County Council, 32, 34, 137, 235, 307, 333, 340, 366, 369, 376; Greater London Council, 383, 401n
London Labour Choral Union, 55n, 86, 117, 136
London Negro Repertory Theatre, 182, 186n, 358
London Theatre Studio, 67, 113
Longitude 49, 316, 329, 359
Lorca, Federico García, 270, 275, 338, 359
Lord Chamberlain, 24, 47, 65, 73, 151, 174, 183, 185, 202, 208, 245, 272, 304, 320, 321, 327, 331, 360
Lorm-Schaffer, Eva, 249
Love, Bessie, 300, 309
Love in Industry, 41, 79
Low, 173, 305
Lower Depths, The, 264, 281, 282, 353
Lowthian, George, 360
Luce, Claire, 279
Lund, Beryl, 305, 309
Luxembourg, Rosa, 39

MacColl, Ewan (Jimmy Miller), 56n, 146, 246, 314, 315, 337, 392

MacColum, Joe, 292, 297, 337, 352, 361
MacDiarmid, Hugh, 289, 373, 392
Machine Wreckers, The, 25
Macleod, Alison, 307
Macmillan, Harold, 359
Macmillan, Nan, 327
MacNeice, Louis, 146
Macowan, Michael, 203
Mad Tom, 397
Magito, Suria, 225
Magnos, Paschoral Carlos, 282
Maitland, Joan, *see* Clarke
Major Operation, 245
Makarenko, Anton, 326
Malaya, guerrilla war in, 327
Malice in Plunderland, 27, 258
Malleson, Miles, 33, 98, 107, 122n, 137, 268, 300, 321, 375
Maltz, Albert, 35, 66, 69, 84, 92, 205, 239, 359, 380
Man and a Woman, A, see Requiem
Man of the Maquis (Salute the Maquis), 285, 291, 294, 394
Man Who Bought a Battlefield, The, 364
Manchester Unity, 246, 250, 363
Mandela, Nelson, 394
Manhattan Brothers, 375
Mankowitz, Wolf, 366, 367, 380
Manning, Hilda, 325
Manning, Leah, 300
Manning, Mick, 311, 320, 321, 330, 333
Manning, Olivia, 341
Manzani, Carl, 85
March of Time, The, 142, 194
Marcus, Frank, 285, 364
Marnik, Burt, 357
Marowitz, Charles, 341, 361
Marriage, 361
Marshall, Herbert (H.P.J.), 56n, 57n, 66, 86, 106, 131, 134-9 *passim*, 145, 150-6 *passim*, 160n, 163, 164, 179, 181, 211, 249, 251, 252, 253, 256, 292, 314, 315, 359, 372, 373
Marshall, Vance, 149
Martin, David, 225, 271
Martin, Kingsley, 159, 304, 344
Martin, Leslie, 338
Marxism, 19, 21, 77, 80, 82, 127, 132-3, 146, 152, 203, 207, 211, 249, 288
Mason, Marjorie, 380
mass declamation, 21, 27, 39, 41, 68, 80-5, 99, 103, 201, 202, 292
Mass Observation, 140, 143, 145, 225
Masses and Man, 25, 56n
Match Girls, The, 212-4, 226n, 243, 294, 295, 297, 323, 339, 351, 394
Mathews, Don, 362
Maxwell, Mimi, 231
Mayakovsky, Vladimir, 106, 364
Mayday theatre group, 385, 391
Mayhew, Henry, 351
McBean, Angus, 150
McBean, Donald, 281
McCarthyism, 59, 64, 292, 314, 334; Hollywood Ten, 59, 357, 389; UK and, 18, 301, 305-6, 320
McClellan, Robert, 282
McClelland, Allan, 351, 352
McCormack, Elizabeth, 179
McCracken, Esther, 267
McGinn, Bernard, 281
McGrath, John, 396, 401n
McGregor, Jimmy, 372
McKeeman, Geoffrey, 89n, 173-4
McLean, Peggy, 167
McLeish, Robert, 282
McMillan, Roddy, 281
Means Test Trifle, 249
Measures Taken, The, 86
Memory of Two Mondays, A, 360
Men Should Weep, 281, 282, 387
Menace of the Comics, The, 292
Menon, Krishna, 236, 309
Mercer, Tom, 351, 353, 391
Meredith, Ralph, 85
Mermaid Theatre, 331, 398
Merseyside Left Theatre/Unity, 56n, 64, 74, 83, 85, 88n, 96, 245,

247, 249, 250, 280, 286, 305, 306, 307, 315, 328, 337
Messinger, Ruth, 361, 363
Met, the (Metropolitan Palace of Varieties), 242, 375
Meyerhold, Vsevolod, 33, 134
Midland Bank Dramatic Society, 207
Mikhoels, Solomon, 238
Miles, Bernard, 291, 366
Milk and Honey, 361
Miller, Arthur, 281, 350, 360, 380
Mind the Baby, 361
miners, 65, 91, 275, 276, 291; South Wales, 33, 81, 139, 151, 272, 276, 285, 295; Durham, 81, 98; Derbyshire, 138, 294; Kent, 294
Miracle at Verdun, 33, 148
Misadventures of Mr Pickwick, The, 351
Mitchell, Robert (Glasgow Unity), 264, 281, 393
Mitchell, Robert (Peter Quince), 166, 167, 168, 173, 182, 185, 186n, 192, 212, 213, 214
Mitchell (Misel), Warren, 22, 240, 283, 307, 332
mobile theatre, Workers' Theatre Movement and, 27, 28; Left Book Club Theatre Guild and, 95, 96, 98; Unity and 17, 20, 44, 45, 47, 51, 104, 124, 140, 177, 183, 263, 289, 291-5, 322, 323, 329, 333, 363, 367-8, 380, 389; Unity on tour, 91, 127, 131, 136, 157, 167, 218, 308; in Second World War, 197-202, 214, 215, 222, 224, 225, 242, 243, 250, 253, 254, 257; Unity professional company and, 267, 272-3, 275, 276; 1960s groups and, 385; *see also* Amazons
Molière, 99, 100, 353, 385
Montserrat, 327
Monstrous Regiment, 396
Montagu, Ivor, 130, 168, 177
Montgomery, E.P., 87
Mooney, Ian, 355
Moore, Stephen, 332
Morgan, Horace, 295
Morley College, 354
Morley, Robert, 158
Morris, Colin, 295
Morris, Gadfan, 292
Morris, Phyllis, 266
Morrison, Elizabeth, 297
Morrison, Herbert, 218, 219, 303, 310
Moscow Art Theatre, 374
Moser, Rose, 229
Mosley, Oswald, 35, 66, 69, 84, 92, 205, 239, 359, 380
Mother, The, 354
Mother Courage and Her Children, 353, 355, 360
Mother Goose, 322, 330-1
Mouse Trap, The, 138
Mr Bolfry, 235, 242
Mr Oligarchy's Circus, 384
Mrs Warren's Profession, 26
Muldoon, Claire, 384, 385
Muldoon, Roland, 384, 385, 388, 389, 401n
Munich, 162, 163, 166, 214, 220
Munro, George, 282
Munroe, Carmen, 358
Murphy, Brian, 360
Murray, Gilbert, 98
Murray, Stephen, 203
Music at Night, 290
music hall, 18, 198, 201-2, 214, 230, 242-4, 292, 293, 295, 327, 336, 337, 351, 368, 374, 380, 384
Musicians' Union, 375
Mussolini, Benito, 166, 169, 170, 173, 174

Nanking Captured, 145
National Council for Civil Liberties, 321, 323, 392
National Council for Labour Colleges, 25
National Council for the Defence of Women and Culture, 230
National Theatre, 18, 284, 287, 333, 352, 353

National Union of Agricultural and Allied Workers, 300, 393
National Youth Theatre, 381, 383
naturalism, 21, 27, 57n, 85, 142, 154, 209, 233, 271, 307, 308, 315, 349
Nazi-Soviet Pact, 94, 103, 121n, 188, 190, 195, 206, 218, 221
Nehru, Pandit, 152, 157
Nekrassov, 265, 333, 339-40, 346n, 355
Neville, Edith, 108
New Builders' Leader, 110
New Left, 345, 371
New Playwrights Incorporated, 316
New Red Stage, 30
New Statesman, 46, 65, 119, 159, 218
New Theater (USA), 41, 56n, 59, 69, 154, 156
New Theatre (Unity and Left Book Club Theatre Guild), 95, 100, 118, 132, 137, 145, 165
New Theatre (Unity 1939), 96, 137, 182, 183, 244
New Theatre (Unity 1945-49), 238, 265, 266, 279, 280-1, 284, 287, 307, 348, 355, 399
New Theater League (USA), 41, 55n, 59, 64, 154
New Theatre League (Australia), 251, 262n, 327, 338
New Theatre League (Britain), 36, 42, 43, 49, 54n, 93
New Theatre Publications, 267, 289
'new variety', 385, 388
new writing, 17, 18, 40, 68, 74, 76, 78, 79, 98, 138, 139-40, 146, 165, 204, 213, 222-3, 233, 239, 249, 307, 315, 327, 329, 336-7, 347, 350, 351, 361-9, 374, 393, 394, 395
New Writing, 175
New Writing for Europe, 208
Newcastle LBCTG, 98
Newmark, Peter, 207
News Chronicle, 150, 157, 175, 181, 219
Newsboy, 41, 79, 141
Newsome, Noel, 275, 276
Newton, Harry, 111, 309, 316
Nicolson, Harold, 157
Night and Day, 119, 133
Night of the Blitz, 245
Nixon, Barbara, 33, 65, 156
No!, 328-9, 331
Noah's Deluge, 99
Noble, Peter (George), 182, 186n, 358
Non-Stop Connolly Show, The, 397
Norris, Benny, 230, 231, 243, 258
North-West London Unity, 264, 273
North-West Spanner, 387
Norton, Bill, 338
Not For Us (Last Fight), 78, 79
Notting Hill riots, 359
Now is the Day, 246

Oakham, Joan, 251
O'Casey, Sean, 18, 96, 100, 107, 112, 138, 190, 201, 204-11 *passim*, 245, 272, 282, 292, 327, 329, 331, 380, 399
O'Connor, Patrick, 285
Occupations, 396
Odets, Clifford, 41-2, 45, 61-4 *passim*, 73, 78, 142, 158, 165, 194, 223, 234, 245, 272
Off the Record, 247
Offshore Island, The, 363
Oh! Freedom, 360
Oh Priceless Heritage, 292
Oh, What a Lovely War!, 360
Oklahoma, 303, 338
Oklopkhov, Nikolai, 33, 134, 183
Old Vic, 48, 50, 159, 235, 286, 309, 366-7
Oliver!, 331, 351
Olympiad of workers' theatre groups, Moscow, 31-2, 33, 35, 36, 134
O'Neill, Eugene, 33, 54n, 187n, 270, 271, 358
On Guard for Spain, 82-6, 96, 97, 119n, 147, 387

One-Act Play Magazine, 145
One and the Many, The, 236, 246
One More Mile, 232, 253, 254
One Third of a Nation, 225,235
Optimistic Tragedy, 245
Osborne, John, 265, 349, 373, 393
Ostrovsky, Alexander, 285
Our Time, 211, 215, 222, 229, 236, 284, 287, 288, 304
Out of Liverpool, 289
Out of the Dust, 295
Over to You, 246
Overruled, 289
Owen (Rowbotham), Bill, 22, 176, 185, 192, 196, 201, 214, 225, 230, 232, 242, 243, 253, 258, 263, 269, 273, 294, 295, 297, 299, 300, 301 (a.k.a. John Spag), 304 (Spag), 307, 308 (Spag), 324, 357, 396, 397
Oxford Unity, 245, 250

pageants, 21, 33, 54n, 67, 82, 89n, 138, 182, 245, 246
Paice, Eric, 293, 322, 323, 331-6 *passim*, 340, 344, 359
Palestine, 271
pantomime, 18, 21, 27, 161n, 165-77 *passim*, 184, 214-20 *passim*, 259, 262n, 322, 335, 336, 350, 351, 359, 389, 390, 399
Papworth, Bert, 142
Paradise Foundry, 386
Pardon My Greek, 273-4
Parker, Charles, 146
Parnell, Val, 281
Parsons, Geoffrey, 165-9 *passim*, 174-7 *passim*, 182, 185, 186n, 192, 196, 197, 214, 219, 22, 223, 225, 273, 274, 301, 304, 305, 309, 316, 319, 322, 330, 335, 345n
Passion, 389
Pastor Niemoller, 185
Paul, William, 99
Peace, The, 78, 385
peace movement: pre-Second World War, 35, 39, 148, 150; post-Second World War, 293, 314, 322, 328, 339, 358, 362, 363, 384
Peace and Plenty, 177
Peace and Prosperity, 136
Peace News, 341
Peace on Earth, 35, 39
Peacemeal, 335-6, 358
Pearn, Johnny, 375
Peasants' Revolt, 81, 323
Peck, Leonard, 13, 249, 292, 305-6 (Leonard Brain), 307, 315, 329, 362
Penn, Colin, 373
Penrose, Roland, 102
Penty, Kate, 247
People Like Us, 359
People's Convention, 214, 218, 219, 220, 222, 246
People's Court, The, 40, 79, 209, 221
People's Entertainment Society, 214, 247-50 *passim*, 262n, 287
People's Palace, 92
People's Plays Ltd, 248
people's theatre, 19, 241, 288
People's Theatre, Newcastle, 91, 119n
Peppin, Geraldine, 168, 236
Peppin, Mary, 168, 236, 324
Percival, Michael, 223
Percy, Esmé, 158
Peter Grimes, 246
Peters, Paul, 33
Phelan, Brian, 359
Phillips, Anton, 359
Phillips, Morgan, 303, 305
Phoenix Theatre, 73, 84, 86, 106, 136, 144
'phoney war', 191, 193, 195, 196, 208
Picture Post, 145, 175, 238, 244, 308
Piece About Peace, A, 293
Pieck, Arthur, 31
Pillars of the Community, 337
Pinkus, Ivor, 338
Pins and Needles, 99, 174, 186n, 254
Piper, John, 147, 373

Piratin, Phil, 378
Piscator, Erwin, 143
Plant in the Sun, 99,119n, 127, 151, 152-9, 168, 182, 197, 245, 270, 274, 307
Plater, Alan, 394, 396
Platts-Mills, John, 304, 370, 375
Players' Theatre, 65, 183, 244, 274
Playboy of the Western World, 380
Pleasure and Repentance, 397
Plebs League, 25
Plunkett, James, 351
Plymouth LBCTG, 96, 98
Poetry and the People, 196
Pogodin, Nikolai, 134, 135
Pole(s), George, 40
Politique des restes, La, see *Scavengers*
Polling, Richard, 86, 266, 290, 309, 311, 333
Pollitt, Harry, 85, 118, 147, 190, 194, 268
Polly, 338
Poole, George, 309
Poole, Philip, 46, 47
Pooley, Arthur, *see* Woolf
Popular Front, 19, 35, 37, 50-52, 54n, 82, 84, 99, 104, 125, 144, 222; Rebel Players and, 42, 44; Unity and, 36, 47, 106, 107, 125, 128, 132, 144, 147, 158, 190, 373; Unity plays and, 60, 64, 154, 166, 169, 176, 206, 324; Left Book Club Theatre Guild and, 93, 94, 99, 104
Popular Theatre, 386
Porgy and Bess, 202
Poulsen, Charles, 323
Pound on Demand, A, 201, 292, 380
Pouschka, Maria, 324
Pransky, Elaine, 355, 360
Priestley, J.B., 203, 224, 232, 247, 266, 276, 284, 290, 311
Pritt, D.N., 107, 122n, 176
Private Hicks, 49, 59-61, 65, 91, 97, 99, 103, 153-4, 156
professional theatre: Workers' Theatre Movement and, 29, 32, 33; Left Theatre and, 33, 34; Rebel Players and, 42; Unity and, 17, 20, 52, 57n, 67, 68, 106, 121n, 124, 137, 147, 158, 163, 165, 176, 177, 183, 189, 190, 238, 240, 241, 253, 259, 265-80 *passim*, 288, 289, 291, 350, 373, 377, 381, 382; Left Book Club Theatre Guild and, 102, 103; Glasgow Unity and, 281, 282, 283, 286; *see also* Unity Repertory Company
Professor Mamlock, 77 (play); 195 (film)
Professor Taranne, 356
Proltet, 29, 33, 38, 45
Prometheus, 272
Prompt, 355
Proud Valley, 151, 182
Puerto Franco, 249, 362
puppet theatre, 22, 77, 198, 330, 368n
Purple Dust, 211, 282
Pygmalion, 213

racial awareness, 21, 37, 38, 152, 154, 181-2, 239, 270, 358-9, 360, 386, 400n
Rafferty, Sean, 301
Ragged Trousered Philanthropists, The, 26, 27, 39, 140, 294, 308, 309, 351, 368, 390, 397,
Rainer, Louise, 183,
Ramsay, Bill, 251
Rattenbury, Arnold, 236, 284
Rayevsky, Im, 374
realism, 21, 27, 40, 63, 133, 144, 150, 154, 166, 178, 195, 268; *see also* socialist realism
Rebel Players, 29, 32, 33, 35, 36-49 *passim*, 54n, 55n, 56n, 57n, 66, 68, 79, 86, 87, 117, 125, 131, 138, 236, 261n, 375,
Recreation Ground, 392
Recruiting Officer, The, 352, 390
Red Dawn (Southampton), 29
Red Flag (London), 29

Red Front Troupe (Dundee), 29
Red Magnets (Sunderland), 29
Red Megaphones (Salford), 29, 36
Red Radio, 28, 29, 33, 36, 49, 55n, 66
Red Roses for Me, 329
Red Stage, 30, 31
Redgrave, Michael, 102, 189, 219-220, 266, 271, 375
Redgrave, Vanessa, 375-6, 377
Reed, John, 389
Reedy River, 338
Rees, Goronwy, 175
Rees, Llewellyn, 268
Reeves, Joseph, 107, 122n
Rehearsal, The, 97, 156
Reigate and Redhill Unity, 247, 250
Reign of Terror and the Great Money Trick, The, 390
Reluctant Prodigy, The, 363
Remembered for Ever, 281
Rent, The, 393
Rent, or Caught in the Act, 391
Requiem (A Man and a Woman), 39, 41, 42, 49, 79, 83, 245, 375
Revolt of the Beavers, The, 246
revue, Workers' Theatre Movement and, 27; New Theatre League and, 43; Unity and, 18, 21, 77, 136, 138, 138, 161n, 184, 262n, 263, 269, 290, 292, 301-5, 309-10, 316-20, 330-1, 335-6, 351, 359, 364, 374, 389, 398; Parsons and Fase and, 177, 185, 215, 223, 225, 274, 301, 303, 305, 316, 322; in wartime, 191-197, 200, 202, 223-5, 232, 245, 247; *see also* 'new variety'
Reynolds News, 45, 49, 56n, 73, 93, 114, 144, 150, 152, 157, 271, 366
Rhodes, Frank, 294, 329
Rhondda Roundabout, 139
Rice, Elmer, 98, 106, 246
Richardson, Bill, 271
Richardson, Ralph, 268
Rickword, Edgell, 44, 121n, 261n
Riders to the Sea, 185, 291
Ridler, Ann, 289
R.I.P. (Rent, Interest, Profit), 40
Risen People, The, 351
Road to Life, The, 326
Robbins, Tessa, 375
Robert Owen, 391, 389, 394
Roberts, Buckley, *see* Buckland, Robert
Roberts, Fred, 131-2, 184
Robeson, Eslanda, 112, 153
Robeson, Paul, 18, 33, 54n, 107, 110, 117, 122n, 137, 151-9 *passim*, 161n, 181, 185, 202, 270, 306, 358
Robin Hood and His Merry Men, 350
Robin of England, 254, 323
Robinson, Eric, 299
Roblès, Emmanuel, 327
Robson, Flora, 106, 137
Rochdale Pioneers, The, (Men of Rochdale), 253, 254, 294
Rock, Caron, 213, 227n, 295
Rocket for the Governor, A, 363
Rogers, Benjamin, 273
Rolland, Romain, 146
Room for Adjustment, 363
Rosenbergs, The, 334-5
Ross, Harry, 73, 189, 235
Rossides, K.P., 359
Roszak, Theodore, 393
Rotha, Paul, 99, 144, 346n
Rotter, The, 363
Rough Theatre, 385
Roundheads and Peakheads, 138
Roundhouse, The, 398
Rowbotham, Bill *see* Owen
Royal Academy of Dramatic Art, 32, 59, 86, 108, 211, 307, 385
Royal Court Theatre, 184, 265, 297, 323, 340, 346n, 350, 363
Royal Shakespeare Company, 220, 333, 352, 361, 368, 393, 397
Rubin, Barnard, 316
RUR (Rossum's Universal Robots), 25, 26
Russell, Billy, 375
Russell, Tony, 214
Russia's Glory: the Red Army, 201

Russia Today Society, 222
Russian for Yes, 328, 358
Russian Question, The, 299
Russians, The, 274
Rutherford, Owen, 236
Ryan, Paul, 397

7:84 (England), 385, 387, 390, 396, 398
7:84 (Scotland), 25, 282, 386, 387, 396
Sabotage!, 223, 233
Sachs, Leonard, 244, 274
Sailors of Cattaro, 34
Saint-Denis, Michel, 50, 67, 106, 107, 113, 122n, 137, 183, 225, 251, 285
Salute the Maquis (Man of the Maquis), 82, 202
Salute the Soviet Union, 82, 109, 118
Salute to the Gentle Sex, 230
San Francisco Mime Troupe, 388
Sandbag Follies, 89n, 191-7
Sandys, Duncan, 176
Sarron, Bernard, 232, 237, 243, 257, 263, 266, 273, 325, 331
Sartre, Jean-Paul, 18, 333, 339, 340, 355
satire, 17, 18, 27, 74, 78, 135, 140, 161n, 169, 174, 193, 195, 218, 304, 339, 351, 356, 357, 362, 364, 399
Sauce Tartare, 177, 304, 305
Saul, Lantz, 246
Say Uncle, 389, 393, 394
Scala Theatre, 66, 87, 102, 108, 202, 223, 232, 291
Scavengers, The (La Politique des restes), 356
Schneider, Harvey, 363
School for Wives, 353, 360
Schuster, Ida, 281
Scott, Benedict, 282
Scott, Paul, 239
Seagull, The, 353
Second Front, 201, 223, 225, 238, 252
Secret, The, 41, 83, 86
See a Man Falling, 374
Seeger, Pete, 357
Selford (Solomons), Jack, 97, 131, 132, 138-9, 140, 184, 186n, 206
Sender, Ramón, 41, 83
Señora Carrar's Rifles (Mrs Carrar's Rifles), 85-6, 164, 165, 354
Servant of Two Masters, 285
Shadow of the Swastika, The (Double Cross/The Worn Shoe), 249, 329
Sharma, Ben, 78
Sharp, Gerry, 280, 295, 311
Shatrov, Mikhail, 390
Shaw, George Bernard, 25, 26, 98, 100, 108, 114, 174, 195, 207, 213, 266, 286, 289, 332, 337, 339, 353, 381
Shaw, Irwin, 69, 99, 148, 158
Shaw, Margery, 339, 361
Shaw Theatre, 381, 382, 383, 391
Sheepwell, The, 237
Sheffield Left Theatre, 95, 97, 98, 121n, 245
Shelley, Percy Bysshe, 100, 196, 205
Shepherd, Jean, 137, 140
Shepherd and the Hunter, 271, 277
Shepley, Ida, 270, 358
Shinwell, Manny, 275, 276
Shoemaker's Holiday, The, 291, 338
Shoemaker's Wife, The, 275, 338, 359
Sholem Aleichem, 357
Shop Window, 202, 232
Shop Window No. 2, 232, 250
Short, Renée, 246
Shufflewick, Mrs, 375
Sillitoe, Alan, 373
Silverman, Sidney, 344
Simonov, Konstantin, 274, 299, 329
Sinclair, Upton, 27
Singing Jailbirds, 27
Singuineau, Frank, 358, 400
Sitwell, Edith, 289

Six Away, 359, 375
Six Men of Dorset, 98, 294, 300, 313n, 323, 387
Sklar, George, 33, 34, 89n
Slater, John, 1121n, 185, 189, 223, 367, 375
Slater, Montagu, 13, 34, 138, 142, 163, 246, 261n, 284, 289, 291
Slickers Ltd, 40, 42, 56n
Sluszny, Jim, 355, 356
Smith, Bob, 330
Smith, Reggie, 341
Snowdon, Lord, 377
Social Service, 32
socialist realism, 21, 31, 57n, 133, 150, 209, 242, 253, 282, 316; *see also* realism
Society for Anglo-Chinese Understanding, 389
Soelberg, Louise, 143, 207
Sole, Molly, 366
Solomon, Ellis, 273
Solomons, Gerry, 309
Some Notes on the Formation of Left-Wing Amateur Theatre Groups, 94
Song of Tomorrow, 245
Soo Bee Lee, 375
South Africa '70, 394
Soutter, Ann, 111, 153
Soutter, Arthur, 169, 382, 397
Soviet Union: role of in 1930s, 37, 128, 133, 162; 1939-41, 188, 190, 195, 218, 247; 1941-1945, 201, 211, 220-4 *passim*; Cold War period, 263, 293, 301, 334, 335; Workers' Theatre Movement and, 27, 31; Left Book Club Theatre Guild and, 103; Unity and, 21, 131, 134, 135, 136, 183-4, 191, 201, 268, 297, 311, 325, 353; Unity plays and, 40-1, 62, 109, 135, 138, 161n, 163, 172, 193, 205, 209, 218, 220, 221, 223, 224, 234, 253, 297, 299, 331, 333, 336, 340-5 *passim*, 364, 390, 392
Spain, 83
Spanish Aid, 85
Spanish Dance, The (Spanish Travail), 84
Spanish Village (Fuente Ovejuna), 211, 235, 236, 237-8 , 240, 244, 245, 257, 274, 321
Spanish war, 35, 128, 146, 149, 150, 153, 162, 190, 206, 363; plays and, 83-8, 90n, 117, 145, 163, 202, 205, 233, 237, 273; solidarity and, 82-3, 84, 86, 87, 97, 99, 136, 146, 153; Republican cultural group, 87
Sparrer's Can't Sing, 266 (film); 360 (play)
Spear, Ruskin, 373
Speight, Johnny, 332
Spewack, Sam and Bella, 272
Spirochette, 253
Spring '71, 355-6, 369, 385
Springhall, Dave, 130, 132
Squaring the Circle, 246, 353
squatters (1946), 201, 273, 282 (Glasgow), 291
Squire, J.C., 109
Squire, Raglan, 109-10, 114
Spender, Stephen, 85, 121n, 139, 146, 147, 160n, 207
St Joan of the Stockyards, 374
St Pancras (Unity and local relations), 108, 290, 292, 337, 350, 362, 367, 378, 381 (Camden), 382, 383
St Pancras Housing Association, 398
Stack, T.B. (Tris), 168, 258, 307
Stage Left, 386
Stalin, J.V., 128, 132, 134, 135, 220, 221, 222, 301, 340, 345
Stampe, Will (Bernie Cohen), 322, 331
Stanislavsky, Constantin, 107, 132, 136, 154, 167, 173, 178, 181, 242, 256, 268, 271, 277, 366
Star Parade, 274
Star Turns Red, The, 204-10, 237, 247, 272, 274, 277
Starched Aprons, 281

Stay Down Miner (New Way Wins), 34
Stephenson, Sir John, 308
Stepney Unity, 103, 264, 273
Sterling, Lance, 168
Stern(e), Joe, 48, 49, 56n, 59, 69, 78, 157, 271, 276
Stern, Trudy, 153, 157
Stevens, Helena (Bartlett), 395
Stevedore, 33, 182
Stewart, Arthur, 373
Stewart, Donald Ogden, 314, 315, 319
Stewart, Ena Lamont, 281, 282
STG Theatre, Poland, 385
STGRU (Socialist Theatre Groups for the Rebuilding of Unity), 396, 397
Stitch in Time, A, 202, 230
Stop Those War Drums, 103
Stoppard, Tom, 369
Storm Warning, 389
Strachey, John, 310, 319
Strangers in the Land, 327
Strauss, George, 107, 122n, 190, 287, 305
Strike, 391
Strike Me Red, 74, 245
Strike Up, 27
subsidy, public (for the arts), 18, 20, 24, 52, 67, 228, 279, 287
Suez crisis, 336, 340-44 *passim*, 395
Sullivan, Tommy, 111
summer schools, 98, 99, 120n, 132, 149, 188, 192, 264, 280, 281, 285
Summerhill, 99, 120n
Summerskill, Edith, 49, 373
Sunderland Left Theatre, 98
Sundgaard, Arnold, 253
Swaffer, Hannan, 224
Sweden, Maurice, 219
Sweeney Todd, 351
Swinging to the Left, 263
Swingler, Randall, 83, 137, 139, 163, 192, 200, 202, 223, 236, 261n
Sword of the Spirit, The, 202, 236
Synge, John Millington, 85, 275, 291, 380
20 Years, 245
Tailor and Garment Workers' Union, 92, 96
Take It As Red, 358, 359
Taming of the Shrew, The, 201
Tank, Herb, 316
Taste of Honey, A, 265 (play); 323 (film)
Tavistock Players, 108, 166, 176, 213
Temptation, 351
Ten Days that Shook the World, 389
Theatre 46, 287, 291
Théâtre du Peuple, 146
Theatre for the People, 96, 137
Theatre is Our Weapon, The, 222
Theatre Newsletter, 275, 284
Theatre of Action, 36, 39, 41, 51, 55n, 56n, 191, 332
Theatre Royal Stratford East, 331, 350, 359, 360
Theatre Today, 284
Theatre Union, 36, 237, 246, 247,
Theatre Workshop. 36, 53n, 56n, 136, 247, 265, 286, 332, 337, 341, 346n, 350, 353, 355, 359, 360, 363, 386
Theatre Workshop, 86
Theatro Technis (Greek Art Theatre), 359, 385
Their Theatre and Ours, 27
Then, 397
There's a Megabutton on My Living Room Floor, 360-1, 363
They Came to a City, 247, 248, 264
They Made Me a Present of Mornington Crescent, 391
They Shall Not Die, 34
Third World Poets, 392
This Our World, 221
This Trampled Earth, 88, 89n, 264, 273
Thomas, Dylan, 289
Thomas, Tom, 26-9 *passim*, 34, 36, 40,42, 43, 47, 56n, 140, 258, 294
Thomson, George, 132, 273
Thomson, Marjorie, 283
Thompson, W.H., 207

Thompson, Paul, 393
Thorne, Clarence, 168
Thorndike, Sybil, 98, 102, 122n, 137, 159, 183, 185, 240, 268, 279, 281, 300, 321, 367, 374-5
Threepenny Opera, The, 86
Thunder Rock, 246, 271, 358
Tigers Are Coming, OK?, The, 394, 396
Till the Day I Die, 98, 223, 245
Timid People, 326
Tinker's Wedding, The, 275
Toller, Ernst, 25, 34, 39, 41, 49, 56n, 83, 143, 185, 245
Tolmers Square Show, The, 391
Tom Barker of Camden and the World, 391-2, 394
Tomalin, Miles, 203, 223, 225
Tomlinson, Paul, 394
Tomorrow will be Different, 282
Torwatletie, 282
Tory MP, 98
Towb, Harry, 283
Townshends, The, 249, 292, 307
Toynbee Hall, 207, 225 (Toynbee Players), 235
trade union and labour movement, 24, 37, 44, 125, 278, 287, 288, 301, 339, 372, 386; Workers' Theatre Movement and, 29; Left Theatre and, 34; Rebel Players and, 39, 42,; Left Book Club Theatre Guild and, 96, 97, 102; Unity and, 19, 21, 23, 47, 66, 67, 92, 93, 94, 96, 105, 110, 122n, 127, 130, 167, 220, 266, 268, 269, 276, 280, 291, 293, 294, 295, 297, 300, 308, 320, 332, 333, 339, 349, 350, 358, 360, 369-75 *passim*, 382, 386, 397, 398; plays about, 18, 25, 27, 40, 59-60, 61-4, 98, 140-4, 154-6, 180-1, 206, 212-3, 246, 252, 258-9, 293, 294, 308, 317, 327-8, 338, 351, 360, 374, 391, 393, 394; *see also* TUC
training, 18, 22, 43, 107, 129, 132, 137, 151, 154, 156, 178, 190, 203, 239, 240, 251, 267-8, 280, 284, 290, 311, 312n, 361, 368, 393
Transport and General Workers' Union, 68-9 (taxi drivers), 141-144 (bus workers), 294, 338 (dockers), 308, 317; *see also* bus workers, dockers
Transport Players, Glasgow, 245
Trease, Geoffrey, 138, 179
Tree, David, 295, 300
Tree of Idleness, The, 359
Tressell, Robert, 26, 308
Trial of a Judge, 146-8, 160n
Tribune, 101, 122n, 144, 191, 253, 265, 331, 339, 344
Trip to the Big Store, A, 202
Tripe and Onions, 351
Triple A Plowed Under, 141
Trojan Women, The (Women of Troy), 98, 337
Trumbo, Dalton, 357
Trumpets and Drums, 353, 354
TUC, 26, 34, 35, 86, 92, 93, 98, 101, 195, 215, 219, 239, 300, 301, 317, 348, 360
Tuckett, Joan, 98, 120n, 387
Tudor, Anthony, 184
Turn It Up!, 330-1, 335
Turn Up the Lights, 195-7, 204
Turner, Jimmy, 45, 46, 48-9, 91, 102, 109, 110, 111, 114, 118, 131
Twelfth Night, 327
Twelve Pound Look, The, 26
Twenty Minutes, 40, 42
Tynan, Ken, 339

UAB – Scotland, 98
United Artists of Lyricon, 251
Unity: Britannia Street theatre (opening), 46-9, (closes) 290; Goldington Street theatre (opening), 108-19, (closes 1967) 380-2, (re-opens) 383-4, (fire) 17, 395, 396
Unity Theatre Club (1936), 47-8, 91, 94; Unity Theatre Club Ltd (1937), 106-8, 124, 129; Unity

Theatre Society Ltd (1939), 184; Unity Theatre Society Ltd (1944, national movement), 18, 103, 190, 237, 241, 244, 247, 250-1, 260, 264-5, 270, 278-81, 289; Unity Theatre Federation (1947), 265, 283-6; Unity Theatre Society Ltd (London only, 1947 on), 308
general council, 107, 128, 152, 159, 190, 203, 204, 224, 226, 280, 284, 311, 348; play department, 98, 99, 131, 138-9, 164, 168, 213, 223, 233, 364; rules and aims, 19, 47, 107, 109, 124, 128, 184, 189, 283, 304, 320, 321; school, 22, 107, 137, 156, 235, 238, 251, 267, 272, 291, 307
harassment of, 18, 189, 306 (Merseyside), 320; club status, 19, 47, 107, 109, 128, 184, 189, 283, 304, 320-1; as cultural centre, 45, 52, 77, 107, 134, 136, 184, 202-3, 239, 289, 358, 368, 388; membership of, 23, 47, 49, 56n, 67, 77, 91, 92-3, 105, 106, 124-30, 131, 132, 157, 175-6, 190, 226, 228, 229-30, 238, 239-40, 247, 250, 251, 264, 279-285, 323, 350, 365, 367, 374, 392, 398; social life of, 22, 45, 107, 125, 126-7, 197, 202, 203, 239, 289, 358, 368, 388
Unity New Play Service, 328
Unity Repertory Company, 20, 182, 253, 260, 265-80, 288, 291, 338
Unity Studios, 274, 289
Unity Theatre Trust, 176, 37-1, 375, 376, 380, 383, 396, 397-8
Unity West End Limited, 184; *see also* Kingsway Theatre
Unna, Harvey, 291
Up and Down the City Road, 391
US, 393
Ustinov, Peter, 253, 281, 285

Valk, Frederick, 355
van Gyseghem, André, 32-3, 46, 48, 54n, 56n, 57n, 59, 68, 102, 107, 137, 138, 139, 141, 148, 150, 151, 161n, 177, 178, 182, 203, 211, 283, 341, 358
van Phillips (John Berry), 168, 192, 193, 194, 196, 200
Vansittart, Sir John, 174
Variety Artistes' Federation, 375
Vaughan, Tom, 356, 364, 369
Vaux, Adrian, 356
Vega, Lope de, 237
vernacular (working-class) drama, 17, 19, 20, 22, 91, 107, 139, 178-9, 235, 268, 308, 336, 399
Viet Review, 389, 392-3, 394
Vietnam – the 'Postwar' War, 394
Vietnam war, 364, 389-90, 394
Vicars, Mervyn, 168
Vickers, John, 150, 156, 182
Vishnevsky, Vsevolod, 245
Visions of Simone Machard, The, 353-4
Voice of Greece, The (Cry of Greece), 82, 292
Volpone, 270, 350
von Wagenheim, Gustave, 138

Wages of Eve, 327-8, 331
Wagland, Frank, 338, 354, 391
Wagland, Pat, 361, 389
Wagland, Reg, 361, 389
Waiting for Lefty, 41-2, 45, 49, 52, 56n, 59, 61-9, 73, 76, 79, 83, 84, 87, 89n, 91, 92, 94, 96, 97, 99, 102, 106, 109, 118, 119n, 134, 135, 139, 142, 148, 153, 154, 164, 165, 171, 194, 197, 203, 274, 285, 387, 390
Wakefield, Shirley, 54n, 56n, 59, 68
Wakefield Tricycle, 392
Waldock, Denis, 177
Walker, Rudolph, 359, 395
Wallace, Hazel Vincent, 240
Wallis, Keene, 86
Wally Pone, 350-1
Walshe, Christina, 132
War and Culture; The Decline of Culture under Capitalism, 44

War Game, The, 363
Ward, Bill, 317, 331
Wardman, Bill, 295
Warsaw uprising, 257
Waterhouse, Keith, 393
Watkins, Peter, 363
Watson, Elizabeth, 156
Watson, Marion, 225
Way of the World, The, 393
We Fight On, 87, 202
We Want Peace (A Plea for Peace), 293
Weaver, Denis, 87
Webb, Rita, 306
Weiss, Fritz, 290
Welfare State theatre group, 387
Wellgarth, Jack, 354
Wells, H.G., 106, 107
Welwyn Garden Festival, 157, 179, 208, 249
We're on the Way, 247
Wesker, Arnold, 348, 349, 350, 363, 375, 380, 399
Wesley, Peter, 225
West, Alick, 132
West Ham United Front Troupe, 34
West Indian Drama Group, 358
Wexley, John, 34
What Happens to Love?, 276
What Next!, 309
What's Left?, 292, 301-6, 320
When the Boys Come Home, 281
Where's that Bomb?, 17, 70-3, 84, 97, 106, 135, 138, 140, 164, 306, 307, 387
White, Edwin C., 137
White, Sam E., 145
White, Wilfred, 111, 188
Whitworth, Geoffrey, 106, 266
Who are the English? ('not English?'), 80-1, 149, 292, 323
Whole World Over, The, 299
Widowers' Houses, 337
Wilder, Thornton, 225
Wilkinson, Ellen, 85, 158, 180
Williams, Tennessee, 353
Willis, Ted (John Bishop), 13, 22, 203, 231-41 *passim*, 246-57 *passim*, 260, 261n, 264-280 *passim*, 284, 285, 289-93 *passim*, 299, 336, 348, 349, 366, 372-3, 381-2, 399; plays by, 87, 202, 222-3, 231, 233-5, 246, 252, 255-6, 266-7, 276, 293, 314, 367
Wilson, Harold, 377, 389, 390
Wilson, Sandy, 175, 244
Windsor Theatre Guild, 264
Winkles and Champagne, 18, 242-4, 248, 254, 257, 274, 290, 292, 299, 300, 306, 316
Winnick, David, 332
Wintringham, Meg, 97
Woddis, Roger, 163, 183, 192, 225, 274, 295, 297, 299, 301, 335, 340, 344
Woking Left Theatre, 96
Wolf, Friedrich, 34, 77
Woman's Honour, A, 26
Women in Parliament (Ecclesiazusae), 273
Women of Kirbinsk, 40
Women of Troy, see *Trojan Women*
Women's Theatre Group, 396
Wood, Charles, 265, 363
Wood, Mrs Henry, 266
Woods, Beryl, 391
Woods, George, 391
Woods, Phil, 394
Woods, S. John, 169
Woolf, Barnet (Arthur Pooley), 192, 193, 196, 200, 223, 225
Word of a King, The, 323, 365
Workers' Circle, 46 (Circle House), 103, 226n,
Workers' Educational Association, 96, 246 (Players)
Workers' Film and Photo League, 36
Workers' Music Association, 36 (as Workers' Music League), 103, 196, 251, 301, 339
Workers' Propaganda Dance Group, 77, 117
Workers' Theatre Movement, 13, 22, 25-52 *passim*, 56n, 57n, 59, 63, 79, 93-8 *passim*, 120n, 145,

176, 184, 217, 292, 401n
workers' theatre, 19, 20, 28, 31, 32, 36, 45, 46, 52, 64, 106, 110, 117, 118, 124, 126, 152, 156, 241, 396
World on Edge, 146, 340-5, 346n, 357, 360, 366, 371, 372, 376, 395
World Youth Festivals: Berlin (1951), 322, 323, 326; Bucharest (1953), 326; Warsaw (1955), 326
Worsley, T.C., 218
Woyzeck, 385
Wren, Mary, 229
Wycherley, William, 384, 393
Wynard, Leslie, 250
Yegor Bulichev, 220
Yellow Star, The, 254-58
Yiddish theatre, 29, 38, 200, 257, 357; *see also* Jewish culture, Proltet
York Shoestring, 397
You Can't Always Be On Top, 360
Young Communist League, 29, 122n, 222, 265, 368
You've Had It, 247
Your Money and Your Life, 292

Zdrachev, Levcho, 353
Zolk, Anna, 180